W9-DHG-955

Historical Dictionaries of Ancient Civilizations and Historical Eras
Series editor: Jon Woronoff

Historical Dictionary
of the Hittites

Charles Burney

Historical Dictionaries of Ancient
Civilizations and Historical Eras, No. 14

The Scarecrow Press, Inc.
Lanham, Maryland • Toronto • Oxford
2004

DS
66
.B87
2004

SCARECROW PRESS, INC.

Published in the United States of America
by Scarecrow Press, Inc.
A wholly owned subsidiary of
The Rowman & Littlefield Publishing Group, Inc.
4501 Forbes Boulevard, Suite 200, Lanham, Maryland 20706
www.scarecrowpress.com

PO Box 317
Oxford
OX2 9RU, UK

British Library Cataloguing in Publication Information Available

Library of Congress Cataloging-in-Publication Data

Burney, Charles, 1930–
  Historical dictionary of the Hittites / Charles Burney.
      p. cm. — (Historical dictionaries of ancient civilizations and
historical eras ; no. 14)
  Includes bibliographical references.
  ISBN 0-8108-4936-4 (alk. paper)
  1. Hittites—History—Dictionaries. 2.
Hittites—Civilization—Dictionaries. I. Title. II. Series.
DS66 .B87 2004
930'.049199'003—dc22
                                        2003026004

53796766

Dedicated to Brigit, for three Hittite years

"I will lift up mine eyes unto the hills"
Psalm 121

Contents

Editor's Foreword

Less well known than civilizations in Mesopotamia and Egypt, the Hittites nonetheless created one of the great civilizations of the ancient world. It was no mean feat to rule a vast empire, establish important cities, preside over a conglomerate of peoples, encourage a flowering of culture and religion and, yes, engage in incessant warfare. Some of this was against attacking enemies, some against relative innocents who happened to be in the way, and part within the royal families. This impressive history spanned nearly five centuries during the second millennium BC, although predecessors and successors stretch over a much longer period. Yet despite the mark they made on ancient history, the Hittites were largely forgotten until curious travelers and then professional archaeologists had excavated important sites, verified some of the crucial events, and deciphered the languages. This *Historical Dictionary of the Hittites* therefore consists of two stories, that of the Hittites themselves and that of the rediscovery of the Hittites.

This volume, like others in the series, provides most of the basic information in a dictionary section with hundreds of entries on important persons (kings, queens and archaeologists), places (temples, palaces and excavations), essential institutions (kingship and cults) and significant aspects of the society, economy, material culture and, inevitably, warfare. These numerous detailed studies are integrated in a broader overview in the introduction, while the time sequences are sorted in chronological charts. The bibliography offers the basis for further reading on related topics. The contribution of photographs is not only to show what has been described but to remind us what the Hittites could accomplish in art and architecture.

This volume was written by Charles Burney, whose interests cover much of the Near East and Caucasus, but focus especially on Eastern Turkey. There he has worked on and directed excavations at Kayalıdere (Urartu) and carried out extensive archaeological surveys. He has written several books on the ancient Near East including *From Village to Empire: An Introduction to Near Eastern Archaeology* and many articles for journals such as *Anatolian Studies* and *Iran*. He also collaborated with the late David Lang, and is the author of the greater part of *Peoples of the Hills: Ancient Ararat and Caucasus*.

During most of this period from 1958 to 1995 Charles Burney was senior lecturer in Near Eastern Archaeology at the University of Manchester. This book has therefore benefited from a long career both on digs and in the classroom and, as a special bonus, the expertise of someone who knows his field and the enthusiasm of someone who enjoys it.

Jon Woronoff
Series Editor

Preface

The preparation of this *Historical Dictionary of the Hittites* has proved to be a challenge, both in the scope of the subject matter and in selection of entries. It is in relation to the latter that I have inevitably exercised individual judgment: no two authors would choose the same topics, and all would be inclined to favor their own particular field of expertise. The philosophy behind this publication is that the civilization of the Hittites can be adequately understood only by reference to all the evidence, not merely to the written records. It is surprising to note how certain publications purporting to bring the Hittites to a wide readership almost totally ignore several lines of research.

Certain topics have had to be restricted, in order to maintain a balance and keep within the prescribed length for the text as a whole. Some may regret that more of the hundreds of Hittite geographical names have not been included, even though their locations remain uncertain. Others may deplore the absence of certain gods and goddesses; but they too are largely obscure. The Hittite laws could not be discussed in very great detail, nor could I include any discussion of the grammar and syntax of the Hittite language. Not every archaeological site could be included, nor could the problems surrounding Indo-European migrations be fully aired. Perhaps the most arbitrary component of this *Historical Dictionary of the Hittites* is the selection of biographical entries, mostly of deceased scholars. Famous names have been excluded where the Hittite connection is unclear.

Now the Hittites are a major subject of study for the philologists, students of ancient languages; for the linguists, trying to reassemble the components of the family of languages to which Hittite belongs; for the historians, endeavoring to understand the royal annals and other texts; for the anthropologists, using contemporary sociology to illuminate aspects of Hittite society; for the geologists, mineralogists and paleobotanists, concerned with the natural resources available to the Hittites, as likewise with their natural environment; for the archaeologists, investigating the material culture of the Hittites, from architecture to portable artifacts, including pottery and metalwork; and for art historians and specialists in ancient technology. Perhaps it is understandable that some prefer to retreat into their own academic foxhole!

xii • PREFACE

I wish to acknowledge help and guidance from a number of different quarters. Dr. Tom Rasmussen (University of Manchester) first suggested this project. James Mellaart, F.B.A, gave generously of his time and immense knowledge in discussion of matters of historical geography: I hope he will forgive my not following his every suggestion in this controversial field. Dr. Jürgen Seeher, director of the Boğazköy excavations, most kindly provided hospitality for two nights in the expedition house, and gave his time to show me round the site of Hattusa, the Hittite capital, in August 2001. Two successive directors of the British Institute of Archaeology at Ankara, Dr. Roger Matthews and Dr. Hugh Elton, have provided accommodation in Ankara.

On a more personal note, I would like to thank Howard Greville for tolerating my idiosyncrasies during nearly four weeks of traveling in Anatolia, and for being there just when most needed!

This publication would not have seen the light of day without the skill and patience of Jonathan Pickup, M.A. (University of Manchester), without whose dexterity on the computers I could not have surmounted the inevitable moments of frustration with my own machine.

I acknowledge permission from Professor David Hawkins to use his map of western Anatolia in Hittite times; and likewise permission from Dr. Jürgen Seeher to reproduce his site plan of Boğazköy-Hattusa. Otherwise the maps and photographs are my own. Turkish names have been given their correct accentuation. I have followed the style set by Trevor Bryce in omitting accents from Hittite names: the most noteworthy effect is that "s" replaces "sh," as in the names of the god Tes(h)ub and the city of Kanes(h).

One specific detail is worth noting: following academic custom, the term Anatolia is used throughout in preference to Turkey. It applies specifically to the plateau and to the highlands to the north, south and east, but not to the coastal regions fringing the Black Sea, the Aegean and the Mediterranean, nor to the lowlands of southeastern Turkey, bordering modern Syria and Iraq.

Finally, I must record my acknowledgment of the tolerance shown by my publisher. Any shortcomings are my own responsibility.

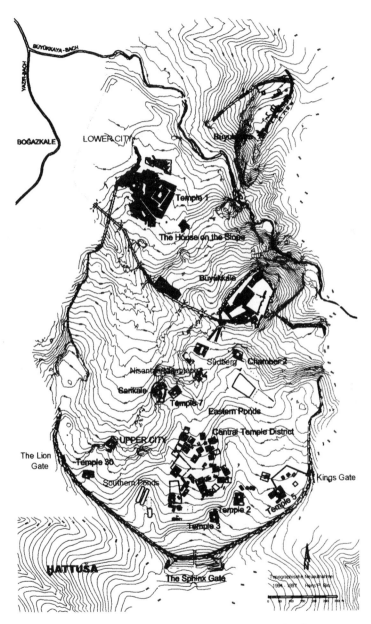

Plan of Bogazköy Excavations after Seeher

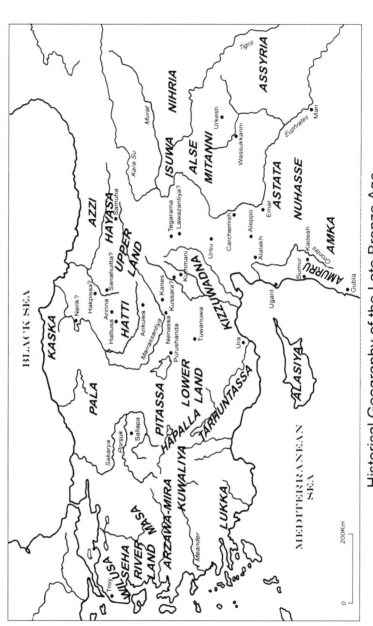

Historical Geography of the Late Bronze Age

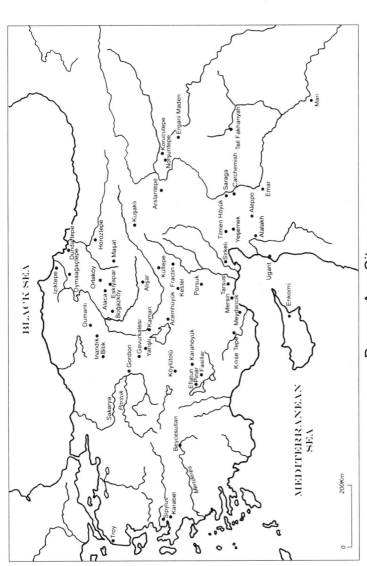

BLACK SEA

MEDITERRANEAN SEA

Troy
Sipylus
Karabel
Beycesultan
Menderes
Sakarya
Porsuk
Köylütolü
Gordion
Yanşli
Kaman
Gavurkalesi
Bitik
İnandik
Dumanlı
Alaca
Ortaköy
Boğazköy
Eskiyapar
Dündartepe
Oymaağaçtepe
İkiztepe
Horoztepe
Maşat
Alişar
Acemhüyük
Fractin
Küllepe
Kestel
Porsuk
Eflatun
Pınar
Fasillar
Karahöyük
Kılıse Tepe
Meydancık
Mersin
Tarsus
Sirkeli
Yeşemek
Tilmen Höyük
Alalakh
Aleppo
Emar
Saraga
Carchemish Tell Fakhariyah
Arslantepe
Noŗşuntepe
Korucutepe
Ergani Maden
Kuşakli
Ugarit
Enkomi
Mari

0   200 Km

Bronze Age Sites

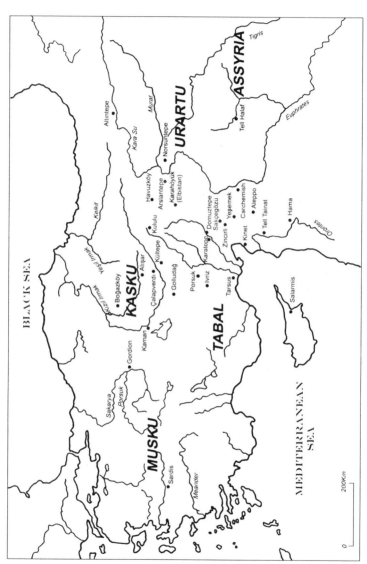

Iron Age Sites

BLACK SEA

MEDITERRANEAN
SEA

MUSKU

KASKU

TABAL

URARTU

ASSYRIA

Altıntepe

Tigris

Murat

Kara Su

Norsuntepe

Euphrates

Tell Halaf

Kelkit

Havuzköy
Arslantepe
Karahöyük
(Elbistan)

Domuztepe
Sakçagözü

Yeşemek

Aleppo

Carchemish

Tell Tainat

Hama

Orontes

Kulula

Kültepe

Karatepe

Zincirli

Kinet

Yeşil Irmak

Boğazköy

Alişar

Çalapardi

Golludağ

Porsuk

İvriz

Tarsus

Salarmis

Kızıl Irmak

Kaman

Gordion

Sakarya

Porsuk

Sardis

Meander

0   200Km

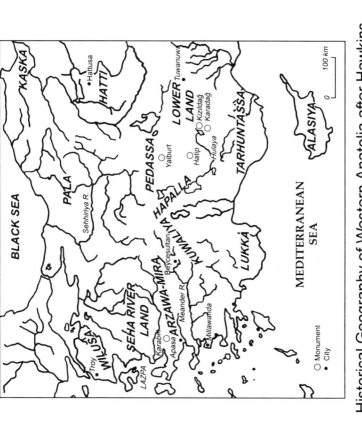

Historical Geography of Western Anatolia after Hawkins

HATTI	EGYPT	MITANNI	ASSYRIA & BABYLON	SYRIA	ARZAWA LANDS
PITHANA ANITTA	**DYNASTY XII** 1991–1785		SHAMSHI-ADAD I OF ASSYRIA 1813–1781	**ALALAKH**	(LUWIYA)
OLD KINGDOM	SECOND INTERMEDIATE PERIOD +HYKSOS 1785–1550		**BABYLON** HAMMURABI 1792-1750		
LABARNA 1650 HATTUSILI I 1650–1620 MURSILI I 1620–1590 HANTILI I 1590–1560 ZIDANTA I AMMUNA HUZZIYA I [1560–1525] TELIPINU 1525–1500			Raid on Babylon 1595		First Hittite Campaigns in Arzawa
	NEW KINGDOM AHMOSE 1550–1525 AMENHOTEP I 1525–1504 THUTHMOSE I 1504–1491 THUTHMOSE II 1491–1479 HATSHEPSUT 1479–1458 THUTHMOSE III 1479–1425	(first ref to Mitanni) PARRATTARNA (CA 1480?) KIRTA SUTTARNA I PARSATATAR SAUSTATAR	KASSITE RULE IN BABYLON 1595-1155	SARRA-EL ABA-EL ILIMILIMMA IDRI-MI	
{ALLUWAMNA TAHURWAILI HANTILI II, ZIDANTA II HUZZIYA II MUWATALLI I} 1500–1400				**UGARIT**	
EMPIRE {TUDHALIYA I/II ARNUWANDA I HATTUSILI II} 1402–1360	AMENHOTEP II 1425–1398 TUTTHMOSE IV 1398–1390 AMENHOTEP III 1390–1336 AKHENATEN 1352–1336 SMENKHARE 1338–1336	(PARRATTARNA II?) ARTATAMA I SUTTARNA II ARTASUMARA TUSRATTA (+ARTATAMA II, SUTTARNA III) SATTIWAZA		AMMISTANRU I	KUPANTA-KURNTA (MADDUWATTA)
TUDHALIYA III 1360–1344 SUPILULIUMA I 1344-1322		SATTURA II		NIQMADDU II ARHALBA	TARHUNDARADU UHHAZITI

HATTI	EGYPT		ASSYRIA	NIQMEPA	(MANAPA-TARHUNDA)
ARNUWANDA II 1322–1321	TUTANKHAMUN 1336–1327			NIQMEPA	(MANAPA-TARHUNDA)
MURSILI II 1321–1295	AY 1327–1323		ASSUR-UBALLIT I 1353–1318	AMMISTAMRU II	(TARGASNALLI)
	HOREMHEB 1323–1295			IBIRANU	(PIYAMARADU)
	RAMESSES I 1295–1294		ADAD-NIRARI I 1295–1264		
MUWATALLI II 1295–1272	SETI I 1294–1279			NIQMADDU III	(TARHUNARADU) WALMU (WILUSA)
	RAMESSES II 1279–1213		SHALMANESER I 1263–1234		
URHI-TESUB 1272–1267	Battle of Kadesh 1274				
HATTUSILI III 1267–1237	Treaty with Hatti 1258			AMMURAPI	
TUDHALIYA IV 1237–1228 1227–1209			TUKULTI-NINURTA I 1233–1197		
ARNUWANDA III 1209–1207	MERNEPTAH 1213–1204				
SUPPILULIUMA II 1207–?1176	RAMESSES III 1184–1152			Destruction of Ugarit	
-FALL OF HATTI-	Sea Peoples 1176		ASSUR-DAN I 1179–1134		
			TIGLATH-PILESER I 1114–1076		

Chronological Table

Introduction

Much has changed since knowledge of the Hittites was based solely on the Old Testament, where the "sons of Heth" are recorded in Genesis 10, Heth being the second son of Canaan and the eponymous ancestor of the Hittite race. It was through the Bible that the modern western world first became aware of an otherwise totally obscure ancient people. Historical records outside the river valley civilizations of Mesopotamia and Egypt were unknown, aside from the Old Testament and much later references in Classical sources, for the most part Greek. It was somewhat ironically a British clergyman, Archibald Henry Sayce, who first began to make the Hittites of the Bible, now known as the Neo-Hittites, better known to the world of scholarship, as well as their predecessors, the Hittites of the Empire centered in Anatolia.

It was not till October 1906 that the Hittites quite suddenly came into the bright sunshine of modern academic research, through the opening of the German expedition's excavations at Boğazköy (ancient Hattusa) under Hugo Winckler and Theodore Makridi. But their recognition of the Hittites as a distinctive people speaking an Indo-European tongue was quickly understood. The centenary of these excavations is fast approaching. The fragments into which so many of the clay tablets had been smashed, however, has made the task of piecing together and translating the texts that much slower and harder than it would otherwise have been.

Meanwhile, the increase of knowledge has, as so often occurs, merely complicated matters. If attention is focused solely on the successive Hittite kings, it may seem easy to identify the Hittite people and their civilization in second-millennium BC (Middle and Late Bronze Age) Anatolia; and the legacy of the Hittite Empire to successor states is now more fully understood. It therefore seemed appropriate to include the Neo-Hittite (formerly "Syro-Hittite") city-states in this *Historical Dictionary of the Hittites*. But archaeological discoveries indicate that the fashion—still followed by some—of using the term "Hittite" for everything in Bronze Age Anatolia has been gravely mistaken, just as "Phrygian" has been misused for the Iron Age. For some decades there was a climate of opinion in the new Turkish Republic for identifying the Hittites as ancestors of the Turks. While many elements over the millennia have naturally gone into the composition of the present-day population of Anatolia, and in that context the Hittites were forebears of the modern inhabitants of Anatolia, neither linguistically nor culturally can the present population be termed in any way Hittite. This is now generally agreed.

Anyone traveling extensively in Anatolia (the greater part of modern Turkey, comprising the whole plateau and surrounding highlands) must become aware of something of the environment in which the Hittites established their homeland, though the areas of forest must have been far more extensive than today. The achievement of the Hittite kings was somehow to impose a centralized administration on naturally centrifugal districts. In so doing they managed to achieve a coalescence of disparate ethnic groups. They ended up, however, with so mixed a population, augmented by repeated arrivals of deportees brought as prisoners of war to work the landed estates, that the government could no longer rely on its subjects' loyalty in the face of enemy incursions. Indeed, under the Empire (ca.1400–1180 BC) the ethnically Hittite percentage of the population may have shrunk to quite a small minority. Attention is therefore drawn to the whole question of identity, which essentially boils down to language and cultural traditions, of which religion forms an integral part. The extreme devotion to rituals and festivals by the Hittite royal family underlines the indivisibility of state from religion, the two being later constructs.

The Hittite Laws help to bring to modern attention a state and society evincing a contrasting blend of harshness with relative humanity, the latter more in evidence than (say) in the famous Code of Hammurabi of Babylon. While much is obscured by magic and superstition, a civilization emerges from the mist as possessing certain appealing traits, while fully proficient in the arts of war and also of international diplomacy. Assessment of artistic talent is usually subjective; but it has to be admitted that the distinctively Hittite elements seen in an eclectic artistic repertoire—notably the sculpture—demonstrate rather more originality than taste. It is unfortunate that Hittite music cannot be adequately understood: like their Hurrian mentors, they may well have been skilled in this art.

While much emphasis tends to be laid upon the political and military vicissitudes experienced by the Hittite state, life would have continued largely unchanged for most of the time in much of the territory under Hittite rule at its most extensive. Such continuity is implied by the evidence gathered from archaeological surveys, with collection of surface sherds from numerous settlement sites: only in metropolitan centers were the latest fashions followed.

Physical environment

The land of the Hittites has changed greatly over the past 50 years or so. Deforestation has been halted by rigorous governmental control, though woodland is far less extensive and the stature of trees diminished since the days of the Hittite Empire. Altitude is the principal factor determining local climate on the Anatolian plateau, temperatures being higher in the Hittite-controlled lands of Syria and Kizzuwadna at the northeast corner of the Mediterranean, closer to sea level. There rainfall is fairly reliable in winter and spring, and densely populated areas included the Amuq (Plain of Antioch). The Hittite homeland escaped the extreme cold of winters in the highlands further east, in parts approaching 2,000 meters above sea level. Most of the Hittite homeland lies at 1,000 to 1,300 meters.

To the north the homeland was fringed by the forest-clad Pontic highlands south of the Black Sea, a rich source of timber and also of copper and other mineral deposits, though many too small and remote to be commercially viable today. Here the rainfall is relatively high, with winds from the north bringing rain along the Black Sea littoral and into the highlands behind even in summer. Hattusa (Boğazköy) itself stood exposed to northerly winds, giving cool weather at times in summer, the winters being bitterly cold.

To the southwest extended the region south of the Salt Lake, today semiarid and probably little different in Hittite times. Much of the Konya Plain (the Lower Land) can be thus described. Immediately to the east the region around Niğde yielded invaluable supplies of tin, compensating for the end of the Old Assyrian trading network.

The Marrassantiya River, now the Red River (Kızıl Irmak), provided a boundary from southeast to northwest for the Hittite homeland. It was, however, no barrier to an advancing enemy, nor were the rivers of Anatolia suitable for navigation. Their seasonal fluctuations are extreme; and they drop sharply from the plateau down to the Black Sea or Mediterranean or, with the Euphrates, into the lowlands of Syria. Consequently, the rivers were of little use for communication.

Did the Hittites choose the rather uninviting territory within the great bend of the Marrassantiya River as their homeland? Or was it the only region relatively empty on their arrival? It is impossible to be sure.

Overland movement with chariots or wagons was easy in the wide, open expanses of central Anatolia. Thus the effectiveness of military deployments and commercial movements was assured. In the mountainous lands to the north and east this did not apply; and there were few natural routes to the Mediterranean. The first runs through the Cilician Gates to the Cilician plain (Hittite Kizzuwadna), where Mersin, Tarsus and Adana are the chief cities today. The second, to the west, runs through the forests of the Taurus range down the Calycadnos (Gök Su) valley to Silifke. The third, further west, reaches the sea by Antalya. Hittite control of Kizzuwadna was essential for access to Syria.

The routes westward toward the Aegean Sea presented no physical barrier, so that it is perhaps remarkable that the evidence for trade with Ahhiyawa (Mycenae) is sparse. That power had its eyes turned to the ports of Syria, notably Ugarit, and en route to Cyprus (Alasiya).

There were less easy routes giving access to parts of the Black Sea coast: the fierce independence of the inhabitants of the hinterland is thus understandable.

Modern roads and means of transport have made comparisons between ancient and contemporary Anatolia largely meaningless. Nowadays every village in Turkey by law has vehicular access to the public road system, a radical change for remoter districts. Today the traditional building materials and methods have largely been abandoned: the old timber-framed houses fall into decay, their owners anxious for the amenities of modern living. It is therefore harder for the visitor to Turkey to envisage aspects of life in Hittite times which were more readily discernible only 50 years ago. The trebling of the population of Turkey since World War II has involved immense expansion of cities and towns. This makes accounts by 19th-century travelers especially relevant, and all the more so for their breadth of interests.

Çorum, Yozgat, Kayseri and Nevşehir are bases from which to explore the Hittite homeland today, while for the Neo-Hittite period Osmaniye lies close to the site of Karatepe and Ereğli to the Ivriz relief.

Political vicissitudes of the Hittite state

The Hittite kings left no king-lists, making it difficult to achieve complete agreement on every detail of chronology. The most straightforward division is between the Old Kingdom (ca.1680–1400 BC) and the New Kingdom or Empire (ca.1400–1180 BC). Description of the 15th century BC as the Middle Kingdom is based solely on linguistic developments during a time of political division and weakness.

Throughout their history the Hittites were never entirely free of threats from surrounding peoples and states all too eager to take advantage of any military, political or economic weakness. The survival of the Hittite state lay as much in the lack of political cohesion among its rivals as in its own strength.

The story begins with the people of Nesa (Kanes), as evidently constituting the earliest documented focus of Hittite power in central Anatolia, not unconnected with the wealth and influence of that city arising from the Old Assyrian trade. At that stage, and indeed stretching back well into the third millennium BC (Early Bronze Age), a network of city-states seems to have dominated much of the Anatolian plateau, controlling trade taken over by the Assyrian merchants.

The earliest in the enduring dynasty which, through one branch or another, was to rule Hatti for some five centuries was Labarna, whose name was so greatly respected as to become a royal title for each succeeding king. Much more is known of his successor, Hattusili I, whose achievements can be reckoned among the most enduring of all the Hittite rulers. Not only did he aspire to military and economic control over the wealthy lands to the southeast, extending from Aleppo to Babylon, but he also endeavored to exalt the status of the kingship, clouded in the final phase of his reign by internecine strife. This was aggravated by a problem destined to recur at times, the absence of a direct male heir. In the end it was his young grandson, Mursili I, who was to continue the expansionist policy in the southeast, culminating in the raid on Babylon (1595 BC). These two reigns mark the emergence of Hatti as a leading Near Eastern power.

Yet at the moment of triumph the assassin's blow was to imperil all that had been gained. The murder of Mursili I by his brother-in-law inaugurated a long period of internecine strife, eventually restrained by the *Proclamation* of Telipinu, laying down regulations for the succession to the throne, which were more or less adhered to thereafter. Successive assassinations had created a demand for law and order.

Military successes marked the reign of Tudhaliya I/II and the dawn of the Empire. He stands indeed in the same rank as his two illustrious predecessors. Yet his achievements were not to prove enduring. This time it was external threats which were to endanger the very survival of the state, brought to a low point by invaders from all directions at once, as vividly described in the annals of Tudhaliya III. Even Hattusa, the capital, fell.

Still, all was not lost. The counter-attacks were led, from before his gaining the throne, by Suppiluliuma, destined to become the most successful of all the Hittite kings, not merely to recover territories recently overrun but also to extend the power of Hatti deep into Syria and across the Euphrates River into Mitanni. The Hittite Empire, now one of the leading powers of the Near East, came into direct confrontation with Egypt, then in a period of relative weakness; and for a brief moment it seemed possible that a political alliance through marriage might have united the two powers under Hittite leadership.

Even at its zenith, however, the Hittite realm was vulnerable to rebellions by vassals and dissension within the royal family. Violence reverberated down the generations. The divisions which ultimately laid low the Hittite power may possibly be traced back as far as the slaying of the heir to the throne of Tudhaliya III by his younger son, Suppiluliuma I. His son Mursili II attributed the plague which ravaged the land for 20 years largely to his father's sins, among which neglect of certain religious festivals weighed as heavily as his fratricide.

Suppiluliuma devoted most of his energies, after regaining the lost lands in Anatolia, to the southeast, to the reduction of minor kingdoms of north Syria and the major diplomatic gain of securing the support of the rich city of Ugarit as a vassal, lured away from its fealty to Egypt. To the east the kingdom of Mitanni was subjugated and the nascent power of Assyria curbed.

The regions north and west of the Hittite homeland demanding attention—the lands of Kaska, Arzawa and their neighbours—remained to be subjugated by Mursili II, the fifth and youngest son of Suppiluliuma, whose interests in Syria were guarded by two older brothers, appointed in their father's reign as viceroys of Aleppo and Carchemish. Mursili II's reign is distinctive for its legacy of royal annals, the principal evidence of Hittite leadership in ancient Near Eastern historiography. It is also remarkable for its two surviving brothers' acceptance of his designation to the throne of Hattusa. Fratricide was not to be repeated.

The annals of the next king, Muwatalli II, have not been recovered, so that question marks hang over these years. Two events stand out: the removal of the seat of government south from Hattusa to Tarhuntassa and the battle of Kadesh, after lengthy mustering of forces. The result was a draw in favor of the Hittites, who regained control of lands in Syria wrested from them by Seti I, the father of Ramesses II. But Muwatalli met a probably violent end soon afterward, the throne passing to his son Urhi-Tesub.

Certainly it was with this reign that a division appeared in the royal family with repercussions over the next half century. Muwatalli seems to have been unaware of the legacy he would bequeath, when he gave his brother Hattusili virtually viceregal powers over a wide tract along the sensitive border with the Kaska lands lying to the north. This became a provocation for his nephew Urhi-Tesub, less experienced in war and peace than his uncle. The usurpation of the throne by the latter followed. There ensued a reign more notable for international diplomacy than military successes, partly owing to the advanced years of Hattusili III, perhaps 50 on his seizure of the throne. There began too an inordinate attention to building and endowing temples, which were to occupy the greater part of the Upper City of Boğazköy (Hattusa). Indeed the major undertaking of restoration of the capital after its sack in the time of Tudhaliya III, begun in the 14th century BC, was continued with renewed vigor by Hattusili III and his son and successor Tudhaliya IV.

By his reign the Hittite Empire was showing signs of decline, most dramatically in defeat at the hands of Assyria. A wide swathe of territory, created as the kingdom of Tarhuntassa in the south, around the Taurus highlands, seems to have become virtually independent under the rule of Kurunta, a son of Muwatalli II. In spite of outwardly friendly relations between the cousins, Kurunta must have believed he had as strong a claim to the throne as Tudhaliya IV. Rebellion ensued, with a short-lived seizure of Hattusa. Tudhaliya IV, however, soon regained his throne. The Hittite Empire was far from expiring, for military activity continued in the far west.

The full range of factors behind the final fall of Hatti is uncertain. Luwian influence at the heart of government is perhaps implied by the adoption of the hieroglyphic script, best suited for inscriptions on rock faces or masonry. The last king of Hatti, Suppiluliuma II, was a vigorous ruler, extending his campaigning even to Cyprus. The Hittite nobility—the essential support through the generations of the monarchy —seems to have perished or dispersed, in part to north Syria, in the obscure events in the early 12th century BC commonly associated with the Sea Peoples. Luwian elements survived, however, at the head of a number of principalities in Tabal (centered on the Kayseri-Sivas region), the old Lower Land and beyond. The direct Hittite legacy was manifested until as late as the eighth century BC not in the former Anatolian homeland but in the Neo-Hittite zone to the southeast, most notably at Carchemish and Malatya.

At Boğazköy itself and elsewhere a "dark age" followed the fall of the Hittite Empire, with clear archaeological indications of newcomers, evidently from the north. Though the break in cultural continuity may have been less abrupt than long supposed, Anatolia was never the same again. The literate, highly organized bureaucracy of Hattusa had vanished forever, its memory not to be recovered until the Germans began excavations (1906).

Neighbors and contemporaries

At various times reckoned as international powers—a status recognized through the title of "Great King" —Aleppo was the earliest such threat to Hittite ambitions, in the days of Hattusili I. Behind it lay Mitanni, in the 16th century BC emerging as a danger to Hatti in the east, being the constant support of Hurrian groups pressing in on the Hittite domain, at one stage even controlling Kizzuwadna and thus cutting the Hittites off from the rich trade of Syria. The kingdom of Mitanni could boast of advanced chariotry and horsemanship, influencing the Hittite army. But it had one fatal weakness, the murderous rivalry between branches of the royal dynasty. Moreover, it lacked naturally defensible borders. In the end, after its defeat by Suppiluliuma I, it was absorbed by the rising power of Assyria.

To the south, the Egyptian New Kingdom extended its rule in Asia as far as the bend of the Euphrates River in north Syria, confronting Mitanni but in due course establishing diplomatic relations by the tried method of royal marriages. Egypt controlled the Mediterranean coast, including the territory of Ugarit. The weak foreign policy of Egypt, from the reign of Amenhotep III (1390–1352 BC) onward, made the small kingdoms of Syria more prepared to switch their allegiance from Egypt to Hatti. But the balance of power in this region depended as much on Egyptian vicissitudes as on the energy of Hittite kings and their viceroys. The advent of the 19th Dynasty brought an aggressive expansion under Seti I (1294–1279 BC), which Muwatalli had to accept. The death of Seti I brought a young new pharaoh, Ramesses II, stronger in courage than generalship. This gave Muwatalli his chance. Amurru and Kadesh were recovered, with the battle of Kadesh leading 16 years later to a treaty which brought international peace to Syria-Palestine until the fall of Hatti.

In western Anatolia Arzawa was a loose coalition only rarely centralized enough seriously to threaten the Hittite homeland. Yet successive Hittite kings found it essential to curb the desires of its vassals for independence or their being drawn into the sphere of Arzawa or even of the Mycenaean state (Ahhiyawa). Mursili II was successful in dividing and ruling these western lands, though recurrent punitive expeditions were called for in later reigns.

The least sophisticated of the Hittites' neighbors, with no tradition of centralized authority, were the Kaska tribes in the Pontic hills to the north of the Hittite homeland. Yet it was these who proved the least tractable of all the enemies of Hatti, never effectively subjugated. Kaska elements came into their old enemy's land on the fall of Hattusa, squatting in its ruins.

Hittite civilization and society

Hittite society reflected the general characteristics of daily life and material culture throughout Anatolia, with shared traditions largely distinct from those of the lands to the south and southeast. Anatolian culture was of course much influenced by the older urban societies of Assyria, Babylonia and Syria. The Assyrian impact was strongest through the activities of the merchants who conducted a highly organized long-distance trade over some three centuries (ca.2050–1750 BC). Later on, Babylon probably had a greater impact, with the importation of scribes to the Hittite court. Hittite rule in north Syria inevitably introduced elements hitherto not found in the Hittite homeland: one example is the winged sun -disk, derived from Egypt.

It is almost impossible to detect socioeconomic differences between Hatti and its neighbors, owing to the lack of written records from the latter. The king, the royal family and the major temples wielded decisive economic power, controlling much of the labor force and exacting taxes in kind from the less dependent inhabitants. Manpower—and womanpower, too, in the fields—was the decisive resource. A chronic shortage of manpower can be only partly explicable by the demands of the army and the intermittent ravages of famine and plague. The temples certainly diverted many men from productive work, though administering extensive estates.

Warfare was an economic as well as a political necessity, with deportation of prisoners of war a regular feature of Hittite policy. This worked adequately so long as the political center stood firm. Once developments began which presaged the final decline and fall of the government centered on Hattusa, the thousands of those who cannot have believed themselves genuinely Hittite were ready to desert their masters.

War could be conducted only through the military caste or nobility surrounding the throne, whose support depended on the qualities of the king ruling at the time. He had perforce to trust his seasoned generals, quite often named in the surviving records, though the first rank under the king was accorded to his heir from a surprisingly early age. Life expectancy even in the royal family was not long, and years of energetic good health even less so. No doubt the rigors of constant campaigning accounted for this. Consequently, many recorded military actions were led by the crown prince of the day or by a younger son. Chariotry provided the shock force whereby the Hittite army could overpower its enemies, most of whom could not afford the outlay required. Infantry were more evenly matched: where chariotry could not be deployed, the issue was liable to be less certain. This is especially evident in conflicts with the recalcitrant northern tribes in their forest-clad hills. These constituted the major and recurrent threat to the very survival of the Hittite state.

Though in origins a military monarchy, the Hittite Empire during its final century became increasingly theocratic, with an inordinate proportion of the resources of the realm and of the king's and queen's time devoted to religious festivals, with endowments to the leading temples. Some see such a trend as an indication of an introverted attitude in the face of growing external threats. Yet the gravest dangers came on the whole from dissension in and around the royal family. Such strife could emerge from the traditional status enjoyed by the queen mother, often to the detriment of her son or stepson. Polygamy, not normal in Hittite society, was permitted the king. A particularly bloody period of assassinations was followed by a largely successful attempt to lay down clear rules for the succession, in the *Proclamation of Telipinu*.

Inevitably the principal inspiration for the arts came from the royal court, and was largely concentrated in the capital city of Hattusa (Boğazköy). There were, however, numerous and widely distributed rock reliefs, located from the Aegean almost to the upper Euphrates River. Many are associated with springs or rivers. The centralized character of Hittite art is demonstrated by the sharing of the same motifs between reliefs and, on a far smaller scale, seals and jewelry. Style of clothing, including footwear, and muscular representations of the human form are both uniquely Hittite. This legacy was perpetuated through several centuries after the fall of the Hittite Empire.

In the more humdrum manifestations of material culture, including pottery and metal tools and weapons, the Hittites are not altogether distinguishable from their Anatolian neighbors. It is, anyhow, inadvisable to attach ethnic labels to artifacts. Admittedly, however, the Late Bronze Age pottery of central Anatolia and some regions to the southeast differs from that found elsewhere in Anatolia, being marked by a monotony resulting from a degree of mass production.

Perhaps some insight can be gained into the outlook of the Hittite population from the gods and goddesses they worshiped, though these had much in common with those revered outside the Hittite lands.

Inevitably the universe and the powers shaping the weather loomed large, with the sun foremost in the pantheon, later displaced by the god of weather and storm. The harvest had to be secured by appointed prayers and rituals. Before battle the omens had to be consulted and the appropriate rituals performed; failure to observe these rituals could make the difference between victory and defeat. Above all, life after death required, especially for the royal family, protracted ceremonies before and after cremation. The divinities of the Underworld were as fearful as their gloomy abode.

The Hittites can nevertheless be credited with certain attitudes which give them an image a fraction closer to modern ideals than that displayed by their supposedly more sophisticated contemporaries elsewhere in the Near East, notably in Syria and Mesopotamia. Women were in some respects, as in the context of rape, better treated than elsewhere in the second millennium BC. Capital punishment was restricted to a minority of crimes and offenses against the moral code. Though slavery became more widespread as time passed, it was not always entirely oppressive for the individual concerned. The gods and goddesses had to be kept satisfied by performance of the precise rituals required by each of them. Wrongdoing brought its punishment even on succeeding generations. Respect for the ancestors was a prerequisite for a successful reign; and later kings of the Hittite Empire showed particular devotion to the memory of their namesakes generations back. Three or four kings bore the name of Tudhaliya, three Arnuwanda and possibly three Hattusili. The last king of the Empire echoed in his name the greatest of all the Hittite kings, Suppiluliuma I. There was thus a strong sense of dynastic identity, not diminished by the ever more prominent influence of Hurrians at the Hittite court.

The economy of the Hittite realm was remarkably centralized, a source of strength under the more successful kings but of serious, even fatal weakness at times of defeat and during the final decline and disintegration. While the Assyrian merchants had introduced a form of private enterprise, the family firm, from Assur to Kanes and in due course to other trading colonies in central Anatolia, the bureaucracy which characterized the Hittite state ensured regular payments in kind to the royal treasury in Hattusa. Its only competitors were the major cult centers, with assured revenues from their estates and from worshipers, from the king downwards. Such centers had a corporate identity enduring through successive generations, in contrast to the vicissitudes of inheritance in individual families. There was special satisfaction at the recovery of the revered shrine of Nerik from the northerners after several generations.

The ethnic and cultural elements contributing to make Hittite civilization what it became in the 14th and 13th centuries BC were essentially fourfold. The Indo-European components were the Hittite and the Luwian. The Hattians, long seen as the indigenous pre-Hittite population of central Anatolia, may in fact have arrived later than hitherto supposed but well before the emergence of the Hittites as a political force to be reckoned with. This is a point of continuing debate. The Luwians, whose hallmark is the hieroglyphic script, became ever more dominant in the population of the Hittite homeland, so much so that Luwian had displaced Hittite as the spoken language early in the Empire; and it was the Luwian traditions which persisted in the so-called Neo-Hittite principalities, which were heirs to the Hittite Empire in the southeast.

The Hurrian contribution to Hittite civilization became particularly prominent in the 13th century BC, after the Hurrian tribes pressing in from the east had ceased to pose a threat to Hatti. The royal family had married into Hurrian bloodstock from the opening of the New Kingdom (Empire), as indicated by personal names. There is no evidence, however, to suggest a less aggressive policy toward lands to the east, including Isuwa across the Euphrates River. It was Puduhepa, the young priestess from the Anti-Taurus region, who systematically introduced—with the full support of her husband Hattusili, before and after his seizure of the throne—the Hurrian pantheon, familiar in the reliefs of the shrine of Yazilikaya. Hurrian influence undoubtedly permeated the royal court in Hattusa, notably in literature and music. How extensive it became outside Hattusa, in the small towns and villages, surely varied with their location. To the north and west the Hurrian impact was weaker.

Who then precisely were the Hittites? It may seem strange to pose this question at the conclusion of this introduction. Questions of identity revolve around cultural factors, notably language, religion and government, far more than around genetic inheritance. Studies of DNA can illuminate the dark recesses of ethnic movements, and thus point toward possible homelands; but in themselves they can reveal little or nothing of the character of the population in question. Those seeking answers to this problem of identity may look to different sources of evidence: to religion through written and iconographic records; to methods of warfare; to the laws and charisma surrounding kingship; and, most complex of all, to clues for the ancestry of Hittite and the other Anatolian languages. This last, the field of linguistics, is a minefield for the unwary or dogmatic enquirer and a discipline approached with understandable caution by the archaeologist. Perhaps it is safest to identify the Hittites with their kings and nobility and royal court, for without these they would not have played their role among the leading powers of the ancient Near East. While absorbing cosmopolitan elements—exemplified by the eight languages attested at Hattusa—they yet retained their Anatolian character, in its ultimate roots Indo-European but long diluted and diversified.

Conclusion

Emerging from the ever-increasing body of data on the Hittites is a kaleidoscope of disparate elements tending to form a picture on which unanimity is never likely to be achieved. The Hittites are worthy of study as one of the great powers of the ancient Near East, as recognized for some decades. Their full identity and achievements in their Anatolian homeland remain tantalizingly elusive in certain respects. It is hoped that this *Historical Dictionary of the Hittites* will lift at least some of the fog and will stimulate further inquiry.

The Dictionary

- A -

ABSOLUTE CHRONOLOGY. The dates of kings' reigns in the different states of the ancient Near East are significant for piecing together the pattern of international relations and the mechanisms of **diplomacy**. King lists give regnal years; but they do not in themselves answer the question of how they should be moved up or down the columns of a chronological table. Babylon, Assyria and especially Egypt provide a framework for Hittite and other chronologies to which all other dates have to be attached. A modification of Egyptian requires the same for Hittite dates. It is the chronology of the 18th and 19th Dynasties of New Kingdom Egypt which is most directly relevant for the Hittite Old Kingdom and Empire.

For the immediately preceding years the reign of Hammurabi, the greatest king of the First Dynasty of Babylon, and the Hittite raid on Babylon under **Mursili I** are the focal points for the absolute chronology of Mesopotamia and surrounding lands. The so-called middle chronology places his reign—known to have lasted 42 years—at 1792–1750 BC, with the Hittite raid at 1595 BC. The high chronology dates Hammurabi to 1848–1806 BC and the raid on Babylon to 1651 BC, while the low chronology gives dates of 1728–1686 BC and 1531 BC respectively.

Based in southern Mesopotamia but extending its sway far north, the Third Dynasty of Ur (Ur III) lasted 108 years (2113–2004 BC). The occurrence of **seals** of Ur III style provides a chronological link with **Kültepe** (*karum* II); but a firmer correlation is between *karum* IB and Samsi-Adad I of Assyria (middle chronology: 1813–1781 BC), through the coincidence of *limmu*-names.

The Assyrian king-list affords a chronological anchor from the mid-second millennium BC, though links with Hittite kings are few before **Suppiluliuma I**.

The dates given here follow the middle chronology for the earlier phases, until the rise of the New Kingdom in Egypt and the rather later beginning of the Hittite New Kingdom (Empire), after which a slightly lower chronology is followed, with the long reign of **Ramesses II** beginning in 1279 rather than 1304 or 1290 BC.

The lengths of each reign are undisputed, apart from one or two question marks in the period of **Tell el-Amarna**, with the complications of coregencies in Egypt. Dates for Hittite kings' reigns before the Empire can only be estimated, with the one fixed point of the raid on Babylon. *See also* **RELATIVE CHRONOLOGY**.

ACEMHÖYÜK (BURUSHATTUM/ PURUSHANDA). This settlement mound, one of the largest in central Anatolia, is situated 14 kilometers west of the town of Aksaray and about 20 kilometers from the south end of the Salt Lake (Tuz Gölü). Excavations have been undertaken there since 1962, under the direction of **Nimet Özgüç**. After a few years' interruption, work was resumed in 1988; and in 1989 the direction of these excavations was passed to Dr. Aliye Özten. The expedition has been under the aegis of the University of Ankara and the Turkish Historical Foundation.

The identification of Acemhöyük with Burushattum of the Akkadian texts and Purushanda of the Hittite texts is generally, though not unanimously, agreed. An alternative identification of Acemhöyük with **Zalpa** "by the sea," with the latter taken to be the Salt Lake rather than the normally accepted Black Sea, lacks credibility. There is a difficulty, however, in that the most prosperous phase of Burushattum, on the textual evidence, seems to have been during the period of **Kültepe-*Karum*** II, when it was particularly prominent, along with the kingdoms of **Kanes** and **Wahsusana**, and when its ruler enjoyed the title of *ruba'um rabi-um,* (King of Kings). The major archaeological remains come from a level contemporary not with Kültepe II but IB.

A deep sounding on the east side of the mound reached an occupation level (10) with some **pottery** paralleled in **Tarsus** Early Bronze II, **Mersin** and **Karahöyük (Konya)**. Painted "metallic ware" is characteristic of the Early Bronze II period at Acemhöyük, in the Konya Plain and in the Taurus Mountains. Another trench, on the south side of the mound, revealed four levels antedating the main palatial building period, from Early Bronze Age onward.

The most important period by far at Acemhöyük is dominated by a large palatial building, initially distinguished as two separate structures, the palaces of Sarıkaya and Hatipler Tepesi, with the latter on a grid plan and functioning largely as a storehouse. This is now seen, however, as essentially one and the same building with Sarıkaya, though the latter includes the most prestigious residential and public quarters. Heavily burnt in the destruction ending its lifetime, from this palace abundant charred timbers were recovered, demonstrating the **timber-frame construction** so widespread through Anatolia and exemplified even more dramatically in the fire which destroyed the approximately contemporary palace of **Beycesultan** V, in the **Arzawa** lands of southwestern Anatolia.

Pine and juniper were the woods most abundantly used at Kültepe and Acemhöyük alike for building work, with rather less cedar and rarely boxwood and oak. The rarity of oak is surprising, seeing it was so commonly in use in Anatolia during the Middle Ages. Timbers at Acemhöyük were not extensively shaped, though peeled by the carpenters.

Though sharing the general Anatolian structural techniques, the palace of Acemhöyük represents a local tradition in many of its features. These are most graphically displayed in the decoration of a bathtub: it seems reasonable to suppose that the major building it depicts is in fact the palace. It has an open façade with two stories of balconies over a socle, with slender supporting wooden posts with large flat capitals, the lower posts being taller than the striped upper posts. Openwork railings serve as parapets for the balconies. Stairs are clearly if sketchily shown in two locations. Solid black, checkerboard or criss-cross linear patterns represent the walls. It has been suggested that the design of this palace indicates close connections with Minoan Crete; but there is a radical difference. While the façades of the palace of Acemhöyük look outward, the Minoan palaces look inward on to a central court.

Bullae and **seal** impressions provide much of the evidence of economic activity here and in other centers, as well as suggesting the functions of various rooms. They occur in almost every ground-floor room of Sarıkaya and Hatipler Tepesi, thus throughout the palace, except in those rooms which were filled with large storage jars (*pithoi*). Bullae impressed with the same seal were found in the same storeroom, especially those containing jars with covers or lids. It might be thought that such lumps of clay, once the goods sealed by them had been unpacked, would be of no further use; but that would be to ignore the necessity of record keeping for business purposes. After removal of incoming merchandise, their bullae or labels were saved, collected in two special rooms and filed on wooden shelves along the walls, forming a commercial **archive**. The bullae arriving at Acemhöyük were attached to various types and sizes of container or package, sometimes secured with string or cord, string holes being visible on some bullae.

The name of the owner included on a bulla inscription can be useful in suggesting the origin of the merchandise. Moreover, foreign rulers occurring on bullae indicate some of the commercial connections of the merchants of Acemhöyük: such are Samsi-Adad I of Assyria (1813–1781 BC), Aplahanda of **Carchemish**, Anum-Hirbi of **Mama** and a daughter of Zimri-Lim of **Mari**. It is the archaeological finds, however, which add weight to the evidence of close trading links with Syria, including ivories and objects of lapis lazuli and rock crystal. One particularly fine example is a carved ivory box with crowded design and with bronze, **iron** and lapis lazuli studs. From the palace, other buildings on the mound and the lower city comes a wealth of metalwork, ivories, terracottas, stone vases and, last but not least, the **glyptic art** of the numerous bullae with their cylinder and stamp-seal impressions in different styles, including the native Anatolian. The stone vessels include some made of obsidian. Among the metalwork are lead figurines, for some of which the molds have been found.

The glyptic art of Acemhöyük, together with that of Kültepe-Kanes, is discussed elsewhere, and has been the subject perhaps of greatest interest and a special concern of Nimet Özgüç. It is worth mentioning here the suggestions that the seals betray in their designs art on a larger scale, such as mural paintings, reliefs in gateways or divine **statues**, the last being the most probable. Whether the seal cutters were inspired by sculptors and painters or vice versa one cannot be sure, although it is hard to believe that works on such a small scale could have been the dominant artistic influence.

One thing is seemingly almost certain, that Burushattum was a leading actor on the political scene as early as the days of **Sargon of Agade** and **Naramsin**, and likewise was playing a major economic role. There is as yet a dearth of documentary evidence for the details of its trading colony (*karum*) in the time of Kültepe II, apart from the **tablets** from that site, where the Old Assyrian **trade** was centered. This seems to have been so, even if Burushattum was every bit as powerful and prosperous as Kanes at that time. In the later period of the Assyrian trade, Kültepe IB, levels of that time were reached outside the mound at Acemhöyük at a depth of seven meters. Thus a lower city, doubtless housing the merchants, stood here at an absolute level some 22 meters below that of the contemporary Sarıkaya palace.

Acemhöyük provides data for the **relative** and **absolute chronology** of central Anatolia in the early second millennium BC (Middle Bronze Age), obtained from comparative dating and physical analyses through radiocarbon and **dendrochronology**. That the palace of Acemhöyük was active at least as late as the conquest of Mari by Samsi-Adad I (ca.1810 BC) is suggested by cylinder-seal impressions of an official known also from Mari and Tell Leilan to the northeast. The data from dendrochronology indicate a dating of 1791 +- 37 BC for the construction of the palace of Acemhöyük, unlikely to have been occupied for less than the minimum life span of 61 years assigned by the same technique to the palace of Warsama, king of Kanes (Kültepe IB). That was built 58 years before the construction of the palace of Acemhöyük, suggesting a dating around 1850 BC for the beginning of Kültepe IB, in turn tending to support not too low a dating for Kültepe II, plausibly ca.2050/2000–1900 BC, with a minimum of a century indicated by the *limmu* names. Accepting the dendrochronological (tree-ring) dating for the palace of Sarıkaya (Acemhöyük), a much longer time-span than widely accepted is implied for Kültepe IB, unless the Assyrian trade is thought to have continued some decades later at Burushattum, until at least ca.1750 BC. That seems unlikely, seeing that Kanes was the main center of that trade in Anatolia. Therefore a date of around 1750 BC for the destruction of Acemhöyük III (the palace) and Kültepe-*karum* IB seems to be indicated, though the recovery of the Old Assyrian trading network evidently came some decades later to Burushattum than to Kanes. The final stages of the Assyrian trade were marked by decline, though at Acemhöyük successive building levels were constructed over the burnt ruins of the palace.

Undoubtedly Acemhöyük must have been a major center of industry as well as trade, though it is rather hard to understand such prosperity located in one of the least hospitable areas of Anatolia, with its low rainfall and the proximity of the Salt Lake. Perhaps this was less saline 4,000 years ago? Its workshops must have been very busy, among them those of the **iron**smiths, producing items such as the throne and scepter presented as a gift or tribute to **Anitta**, king of Kanes.

The Old Assyrian trade never recovered from the unrest of the immediate sequel to its ending ca.1700 BC or slightly earlier. Many cities, among them Burushattum, vanished for good, unlike **Hattusa**. When commerce revived, it took a very different form, being controlled by the palace, the centralized administration of the Hittite kingdom.

ADAD-NIRARI I (1295–1264 BC). He continued Assyrian expansion westward toward the Euphrates River, capturing the city of Taide, which had replaced **Wassukanni** as the capital of **Mitanni**. He was rebuffed by **Urhi-Tesub** on writing to him in terms of "brotherhood." **Hattusili III** characteristically adopted a more conciliatory stance toward the rising power of Assyria, accepting the loss de facto of **Hanigalbat**.

AGRIG. Most references to this official occur in the Hittite records broadly defined as "**festival** texts," the *agrig* fulfilling the functions of a quartermaster, responsible for the **food**, drink and other rations required by the local **temple** and described in detail. Unlike the senior palace officials, military commanders and high priests, normally recruited from the extended royal family, the *agrig* did not enjoy high social status. Lists and sequences of *agrigs* show some geographical clustering, but these were not itineraries. At least 29 in all are recorded and maybe a few more. The major clusters were in the north, including **Nerik**, **Hanhana** and **Kastama**, and in central Hatti, with three near **Hattusa**, including **Ankuwa**. Other centers with an *agrig* were located in eastern Hatti, in the **Upper Land** and southwest of **Samuha**; and widely scattered centers in the **Lower Land** included **Tuwanuwa**. It seems clear that these centers, given the function of the *agrig*, were associated with cults of differing importance.

AHHIYAWA. Few topics have aroused greater controversy than the identity and location of this land. In the 1920s **Emil Forrer** equated Ahhiyawa with the Homeric Achaia, observing that Homer refers not to Greeks but to Achaeans. His view attracted both supporters and skeptics. Locations for Ahhiyawa have been proposed for the western mainland of Anatolia, the Aegean islands, Thrace and the mainland of Mycenaean Greece. In fact most specialists have envisaged its extending over more than one of these. The least plausible location would be entirely on the Anatolian mainland. With the title of "Great King" for the rulers of Ahhiyawa, it cannot have covered only a very restricted area; and western Anatolia now appears fully occupied by the various components of **Arzawa**, before and after its division by **Mursili II**. Likewise a carefully argued case for locating Ahhiyawa as an island realm with a narrow coastal strip on the Anatolian mainland from **Millawanda** southeastward, centered perhaps in the island of Rhodes and subsisting in large part by its command of the sea route from the Aegean to Cyprus and the Levant, lacks credibility. How could such a limited territory be ruled by a Great King?

Essential to the location of Ahhiyawa are references to men fleeing across the sea, notably Uhhaziti of Arzawa and, most explicitly, Piyamaradu. This would fit a location of Ahhiyawa in Thrace, but that goes against identifying Millawanda as Miletos. This leaves only Mycenaean Greece, a location fitting the archaeological evidence of a Mycenaean presence at Millawanda and elsewhere along the Aegean coast. The language of Ahhiyawa would therefore have been Mycenaean Greek rather than, for example, **Luwian**, as would have been likely if Ahhiyawa were to be centered between Miletos and Rhodes. This may still have been spoken by most of the population of that region, even though for a time at least it was under Mycenaean control, without being part of the central homeland.

The difficulty of determining Hittite relations with Ahhiyawa lies largely in the fundamental divergence of their interests, the one being a land-based power with only intermittent maritime interests, and those largely near the end of the Empire, and the other being concerned with command of the maritime **trade** routes through the Aegean and the east Mediterranean. Whereas the Hittite Empire stood as one of the great powers of the Near East and precursor of the Assyrian state and other powers of the first millennium BC, Ahhiyawa (Mycenae) in economic terms foreshadowed the Phoenician cities and their adventurous sailors. It seems a reasonable guess that the rulers of Ahhiyawa saw the outside world very differently from the kings of Hatti, nor were their priorities similar.

Both textual and archaeological evidence, the latter mainly in the form of **pottery**, indicate that the area of closest contact between Ahhiyawa and the Anatolian mainland was around Apasa (Ephesus), the royal center of Arzawa, where excavations are revealing Late Bronze Age occupation levels. The close involvement of Ahhiyawa with Millawanda is quite well documented. The pottery found along the Aegean littoral, from **Troy** southward as far as the island of Rhodes, suggests an ethnic and cultural mix, demonstrated by pottery of Anatolian, Mycenaean and Minoan affinities. Pottery from the northern and central littoral is largely Anatolian, while in the south there is a large percentage of Mycenaean wares. In addition to this ceramic evidence, such sites as Trianda and Lindos on Rhodes were likely palatial centers; and Iasos was a flourishing community with a rich cemetery. Rhodes would have benefited from its position guarding the sea route from Mycenae to **Ugarit** and other ports in the east.

References to Ahhiyawa occur in Hittite texts over almost two centuries. The earliest is in the Madduwatta Text, of the time of **Arnuwanda I** (ca.1380 BC), when Attarisya (Atreus?) was king of Ahhiyawa, mentioned in the Hittite text as "the man of Ahhiya," the early form of the name. He clearly commanded considerable forces by land and sea, for he is recorded as having many **chariots** as well as raiding **Alasiya (Cyprus)**, which became a major focus of Mycenaean settlement and trade. Then come the **annals** of Mursili II, when Apasa, Troy and Millawanda were all coastal towns. In the reign of **Hattusili III** the Tawagalawa letter was in effect an appeal to the king of Ahhiyawa to hand over the renegade Piyamaradu, whom the Hittite king had failed to capture: this was a tacit admission of failure. But Hattusili had other priorities, and did not wish for further entanglement in the west. Under **Tudhaliya IV** the text entitled "Sins of the **Seha River Land**" finds the king of Ahhiyawa supporting the ruler of that land, Tarhunaradu. The last important reference to Ahhiyawa comes in the Sausgamuwa **treaty** made by Tudhaliya IV with the vassal king of **Amurru**, containing a prohibition of Assyrian use of his ports—at a time when Hatti and Assyria were at loggerheads—and by implication an obstacle to Ahhiyawan sea trade with the region by then equivalent to modern Lebanon. This is the famous text in which the king of Ahhiyawa—along with those of Egypt, Babylon and Assyria—is included by the Hittite king in the top rank of international affairs, being granted the title of Great King, the name of Ahhiyawa being then deleted. Much discussion has revolved round this deletion. Was it a mere scribal error? Hardly likely! A mark of a change of attitude by Tudhaliya IV and a desire to demote Ahhiyawa? Conceivably. The result of a sudden decline in the power of Ahhiyawa in western Anatolia? This seems the most probable explanation. Relations between Hatti and Ahhiyawa had been cool but relatively peaceful. This changed with the successful intervention by Tudhaliya IV, when Ahhiyawan control over Millawanda ceased, thus causing the loss of its one major foothold on the Anatolian mainland. Tudhaliya's main concern, however, was to exclude Ahhiyawa from the Near East at a time when Assyria was the major threat to Hatti. Thus Ahhiyawa automatically ceased to be a great power, whatever the circumstances in the Mycenaean homeland.

AKURGAL, EKREM (1911–2002). While primarily known as a Classical archaeologist and art historian, he was formerly director of the School of Fine Arts in the University of Ankara. He has published general works on Hittite art and architecture: *The Art of the Hittites* (1962) and *The Birth of Greek Art* (1968), the latter largely devoted to Neo-Hittite civilization.

ALACA HÖYÜK: EARLY BRONZE II TOMBS. Situated 25 kilometers north of **Boğazköy**, this easily accessible site is nevertheless far less visited than its more famous neighbor. This was the site of the major pre–World War II Turkish-run excavation, directed by the late **Hamit Koşay**, who, as director of the Hittite Museum (as it was then called) in Ankara, the new capital of the Turkish Republic, organized the display of the major finds from 13 tombs, attributable to a stage during the third millennium BC. On the high chronology, these tombs fall within the years ca.2800–2600 BC, though still often dated to the later third millennium BC.

While the site was settled already in the fourth millennium BC, the earliest major discovery is the cemetery of 13 pit graves, each most probably with a canopy supported by corner posts surmounted by a "standard" in the form of a stag or a bull or a trellised disk, so called from the rather implausible suggestion that they were carried in procession before the burial; another theory is that they were mounted on wagons, but no traces of such have been found. The bulls and stags, with massive dowels for attachment to the tops of the corner posts, were of **copper**, inlaid and sometimes partly sheathed in electrum. Concentric circles may have had some esoteric significance.

Any belief that the trellised disks are solar emblems, representing a cult of the Sun-God or Sky-God, must stimulate debate concerning the whole question of early Indo-Europeans in Anatolia, their date of arrival and geographical limits, in this case in the third millennium BC. Without doubt this group of richly furnished tombs, sited at the edge of the town, demonstrates the cultural interface between Anatolian (Near Eastern) craftsmanship and northern (steppe) **burial customs.** A similar phenomenon appears elsewhere, notably at Maikop in the Kuban valley, north of the northwestern Caucasus. The skills of the indigenous population are particularly evident in the metalwork, while the northern traditions are discernible in the pit graves, roofed with **timber** and then covered with earth, with remains of animal sacrifices above. There was, however, no tumulus (kurgan) above ground: in this respect the northern tradition had been modified. Each tomb must have had its own marker, for none overlap.

It does seem very possible that those buried in these tombs

were Indo-European intruders from the north or possibly from the west, ruling over a more sophisticated central Anatolian population. **Swords**, daggers, maceheads, battle-axes and **spears** may indicate a warrior class. It may not be going too far to suggest these were Hittites who had gained political power over the indigenous **Hattians**, inhabitants of the great bend of the Halys River (**Marrassantiya**), though the Hattians may have arrived after the initial Hittite migration into the Anatolian plateau. Thus may have begun the long process of cultural assimilation. Alaca Höyük was not the only manifestation of the cultural interface between the steppes and the Near East, a phenomenon seen from **Troy** in the west to Horoztepe in central Anatolia and beyond.

The Alaca craftsmen had mastered hammering and casting in open and closed molds and by the lost wax (*cire perdue*) method, used for the difficult casting of a copper stag and "standard" combined. A technique widely used in Anatolia in the third millennium BC, as at Alaca, was the casting of arsenical bronze, producing an attractive silvery surface. Hollowing or sinking and raising, for making metal vessels, was also evident, in fluted jugs and goblets of **gold**, **silver**, electrum, copper and bronze. These demonstrate close parallels with contemporary **pottery**, as occur widely, though fluting is more typical of Early Bronze Age pottery from western rather than central Anatolia.

The skills of the Alaca goldsmiths, whose work is seen in the 13 tombs, bear comparison with those of the craftsmen of the approximately contemporary "Royal Cemetery" of Ur, in southern Mesopotamia. A variety of techniques is apparent. Chasing, but not engraving, was practiced, together with soldering, sweating, inlay and repoussé work. Troy is the richest site for comparative material (in Troy II).

Only cemeteries are likely to yield items of gold and silver. The discoveries at Alaca Höyük surely indicate that it lay within the range of distribution of metalworking skills common to much of the Near East in the third millennium BC.

The Early Bronze II town of Alaca Höyük was destroyed by newcomers, who appear not to have settled in the area, the site being only intermittently occupied until ca.1850 BC. When the town rose to prominence again, it had become a principal center in the Hittite state.

ALACA HÖYÜK: LATE BRONZE AGE. The most impressive remains are the reliefs carved in andesite. The originals are now in

Ankara in the Museum of Anatolian Civilizations, with excellent replicas in their place. These reliefs certainly are older than those of **Yazılıkaya**. There is, however, a similarity in the overall arrangement of two processions from left and right meeting in the center, the **Storm-God** at Alaca Höyük being on the left and a seated goddess on the right.

In favor of the dating of these **sculptures** to the reign of **Muwatalli II** (1295–1272 BC) rather than to a date around 1400 BC is the undoubted Egyptian inspiration for the two guardian figures flanking the inner entrance to the focal sector of the town, giving it the modern appellation of the Sphinx Gate. These figures have heavy wigs and long hairstyle: it has even been suggested that they may have become an ideal of feminine beauty for the Hittite ruling class. Be that as it may, the Lion Gate in the outer perimeter of the central enclosure probably marked the beginning of a processional road to the inner entrance, the Sphinx Gate. This in turn leads into what may best be described as a **temple**-palace, protected by a defensive perimeter. Within the Sphinx Gate was a courtyard giving access to a small square drained by a sewer. Beyond is a large rectangular area with porticoes alongside. On the right was a public building, evidently the palace, including private quarters, governmental offices and a temple. At the end of this open space was a **postern tunnel** leading outside the walls, and bringing to mind that in the perimeter wall of the Upper City of **Boğazköy-Hattusa**. Alaca was indeed a major city with an area of 40,000 square meters and a diameter of 250 meters, prospering through successive Hittite phases. Alaca IIIa ended about the time of the death of **Mursili II** (1295 BC); and Alaca II continued till the fall of the Empire. The **fortifications** befitted this prestigious city and **cult center**, having towers along the city wall and a strong gateway.

The reliefs adorning the base of towers flanking the Sphinx Gate are notable for their secular content and style. On the side of the right-hand figure of the Sphinx Gate, where the sphinxes are carved in frontal view only, a double-headed eagle, grasping two rabbits or hares, was surmounted by a robed figure, possibly a king or a goddess: this motif occurs already on Old Assyrian **seals** from south central Anatolia. A readily recognizable scene depicts a king and **queen** worshiping the Storm-God, represented by a bull on a high stand with an altar in between. Elsewhere goats are being taken for sacrifice. Some of the Alaca Höyük reliefs are of typically processional figures; but others are altogether secular in spirit. Musicians and acrobats, the latter depicted swallowing a

sword or climbing a ladder, are altogether less usual themes in the art of the ancient Near East, implying perhaps a less dominant role for the court religion than appears at Yazılıkaya two generations later. Higher on the façade are hunting scenes, including wild boar, especially vigorous in style. These scenes, as well as the sword-swallower, point to a very possible association with the cult of the goddess **Teteshapi**, attested by 40 or more **tablets** from Hattusa: her **festival** was marked by **music**, dancing, games and acrobatics, her cult being centered at **Tawaniya**, with which Alaca Höyük may conceivably be identified. The Hattian identity of Teteshapi reinforces a dating for the reliefs before the 13th century BC.

There are very strong arguments, however, for identifying Alaca Höyük with **Arinna**. Alternative identifications, as with **Zippalanda** or **Kussara**, are less plausible. Considerable wealth must have accrued to this, the most revered of all Hittite cult centers, with economic activity exemplified by workshops attested in the texts.

ALALAKH (TELL ATCHANA). This large settlement mound, with an area of 750 x 300 meters, stands just east of the River Orontes, in the Amuq plain. From the Early Bronze Age until the end of the Late Bronze Age the excavations, directed by **Sir Leonard Woolley**, revealed a sequence of 17 levels of occupation, the earliest being below the modern water table, contemporary with references to Alalakh in the **archives** of Ebla.

Successive palaces and **temples** were excavated, the earliest palace (ca.2000 BC) being followed by that of Alalakh VII. The city was then a vassal of Yamhad, the kingdom of **Aleppo**, ruled by Yarim-Lim, a contemporary of Hammurabi of Babylon. Some of the 500 Akkadian **cuneiform tablets** come from this building, recording **trade** with Syria, Babylonia and **Alasiya (Cyprus)**. This palace had two or three stories, some rooms having wall paintings showing parallels with Minoan Crete. Basalt was used for orthostats as a dado for the rooms and courtyard of the most important of the three sections of this palace, as well as for column bases and door sills: it was to be the favorite material for the mason and sculptor in north Syria for 1,000 years to come. The combination of stone, **timber** and mudbrick was more typical of Anatolia than of the Levant or Mesopotamia. Ivory inlays were produced at Alalakh, with some of the storerooms containing elephant tusks.

The following period, after the destruction by **Hattusili I**, saw Alalakh a vassal of **Mitanni**, having broken free from the suzerainty of Aleppo. This period is illuminated by the colorful autobiography inscribed on the **statue** of Idri-Mi set up by his son, Niqmepa, who built the palace of Alalakh IV. This building was designed as an early version of the *bit hilani*, with the living quarters on the upper floor, as with the palace of Alalakh VII. The tablets from the palace of Niqmepa cast light on administration of the territory, on foreign relations and on legal cases. This palace was in its turn destroyed by a Hittite attack, probably under **Tudhaliya I/II**, in his campaign to reassert Hittite authority in Syria.

Alalakh remained under Mitannian rule until its conquest by **Suppiluliuma I**, when it was incorporated into the **viceroyalty** of Aleppo. Inscriptions, **seals** and a stela attest Hittite rule, under which Alalakh remained until its final destruction in the early 12th century BC by the **Sea Peoples**. It was not reoccupied.

ALALU. The ruler of heaven and the **gods**, he was the first in the succession described in the **Hurrian theogony**; and he is attested in a Babylonian list of gods as one of the ancestors of **Anu**.

ALASIYA (CYPRUS). The island appears intermittently in the affairs of the Hittite state, which at least from the time of **Tudhaliya I/II** (ca.1400 BC) was claimed by Hatti as a vassal. The troublesome Madduwatta, of this same time, recruited ships from **Lukka** for an attack on Alasiya, provoking a protest from **Hattusa**.

The account of the attack on Alasiya by **Tudhaliya IV** is preserved on a **cuneiform tablet** of his son **Suppiluliuma II**, a copy of two **Luwian hieroglyphic** inscriptions. This campaign was successful, with **deportation** of royal family and prisoners and seizure of **gold**, **silver** and other goods. Alasiya was rich in **timber** and **copper**, both in constant demand in Hatti. But the obvious reason for this otherwise eccentric campaign was the threat of seaborne attacks on the shipments of corn from Egypt and Canaan to the Anatolian **granaries**. Piracy was a recurrent hazard to Mediterranean shipping in the second millennium BC: possibly elements later to form the **Sea Peoples** were already arriving in Cyprus.

Suppiluliuma II engaged the Alasiyan fleet in a sustained sea battle, when the Hittite fleet, probably of ships from **Ugarit**, defeated the enemy, as subsequently also in a land battle. Alasiya is listed in the famous account of Ramesses III of the coming of the Sea Peoples, and was clearly seen by the last Hittite kings as a serious threat to vital maritime imports as well as to Ugarit, a major vassal. *See also* **TRADE**.

ALEPPO. The second city of present-day Syria, the ancient city was centered on the mound crowned by the great medieval castle of Salah-ed-Din, built by Crusader prisoners from the Horns of Hattin (1187 AD). To this day it remains a major focus of **trade**. In the second and first millennia BC it was a major **cult center** of the **Storm-God** Hadad, identifiable with the Anatolian **Tesub** and the Canaanite-Phoenician Ba'al.

Aleppo was regarded by **Hattusili I** and **Mursili I** as a serious obstacle to Hittite ambitions for political and economic expansion southeastward. It had already played a significant role in the Near East as center of the kingdom of Yamhad in the time of Hammurabi of Babylon (1792–1750 BC): while, according to one text, 10 to 15 kings were following Hammurabi, 20 kings were following Yarim-Lim of Yamhad. The high status of Aleppo is recorded in the **treaty** between **Mursili II** and Talmi-Sarruma, which includes an account of relations between Aleppo and the Hittite state. It narrates that in former years Aleppo had a "great kingship," to which Hattusili, the Great King of the land of Hatti, had put an end, with further destruction inflicted by his grandson Mursili. Thus it appears that the Hittites had at first ranked the kings of Yamhad (Aleppo) as their equals.

With the Hittite conquests in Syria under **Suppiluliuma I**, Aleppo became one of two **viceroyalties**, together with **Carchemish**, initially held by a son and then a grandson of the great king. Aleppo was militarily more secure than Carchemish, not facing any direct threat from a great power.

Aleppo continued as a major city in the Iron Age, to which dates the **temple** of the **Weather-God** currently being excavated by a German expedition led by Kay Kohlmeyer. Over 26 relief-blocks have been uncovered, decorated with characteristic Neo-Hittite subjects, including the Weather-God clasping thunderbolts, a charioteer, a bull with the sacred tree, a god armed with a bow, a god seizing a prisoner by the hair and a scorpion-man. The style of some of the blocks is not dissimilar to that found at **Guzanu (Tell Halaf)**. The excavator assesses the reliefs as dating to the early first millennium BC, antedating those of **Sakçegözü** and demonstrating a symbiosis of **Luwian** and Aramaean traditions.

ALIŞAR III (CAPPADOCIAN) WARE. Typical of the Early Bronze III period of the later third millennium BC, notably at **Alışar Höyük** (Level III) and the city mound of **Kanes** (Levels 13–11).

Forms comprise cups, bowls, jugs and jars, the last two ranging in height from about 40 centimeters to one meter. A degree of continuity from Early Bronze II (formerly termed the Copper Age) and down into the subsequent Middle Bronze Age is apparent, especially at Kanes.

This ware is handmade, with a rich variety of painted designs, albeit based on rather few motifs. These are arranged in continuous bands or separated into defined areas, or metopes, divided by broad vertical bands or by narrow lines, straight or wavy. A reddish slip usually covers the interior of the cup or bowl, making a stripe below the rim outside, a lighter slip covering the exterior.

This **pottery** is often termed Cappadocian, from its arrival on the antiquities market at the same time as the **tablets** plundered from the site of the *karum* of Kanes, which drew **Bedrich Hrozny** to undertake his excavations.

ALIŞAR IV WARE. Misnamed Phrygian, the repertoire of this ware nevertheless includes similarities of form to **Iron Age gray ware**, notably the channel beneath the inside of the rim, a telltale sign of Iron Age date. Most **pottery** is wheelmade, with painted pottery exceeding the finer qualities of plain ware. Painted decoration is the most obvious feature of this ware, with black, dark brown, brown and red paint on a buff ground. Among larger vessels the storage jar, or *krater*, is typical: decoration includes fine lines drawn with a brush well loaded with paint and thickening the line as it was withdrawn. Concentric circles were compass-drawn. Stags with "feathered" antlers are distinctive of this period.

The distribution of Alışar IV ware covers a very wide zone across the old Hittite homeland in and around the bend of the **Marrassantiya**, the Pontic region near the Black Sea, formerly the **Kaska** lands, and southeastward to the upper Euphrates, where it occurs at **Malatya (Arslantepe)**. There is a tendency erroneously to attribute most pottery of this class to the eighth century BC. There is, however, a considerable ceramic continuity into the Persian and Hellenistic periods (Alışar V).

ALIŞAR HÖYÜK. This large settlement mound is now generally identified with **Ankuwa**, though previously with **Kussara**. It is situated between Sorgun and Kayseri, 15 kilometers northwest of Sarıkaya. This site was excavated by the Oriental Institute of the University of Chicago between 1927 and 1932, under the direction of **Erich Schmidt** and **Hans Henning von der Osten**. This was one of many expeditions funded by the Oriental Institute through Rockefeller munificence, running simultaneously in the Near East, in Egypt, Palestine, Syria, Iraq, Iran and Turkey.

Many occupation levels were distinguished on the summit and in the lower areas of this extensive site, the separation of the areas of excavation contributing to a certain eccentricity in the numbering of the main successive periods. The earliest occupation, dating well back into the fourth millennium BC, was followed by Early Bronze Age levels. Then the sequence of periods jumps from I to III, the later Early Bronze Age, approximately the second half of the third millennium BC, followed by Alışar II, the Middle Bronze Age or early second millennium BC. The site appears to have been deserted during the Late Bronze Age, the time of the Hittite state, although this fact was not recognized by the excavators, at a time when knowledge of Anatolian prehistory was in its infancy. The site was reoccupied during the Iron Age and down into Hellenistic times (Alışar IV–V).

The painted **pottery** of Alışar III is the most distinctive feature of this period, being thus named or, alternatively, Cappadocian ware: cups and large jars are the most typical forms, the vessels being handmade. The following period, Alışar II, yielded evidence of an Assyrian *karum*, one of the network of trading colonies centered on **Kültepe-***karum* IB (ca.1850–1800 BC). **Tablets** of this time from Alışar Level 10TC mention both **Pithana** and his son **Anitta**, rulers of the city of **Nesa (Kanes)**. The abrupt end of this **trade** throughout central Anatolia may well have contributed to the abandonment of the whole settlement, which had been heavily fortified, especially in its gateways.

The reoccupation, some time after the fall of the Hittite Empire, is marked by distinctive painted pottery, with forms largely similar to those of the so-called Phrygian gray ware so widespread in western Anatolia and the Konya Plain. Though complete pots of this Alışar IV painted ware are readily distinguishable from the painted Alışar III vessels, small sherds collected on the surface of sites can be hard to differentiate, although the general context usually clarifies matters.

ALP, SEDAT. Turkish Hittitologist in the University of Ankara. He has directed excavations at **Karahöyük (Konya)**, intermittently since 1953; and has also carried out investigations at **Kululu**.

ALSE. A land lying between **Isuwa** and the heartland of **Mitanni**, whose ruler allowed **Suppiluliuma I** to march through from his conquest of Isuwa to **Wassukkanni**. Mitannian rule must have been resented, for Alse joined in the devastation of the kingdom by **Assur-uballit I (1354-1321 BC)** of Assyria, carrying off and brutally executing the **charioteers**, finally destroying the **army** of Mitanni.

ALTINTEPE. An Urartian citadel in the Erzincan plain, not far east of the modern city and one of two adjoining Iron Age hill sites. Excavations were conducted under the direction of **Tahsin Özgüç** (1959–1966). Its most notable features are a square **temple** of the standard Urartian design and a large columned hall. Large storage jars are incised with annotations of content and capacity in "Hittite" (**Luwian**), not Urartian **hieroglyphs**.

This citadel guarded the northwest frontier of the kingdom of **Urartu**, though the **trade** route on which it stood was never as important as the more southerly routes.

AMARNA. The term commonly applied to the period, **religion** and art of the reign of the heretic pharaoh Akhenaten (1352–1336 BC). *See* **TELL EL-AMARNA (AKHETATEN)**.

AMMUNA. Though the *Proclamation* of **Telipinu** depicts a reign of utter disaster and disintegration, this may not have been true throughout his rule, for he campaigned from **Arzawa** in the southwest to the Euphrates River in the east. But an array of subject and neighboring territories seem to have banded against Hatti, including Arzawa and Adan (iy) a in **Kizzuwadna**. The loss of the latter, along with Hahha (Lidar Höyük), deprived the Hittite kingdom of its grip on north Syria with its resources. **Hurrians** and probably already northerners from **Kaska** were encroaching on the Hittite realm, with even the homeland endangered. Though Ammuna died of natural causes, bloodshed followed his death.

AMURRU. Previously a term applied to a wide zone over which the pastoralist Amorites roamed in the later third millennium BC, it had—from the time of the **archives** of **Mari** and **Alalakh**—become restricted to a region of central and southern Syria and finally to the territory between the upper Orontes valley and the Mediterranean coast, thus including modern Lebanon and lying south of the kingdom of **Ugarit**. Earlier it had been associated with the **Habiru**.

Relations between Amurru and Egypt underwent marked changes, from its conquest by Thutmose III (1479–1425 BC) through the seizure of power with the help of marauding Habiru by one named Abdi-Asirta to the succession of his son Aziru. Fifteen of his letters to the pharaoh Akhenaten (1352–1336 BC), his overlord, survive. Gradually Aziru came to switch his allegiance from Akhenaten to **Suppiluliuma I**, who already had his own nominee as Hittite vassal at **Kadesh**. Though obliged to go to Egypt for a year or more, Aziru was finally released to defend Amurru against a probable Hittite attack. Instead, Aziru made a **treaty** with Suppiluliuma, his position reinforced by alliances with Niqmaddu of Ugarit and Aitakkama of Kadesh. He remained a loyal Hittite vassal to his death.

Seti I of Egypt (1294–1279 BC), launching an aggressive policy in Asia to regain the Empire of the 18th Dynasty, achieved the reconquest of both Kadesh and Amurru, which **Muwatalli II** was obliged, however reluctantly, to accept. The major Hittite gain from the **battle of Kadesh** (1274 BC) was indeed the regaining of Amurru. **Ramesses II**, however, in his eighth and ninth years again marched into the Hittite zone, down the Orontes valley. Until the treaty between **Hattusili III** and Ramesses II (1258 BC) there remained the threat of another confrontation between the two great powers.

Although Muwatalli II removed Bentesina, ruler of Amurru (ca.1290/1280–1235 BC), he was eventually reinstated by Hattusili III. His standing was improved by a double **marriage** between the Hittite royal family and that of Amurru. After the death of Bentesina **Tudhaliya IV** confirmed the succession of his son Sausgamuwa by treaty. Complications arose when Ammistamru of Ugarit divorced the sister of Sausgamuwa, in a bitter dispute possibly arising from her adultery. A dispute between two leading vassals was most unwelcome in Hattusa.

Amurru is mentioned at the fall of the Hittite Empire, when Ramesses III's inscription on the walls of his **temple** of Medinet Habu states that the **Sea Peoples** set up a camp in one place in Amurru, devastating the land.

ANATOLIAN RELIGION: EARTH AND WATER. While the predominant deity in the pantheons—**Hattian**, Hittite, **Luwian** and **Hurrian**—of the second millennium BC is most widely reckoned to have been the **Weather-God** or **Storm-God**, greater emphasis is sometimes placed on the **god** or gods of earth and especially of water, notably in the Hattian pantheon. This certainly had far-reaching impact on Hittite religion, so much so that it is hard to separate the two, although the Hurrian pantheon is readily distinguishable.

Water divinities were associated especially with springs and holes in the ground, where Hattian rituals were particularly performed. Earth was linked with a goddess rather than a god, comparable with the "Earth Mother" or Demeter/Gemeter of the Classical world, and thus naturally with fertility of the crops. It is in such a context that one may approach the reliefs of **Eflatun Pınar** ("Plato's Spring").

It does seem possible that Indo-European elements were less prominent in Hattian-Hittite religion than might have been expected, if sky-, mountain-, storm- and weather-gods were not placed in the highest rank. Yet Taru, a Storm-God, had as his consort the **Sun-Goddess** of **Arinna**, this pair heading the Hattian pantheon. Thus it is difficult to argue that chthonic elements, worship of earth and water from the earth, predominated over those associated with the sky. Perhaps the former were essentially the focus of ritual for the rural poor, not requiring the construction of shrines or the support of a priesthood.

The limitations of the evidence still challenge the specialists, the archaeological data, including the **glyptic art**, naturally being susceptible to speculation and differences of interpretation. Moreover, the textual records are related almost exclusively to ritual and cult: mythology independent of these, such as would have been transmitted from one generation to the next, has not survived. The available picture of Hittite-Hattian religion and related literature is therefore far from complete. Let it not be forgotten that the word *DU* ("god") is probably related to **Proto-Indo-European** *deus*. The chthonic aspect of Anatolian religion persisted through and indeed beyond the time of the Hittite Empire, evident in the rituals associated with the **Underworld** and in the role of **Nergal**, prominent in the reliefs of **Yazılıkaya**.

ANCESTOR CULT. Reverence for forebears in Hittite society normally focused on the **gods** and the kings, with close association with the **Underworld**, presided over especially by the goddess **Lelwani**. The center of attention in the Underworld was the sacred cultic ditch, references to which indicate a feature varying between a deep hole resembling a well and a shallow, narrow incision with a cup-like depression, such as occurs widely carved into rock-cut shrines. The cultic ditch was the abode of gods and dead kings alike.

The Hittite kings were never deified during their lifetime, but became divine at the moment of death, thus differing from other rulers, including the pharaohs of Egypt. A new king owed a special debt of veneration for his dead father and predecessor on the throne; and this seems curiously accentuated where there was an identity of name, notably as between **Tudhaliya IV** and **I** and between **Suppiluliuma II** and **I**, separated by several generations. The name always had a deep meaning, almost magical, in the ancient Near East, reflected in the deliberate obliteration of the name of the god Amun by the heretical pharaoh Akhenaten in New Kingdom Egypt and by the subsequent erasures of his own name. Moreover, the psalmists frequently refer to blotting out the name.

It seems that the gods of the Underworld had more direct connection with the royal funerary rituals than did those of agriculture, notably **Telipinu**, the god generally responsible for the fertility of the soil and thus for human sustenance. Yet one text credits this god, son of the **Storm-God**, with the foundation of the Hittite kingdom. Moreover, in the eighth day of the royal funerary ritual, the image given to the king is that of a shepherd, accompanied by the pious prayer that his livestock may graze unharmed in his meadow.

Of course patriarchal succession had its roots in the earliest Indo-European tribal communities, and veneration for his royal ancestors had the objective of strengthening the king's claim to legitimacy. The cult of the ancestors was linked not only to the gods of the Underworld and of agriculture but also to the solar cults of earth and sky, the latter particularly ancient among the Indo-Europeans. The gods were conceived as above, though not far removed from, the king, as he was above his subjects. Indeed, one myth told of a **marriage** between a goddess and a mortal, which gave birth to the Hittite people. Marriage between a Hittite divinity and a man from the enemy side, however, was literally fatal in its outcome.

The development of the ancestor cult among the Hittites, most evident in the royal family, had its roots in several ethnic backgrounds, initially **Hattian** from the central lands in and around the Halys basin and then also **Palaic**, from Paphlagonia adjoining the Black Sea, **Luwian** from the Taurus region and eventually **Hurrian** from **Kizzuwadna**. Thus it reflected the heterogeneous character of the **religion** of the Hittite state, in due course codified as the official **pantheon**, the "thousand gods."

In one ritual, on the 16th day of the Spring Festival, devoted to the War-God, after the meat offering and libations in the sacred places of the **temple**, a final libation was poured out by Tudhaliya IV at the **statue** of his father **Hattusili III**, who had become his ancestor and thus a god. The sense of dynastic continuity was thereby reinforced. *See also* **ANATOLIAN RELIGION: EARTH AND WATER.**

ANITTA. The son and successor of **Pithana**, through the record he left in the Anitta Text he is the earliest king whom we may term Hittite, even with a questionmark over this description. His reign is reasonably well documented, albeit from one main source, the so-called Anitta Text. This was in the original probably written in "Hittite" (Nesite) **cuneiform** rather than in Old Assyrian.

The conquests of Pithana and Anitta in due course extended from **Zalpa** in the Pontic region near the Black Sea southward to Ullamma, the **Lower Land** of later sources. These territories were inhabited by different ethnic groups, perhaps aware of their differences mainly through **language**. A sense of territorial identity had been strengthened as a result of the trading network established by the Assyrian merchants, with the opportunities afforded for levying local **taxes** on the merchandise.

Almost inevitably Anitta soon faced a major rebellion, requiring firm and continued military responses. One of these rebels was Piyusti, king of Hatti, whose royal seat, **Hattusa**, was captured and destroyed, though only after a long siege had reduced the inhabitants to starvation. A curse was laid on the site by Anitta: "On its site I sowed weeds. May the **Storm-God** strike down anyone who becomes king after me and resettles Hattusa."

This recalls the later sowing of salt on the site of Carthage by the victorious Romans. This destruction is archaeologically attested in **Boğazköy: Büyükkale** IVd and **Kültepe-Kanes** IB.

Anitta had not finished his campaigning, for he next had to march south against Salatiwara, a city on the road from the kingdom of **Wahsusana** to that of **Burushattum**. He interrupted his military activities by building **fortifications** and several **temples** in Kanes, the latter used for storing booty. A sense of royal prestige and propaganda is hinted at by the importation of a varied range of animals, from lions and leopards to wild pigs and goats: the novelty of a zoological collection appealed to a number of Near Eastern rulers, including Assyrian kings. Word would get around, all the more quickly in a society where the overwhelming majority was illiterate.

On his second southern campaign Anitta carried off much **silver** and **gold** from Salatiwara, as well as soldiers and 40 teams of **horses**. Finally he marched against Purushanda (Burushhattum in the Old Assyrian merchant **tablets**). Its king, albeit ruling a widely respected realm, had the wisdom voluntarily to submit to the upstart Anitta, king of Kanes, bringing gifts including a throne and a scepter of **iron**. Perhaps owing to his submission, he was treated honorably: his precise status thereafter is unknown; but the control of Burushhattum was a prestigious addition to Anitta's power.

It is remarkable how rapidly Anitta's conquests dissolved after his death, followed by the collapse of the Assyrian merchant colonies, Kültepe-Kanes IB and its contemporaries. Yet a precedent had been set for the more enduring achievements of **Hattusili I** and his successors.

ANKHESENAMUN (ANKHESENPAATEN). A remarkable event occurred in the later years of the reign of **Suppiluliuma I**, an event over which hangs the mystery of an unsolved crime, and which had unforeseeable and disastrous consequences.

Tutankhamun, the young Egyptian king, had died at the age perhaps of no more than 18 years, leaving a young widow, Ankhesenamun (Ankhesenpaaten before the restoration of the cult of Amun), depicted in **silver** on the back of an ornate chair from the tomb of Tutankhamun, whose treasures are now displayed in the Cairo Museum. This Egyptian queen, who had no children, felt herself under dire threat from those who would try to seize the throne, notably the priest Ay, who was much her senior and whom she had no wish to marry.

It is to the *Deeds of Suppiluliuma* that one must turn for the extraordinary approach by the Egyptian queen to the Hittite king, all the more remarkable given the recent hostilities between the two kingdoms. The death of the Egyptian pharaoh Niphururiya is mentioned, an exact rendering in the **cuneiform** script of Nebkheperure, the prenomen of Tutankhamun. In the *Deeds* is the queen's request, almost curtly stated: "I have no sons. But they say you have many sons. If you would give me one of your sons, he would become my husband. I will never take a servant of mine and make him my husband!"

This request came to Suppiluliuma by a messenger from Egypt, as he was making ready his final attack on **Carchemish**. "Such a thing has never happened to me in my whole life!" he exclaimed. He sought the advice of his nobles, and then decided to dispatch his chamberlain to Egypt, to discover the full facts, having presumably realized the far-reaching political implications: the possibility of the union of the two great kingdoms, Egypt and Hatti, the one in a slow decline and the other reaching its zenith.

The reaction from Ankhesenamun was swift and sharp, demanding to know why her word was doubted. Her letter in turn provoked the anger of Suppiluliuma, who recalled the treacherous attack on **Kadesh** and the consequent Hittite retaliation against Amka, in Egyptian territory. In the *Deeds* he responded that his son: "...will in some way become a hostage. You will not make him king!" Then an experienced Egyptian diplomat, Hani, spoke in very conciliatory, even ingratiating tones, finally winning Suppiluliuma over, the text of the *Deeds* expressing matters thus: "Since my father was kind-hearted, he complied with the word of the woman, and concerned himself with the matter of (supplying her with) a son."

Suppiluliuma had five sons, but the only one available, because not assigned specific responsibilities, was the fourth son, Zannanza, who was sent on his way to Egypt, his father having assured himself that the young man would come to no harm. When news reached him at **Hattusa** that his son had been killed, it was inevitable that he would seek revenge against Egypt and specifically against Ay, the one-time adviser of Akhenaten and now the new pharaoh. On the principle of *cui bonum*? he was the prime suspect beyond doubt, though there seems no proof of his guilt. He certainly did not want a confrontation with Hatti: that is the one point in his favor.

Hittite forces were dispatched to southern Syria under the command of the crown prince, the future **Arnuwanda II**, and thousands of prisoners of war were taken and sent back to the Hittite homeland. With them they took the **plague** which was to afflict Hatti for up to 20 years, carrying off both Suppiluliuma and his immediate successor and leaving the throne to his youngest son, **Mursili II**. Thus did momentous events follow from the premature death of Tutankhamun and the spirited effort by his widow to find a new royal husband. She had in the end to be content with Ay.

ANKUWA. A town located probably approximately halfway between **Nesa** (Kanes) and **Hattusa**, this can arguably be identified with **Alışar Höyük**, and more specifically with Alışar 10TC-TB, contemporary with **Kültepe** Karum IB. It was the site of a royal palace favored by the Hittite kings as a winter residence, presumably owing to its milder climate compared with Hattusa. One consignment of 70 kilograms of **copper** was sent to Hattusa in the 13th century BC, originating from Ankuwa, although normally goods were sent to Hattusa from Ankuwa as tribute (*mandattu*) in fairly small quantities.

The archaeological record, however, attests a period of abandonment of the site of Alışar Höyük during the Late Bronze Age, between Alışar II and Alışar IV. This presents something of a problem, therefore, in relation to the identification of Ankuwa, since its role in the days of the Hittite state is documented solely in the surviving written records from Hattusa, without archaeological support. Yet it must be remembered that large areas of the mound of Alışar Höyük, excavated before the modern techniques of surface exploration had been developed, have not been investigated.

ANNALS. This, the most readily understandable if not necessarily entirely reliable form of **historiography**, was developed by the Hittite kings before any others in the Near East, beginning with the opening of the Empire period, under **Tudhaliya I/II** and for later reigns. The annals of **Arnuwanda I**, **Suppiluliuma I** (composed by his son) and, most outstanding of all, **Mursili II** have been preserved; but those of **Muwatalli II** have not yet been recovered. The annals of **Hattusili III** survive only in fragmentary form. For **Tudhaliya IV** and **Suppiluliuma II** there are no **cuneiform** annals, the fashion changing radically to **hieroglyphic** inscriptions in the **Luwian language**.

ANU. Mesopotamian Sky-God, who features in **Hurrian** mythology. He overcame **Alalu** as King of Heaven, being ousted in turn by his son **Kumarbi**. Like other dethroned **gods**, he was consigned to the **Underworld**.

ARCHERY. At its most deadly as a **chariot**-borne mode of attack during the battlefield charge, the light infantry also used the composite bow, made of strips of wood and horn glued and bound together. In reliefs the bow is depicted either in triangular form or with its ends curving outward. It had been introduced into Anatolia most probably from **Mitanni** or its **Hurrian** precursors, but conceivably as early as the Akkadian period. The manufacture of the composite bow was costly in time and the craftsmen's skills, and it required selected materials: it would hardly have been available to the poor;

and its possession carried a certain prestige. Arrows were of bronze, with a tang attaching the head to a wood or reed shaft and sometimes barbed. Arrows were not made of **iron** widely in the Near East before the eighth century BC, for it was too valuable to be thrown away. Quivers were made of bark or leather, probably taking up to 30 arrows.

ARCHITECTS. There are a few Hittite texts which cast light not only on **building methods** and materials but also on the responsibilities and remuneration of the architect. Such texts are essentially foundation rituals, involving many sacrifices. Archaeological evidence reflecting these texts occurs at **Hattusa** and elsewhere, as at **Maşat Höyük**.

A unique foundation ritual of the 13th century BC may refer to a private house rather than a **temple**, though it is noteworthy that three pillars are described, the same number as in the stoa of **Temple I** at Hattusa. If these pillars (or, more precisely, piers) can be equated with those set on the massive stone footings of Temple I and elsewhere, these will be the pilasters which are a basic element of Hittite architecture, in effect part of the **timber** frame, supporting the roof. A sacrifice for the foundation stones—comparable in intent with the foundation deposits so common in Mesopotamia—and a magical formula to ward off evil from the building are included in this text from Hattusa.

The architects must have been young and energetic, their agility indicated by a passage in the above-mentioned text:

> When the workmen haul the beams up to the roof, the architect who builds the house is the one who shall climb up the rope to the roof. He goes up the rope to the roof (?) twice and [he goes] down twice. While he is climbing the rope, the singers run around the **hearth**. The third time [the architect] cuts the sling. When the architect cuts the sling, the cheer-leader claps his hands. But there is a sash dangling from the roof beam. In this sash are bound an **ax** of **silver** and a knife of silver. Now that sash too he cuts off. Then the architect comes down by the rope, and he bows to the owner of the house. When he goes to his own house, the architect takes the ax of silver and the knife of silver for himself (as his fee).

ARCHITECTURE. *See* **ARCHITECTS; BUILDING METHODS; CYCLOPEAN MASONRY; TIMBER AND TIMBER CON-**

STRUCTION.

ARCHIVES. For efficient business administration, filing systems for clay **tablets** were essential, being exemplified by those in the house of one of the Assyrian merchants at **Kanes** in *karum* II: opened correspondence was kept in orderly rows in the storeroom separate from the unopened tablets, still in their envelopes and with their **bullae**. In another merchant's house letters were kept quite separate from loan documents, probably in another room or even another house. The texts often refer to mobility of documents, and by implication to their storage. On the death of a merchant or his permanent return to Assur, all or part of his archives were taken thither. Documents might be circulated or moved about within Anatolia. Legal requirements often necessitated dispatch of tablets to or from Assur. Memoranda of original texts mainly concerning Assyrians in summary or complete copy were sent to Assur. Twenty-four tablets, mostly credit or debt notes or bonds, survive from the records of a lawsuit between two merchants, the complainant alleging theft of sealed tablet containers from the "guest house."

In *karum* II at Kanes the Assyrian merchants' houses have yielded many more tablets than those of the Anatolian merchants, housed in areas in the north and south respectively of the *karum*. The local traders were surely not less literate so much as less in need of extensive correspondence with Assur. Not every house had tablets, numbers varying greatly. In the larger houses a "store" room tended to serve as the archive, with other tablets—perhaps those most likely to be required for reference—in the "main" room. In smaller houses available spaces in the living quarters had to be used for storing tablets. Containers for tablets might be **pottery** jars, boxes or baskets. Tablets were also stored on shelves, as, for example, at Ebla and **Hattusa,** on straw matting, in rows or in stacks. Boxes of tablets could be sealed and held in a "safe" or sealed room. Labels were often found with tablets.

As yet the published data do not make it possible to connect **seals** with those officials or traders in charge of archives. Two difficulties are the rarity of fathers' names and the method of storage of the tablets.

In marked contrast with the individual or family basis of the Old Assyrian archives at Kültepe-Kanes, with tablets of the *karum* IB period found also at Hattusa and **Alışar Höyük**, the archives of the Hittite Empire—mainly from Hattusa but also exemplified by tablets from **Maşat Höyük** and **Ortaköy** and other cities outside the homeland but under Hittite control—illuminate the administration of a far-flung state, with its powerful bureaucracy. The most important of those archives only partly relevant to Hittite affairs have been found in a number of the major buildings of **Ugarit**.

Shelving has naturally not survived, but the manner in which tablets had fallen, as found by the excavators, makes this method of storage and filing apparent, notably at Ebla in Syria in third-millennium BC context.

It is on **Boğazköy: Büyükkale** that the major royal archives of Hattusa have been recovered by the German excavators, from their first season (1906) onwards. That first discovery was made in Building E in the royal residential quarters and on the slope in front. Other archives were found in Buildings A and K, north of the East Gate. Yet more tablets were recovered from **Temple I (Boğazköy)**. As **Jürgen Seeher** puts it:

> The archives of clay tablets found in Buildings A, E and K have played a most important role in our research of Hittite history. The hundreds of tablets that had been stored on wooden shelves here have perpetuated not only contracts and official documents but oracular prophecies, instruction in cult practice, folklore, collections of legal decisions and historical texts as well. While most of these survived the burning of the palace complex, the information included in the archives of wooden tablets has been lost for ever.

In the archive rooms of Hattusa mud-plastered stone benches were surmounted by the wooden shelves, where the tablets were originally arranged by their content and labeled, under the supervision of the "tablet librarian." Comparable duties were assigned to those responsible for the wooden tablets. During the final years leading to the downfall of Hatti, however, this orderly filing was probably discontinued.

The archives at Hattusa included that in the House on the Slope and, more significantly, thousands of tablets and fragments from the storerooms outside the southeast side of the **temple** proper in the Temple I precinct. It was here that, among other texts, **treaties** were kept, perhaps from their association with the **gods**.

One disruption brought about by the rebellion by **Kurunta** was widespread disturbance of the archives of Hattusa, especially those on Büyükkale. The tablets therefore cannot have been excavated in their original filing order. Likewise the move to and back from **Tarhuntassa**, under **Muwatalli II** and **Urhi-Tesub**, doubtless involved transfer of archives.

The archives of Ugarit comprise six in the palace and many in private houses, including that of Urtenu, a powerful figure close to the throne in the last decades of the city's history. Foreign relations are attested, principally with Hittite centers (Hattusa, Tarhuntassa, **Carchemish**, Usnatu, **Kadesh** and **Emar**) but also with Egypt, Canaan (Beirut and Sidon), Assyria and the land of Suhi, on the middle Euphrates. As the central Hittite power weakened, Ugarit was becoming increasingly restive.

ARIK, REMZI OGUZ. Codirector, with **Hamit Koşay**, of the first campaign of excavations at **Alaca Höyük**. He also directed excavations at **Göllüdağ**.

ARINNA. One of several major **cult centers**, this became probably the leading holy city of the Hittites by the time of the Empire. Like so many sites recorded in the texts, it is yet to be located with certainty, although anywhere outside the central Hittite homeland is ruled out by a reference to Arinna as being situated within one day's march of the capital, **Hattusa**. A location west of another shrine, **Nerik**, would place Arinna just west of the lower **Marrassantiya** River, approximately north-northwest of Hattusa. Surely more plausible a location would be at **Alaca Höyük**, a short day's march north-northeast of Hattusa, where there is clear archaeological evidence of its status in the Empire, as well as earlier remains likely to have relevance to the cult of Arinna.

The origins of Arinna undoubtedly lie in the **Hattian** traditions and pantheon rooted in the prehistory of central Anatolia and eventually by stages adapted by the Hittite state. The early pantheon of Arinna includes the Sun-God, **Sun-Goddess** and **Storm-God**. The Sun-Goddess of Arinna was considered to be married to the Storm-God of Hatti, both helping the Hittite king in battle. In the six-year **annals** of **Hattusili I** we find not the Sun-God but the Sun-Goddess of Arinna, making her earliest textual appearance. Hattusili I brings back booty to her **temple**, as well as to those of the Storm-God and Mezulla, divine daughter of the Sun-Goddess. Though this text survives only in late copies, there are sound arguments against any suggestion that the name of Arinna was a later insertion by a **scribe**. The Sun-Goddess of Arinna, later often named **Wurusemu**, was certainly Hattian: her relationship to the Hattian sun-deity Estan, especially if she is also a goddess, remains problematical.

It is in the early 13th century BC that the documentation for Arinna and its Sun-Goddess is particularly clear, at a time when— largely on the initiative of the Great Queen **Puduhepa**, wife of **Hattusili III**—both **Hurrian** and Hattian divinities were being assimilated into the large and varied Hittite **pantheon**, the so-called "Thousand Gods of Hatti." Puduhepa addresses this leading divinity simply as "Sun Goddess of Arinna." Hattusili III had a prayer to her composed following his deposition of his nephew **Urhi-Tesub (Mursili III)** and his seizure of the throne: "O Sun Goddess of Arinna, lady of the land, queen of heaven and earth, the lady of the king and the **queen** of the Hatti lands, the light of the country of the Hatti. . . . " More personal and informative is another prayer, composed by Puduhepa herself:

> O Sun Goddess of Arinna, queen of all the lands! You bear the name of the Sun Goddess of Arinna in the country of the Hatti, but in the country which you created, the country of the cedar trees, your name is **Hepat**, and Puduhepa has always been at your service.

"The country of the cedar trees" has to be the eastern Taurus range rather than the Lebanon. While Hepat was indeed goddess of the Hurrians, the Hattian ancestry of the Sun-Goddess of Arinna has already been stressed. She was no Hurrian. Here was a strong political agenda.

ARMOR. This, with protective clothing as an alternative, was in common use, though it is usually hard to determine for sure whether it is being depicted. The figure in the King's Gate at **Hattusa** may be wearing a sleeveless shirt of scale armor: pieces of bronze scale armor have been excavated at Hattusa; and two probable **iron** armor scales were found at **Korucutepe**. Chain mail was also used, and may conceivably be represented at the King's Gate, although it is more probably chest hair that is indicated. The long, ankle-length clothing of the Hittite infantry depicted on the Egyptian reliefs of the battle of **Kadesh** could represent chain mail, seeing that they are not carrying **shields**.

ARMY. The Hittite state should not rightly be termed militaristic, for the kings did not glory in war after the manner of Egypt and Assyria: no reliefs survive depicting a Hittite king on the battlefield, and, for example, the only pictorial records of the engagement at **Kadesh** are to be found in Egypt. With the possible exception of **Hattusili I**, Hittite kings did not revel in the bloodshed suffered by their enemies. Nevertheless, war was the natural condition of men: there was no ideal vision of peace. Moreover, war benefited the state, both in material plunder and in subsequent tribute, as well as essential augmentation of manpower through prisoners of war.

The king was commander in chief, leading his forces on campaign but always, it seems, avoiding exposure to mortal danger on the battlefield. This was not out of timidity but for sound political reasons: the risks to the internal security of the kingdom from a sudden royal death were far too great to bear contemplation. If engaged elsewhere or in ill-health, the king would delegate supreme military command to his designated successor, the crown prince, whose first exposure to campaigning might come as early as about 12 years of age. The crown prince was succeeded in rank by the king's brothers. Perhaps the outstanding example of successful delegation occurred under **Suppiluliuma I**, whose eldest son, later to become **Arnuwanda II**, became a seasoned commander in his father's reign, while two other sons became **viceroys** of **Aleppo** and **Carchemish**.

The Hittite army carried out nonmilitary duties when not on campaign, such as helping with construction works or even on occasion at **festivals**. Senior commanders might be selected as governors, as was Hannutti, appointed by Suppiluliuma—before or after his ascending the throne—to administer the strategically important **Lower Land**. Individual generals are named quite often in the Hittite records, usually but not invariably in the context of successful operations.

Officers of rather lower rank, roughly equivalent to colonel, would be in command of about 1,000 men. The great majority of soldiers were infantrymen, up to 90 percent, the remainder forming the elite **chariotry**. The few **horse** riders were deployed as scouts and dispatch riders: the army had no cavalry. This was, by ancient Near Eastern standards, a disciplined, well-trained force, the training of the charioteers being particularly rigorous, as implied by the famous manual of **Kikkuli**. For junior officers and those in the ranks there was a stern oath-taking ceremony: those breaking the oath were to become as women!

While most of the troops were required on campaign, spending winter in barracks in **Hattusa**, some units were deployed along the borders, especially confronting the **Kaska** tribesmen in the north, under the control of officers with the title of "Lord of the Watch-Tower."

Specialist training was desirable for **sieges**, though this does not seem to have been a strong point with the Hittite army. Nevertheless, this was the natural sequel to defeating an enemy on his own ground.

Undoubtedly the demands of the army for manpower were a constant drain on a realm in large areas underpopulated. For many years this drain could be countered by **deportation** and resettlement, mostly of prisoners of war, who might be employed on the land, in building works and even assisting at festivals. With the 20-year **plague** afflicting the realm from the final years of Suppiluliuma I, however, came a disaster from which to a degree the Hittite Empire probably never fully recovered. Recruitment to the army must have been affected. For a normal campaign against a rebellious vassal or hostile neighbor 10,000 soldiers sufficed, their discipline and **weaponry** usually assuring victory. No fewer than some 47,500 troops were led by **Muwatalli II** against **Ramesses II** at Kadesh; but these included units from Syrian vassals, notably **Ugarit** and **Amurru**. A considerable time had been required in preparation for this major campaign.

ARNUWANDA I (ca.1380–1360 BC). A capable and trustworthy successor to **Tudhaliya I/II**, who must have made him coregent, a fact indicated by his bearing the title of Great King *before* his accession. Tudhaliya called him his son; but this raises the problem of a brother-sister marriage, strictly prohibited under the **Hittite Laws**. Arnuwanda's wife was Asmunikal, daughter of Tudhaliya and his wife Nikkalmati. The likeliest explanation is that Tudhaliya made his son-in-law his adopted son, in the absence of a legitimate male heir: this device was permitted by the **Telipinu** *Proclamation*. It was a wise choice, for Arnuwanda became a seasoned campaigner, like his grandson **Suppiluliuma I**, with considerable achievements to his credit before ascending the throne. Yet he faced mounting dangers.

In the lands of **Nerik, Kastama** and other areas in the north numerous **cult centers** were looted and destroyed, in spite of prayers uttered in the joint names of Arnuwanda and Asmunikal. A series of **treaties** was drawn up with the **Kaska** people, though to little avail.

In the southeast Arnuwanda endeavored to shore up his power. A treaty was drawn up with the city of **Ura** on the Mediterranean coast in Kizzuwadna. He also took steps to punish Mita of Pahhuwa, a city near the upper Euphrates. His offense was to have married the daughter of a known enemy of Arnuwanda, who summoned neighboring cities to his aid, ordering them to move against Pahhuwa, failing surrender of the errant Mita. The outcome is not known; but some comparison with the Indictment of Madduwatta is appropriate. In both regions Hittite propaganda was brought into play.

In Syria there was a resurgence of **Mitanni**, eventually sealed by a diplomatic **marriage** alliance with Egypt, providing a political settlement excluding Hittite intervention anywhere in Syria. Egypt secured all the territory as far north as **Kadesh** and to **Amurru** and **Ugarit** on the Mediterranean coast.

ARNUWANDA II (1322–1321 BC). The eldest son and heir of **Suppiluliuma I**, he had become an experienced commander, leading an **army** against **Carchemish** to prepare for the **siege** by his father and later a foray into Egyptian-controlled territory. Succeeding to the throne in **Hattusa**, he died soon afterward, most probably a victim of the **plague**, as his father before him.

ARNUWANDA III (1209-1207 BC). Up to 45 **seal** impressions in the "seal **archive**" of Nişantepe are attributable to this obscure, brief reign. Serious unrest had erupted, and continued after his brother's accession. Arnuwanda III was childless, leaving the throne clear for his brother **Suppiluliuma II**, who was probably very anxious to avoid internecine strife within the royal family and their respective supporters. This can explain his vehement disclaimer of any hand in the death of Arnuwanda III. *See* **BOĞAZKÖY: NIŞANTAS AND ENVIRONS**

ARZANA-**HOUSES.** These were hostelries or inns, dispensing **food**, beer and **wine**, as well as a drink of uncertain character. **Music** and entertainment might be provided, and royal guests could be entertained. While there are scant references in official documents, data can be gleaned from legal, literary, ritual and **festival** texts. The precise character of the *arzana*-house nevertheless remains obscure: there are no records of payments for food or drink. Thus they may have been attached to the local **temple**, though this suggestion is hard to reconcile with references to their being sited on a road at a moderate distance outside the city wall. Prohibitions against construction of an inn up against the city wall imply that this did occur. All in all, a secular context seems most likely. If the *arzana*-house could serve also as a brothel, discretion has prevailed.

ARZAWA. Centered in the fertile Aegean hinterland, with its capital at times located at Apasa (later, Ephesus), this could be regarded as the precursor of the kingdom of Lydia in the Iron Age. It formed a major part of the lands known to the Hittites as **Luwiya**, the spoken language being **Luwian**. Arzawa suffered from inherent disunity, with rival rulers claiming sovereignty with varying success at different times. Although hardly anything would be known of Arzawa without the Hittite records, most notably those of **Mursili II**, this kingdom enjoyed a brief prominence with the discovery of the **Tell el-Amarna (Akhetaten)** tablets in Egypt. These include an exchange of correspondence between the Egyptian pharaoh Nimuwariya (Neb-kheper-Re/ Amenhotep III) and **Tarhundaradu**, king of Arzawa, revealing acceptance by the former of the Great King status of the latter, at a time of great weakness of the Hittite kingdom. Indeed, the language of Arzawa was briefly expected to be that of the **archives** of **Hattusa**!

Hittite-Arzawan relations are recorded from the time of **Tudhaliya I/II**, with the names of several Arzawan rulers preserved, though probably not all of them. Relationships are often unclear. Among the enemies of Tudhaliya and his successor, **Arnuwanda I**, was "the man of Arzawa," Kupanta-Kurunta, who was involved with Madduwatta, first as enemy and later as prospective son-in-law, political marriages of course being an accepted device. Tudhaliya I/II's triumph over a coalition of 22 allies, possibly led by **Assuwa**, secured Hittite supremacy in the west for some years but not indefinitely.

Indeed in the following generation, under **Tudhaliya III** (ca.1360–1344 BC), Arzawa was to reach the zenith of its power, thanks to disastrous invasions of Hatti. The defeated Hittites expressed the crisis in dramatic terms: "From the **Lower Land** the Arzawan enemy came, and he too ravaged the Hatti lands and made **Tuwanuwa** and **Uda** his frontier."

The fall of Tuwanuwa (Tyana) into Arzawan hands is attested by the *Deeds* of **Suppiluliuma (I)**, by whom it was recovered, while he was in military command as crown prince acting for his father. The *Deeds* are too fragmentary to give a full narrative of

Suppiluliuma's own campaign into Arzawa, though several territories are mentioned, including **Pitassa (Pedassa)**, west of the Salt Lake, **Mira** and **Hapalla**. This is the earliest mention of Mira. Uhhaziti, king of Arzawa, is now first mentioned, in the *Deeds*.

The accession of the youthful Mursili II was marked by widespread rebellions, that in Arzawa being especially serious, the anti-Hittite disaffection being finally quelled in the 12th year of the reign. After dealing with trouble in the north (**Kaska**), Mursili turned his attention to the west, the *casus belli* being the refusal by the Arzawan ruler Uhhaziti to surrender Hittite fugitives, a frequent pretext for war. His Extended Annals record that Mursili II approached Arzawa via the Sehiriya River, then on to **Sallapa**, situated perhaps not far from Eskişehir, and finally to victory over Piyama, son of the Arzawan king, at Walma on the River Astarpa, near modern Afyon. Though still well inland, Mursili made a rapid, apparently unopposed, advance into the heart of Arzawa, reaching Apasa. Meanwhile Uhhaziti had fled across the sea to the islands, the population fleeing likewise. The onset of winter compelled Mursili to withdraw to winter quarters on the River Astarpa, whence he returned the next spring, after Uhhaziti had died "in the sea." He was then able to move his forces against the northern sector of the Arzawan homeland, the **Seha River Land**. Renewed rebellion broke out in the 12th year of Mursili II, Arzawa inciting Mashuiluwa, king of Mira-**Kuwaliya**, to join him against Hittite rule. Perhaps owing to memories of the Hittite success early in the reign of Mursili II, he did not gain wide support, and was deposed in favor of his son Kupanta-Kurunta, a young man whose popularity among his own people secured him the support of Hattusa, Mursili drawing up a **treaty** with him. He imposed one and the same oath on Kupanta-Kurunta and on the rulers of the Seha River Land and Hapalla. The power of Arzawa was never again to reach its former extent. The kingdom was in effect divided into vassal states, the three main ones being Mira with Kuwaliya, the Seha River Land with Appawiya and Hapalla. A fourth vassal state appears in the treaty of **Muwatalli II** with Alaksandu, ruler of **Wilusa**.

Thenceforward peace endured into the next reign, when **Muwatalli II**, preoccupied with planning the campaign against Egypt, had to send Gassu, a senior commander, to quell unrest largely incited by Piyamaradu. During the civil conflict between **Urhi-Tesub** and his uncle **Hattusili (III)** Arzawa remained mostly loyal to the former. Owing in part to the machinations of **Ahhiyawa**,

Hattusili III was not very successful in restoring Hittite control in the Arzawa lands, a task achieved later by his son **Tudhaliya IV**. Hittite rule remained far from popular in the west, even though Mursili II had reduced Arzawa to a rump, Uhhaziti at that time being ruler of "Arzawa Minor," centered on Apasa (Ephesus). This fertile territory eventually became the heart of the kingdom of Lydia, with its capital at Sardis, one of several examples of the impact of the environment on political and economic developments over many centuries in Anatolia. The last reference to Arzawa occurs in the Medinet Habu inscriptions of Ramesses III in Upper Egypt, recording its sharing with Hatti the devastating impact of the **Sea Peoples**.

ARZIYA. A land adjoining the territory of **Carchemish**, subdued by Telipinu—second son of **Suppiluliuma I** and **viceroy** of **Aleppo**— in a successful campaign designed to thwart the ambition of Tusratta, king of **Mitanni**, to regain territory west of the Euphrates River lost to the Hittites.

ASSEMBLY. This body, known as the *panku* or sometimes as the *tuliya*, has attracted more attention among modern specialists than it really merits, often being credited with genuine political power, at least in the Old Kingdom, with its role later diminished, as the monarchy became more attuned to the traditions of Syria and Mesopotamia, not to say Egypt.

While there is some slight truth in this view, in reality the *panku* had strictly limited judicial functions, and could always be overridden by the king. **Hattusili I** advised his grandson and heir, **Mursili I**, to refer anyone committing a major crime such as murder to the *panku*, while always reserving the final verdict to himself. The functions of the assembly may therefore be seen as largely ceremonial, with any real powers lost in the mists of the Indo-European background, in preliterate times.

The assembly was convened only when the king desired, thus very irregularly, indeed rarely in the **Middle Kingdom** and under the Empire. It did not comprise the great men or nobility, as formerly supposed, nor any single social class, but rather the higher state bureaucracy, augmented by members of the royal household. As the *Proclamation* of **Telipinu** phrased it: "Now, from this day in **Hattusa**, may you observe this order, you palace officials, members of the guard, 'golden grooms,' cupbearers, waiters, cooks, heralds, charioteers and commanders of thousands." These evidently composed the assembly. Small wonder that it would not attempt to resist the wishes of the king, their master!

The term *panku* can refer to bodies of men or of troops or even carry the meaning of the Greek *hoi polloi*, the common people, while the largely synonymous term *tuliya* occurs most often in reference to **gods** witnessing a **treaty**.

There is no evidence of an elective system of kingship, the hereditary principle being laid down in the *Proclamation* of **Telipinu**, announced before the *panku* specially summoned by the king to hear his decisions on the succession to the throne. This may be seen as the most significant of all recorded sessions of the assembly.

One point remains problematical: this is the precise relationship between the nobility and the state bureaucracy, for recruitment to which aristocratic birth, as in Pharaonic Egypt, does not seem to have been a prerequisite.

ASSUR-UBALLIT I (1353–1318 BC). Assyrian king who began the revival of Assyrian power, his reign inaugurating the Middle Assyrian period. He weakened the power of **Mitanni**, after its decisive defeat by **Suppiluliuma I**.

ASSUWA. This land has frequently had its name compared with the Roman province of Asia, which lay in the same northwest Anatolian region. Various locations have been proposed: north of the heartland of **Arzawa**, in **Wilusa** or at varying distances east of the Sea of Marmara. If the name is indeed reflected in the Roman province, it could be supposed that Assuwa was an important territory in the Late Bronze Age. No such location, however, can be pinned down.

Rather it appears that Assuwa must have been a name applied in some sense as an alternative to Arzawa, though embracing territories further north. **Tudhaliya I/II** describes it as the leader of a confederacy of 22 allies, extending from the **Lukka** Lands northward: with his stunning victory over this coalition of doubtless ill-assorted units, he claims to have destroyed the land of Assuwa, returning to **Hattusa** with immense booty. A bronze longsword found in 1991 near the Lion Gate at Hattusa has a dedicatory inscription of Tudhaliya to the **Storm-God** after a victory over Assuwa. This **sword** is of a type indicating a workshop in western Anatolia or the Aegean lands, and was presumably part of the booty. Curiously, Assuwa does not feature in later Hittite records.

ASTATA. A kingdom straddling the Euphrates River around the great bend, where it turns southeast to flow into Mesopotamia. This land was situated in a sensitive area, on the ancient **trade** route from the Mesopotamian cities up the Euphrates into Syria and beyond. Whosoever controlled Astata would gain great economic benefits. During the reign of **Tudhaliya III**, when Hittite power was starting to recover, Astata appealed first to **Mitanni** and then to Hatti against the encroachments of **Aleppo**, in each case gaining a favorable response.

Astata comprised a number of excavated sites in the basin of the Tabqa Dam, not only **Emar** but also Ekalte (Tall Munbaqa), Azu (Tall Hadidi), Tall as-Sweyhat, Tall al-Qitar, Tall Frey and Tall Halawa. Almost every text from these sites can be dated to the Late Bronze Age (ca.1600–1200 BC), making them relevant to the power politics involving Mitanni, Egypt, Hatti and Assyria, especially from **Suppiluliuma I** (ca.1344–1322 BC) onward.

Sarrikusuh (Piyassili), third son of Suppiluliuma, successfully campaigned across the Euphrates from **Carchemish**, together with Sattiwaza, in order to restore the latter to the throne of Mitanni. This had become a much reduced realm, partly because, under a **treaty** imposed by Suppiluliuma and binding Sattiwaza in a firm alliance with the **viceroyalty** of Carchemish, four towns of Astata on the west bank of the river and three on the east were transferred from Mitannian control to the viceroyalty of Carchemish under Sarrikusuh. When he died suddenly on a visit to an Anatolian shrine, his nephew **Mursili II** had to march into Syria to quell a revolt, beginning his task with Astata, thus securing his left flank.

Discoveries in Astata, particularly Emar, have added to understanding of the **Hurrian** impact on much of the Near East. Hurrian society in Astata was both patriarchal and patrilineal.

AXES. Many axes will have been used in furtherance of **timber construction** of buildings rather than as battle axes. These are most graphically represented by the weapon carried by the figure in the King's Gate at **Hattusa**. This has spikes above the shaft hole, and in appearance resembles forms found in the Caucasus and Iran, illustrating the international character of the metal industry. The wooden shaft is curved. Axes were of bronze shaft-hole type or the more primitive design, with a flat blade pushed into a split wooden shaft and bound with leather thongs. Axes of **iron** were appearing in the last years of the Hittite Empire.

AZZI (-HAYASA). Often synonymous with **Hayasa,** but should be located immediately to the north, as far as the Black Sea coast. Here the fortress of Aripsa, captured by **Mursili II,** may be identified with Giresun, on an isthmus beside the sea. The **annals** of Mursili II are the chief source for data on Azzi-Hayasa, though it appears earlier in the Hittite records. **Tudhaliya III** relates how the Azzian enemy came from afar and sacked all the **Upper Land,** making **Samuha** his frontier. Then the Hittite counter-offensive began with attacks on **Kaska** and Azzi-Hayasa, described as a kingdom. After defeating the king of Azzi-Hayasa near the city of **Kummaha, Suppiluliuma I** established it as a vassal state by **treaty** with its ruler Hukkana. Mursili II had trouble with Azzi-Hayasa from his seventh till his 10th year, after an attack on the land of Dankuwa, led by its king, Anniya. After a delay to obtain the **omens,** Nuwanza, a highly experienced general, finally defeated Azzi-Hayasa, restoring the Upper Land to Hittite rule in the king's ninth year. But it took another campaign the following year for Mursili II again to reduce Azzi-Hayasa to vassaldom. This unruly mountain population was never well disposed to the Hittite power, and with Kaska was always a potential menace. Later, **Tudhaliya IV** refers to Azzi as enemy territory.

- B -

BEAD-RIM BOWLS. These are among the most widespread Anatolian **pottery** forms in the second millennium BC, a chronological hallmark for anyone undertaking an archaeological survey, with collection of surface sherds. Sites such as **Beycesultan,** where the influence of metal prototypes is particularly evident, have yielded countless examples. A metal vessel would have a dangerously sharp rim, if not folded outward: this has the further advantage of strengthening the vessel. Bead-rim bowls of fired clay, normally in red or buff ware and wheelmade, imitate the folding outward of the metal rim, with varying depth of fold. This is by no means an exclusively Hittite category.

BEYCESULTAN. This large settlement mound in the upper Menderes (Maeander) valley was excavated for six seasons (1954–1959) by an expedition directed by **Seton Lloyd,** assisted by **James Mellaart,** under the auspices of the British Institute of Archaeology at

Ankara. This site has two summits, and extends for over 500 meters from west to east. Surface **pottery** had indicated occupation of the Late Bronze Age, the period when **Arzawa** flourished as the rival of the Hittite power in the west. Although hopes of discovering an **archive** of **cuneiform tablets** were not to be fulfilled, and identification of the site remains less than certain, the results were to prove significant in a less colorful manner.

Beycesultan is one of two sites, along with **Mersin**, providing a long, unbroken stratigraphic sequence of occupation levels over millennia. Though its origins are much later than those of the Mersin settlement, in the early fifth rather than the early seventh millennium BC, it continued as an important community almost to the end of the second millennium BC, well past the time of the fall of **Hattusa**.

Excavations on the western summit revealed a sequence of 21 Late Chalcolithic levels (XL–XX), followed by Early Bronze (Levels XIX–VI), Middle Bronze (V–IV) and Late Bronze Age occupation (III–I). Pottery provides most of the evidence for cultural changes in the Early Bronze Age, with burnished wares comparable with those of **Troy** I giving way in the third and final period to red, highly fired pottery often betraying the influence of metal vessels, with features such as imitation rivets.

The suggestion has been made that the drastic changes in pottery from Early Bronze II to Early Bronze III at Beycesultan can be associated with a specific group of newcomers, the **Luwians**. At a time when it seemed probable that this Indo-European people had arrived in western Anatolia from the Balkans early in the third millennium BC as the first wave of Indo-European immigrants, preceding the Hittites, this was a very reasonable theory. With the raising of the approximate dating for the first Indo-European arrivals in Anatolia, however, this may require some reconsideration. The houses of the Early Bronze III period included some of the distinctive but simple *megaron* plan, with porch and central hearth, indicating a west Anatolian architectural tradition.

Already in the first season of excavations remains of a major burned building were being investigated on the eastern summit. This proved to be a structure rightly described as the burnt palace of Beycesultan V, the most striking example in Anatolia of Bronze Age **timber construction**. As a result of the fire which raged through the building after it had been very thoroughly looted, the walls had sunk down below the earth floors. Along the walls ran cuts which Seton Lloyd surmised to be heating ducts.

The limestone footings had been calcined by the heat, the massive timbers carbonized and the courses of mud brick vitrified. Nevertheless, it proved possible to reconstruct much of the design of this palace, which had at least two stories, a staircase, mural paintings and a courtyard lined on all four sides by colonnades. There are parallels, though not close, with Minoan Crete. This burnt palace was approximately contemporary with the Old Assyrian colonies of central Anatolia, including the *karum* of **Kanes**, and was clearly the residence of an important dynasty, occupied for some generations. It seems virtually certain that there must have been a link with Arzawa; and its destruction may well have been the work of a Hittite force in the early Hittite Old Kingdom. A long period of poverty ensued (Beycesultan IV).

The Late Bronze Age at Beycesultan marks a decline in the importance of this site, though further excavation might reveal that the buildings of Levels III–I represent not merely a residential area, complete with stables and a shop selling **wine**, but a palace, albeit less magnificent than that of Beycesultan V. The pottery is highly distinctive and quite different from any found in the lands under Hittite control, including stemmed goblets resembling in form champagne glasses. The clay used by the potters contained mica, giving a sparkle to the surface of the vessels: this was used very deliberately, yellow mica imitating **gold**, red mica like **copper** and mica giving the effect of **silver**. From such hints one may guess the wealth of metal vessels which have perished.

In Beycesultan I, the final level—apart from Byzantine occupation over much of the mound—comes a hint of a refugee movement, like those of earlier times in Anatolia, in the changes in pottery. Beak-spouted and foliate-mouthed jugs of central Anatolian forms and wares make their appearance. Thus can be detected a faint echo from the downfall of the Hittite state, Beycesultan coming to an end ca.1050/1000 BC.

As for identification of Late Bronze Age Beycesultan, and by implication the city with the burnt palace of Level V, the city of Salawasa in Arzawa is a good candidate. It was from here that **Tudhaliya I/II** rescued the wives and children of Madduwatta, held captive by the king of Arzawa.

BIBLE. The biblical evidence for the Hittites is limited, with a number of brief references to their land and to individuals, many living in the land of Canaan, later the home of the Israelites. This evidence is, however, of some interest, if only because the Old Testament provided the only knowledge of the Hittites until the records of ancient Egypt, most notably the account of the battle of **Kadesh**, became known following the decipherment of the hieroglyphs.

Of course the picture became infinitely clearer with the discovery of the royal **archives** of **Hattusa.** It was at last evident that the Hittites of the Old Testament were largely Neo-Hittites of the postimperial age. It seems likely that elements of the population of Hatti proper in Anatolia on the fall of the Hittite state found their way southward through Syria into Palestine (i.e. the Israelite lands). Hittites are listed as one of the peoples of Canaan, though such references seem to be anachronistic, in particular the mention of Hittites as occupying Hebron (Genesis 23). There are scattered references to the land of the Hittites, among them the promise to the Israelites of the territory "from the wilderness and this Lebanon even unto the great river, the river Euphrates, all the land of the Hittites" (Joshua 1:4). King David's domain in the north bounded "the land of the Hittites towards Kadesh" (II Samuel 24:6). There were two Hittites in David's entourage, albeit both with Semitic names, Ahimelech and **Uriah** (II Samuel 11). Solomon, requiring **horses** and **chariots,** obtained the former from Que, the western part of the former **Kizzuwadna,** and the latter ready-made from Egypt. Thus he acted as a middleman (I Kings 10: 28ff.). Hittite women were included in his ample harem (I Kings 11:1). Later, we read of Ezekiel often reminding Jerusalem that the Amorite was her father but a Hittite her mother (Ezekiel 16:3,45).

For the earliest reference to the Hittites in the Old Testament we can turn to Genesis 10:15, in the so-called Table of Nations, where Heth appears as a son of Canaan, being the eponymous ancestor of the Hittites. For another early reference, a case can be made for "Tidal king of nations" as being identifiable with **Tudhaliya I/II**. Tidal/Tudhaliya may therefore be dated to around 1400 BC. He is recorded as accompanying the alliance led by the king of Elam named Chedorlaomer, and, whatever the historicity of this account, he was probably the effective founder of the Hittite New Kingdom or Empire, in a disturbed period of ancient Near Eastern history.

BIT HILANI. This was a building plan characteristic of north Syria from the second millennium BC, being found at **Alalakh**, in the palaces of Levels VII and IV. It is, however, most typically Neo-Hittite, notably at **Zincirli**, **Carchemish** and **Guzanu (Tell Halaf)**. The *bit hilani* comprised a portico with one to three columns, sometimes in human form, giving access to a broad room, probably the throne room, with rooms or stairs to one side of the portico.

Sargon II of Assyria (722–705 BC), in his inscription recording the construction of his palace in his new foundation of Khorsabad (Dur-Sharrukin), refers to "a portico patterned after a Hittite palace, which they call a *bit hilani* in the Amorite tongue." The term "Hittite" here means north Syria, more specifically the territory around **Carchemish**. Tiglath-Pileser III and Sennacherib were other Assyrian kings mentioning the *bit hilani*.

The visitor to Syria today will see the entrance to the Aleppo Museum, a reconstruction of the portico of the *bit hilani* at Tell Halaf.

BITIK. A site near Ankara best known as the findspot of a fragment of a large polychrome relief-decorated jar. It depicts a scene comparable with the better-preserved four-handled jar from **Inandiktepe**, likewise dating to the Hittite Old Kingdom. The top surviving scene shows a man lifting a woman's veil and offering her a drinking bowl, perhaps in the context of a sacred **marriage**. Below is a row of worshipers; and below them a possible dance with daggers.

BIT KARIM. This was the head office for administration of the Old Assyrian **trade** centered on **Kültepe-Kanes**. Though frequently mentioned in the **cuneiform tablets** forming the business records, it has yet to be located through the excavations.

BITTEL, KURT (1908-1991). Arriving at the age of 23 at the site of **Boğazköy**, still relatively remote, he directed the German excavations until 1939 and from 1952, handing over to **Neve** as field director (1963), while retaining overall control to 1978. His excavations were centered on Büyükkale and the Lower City. He brought modern methods to the excavations, employing **Güterbock** as epigraphist in defiance of Nazi policy (1933–1939). A broad minded and respected scholar, he published many excavation reports and general works. He was the first director of the German Institute in Istanbul (1938–1944, 1953-1959), then President of the German Archaeological Institute (1960-1972). His contribution to Hittite archaeology will not be surpassed.

BOEHMER, RAINER MICHAEL. Longstanding member of the German expedition at **Boğazköy**, international authority on **glyptic art** and author of the major report on seals from **Hattusa**.

BOĞAZKÖY: BÜYÜKKALE. This was the royal citadel, the most important area of **Hattusa** throughout its checkered history, from the rebuilding by **Hattusili I** onward. Unassailable from its north and east sides, this rocky outcrop was far more accessible from the south and west. **Hantili II** sought to remedy this weakness by building a defensive wall eight meters thick. The buildings within the citadel were by and large not preserved above floor level, presenting a challenge to the excavators overcome by their architectural vision, in the best tradition of German archaeology in the Near East over the past century.

A causeway 85 meters long led up through the main south gate, its mud brick superstructure erected on top of the stone walls beneath. Possibly wooden planks over the surface were laid to facilitate the ascent of **horse**-drawn **wheeled vehicles** into the citadel. Across a first court, a gate led into the lower court, the second in a series of four courts of differing areas: long colonnaded walks, or stoas, extended along the southeast and northwest sides. Buildings M, N, H, A and G around the lower court housed palace officials and the palace guard.

An impressive gateway, with central chamber, gave access to the central court of Büyükkale, lined with colonnades. Another gate, in the north corner of the lower court, allowed admittance to the heart of the citadel. To the left of the approach to Building D (the palace) stood Buildings B and C, evidently serving as palace chapels. In the middle of Building C a pool—six by five meters and over two meters deep—contained many pots, clearly votive offerings.

The largest structure, to which important visitors seeking an audience with the king would have been led, was Building D, the royal palace, not preserved above floor level. The "basement" had an area of 39 by 48 meters, with five long partition walls acting as foundations for the five rows of wooden columns, 25 in all, supporting the roof of the great reception or audience hall, 32 meters square. Such a columned hall—compared by **Kurt Bittel** with the far larger Coronation Hall at **Tell el-Amarna (Akhetaten)** in Egypt—was not typical of the Near East at this time. Direct Egyptian architectural inspiration is unlikely. The main entrance to the palace was on its southeast side. Beyond the palace stood Buildings E and F, the private quarters of the king, with a striking view over the city to one side and the gorge below. The first discovery of an **archive** of **tablets** was found in the very first season of excavations (1906), within and on the slope in front of Building E. The upper court of the citadel, east of the palace, was surrounded by poorly preserved colonnades.

Other archives were found in Buildings A and K, with a large pool (24 meters long) nearby, for cultic purposes but perhaps also for extra **water supply**: sloping embankments were paved with limestone. A small third gate, in addition to an east gate and the main south gate, gave direct access to the city below from Büyükkale and also to a spring, the only immediate source of water for the citadel. Thus this small entrance was vitally important.

BOĞAZKÖY: BÜYÜKKAYA. Prehistoric occupation has been examined during the fairly recent excavations on this steep-sided hilltop in the northeast of the area of **Hattusa**. Occupation deposits of the sixth millennium BC had been disturbed by two phases of late–third millennium BC occupation.

On all three plateaux within the area of the summit of Büyükkaya were found settlement remains of the Hittite Old Kingdom, again much disturbed. The east wall, dating ca.1400 BC at the latest, was the earliest defensive wall. A large building complex of the Hittite Empire presumably served an administrative function, standing on the south spur of the upper plateau on Büyükkaya.

Remains of squatters' habitations have been found on Büyükkaya, and can be dated to the earliest period of the Iron Age, the so-called dark age following the fall of the Hittite Empire and lasting until ca.900 BC. Primitive dwellings and handmade pottery mark this as a retrograde culture with nothing in common with the Hittite city before. Significantly, this material culture has much in common with that of the Early and Middle Bronze Age centuries earlier. No trace suggesting conquest was found. Rather were these squatters, very probably people from **Kaska** in the north, who had moved into the homeland of their old enemy. There is a complete dearth of inscriptions, suggesting illiteracy.

BOĞAZKÖY: CHRONOLOGY. The sequence of occupation is best distinguished on **Büyükkale**, with eight periods, to be summed up thus: (1) Pre-Hittite (Early Bronze Age) (Büyükkale V); (2) Colony period (Büyükkale IVd); (3) Hittite Old Kingdom (Büyükkale IVc); (4) Early Empire (Büyükkale IVb-a); (5) Later Empire (Büyükkale IIIc-a); (6) Early Phrygian (Büyükkale IIb-a); (7) Late Phrygian (Büyükkale Ic-a); (8) Hellenistic-Roman building period.

BOĞAZKÖY: CUNEIFORM TABLETS. The larger proportion of these were recovered in the pre–World War I excavations of **Hattusa**, and were taken to Germany for study. With the onset of World War I, the world of scholarship outside Germany did not become acquainted with the Hittite **archives** until after 1918. While philologists from other countries—some being refugees from the Nazi regime—have made significant contributions over the years, it is German Hittitologists, such as **Heinrich Otten**, who have labored unremittingly at the task of transliteration and translation of the texts, along with the even harder task of piecing together the thousands of fragments into which these clay tablets had been shattered.

Since World War II these tablets have been returned to Turkey, the majority to Ankara and the rest to Istanbul. They have been published in two series. The earlier volumes of *Keilschrifttexte aus Boghazkoi* (KBo) publish tablets from the early seasons before World War I. This series was revived for publication of tablets from the post–World War II seasons, all being deposited in the tablet collection of the Ankara Museum. The second series— *Keilschrifturkunden aus Boghazkoi* (KUB)—comprised 58 volumes by 1989, being published in Berlin from 1921. It has covered tablets excavated in the early seasons and for some years housed in the Pergamon Museum in Berlin.

BOĞAZKÖY: EARLY TRAVELERS. The ruins of Boğazköy were unknown to foreigners and unappreciated locally until 28 July 1834, when Charles Texier, a young French traveler, first set eyes on the site. He spent a considerable time in Anatolia, his first journey being undertaken in 1833–1837, and longer at Boğazköy than most subsequent visitors in the 19th century. Given the Classical upbringing of his time, it is scarcely surprising that he identified it with the city of Pteria, recorded by Herodotus; but this is now far more plausibly located at Kerkenes Dağ, not far from Yozgat. It is worth noting that Texier made the first suggestion about the reliefs of **Yazılıkaya**, associating them with the Amazons of Classical mythology.

Brief, two-day visits were made by William Hamilton (1836) and years later by Heinrich Barth and Andreas Mordtmann (1858). Members of the expedition led by Georges Perrot, of Perrot and Chipiez fame, spent one week at Boğazköy (November 1861). Edmond Guilaume, an artist, drew the reliefs, while Jules Debet, a medical doctor, was an early practitioner of photography. A later two-day visitor was Rev. Henry J. van Lennep, "30 years a missionary in Turkey" (1864). Others visited the ruins, including representatives from the Prussian Academy who made squeezes of the Yazılıkaya friezes (1882). But the initial impact of Charles Texier's account was unsurpassed until the brief excavations by **Ernest Chantre** led to the recovery of **cuneiform tablets** (1893). It was then inevitable that Boğazköy would attract a major expedition, as occurred from 1906 under **Hugo Winckler.**

BOĞAZKÖY: EXCAVATIONS. It would not be a gross overstatement to equate the history of Hittitology with the story, still unfolding, of the excavations at Boğazköy by the German expedition. The romantic aura that some may see surrounding the early travelers in Anatolia, at this site beginning in 1834 with the rediscovery of the ruins by **Charles Texier**, may have departed; but **Hattusa**, the ancient capital of the kings of Hatti, will always impress the visitor, if only by its commanding landscape, **cyclopean masonry** and sheer scale.

In strict truth the history of these excavations began in 1893–1894 with the very limited trenches dug by **Ernest Chantre** in **Boğazköy: Büyükkale, Temple 1** and **Yazılıkaya,** resulting in the discovery of fragmentary clay **tablets** written in the **cuneiform** script and Akkadian language. The fierce conflagration at the destruction of Hattusa in the early 12th century BC caused the clay tablets to be baked hard and thus to survive even the methods of the early excavators.

Fortunately scholarship, save only in time of war, is international. Among the many clay tablets recovered by happy accident from **Tell-el-Amarna (Akhetaten)** in Egypt were two letters, from a correspondence between the Pharaoh Amenhotep III and a king of **Arzawa,** a land till that moment unknown to the modern world. The philologist J.A. Knudtzon deciphered these, and recognized that they were written in an Indo-European language. This discovery, in 1901, was quickly followed by the realization that the language of these two Amarna letters was closely comparable with that of the tablets found by Chantre at Boğazköy-Hattusa.

This was enough to send **Hugo Winckler,** a German Assyriologist, together with **Theodore Makridi,** the second director of the Istanbul Museum, to Boğazköy in 1905, in search of Arzawa. The following year—after the personal intervention of Kaiser Wilhelm II—the application for a permit to excavate this site was refused the front-runner **John Garstang** and granted instead to

Winckler. Excavations began promptly, in 1906, under the auspices of the Istanbul Museum but partly funded by the Deutsche Orient-Gesellschaft (D.O.G.). Very soon they found thousands of clay tablets and fragments on the west slope of the royal citadel of Büyükkale. Winckler at once recognized the title "Great King, King of Hatti." The identification of Boğazköy as the Hittite capital Hattusa was clinched beyond any doubt.

Excavations continued in 1907, 1911 and 1912, being extended to some of the storerooms of Temple 1. By then some 10,000 tablets had been found, providing a large enough corpus for the systematic development of Hittitology by German scholars, a task continued through World War I. In 1907 a team of archaeologists and architects, the latter from the earliest days of excavation in the Near East prominent in German expeditions, worked under the auspices of the German Archaeological Institute and directed by **Otto Puchstein**. Their task was to survey the walls of the **Boğazköy: Upper City** in particular, with five gates and five **temples** then known, and to carry out some excavations. This they did with remarkable dispatch, the results being published by Puchstein in 1912.

The ensuing break in excavations at Boğazköy, not resumed until 1931, was by no means entirely unfortunate, for it allowed the direction of the fieldwork to pass to the next generation in the person of **Kurt Bittel**, whose lifetime's work it became. He was destined to lead the German expedition at Boğazköy over many seasons (1931–1939 and 1952–1977) until his retirement. Like most cuneiformists, Winckler had been interested only in tablets, a specialism balanced by the exclusive concern of Puchstein with the monumental architecture, especially the defenses. There was an urgent need to determine the stratigraphy of the site by modern excavation methods, not easy at Boğazköy, being as it is a hill site rather than a stratified mound. In this respect it more closely resembles Anatolian sites of the Iron Age rather than the Bronze Age. Temple 1 and Büyükkale were among the principal areas of work under Bittel.

Peter Neve, a dedicated architect and archaeologist, turned his attention to the Upper City, including the temple area and **Boğazköy: Südburg**, from the 1978 season. He also carried out extensive conservation on the defenses, going further by reconstructing considerable lengths, an operation requiring funding at this present stage beyond the expedition's resources. The present director since 1993, **Jürgen Seeher**, has carried out extensive excavations on

Boğazköy: Büyükkaya, thus filling in gaps in the known story of settlement at this immense and diversified site. Among his results in the Upper City has been the excavation of a number of **granaries** and ponds designed for **water supply** for the whole of Hattusa, with results affecting the **absolute chronology** of Hattusa, especially the Upper City.

Although the work at Boğazköy remains essentially a German undertaking, for many decades in highly experienced hands both on site and in post excavation work on artifacts ranging from **pottery** to tablets, there has been collaboration with scholars of other nationalities, notably American, French, Italian and British, the last recently in the person of **David Hawkins**. He deployed his expertise in deciphering the **hieroglyphs** of the Südburg and **Boğazköy: Nişantaş** inscriptions.

It goes without saying that the excavations at Boğazköy are the focus of attention above all others for everyone interested in Hittite civilization. Even today, however, the overriding concern of Hugo Winckler still remains to some degree dominant, for most of the publications are related to the tablets and rock inscriptions. The ubiquitous attention to pottery and other artifacts in the archaeological profession can help to place Hattusa in its wider Anatolian Late Bronze Age context.

BOĞAZKÖY: IRON AGE. Though the great days of **Hattusa** as center of the Empire were never to return, there are widespread indications of later occupation on **Boğazköy: Büyükkaya, Büyükkale** and elsewhere. While it is not till the ninth century BC that significant building works are found, humbler traces of occupation abound. The concept of a "dark age"—a term which often implies modern ignorance of the past rather than cultural backwardness—of three centuries or more after the fall of the Hittite Empire has largely been discarded, on the evidence of excavated sites, notably Boğazköy and **Gordion**. On Büyükkaya there are traces of squatters, relatively primitive newcomers living in simple dwellings and making **pottery** by hand, a complete break with the Late Bronze Age. These may well have been **Kaska** tribesmen, arriving after rather than causing the fall of Hattusa. Comparable Early Iron Age occupation occurs near the House on the Slope in **Boğazköy: Lower City**, on Büyükkale and around **Temple** 7 in **Boğazköy: Upper City**.

Early in the Middle Iron Age (ninth–eighth centuries BC) Büyükkaya grew into an extensive settlement across the whole of that rocky hill. By the eighth century BC parts of Büyükkale and the Lower City were also occupied.

Then in the Late Iron Age (early to mid–seventh century BC, alternatively termed the later Phrygian period) Büyükkale was encircled by strong **fortifications**, a massive wall with rectangular towers. There were no major public buildings; but gradually the interior came to be filled with houses. The population was now largely concentrated on Büyükkale, Büyükkaya and the Lower City being almost deserted. Further south the Southern Citadel (**Boğazköy: Südburg**) was built, with stone footings four meters thick, and houses above the East Ponds and near **Boğazköy: Nişantaş**— all in the eastern half of the Upper City. The defenses of Büyükkale were very possibly built in the face of danger from the Cimmerian invaders sweeping across Anatolia from the Caucasus soon after 700 BC.

A fine statue of Kybele, the Phrygian goddess equivalent to the Neo-Hittite **Kubaba**, was found at the southeast gate of the Iron Age fortress of Büyükkale. Cultural links with the west, the Phrygian heartland, are exemplified by sherds incised with Phrygian script and by a few sherds of East Greek imported pottery.

From 585 BC Boğazköy—along with all central Anatolia east of the western reaches of the Halys River (**Marrassantiya**)—came under the rule of the Medes, followed by that of the Persians (547–336 BC). Political changes had little initial impact on life in Boğazköy, the site mistakenly identified by **Charles Texier** with Pteria, conquered by Croesus of Lydia in a campaign ending with the complete victory of Cyrus over Croesus and the annexation of Lydia to the Persian Empire (547 BC).

BOĞAZKÖY: LOWER CITY (OLD CITY). While the earliest occupation dates back well into the Early Bronze Age, the earliest notable structures are the houses of the Old Assyrian *karum* of Hattus, one of the trading colonies established in the time of **Kültepe-Kanes** IB (18th century BC). By the 16th century BC the Lower City had been protected by a **fortification** wall.

The major excavations in the Lower City have been concentrated in **Temple 1** and in the extensive residential quarter to the west, between it and the defensive wall, as well as in official housing to the south. The earlier houses had a central open court. Conceivably for reasons of **climatic change**, the "vestibule house" with roofed living area came into fashion. Housing did not reflect status, for priests, civil servants, industrial workers and merchants lived side by side, with the agricultural population living in the countryside.

The standard of urban living was far from unbearably primitive. Ovens and open fireplaces provided for cooking and warmth in the long Anatolian winters, while water came from neighboring fountains or perhaps piped from the reservoirs for **water supply** constructed high in **Boğazköy: Upper City**. Some houses had bathtubs of fired clay. Drains beneath the streets served as sewers.

One hundred meters southeast of Temple 1 stood the House on the Slope (*Haus am Hang*). This steep slope up toward the Citadel (**Boğazköy: Büyükkale**) was included within the old Lower City and occupied by various terraced buildings, the House on the Slope being the best preserved and largest, with an area of 36 by 32 meters with two stories. On the upper floor was a hall clearly for public purposes, 17 by 13 meters. Domestic needs and storage were provided for on the ground floor. Here a large **archive** of **tablets** was recovered in the early seasons of excavation. The mud brick walls have largely survived, owing to the fire which destroyed this administrative building, perhaps deliberately torched during the unrest at the time of the short-lived usurpation by **Kurunta**.

BOĞAZKÖY: NIŞANTAŞ AND ENVIRONS. Along with Sarıkale and Yenicekale, Nişantepe is a rock outcrop in and **Boğazköy: Upper City**, on whose summit are only traces of the Hittite structure, perhaps of a defensive character, including cuts in the rock making it possible to trace the line of the walls. This is a fortuitous similarity with some of the later fortresses in the kingdom of **Urartu**. At the foot of the rock there originally stood a gateway approached by a ramp and flanked by sphinxes. On the southeast side was the major Nişantaş rock inscription.

To the north of the rock of Nişantepe stood two buildings forming the North Complex and facing **Büyükkale**. Behind this on the slope stood the West Building, of which only the basement cellars survive, the fierce fire of the destruction preserving over 3,000 clay **bullae** with their **seal** impressions. Bags, baskets, sacks and other containers were tied around the top with string or strips of leather thong, then having a lump of clay pressed on them. In turn a stone or metal seal was then impressed on the clay, normally marking the sealed containers as belonging to the royal administration. The fire had preserved these bullae, though nothing else, in the basement stores where they belonged, baking the clay hard.

More than half the bullae have royal seal impressions of all the great Hittite kings from **Suppiluliuma I** onward. These have typical bilingual stamp-seal designs, inscribed in **cuneiform** and **hieroglyphs**. Particularly common are those of Suppiluliuma I, **Urhi-Tesub** and **Tudhaliya IV**. **Kurunta**, son of **Muwatalli II**, is represented, clear evidence of his status as Great King. The seal impressions of **Hattusili III** have him usually represented jointly with **Puduhepa**. King and **queen** seals occur also for Muwatalli II and his son Urhi-Tesub (Mursili III). It seems possible that this was a reflection of Egyptian influence, in the years preceding the battle of **Kadesh**, for at this time Tiy and Nefertiti were queens exercizing undoubted influence on affairs of state in Egypt in the reigns of Amenhotep III and Akhenaten.

The other bullae were of high officials, most of them **scribes** and including royal princes with governmental responsibilities. Earlier in date are **land grants**, with seal impressions of kings of the late Old Kingdom, including **Hantili II**, Huzziya II and **Muwatalli I**. These needed to be filed and kept indefinitely.

The bullae in this building were filed in some typological and chronological order. Thus this west building below Nişantepe evidently housed a palace **archive**.

BOĞAZKÖY: SÜDBURG. Beneath the remains of the Iron Age Southern Citadel (*Südburg*), in the northeast area of **Boğazköy: Upper City**, were excavated two semi subterranean chambers, the second of which (Chamber 2) is the better preserved and includes a **hieroglyphic** inscription. The blocks indicate that the whole inscription has been preserved. It is carved in **Luwian** hieroglyphs of less refined character than those of the inscriptions of **Tudhaliya IV** at **Yalburt** and **Emirgazi**, suggesting some haste by the sculptors working for **Suppiluliuma II**. The form of the royal name indicates a probability of that king rather than **Suppiluliuma I**; and the evidence elsewhere indicates that hieroglyphic inscriptions did not come into vogue before Tudhaliya IV, the earliest datable example being **Aleppo** I, of Talmi-Sarruma, grandson of Suppiluliuma I and successor of his son Telipinu as **viceroy** of Aleppo.

The inscription refers to a "divine earth road," implying an entrance to the **Underworld** and thus a shrine dedicated to a chthonic cult. Sited near the eastern ponds or reservoirs. The true character of these two chambers is now apparent: they had at first been interpreted as tombs within tumuli, and indeed had been protected by earth heaped over them at the time. The stones robbed had been used in the Iron Age for the Southern Citadel built nearby.

On the rear wall of the second chamber is a relief of the Sun-God holding a **lituus** and a modified Egyptian *ankh*, the sign of life. Above the god's head is a winged sun disk. On the left wall is a relief of Suppuluiuma II as a warrior armed with bow, **sword** and lance: he wears the typically Hittite shoes with turned-up toes and a horned headdress. This last is unusual, since this symbol of divinity had not hitherto been associated with a Great King before his death, when he "became a god." The finish of the relief carving suggests that much detail was left to the painters.

BOĞAZKÖY: UPPER CITY. The former belief that the Upper (Southern) City of **Hattusa** was largely built in the early Empire rather than in its last decades under **Tudhaliya IV** and **Suppiluliuma II** is now supported by recent data in the form of radiocarbon determinations from the highest area of the Upper City, where a group of five ponds has been investigated by **Jürgen Seeher**. It never seemed plausible to suggest that all the construction work in the Upper City, including the **fortifications** 3.3 kilometers in length, could have been completed in one generation. While the **temples** were built under the later kings, probably beginning with **Hattusili III**, it would surely have been in character for those energetic warriors **Suppiluliuma I** and **Mursili II** to undertake the formidable task of fortifying this vast extension to the area of Hattusa, even though no record to this effect has yet been found.

The outstanding features of the defenses are three ornate gateways: the Lion Gate, Sphinx Gate and so-called King's Gate, from west to east. The lions carved in relief at the Lion Gate, not especially ferocious in aspect, would have greeted people arriving at the city from the south: they are in the long Near Eastern tradition, originating in Mesopotamia, of guardian lions. The figure at the King's Gate in exceptionally high relief—often described as quintessentially Hittite—is facing inward, toward those leaving the city. He is almost certainly a **god**, with his battle-**ax** indicating warlike character: he may be **Sarruma**, the special protector of Hittite kings, and very possibly an addition to the original gateway. Another distinctively Hittite element is the use of massive "whalebone" monoliths on either side of the gate, with **cyclopean masonry** on either side.

While the overall layout of Hattusa supports the theory of a predominantly religious and ritual role for the Upper City—with temples there and administrative and residential quarters in the Lower City and the royal palace on **Boğazköy: Büyükkale**—the oldest and by far the largest of all the shrines, **Temple 1**, was sited in **Boğazköy: Lower City** and probably built by Hattusili III. It is difficult to believe that the Upper City had no secular function: it may not have become so devoted to religious celebrations until the reign of Tudhaliya IV. A major occasion would have been the spring **festival** (*purulli*), starting from Temple 5, when the **statues** of the gods would have been carried in public procession out of the Upper City by the King's Gate, along the outside of the defenses and back through the Lion Gate, perhaps ending at Temple 30. The Sphinx Gate (Yerkapi), at the highest point along the circuit of the fortifications, led directly to the central temple area: the least accessible of the three gates, it was probably the least used.

The need for internal security inside the city is implied by the erection of the strongholds of Sarıkale and Yenicekale on the top of rocky outcrops within the Upper City, built of cyclopean masonry.

BOSSERT, HELMUTH THEODOR (1889–1961). German archaeologist and Hittitologist. Professor and director of the Department of Near Eastern Studies in the University of Istanbul. Together with Halet Çambel and Bahadir Alkim he found the site of **Karatepe**, directing excavations there and working at the decipherment of the **Luwian hieroglyphs**.

BUILDING METHODS. The Hittites employed the usual Near Eastern methods of wall construction in undressed stone and mud brick, sometimes with timber reinforcement, for the houses of the population as a whole. For the flat roofs of houses and public buildings alike, wooden beams, matting and mud were used. For the most massive walls, notably **fortifications**, casemate construction was used, saving time and effort: the compartments thus created were normally filled with rubble. An imposing effect was achieved with **cyclopean masonry**. Blocks were fitted closely, even though this often required specially carved irregularities. Local stone—limestone at **Hattusa**—was in general use, though granite was employed for the footings of the sanctuary of **Boğazköy: Temple I**.

Two idiosyncratic features appear in the masonry of Temple I and other buildings in Hattusa. One is the custom of forming the junction of pavement or floor with wall by cutting the corner from one and the same block, bronze chisels being the tools of the period. The other is the use of the drill, evident in numerous drill-holes in the tops of masonry: given the great weight of these blocks, at first sight this seems wholly unnecessary. Yet these drill holes may have been associated with the massive timber frame construction with mud brick filling for the walls standing on their stone footing, all that survives today. **Timber construction**—an essential element of Hittite architecture—alone depended on bringing raw materials from a distance to Hattusa.

Corbeling was used for **posterns** and for the great gateways of **Boğazköy: Upper City**. More remarkable is the construction at Hattusa of the oldest known stone-built domes in the ancient Near East, roofing two semi subterranean chambers, Chamber 2 being the better preserved. Its pointed vault has been described, however, as rather unstable. These are true vaults, unlike (for example) the chamber tombs of **Ugarit** and its port of Minet el-Beidha, with corbeling carved in the form of round or pointed vaults.

BULLA(E). A Latin term in general use to denote lumps of clay used to seal the contents of any container, the clay then being impressed with a **seal**. When subject to burning, the clay is fired, preserving the seal impressions very well.

BURIAL CUSTOMS. The majority of Anatolian cemeteries of the second millennium BC date to the Middle Bronze Age, though some continue through the Late Bronze Age, with a tendency to shift from inhumation to **cremation**. The two burial customs often coexisted. The normal custom was for extramural cemeteries, which consequently have in many places yet to be located, if not destroyed by recent tomb robbers.

Intramural burials represent the survival of an earlier, prehistoric tradition, rather stronger in central Anatolia, though found also in the west. Perhaps here can be seen evidence not simply of family continuity but also of an **ancestor cult**. Intramural burials, largely of children, occur at **Hattusa, Maşat Höyük, Acemhöyük**; at Karaoğlan (near Ankara) and Polatli (near **Gordion**); further west at Demircihöyük and Bozüyük; in southwest Anatolia at Kusura, **Beycesultan** and Aphrodisias; and at **Troy**.

While at Osmankayasi (**Boğazköy**) and at Ilica, 70 kilometers west of Ankara, inhumations and cremations are both found, as likewise at **Karahöyük (Konya)** in the Middle Bronze Age, at **Gordion** only inhumations occur. Numerous Middle Bronze burials have been excavated at **Ikiztepe** on the Black Sea, at **Alışar Höyük** and at **Kültepe (Kanes)**.

Inhumations might be simple earth burials, in stone-lined cists or in large jars (*pithoi*): contracted and facing southeast, these continued the Early Bronze Age tradition evident, for example, at Karataş-Semayük in the Elmali plain in the Taurus zone of the southern Anatolian plateau. Their grave goods indicate the cists as the burials of the upper class, with *pithos* burials for poorer folk.

No Hittite royal tomb has yet been identified. In contrast with Egyptian funerary customs, for the Hittite monarchy—once the **royal funerary rituals** had been performed—the physical body had no enduring significance. Were it otherwise, cremation would not have been invariable for royal obsequies.

BURUNKAYA. A **hieroglyphic** inscription found in 1971 on the west slope of a hill of this name northeast of modern Aksaray. Here, as in the **Karadağ-Kızıldağ** inscriptions, appear the names of Hartapu and his father Mursili.

BURUSHATTUM, PURUSHANDA. *See* **ACEMHÖYÜK.**

BÜYÜKKALE. *See* **BOĞAZKÖY: BÜYÜKKALE.**

BÜYÜKKAYA. *See* **BOĞAZKÖY: BÜYÜKKAYA.**

- C -

ÇALAPVERDI. A very large hill fort situated not far from **Alışar Höyük**, on the north side of the Kızıl Irmak (**Marrassantiya**), commanding the old route from central Anatolia to Erkilet and Kayseri. It stands on a steep-sided, naturally defensible hill. In parts of the site there are six meters of occupation deposits, covering the Iron Age, Hellenistic and Roman periods. This is one of the major Iron Age strongholds, comparable with **Göllüdağ**, **Kululu** and **Havuzköy** and the later vast stronghold of Kerkenes Dağ, near Yozgat. Çalapverdi has yielded typical Iron Age painted **pottery**. It stood on the northern periphery of **Tabal** and the northernmost limit of **hieroglyphic** inscriptions.

CANBY, JEANNY VORYS. Ph.D. from Bryn Mawr College, followed by teaching at several U.S. institutions. She has published widely on Hittite art, and has participated in the excavations at **Gordion**, **Kültepe**, **Boğazköy** and elsewhere.

CAPPADOCIAN WARE. *See* **ALIŞAR III WARE.**

CARCHEMISH/KARKAMIS. This city, on the west bank of the Euphrates, stood at the crossroads of the ancient Near East, where major trade routes—north-south along the river and east-west from Mesopotamia to the Mediterranean—meet. Today this large site is divided by the Istanbul–Baghdad railway, marking the modern frontier between Turkey and Syria, the overriding factor in the discontinuing of the excavations in the early 20th century.

In the written records, for the most part clay **tablets** in the **cuneiform** script, Carchemish appears from the mid–third millennium BC onward, disappearing from the historical scene only at the end of the seventh century BC. Beginning with the **archives** of Ebla in Syria and later of **Mari**, there ensue references to the city in the tablets found at **Hattusa,** **Ugarit** and **Emar (Tell Meskene).** The Assyrian **annals** also include such references, from the time of the Hittite Empire until the final destruction by Sargon II of Assyria (717 BC).

In the mid–second millennium BC (ca.1750–1350 BC) Carchemish found itself successively within the sphere of influence of **Aleppo,** Hattusa and **Mitanni.** At the siege of **Ursu** it sided with Aleppo against **Hattusili I**; but by the reign of his successor, **Mursili I,** Carchemish must have come under Hittite suzerainty. Under **Hantili I** it seems to have rebelled, soon coming within the control of the expanding kingdom of Mitanni, an ill-documented development. Two Hittite **treaties** included retrospective references to the earlier history of Carchemish.

From the time of **Suppiluliuma I (1344–1322 BC)** Carchemish came under Hittite rule until the fall of Hatti in the early 12th century BC, and indeed continued long after to preserve much of its Hittite heritage. With the conquest of the Syrian kingdoms from Aleppo to Kadesh in his Second Syrian War, Suppiluliuma reduced Carchemish to little more than the city itself, seizing its surrounding territory. Yet it was only some years later, during the "Hurrian War," that Carchemish itself was taken, after a week's siege. Suppiluliuma respected the **temples** on the citadel, including that of the goddess **Kubaba**; but the lower town was sacked and 3,330 prisoners taken off to Hattusa. The defensive rampart encircling the lower town contains Middle Bronze Age sherds in its earthen fill, so that the archaeological evidence will fit with dating this to the time of Suppiluliuma I, to the new Hittite regime rather than to the defenders of the city against the Hittite attack, who of course would not have had the necessary time for such a construction.

The long history of the **viceroyalty** of Carchemish then ensued, with the appointment as "king" of Carchemish of Piyassili (Sarri-Kusuh), the third of the five sons of Suppiluliuma I. His responsibilities from the first were primarily military, opening with a campaign in Mitanni. The boundaries of the territory of Carchemish were extended by addition of towns of the country of **Astata**, on both sides of the Euphrates; on the west side only **Mukis** can be identified.

While eight kings ruled in Hattusa, from Suppiluliuma I to II, only four—Sarri-Kusuh, Sahurunuwa, Ini-Tesub and Talmi-Tesub—ruled in Carchemish, over a time span of some 150 years. Their dates are attested by synchronisms with Hittite and other kings. Sarri-Kusuh had the task of ensuring Hittite control of Carchemish following the setbacks of the deaths in rapid succession from the **plague** of Suppiluliuma I and his eldest son and successor, **Arnuwanda II (1322–1321 BC)**. By the third year of **Mursili II**, however, Sarri-Kusuh was able to go to the assistance of his brother in Anatolia, the threat from Assyria having been warded off. The next problem in Syria came with the king of **Nuhasse**, a principality bordering the lands of Carchemish and Ugarit. Egypt was still capable of interfering in Syria, though a shadow of its power in the days when Tuthmose III crossed the Euphrates, mentioning Carchemish (ca.1447 BC). At Egyptian instigation Nuhasse rebelled against Carchemish. A Hittite army commanded by Kantuzzili marched to suppress this revolt, while Sarri-Kusuh made an agreement with Niqmaddu II of Ugarit to attack Nuhasse. For a time peace was restored. But in his ninth year Mursili II was joined by Sarri-Kusuh at the **festival** of the goddess **Hebat** at **Kummanni**, where he died.

Mursili II was obliged to go in person into Syria, after rebellion by Nuhasse and Kadesh, to stave off a further threat of attack from Assyria and to install his nephew, Sahurunuwa, the son of Sarri-Kusuh, as viceroy in Carchemish, to which Mursili transferred some of the territory of Ugarit on the sea coast.

After the accession of **Muwatalli II** Carchemish was again endangered from Assyria and by the threat from Egypt posed by the capture of Kadesh by Seti I, father of **Ramesses II**.

This threat was removed in the fifth year of Ramesses by the outcome of the battle of **Kadesh**; but in the east the Assyrian king **Adad-nirari I (1295–1264 BC)** claimed in his annals to have conquered the cities of **Hanigalbat** (Mitanni), including Harran, "as far as Carchemish of the bank of the Euphrates."

Ini-Tesub probably reigned the longest of the sequence of Hittite viceroys during the Empire, and is the best documented at Ugarit, with four different **seals** and legal documents and letters of the reign of Ammistamru II from Ugarit. In some legal cases the king of Carchemish acted on his own authority, in others subject to the leadership of the Hittite king. Ini-Tesub moreover controlled affairs in Emar, as indicated by the tablets found there.

The reign of Talmi-Tesub, last ruler before the downfall of Hatti, is attested in only a few texts. He must have been in power in Carchemish when the attack by the **Sea Peoples** occurred. Unlike Hattusa and Ugarit, however, there was scant archaeological evidence at Carchemish to prove a massive destruction. The levels of this period were scarcely investigated by the British Museum expedition. It seems very possible that the reference by Ramesses III of Egypt to the devastation brought about by the Sea Peoples might have indicated Hittite-ruled north Syria rather than the city of Carchemish itself. Be that as it may, it was not very long before Carchemish revived to become one of the leading cities of the Neo-Hittite world during the Iron Age.

CARCHEMISH IN THE IRON AGE. Nearly all the archaeological evidence, from the British Museum excavations, pertains to the Neo-Hittite period, in effect from the early 10th to the later eighth century BC. Yet this is frustrating in its incompleteness, owing to the political circumstances preventing continuation of the excavations and also to the damage caused by buildings of the Roman period, when the town was named Europos.

The excavated buildings give only rather indirect hints of the prosperity of a city standing at a commercial crossroads, as it had done in the third and second millennia BC. Few structures were excavated at all completely, the emphasis being on uncovering the sculptures of the facades: interiors were indeed left largely untouched. Quite apart from this, the city had been plundered by Sargon II of Assyria (717 BC), later falling to the Babylonians (605 BC), so that the chances of finding treasures were virtually nil.

It is an irony that one must turn to the **annals** of the Assyrian enemy for a record of the wealth exacted as tribute from Carchemish, notably by Assurnasirpal II from its ruler Sangara (ca.870 BC). The list is impressive, including 20 talents of **silver**, daggers and a couch of **gold**, 100 talents (three tons) of **copper** and 250 talents (seven and a half tons) of **iron.** Other tribute included metal vessels and the contents of the royal palace "whose weight could not be computed." Mention is made of beds, chairs and tables of box-wood, the last inlaid with ivory, as well as elephants' tusks, at a time when the Syrian elephant was about to become extinct through generations of hunting for its ivory. The significance of **textiles** for the economy of Carchemish is illustrated by the inclusion of garments of linen and brightly colored wool and of blue and purple wool, the purple dye doubtless coming from the Mediterranean coast. A ceremonial **chariot** is mentioned in the list of tribute. War chariots were also taken, as well as human tribute in the form of 200 young women, cavalrymen and infantry to reinforce the Assyrian army. Military reinforcements in the shape of prisoners of war were likewise taken from Carchemish by Sargon II on his capture of the city. The tribute exacted from Sangara of Carchemish demonstrates its great wealth at the height of its prosperity, under the dynasty of Suhis (ca.970–870 BC), to which the majority of the excavated monuments can be ascribed.

Links with the well-attested historical **chronology** of Assyria, especially the royal annals, and the internal chronology of the **hieroglyphic** inscriptions provide the epigraphic evidence for dating the buildings and their **sculpture**, assisted by stylistic analysis of the sculpture. The archaeological horizon is entirely Early Iron Age. Over 50 years of study of the material from Carchemish is achieving a growing consensus, with two extreme dissidents (**Ekrem Akurgal** and David Ussishkin).

The **hieroglyphic** inscriptions of Carchemish, with correlations with Assyrian chronology, make it possible to determine the successive dynasties and individual rulers. After two early rulers meagerly documented came the House of Suhis, comprising Suhis I, Astuwatamanzas, Suhis II and Katuwas, preceding Sangara and spanning the years ca.970–870 BC. Following Sangara came the House of Astiruwas, comprising Astiruwas, Yariris (Araras) and Kamanis, this sequence being confirmed by the inscriptions of Korkun, and dated between Sangara and Pisiri, ca.840–740 BC. Finally came "son of Sastu(ras)," on the later inscriptions of the Great Staircase, plausibly identified with Pisiri, ca.740–717 BC.

The excavations were concentrated in an area of the Inner City just below the Citadel, extending westward from the west bank of the Euphrates. On the Citadel little could be recovered, owing to the deep disturbance caused by the Roman buildings: here must have stood the royal palaces of the Hittite **viceroyalty** and of the Neo-Hittite successors, as well as the **temple** of the patron goddess of the city, **Kubaba**, attested in the texts. A processional stairway, with two inscriptions of Katuwas, son of Suhis II and the greatest royal builder of the city, must have led up to the Citadel. Badly damaged reliefs in the gate of this Great Staircase, however, can be stylistically compared with a fragment of a colossal **statue** with inscribed base from the south gate of the Inner Town as well as with sculptures from other Neo-Hittite sites, giving a dating to the period of Tiglath-Pileser III—Sargon II of Assyria, ca.745–705 BC. Just as the Assyrian tribute–lists provide the most vivid evidence of the wealth of Carchemish and indeed many other cities, so the decorated bronze bands of the gates of Balawat, now displayed in the British Museum, depict the **fortifications** of the Citadel with parapets, towers and arched gates, associated with an undated campaign early in the reign of Shalmaneser III of Assyria (859–824 BC).

The Water Gate, giving entry from the river close to the revetted river wall, was at first dated back in the Late Bronze Age by the excavator, **Leonard Woolley**, but this dating has now been brought down into the Neo-Hittite period, along with the other excavated structures. The Water Gate could be reconstructed from the remaining south portion.

A road led from the Water Gate to the square at the foot of the Great Staircase, next to which stood the Temple of the **Storm-God**, identified by an inscription of Katuwas recording its restoration, thus indicating a date in the 10th century BC for its original construction. Its plan, with the sanctuary approached through an outer and an inner cobbled court, demonstrates some similarities to the temple of Solomon at Jerusalem, almost contemporary: a common Canaanite origin rather than any direct connection must be the explanation.

Along the southeast façade of the Temple of the Storm-God stretched the Long Wall of Sculpture, whose inscriptions show that it was entirely the work of Suhis, certainly the second king of that name. This is a victory procession, commemorating battles described in the accompanying inscriptions of Suhis II, whose wife Watis appears in the procession of **gods and goddesses**, followed by **chariotry** and infantry. An interesting detail is the crested **helmet** of the spearmen, a design not found in the Assyrian army until the time of Tiglath-Pileser III (744–727 BC). Any suggestion of Greek influence can be dismissed outright! This is the most significant sculptural series attributable to the first of the three phases of stylistic development at Carchemish. The suggestion that such reliefs betray the influence of New Kingdom Egyptian monumental or public art is arguable, if not altogether convincing. More significant is their dating, not later than ca.900 BC and perhaps rather earlier, for this precludes direct Assyrian influence, seeing that the first of the Late Assyrian palaces, the North-West Palace of Assurnasirpal II at Nimrud, was not built for another generation. Neo-Hittite sculpture has its detractors, its limitations in part attributable to the inflexible character of basalt; but, whatever their shortcomings, the sculptors cannot accurately be accused of producing merely provincial Assyrian works. The chronological evidence is against such a charge. By the eighth century BC matters had changed, though the Assyrianizing style by then in fashion is barely reflected at Carchemish, the leading custodian of the Hittite heritage.

More or less facing the Temple of the Storm God across the square ran a series of relief-carved orthostats termed the Herald's Wall, so named presumably from the symmetrical design of each slab, with echoes of Sumerian art of a much earlier period as well as **Hurrian** influence, among the characters portrayed being the bull-man. The slabs alternate dark and light, basalt and limestone. There is no narrative theme here. Rather than a survival from earlier centuries, as once suggested, the Herald's Wall probably dates from the reign of Katuwas. This too belongs to the first stylistic phase. The second phase is represented by the reliefs of the so-called Royal Buttress, which date to the reign of Yariris, being an addition to the original structure by the entry to the "Lower Palace," extending south. The third and final stylistic phase is represented on the Great Staircase by the additions attributable most probably to Pisiri.

The perimeter wall of the Outer Town, very probably dating to the 10th century BC, is barely discernible for much of its course. Within this area was excavated a house with vivid evidence of its destruction by the Babylonian army (605 BC). At the same time the **Gold** Tomb in the Northwest Fort, at the north end of the Citadel, was looted. This yielded clear proof of the long-lived survival of Hittite artistic tradition from the time of the Empire, with a wealth of tiny gold appliqué ornaments, many reproducing designs from **Yazılıkaya**, including the king embraced by his protective god, **Sarruma**. It is remarkable that these had survived over a century after the sack of Carchemish by Sargon II. The memory of "Great Hatti" could not so easily be obliterated.

CENTRAL ANATOLIA BEFORE THE HITTITE OLD KING-DOM. There was a complex pattern of principalities throughout the lands from the great bend of the **Marrassantiya River** (Kızıl Irmak) southward to the Taurus Mountains and southwestward to the Konya Plain. Relations in one form or another, military or commercial, are attested with Mesopotamia from the 24th until the 18th century BC. The evidence for these relations ranges from the legendary to the matter-of-fact, the former best exemplified by the *King of Battle* text found with the **cuneiform tablets** from **Tell el-Amarna** in Egypt, recounting the achievement of **Sargon of Agade** in marching as far as Burushanda/**Burushattum (Acemhöyük)**, near the Salt Lake. The latter category is abundantly preserved in the tablets from the *karum* of **Kültepe-Kanes**.

While the *King of Battle* text is a millennium after the events described, and thus questionably reliable, inscriptions from the reign of Sargon's grandson **Naramsin** record revolts over a vast zone from Anatolia to the Gulf, involving in one case 20 and in another 17 kings. Naramsin was victorious in nine battles. His account indicates that certain central Anatolian communities—Kültepe, **Boğazköy**, **Alışar** and Acemhöyük—were already prominent in the Akkadian period, before the foundation of the pre-Assyrian trading post at Kültepe-Kanes (*karum* IV). Whatever the precise facts, which seem unlikely ever to be recovered, interference by the Akkadian dynasty in the affairs of Anatolia may well have provided information handed down the generations and taken up some three centuries later by enterprising Assyrian merchants.

There was a brief inclination among specialists to interpret the Old Assyrian **trade** with its colonies in the context of an Old Assyrian Empire in Anatolia, foreshadowing Assyrian imperial expansion many centuries later. Even then, however, Assyrian territorial control north of the Taurus range was extremely limited, if it existed at all. The theory of foreign rule over the Anatolian plateau, with a network of roads built along Roman lines, in the early second millennium BC was based on misconceptions, one being that there was textual evidence that the rulers of the petty Anatolian kingdoms were compelled to swear fealty to the city of Assur. The truth was the reverse, that the merchants were obliged to follow the orders of the local rulers. Common sense should have indicated the absurdity of this theory.

Over 30 Anatolian principalities are mentioned in the Old Assyrian texts, with Hatti and Harkiuna appearing in the **Anitta** text. Three kingdoms—Kanes, **Wahsusana** and Burushattum—were particularly prominent in the 20th century BC, contemporary with Kültepe-*karum* II, the ruler of Burushattum being entitled *ruba'um rabi'um*, "Great Prince," literally "King of Kings." The status of the other principalities of this period, independent or in vassalage, is uncertain. One Old Assyrian text reveals a **treaty** relationship between Kanes and Wahsusana, which may have been a major vassal of Burushattum. Such treaties were quite distinct from those between the Assyrian merchants and the local rulers.

For the period of reoccupation of the *karum* of Kanes and extension of the Old Assyrian trading network beyond it (IB), a letter written by Anum-Hirbi, king of **Mama**, to Warsama, king of Kanes, is very informative. Each kingdom controlled a number of vassals, this letter distinguishing vassal (*sarrum*) from suzerain (*ruba'um*). Under Inar, father of Warsama, the two had been in conflict; and, after an interval of peace sought by both sides, trouble broke out again, ostensibly from the behavior of vassals. It was especially in the interests of Kanes to safeguard the Assyrian trade route which Mama evidently commanded.

Evidence concerning the native Anatolian kingdoms and their vassals can be garnered from the approaches made by the Assyrian merchants, as revealed in the **tablets**. For them the term "palace" was commonly in use, clearly signifying the local power, often intervening in the trade to the irritation of the merchants: on one occasion Assyrians went in a delegation to the palace of **Hahhum**. References to wars do not occur directly in the Old Assyrian tablets, possibly from a desire to avoid any loss of confidence back in the city (Assur), which could damage trade. Quite a modern note! But there are references to "troubles."

Each Anatolian city was recognized by the Assyrian merchants as being under the authority of a king (*lugal*) or a prince (*ruba'um*), Akkadian terms. Various official ranks are attested beneath the ruler, the highest ranking being the "grand chamberlain" (*rabi similtim*), literally, "great one of the staircase." The other officials indicate the predominance of agriculture in the economy: not being of the first concern for the Assyrian merchants, however, it is poorly documented. The same is true of industry. The service industries rather than manufacturing, that is, trade and finance, are the main subjects covered by the tablets. These, moreover, come disproportionately from the later years of *karum* II at Kanes.

Assyrians could and did open accounts in the palace, which thus functioned as a bank rather in the manner of the *karum*. The palace was often involved in the seizure of bankrupt stock. Goods, including **textiles**, were often assigned to the palace. Assyrian and Anatolian merchants followed organizational and commercial practices not so very different, though, with a long Mesopotamian tradition behind them, the Assyrians had refined their methods.

CHANTRE, ERNEST. His significance in the development of Hittitology rests on the brief excavations he carried out at **Boğazköy** (1893), when he discovered the first **tablets** which could be firmly attributed to this site, even though their **language** was not yet identifiable. This discovery naturally awakened interest in Boğazköy among scholars. He published *Recherches Archéologiques dans l'Asie Occidentale—Mission en Cappadoce 1893–4* (Paris, 1898).

CHARIOTS AND CHARIOTRY. Charioteers have traditionally been seen as the shock troops who commanded the open battlefield, most famously at the battle of **Kadesh** in Syria, the scene of the confrontation between **Ramesses II** and **Muwatalli II**, pharaoh and Hittite king respectively. Ramesses claims to have faced no fewer than 2,500 Hittite chariots, each with a crew of three, driver and two armed men. Whatever the accuracy of this number, it is certain that the chariotry formed the elite wing of the Hittite **army**. In texts from the 17th century BC onward charioteers are listed in records of personnel before the infantry, although by the 13th century BC, curiously, the order is reversed. This has no known significance.

The Hittites were not alone in developing chariotry as the leading military wing. It appeared in New Kingdom Egypt from ca.1550 BC as a clear innovation, though it was not widely used throughout the ancient Near East for some generations: for example, **Shalmaneser I (1263–1234 BC)** is the first Assyrian king to record deployment of chariots on the battlefield.

It is mistaken to assume that chariots were deployed only in open battle; and still more so to suggest that they were responsible for the use of the glacis in military architecture. Control of cities and towns was an essential method for the Hittite kings of securing control of new territories. To this end **siege warfare** was a frequent and often protracted phenomenon. But chariots would have been useless as assault vehicles against **fortifications**, let alone as a method of undermining city walls: it was against undermining that the glacis was built, not against chariotry. A Hittite account of the siege of the city of **Ursu**, in the southeast, makes it clear that chariots were deployed as backup for the besieging force, to secure surrounding areas and cut off supplies from reaching the garrison.

Chariots also served nonmilitary functions, notably in hunting and as parade vehicles. Possession of **horses** and chariots was surely a mark of wealth and social standing.

Chariots must be distinguished from the heavier four-wheeled wagons and two-wheeled carts with solid wheels. The evidence for the development of the spoked wheel in Anatolia comes from small-scale representations on **seals** from the Old Assyrian merchant colony of **Kanes (Kültepe)** near modern Kayseri, ca.2050–1750 BC, with depictions also of the more primitive crossbar wheel, surely the precursor of the spoked wheel. In the light of the evidence from central Asia, it may be significant that a rather earlier instance of the crossbar wheel occurs in northeastern Iran, at Tepe Hissar, dated ca.2350 BC. The Hittite army was making full use of chariots by the reign of **Hattusili I (ca.1650–1620 BC)**, probably of the six-spoked wheel design depicted later in the Egyptian reliefs of the battle of Kadesh. The bent-wood technology essential for constructing chariots must have become established in Anatolia some generations earlier than Hattusili I. Manufacture of heavy, solid-wheeled vehicles was a simpler affair. The Hittite chariots were protected with leather. Their crew comprised driver, spearman and shield bearer.

The rapid dissemination across the Near East, including Egypt, of the horse-drawn chariot is attested from ca.1700 BC. The argument is between those suggesting an independent development of the Near Eastern chariot from the heavy, disk-wheeled ox cart and proponents of an Indo-European, more specifically Indo-Aryan, origin. The wide dispersal of Indo-European words for "wheel" (*ratha, rota* etc.), "shaft-pole," "axle," "yoke" and "harness" has influenced discussion. Perhaps it would be wiser to make a contrast simply between a Near Eastern and an intrusive origin, the latter not exclusively Indo-European. The archaeological evidence, though not abundant, may be said to support the argument for an intrusive, non–Near Eastern origin of the chariot, while the remarkable rapidity of its spread in the early second millennium BC also suggests its importation. The crucial innovation was the spoked wheel, widely attested, initially with only four spokes, in New Kingdom Egypt, known to have imported horses and chariots from **Mitanni**.

While the bulk of the evidence from central Asia—arguably the original homeland whence the Hittites derived their chariots—points to the major role played by horsemen and chariotry, there are certain caveats to be noted. The light two-wheeled vehicles, so much more maneuverable than the cumbersome four-wheeled wagons, are, with many other items, widely depicted in rock drawings found for the most part in remote mountain valleys over a vast expanse from Mongolia and the Altai to Kirghizia and the Pamirs. Several of the scenes with two-wheelers appear to depict the rounding up of cattle. The construction of the two-wheelers was normally flimsy, to a degree that they would not have had a long life. Certainly for most of the time the majority of these vehicles were used for peaceful, everyday purposes, such as transporting family belongings from one tented encampment to the next, with a move to fresh pastures.

The horse-drawn chariot seems first to have arrived south of the steppes with the Indo-Aryan migration. One group entered India and the other northeastern Iran, the latter perhaps by ca.3000 BC. It is noteworthy that early sources from India accord a special status to the cartwright as well as to the smith. It has been postulated, with good reason, that the Indo-Aryans first introduced or developed chariotry in Iran; and that it was adopted by the **Hurrian** and Kassite populations occupying much of western Iran. Chariotry was playing a significant role in the Near East by the 13th century BC and indeed earlier. The subsequent defeat in the later 12th century BC of northern invaders, the **Mushki**, by Tiglath-Pileser I of Assyria, when he captured 120 chariots, and Late Assyrian dependence on a supply of horses from such regions as the Urmia basin of northwestern Iran are relevant.

The spread of the lightly constructed chariot—suited to parades, hunting and raiding as well as to the battlefield, where it was controlled by the blowing of trumpets—westward to central Europe (Slovakia) and eastward to Vedic India and even to China during the Shang period (ca.1850–1027 BC) emphasizes the immense span of Indo-European activity.

Although the Hittites can hardly be credited with inventing chariotry, once it had arrived upon the scene in the ancient Near East they deployed it to excellent effect on campaign. If they had left us a pictorial and written record to compare with the vainglorious inscriptions and reliefs of the Egyptian kings, the Hittite achievement in this sphere of warfare would be given the recognition it deserves.

CHRONOLOGY. *See* **ABSOLUTE CHRONOLOGY; RELATIVE CHRONOLOGY**

CISTERNS. Water supply was naturally vital for all communities, not least for those in towns liable to suffer a prolonged **siege**. Cisterns, cut out of the bedrock, are a common feature of the fortresses of **Urartu** in the Iron Age, but fewer examples are known from the second millennium BC. At **Hattusa** cisterns about two meters across and 2.7 meters deep were cut into the rock on **Büyükkale** and Sarıkale. At **Troy** VI, in the northeast corner of the citadel, a cistern four meters square and nine meters deep was cut into the rock and defended by a great tower of limestone masonry no less than nine meters high.

CLIMATIC CHANGE. Nowadays a common topic of discussion, much of it ill-informed and overstated. Given the fact that present-day trends are by no means altogether clear, taking Earth as a whole, any comment on climatic changes four or five millennia before our time has to be treated with some caution. Nevertheless, there are indicators which can hardly be ignored, sometimes of abrupt change.

Volcanic eruptions have more than once occasioned dramatic falls in temperature; and one such occurred round about 2250 BC, striking traces of which have been found in cores obtained from the depths of the Greenland ice sheet, in the form of volcanic ash. Whether or not a violent eruption was the sole cause of climatic change at this time, it has been detected in a wide zone including the Near East. The effects may have been most dramatic in Egypt, contributing to the collapse of the Old Kingdom, with records of **famine** and the likelihood of low levels of the Nile flood over a prolonged period. It is conceivable that climatic factors had an impact on political changes in Mesopotamia from the Akkadian period until the Third Dynasty of Ur, approximately 2370–2000 BC.

The effects of climatic change in Anatolia in the late third millennium BC are not documented in any written records, although there was a collapse of settled life over wide areas during the Early Bronze III period. Hardship from failure of harvests would almost certainly have contributed to political unrest, and may have helped the growth of the Hittites as a force to be reckoned with in central Anatolia.

There is some evidence of low solar activity and thus a relatively cool and rainy period in the Near East from mid–15th to mid–13th century BC. The picture is more certain for the final century of the Hittite Empire, some of the clearest data coming from **Ugarit** and pointing to a period of drought and high temperatures, in contrast with the cold, dry conditions of a millennium earlier described above. This climatic phase lasted until ca.900 BC, and may have been a factor in the decline of Assyria and Babylonia. **Claude Schaeffer** recorded a soil layer up to two meters deep all across the excavated areas of Ugarit: this consisted of fine powdery light yellow or whitish particles. This did not seal the buildings destroyed at the fall of the city: rather, they were built into it.

Grain shortages in the Hittite Empire became serious from time to time before the onset of the three centuries or so of hot, dry conditions; but they were surely aggravated, an additional factor in the final decline and fall of Hatti.

COPPER. Copper-working can be dated back well before the Bronze Age to the eighth millennium BC at a few widely scattered settlements in and beyond Anatolia. By the mid–third millennium BC it was becoming far more widespread and on a larger scale, although most sources mined were too small or too inaccessible to be commercially viable today, an exception being **Ergani Maden**, near Diyarbakir (whose Turkish name means "copper walls"). By ca.2800 BC copper was being mined at Közlü, not very far from **Ikiztepe**. Unalloyed copper was then still widely in use, arsenical bronze being the most popular alloy in the third millennium BC, exemplified by the contents of the rich tombs of **Alaca Höyük**. This was superseded by **tin** bronze, from the period of the Old Assyrian colonies onward.

For the Assyrian merchants at **Kanes** and elsewhere copper was the third largest item of **trade**, after tin and **textiles**, its value averaging 130:1 in **silver** shekels. The Assyrians distinguished several grades of copper, from "washed" and "refined" to the inferior grades, classed as "black," "poor" or "in pieces." Refining centers were not clearly distinguished from sources. It is hard to believe that the copper trade was mainly carried on only within Anatolia. Once sources in Oman became less accessible, the cities of Mesopotamia turned to Anatolian sources, though overland was more expensive than seaborne transport.

From the Hittite Old Kingdom onward trade was altogether less extensive and less sophisticated in organization than under the Assyrian merchants. Unfortunately textual records for commercial activity and industrial production in the countryside outside the control of the palace at **Hattusa** are very limited. Copper, however, was a prominent item in dealings between those cities and towns remaining active throughout the centuries of Hittite power. It was moreover one of the resources for which the local centers had to account to Hattusa in the form of **taxes**. One city sent 190 kilograms of copper and 22 kilograms of tin; but payments were usually much smaller. Sickles, arrows, horse bits, vessels, knives, **axes** and hatchets are listed as gifts or as tribute (*mandattu*). Thus copper-working obviously flourished under Hittite rule, even though inadequately recorded.

CREMATION. Cremation was once regarded as a hallmark of the Iron Age, a distinctive tradition marking out those practicing it from those with a custom of inhumation. Now, however, there is widespread evidence of the coexistence of cremations and inhumations even in the same cemetery. This variety of **burial customs** may appear surprising, as differing concepts of the **Underworld** are implied.

Cremations usually take the form of jars containing the burnt remains of the dead. Several hundred were found at Gedikli, in the Islahiye district of Gaziantep province in southeastern Anatolia, and were dated by the excavator to the 22nd to 20th centuries BC. It was then suggested that here was a link with the arrival of the first Indo-Europeans in Anatolia, a development now dated considerably earlier. However that may be, it is now quite clear that cremation was not an innovation of the Iron Age, even though large cemeteries comprising only cremations do not appear till that period.

In Bronze Age Anatolia cremations occur at several sites, including **Troy** VI (where they were first discovered), Ilica and **Karahöyük-Konya** I. Most noteworthy, however, is the rather small cemetery of Osmankayasi at **Boğazköy (Hattusa),** rediscovered by the German expedition in 1936. It is located across the gorge north of Hattusa and north of **Büyükkaya**, lying not far west of **Yazılıkaya.** This cemetery has been dated ca.1800–1400 BC, the stratigraphy revealing three phases for the 54 cremations and 36 inhumations identified in the shelter of overhanging rocks. Ceramic parallels begin in the period of **Kültepe-*Karum*** IB.

The pots were mostly used as urns for the ashes, fewer being tomb gifts. Horses and donkeys had not been incinerated, and were surely ritual offerings. Archaeologically these can be observed elsewhere, as in the Caucasus and Greece, and philologically in Hittite funerary texts. Dogs too are found, as well as food offerings of pigs, sheep and cows. The human bones were not completely incinerated, making it possible to ascertain the interesting fact that a high percentage of adult-and-child cremations occurs. The significance of this can only be a matter for speculation.

Comparative evidence occurs in two categories. The **pottery** shows close parallels with **Tarsus** to the south, while the analyses of the skeletal data indicate parallels between some of the Hittite men and the inhabitants of Tepe Hissar III in northeastern Iran.

The **royal funerary customs** of the Hittites involved cremation, known only from their rituals as described in the texts: such cremations are yet to be found. An indirect reflection of their wealth may be detectable in the later (Neo-Hittite) "**gold** grave" at **Carchemish.**

Two extensive Neo-Hittite cremation cemeteries were found in the British Museum excavations at Carchemish, in the Yunus cemetery, and in the Danish excavations at **Hama (Hamath).** There four phases were distinguished, the first two dating from the coming of the **Sea Peoples** (ca.1170 BC) to the end of Hama Period F (ca.900 BC), the third to the ninth century BC and the fourth to ca.800–720 BC. The grave goods tend to suggest a progressive decline in the social status of this cemetery.

Comparisons with Homeric customs are suggested by offerings of meat put beside the urn containing the ashes of the dead, a practice evident elsewhere and demonstrating belief in an afterlife, apparently not inconsistent with cremation. Otherwise this must surely have been far less popular as a funerary custom, given the almost universal expectation of some kind of life after death.

CULT CENTERS. Two intact **tablets** from **Hattusa** preserve a long prayer of **Muwatalli II**, invoking the aid of every conceivable divinity of Hatti. The order in which these are listed is clearly related to rank in the Hittite **pantheon**, with geographical sequence also a factor. Their cult centers are also recorded beside their names, though in many cases several deities are bracketed with one center. "Gods, goddeses, mountains and rivers" are regularly mentioned. The purpose of this prayer, however, is uncertain.

While the Sun-God and **Sun-Goddess** of **Arinna** take precedence in the hierarchy associated with the preeminent cult center of the Hittite realm, the **Storm-God** (alias Weather-God) takes third place, followed by a variety of deities and by unnamed mountains and rivers. The primacy of the Storm-God, however, can be seen in his being accorded first mention in connection with the great majority, though not all, of the other cult centers in this prayer.

Other cult centers listed in this royal prayer comprise:

Samuha; **Aleppo** (Halap); **Katapa**; Hattarina, Pirwa and Askasepa; **Zippalanda**; **Kummanni**; Sanahuitta; **Nerik** and **Kastama**; Hatenzuwa and Takupsa; **Sarissa**; Hurma; **Lawazan-tiya**; Pittiyariga and **Uda**; Parsa; **Hissashapa** and Kuliwisna; Kar-ahna; **Sugziya**; Lihsina; Turmitta; **Nenassa**; **Hupisna**; **Tuwan-uwa**; Illaya; Suwanzana; **Arziya**; Hurniya; Zarwisa; Sahhaniya; Pahtima, Sahhuwiya and Mallitaskuriya; Harziuna; **Sallapa**; Ussa and **Parsunta**; Wasutuwanda and Innuwita; Alazhana, **Hahana** and Ammama; Tawiniya and Katahha; Waskhaniya; **Landa** and **Hattena**; Harbisa and Kalimuna; **Hakpissa**; **Ankuwa**; Neni-sankuwa, Duruwaduruwa and Iksuna; Sullama, Hatra and **Isuwa**; **Tegarama**; Paliya; Tupazziya; Kariuna; Apzisna; Kalasmitta; **Tapikka**.

The Storm-God appears in this list in a number of guises, re-lated to thunder, the (**army**) camp, the **Underworld** and prosperity, the last clearly through rain on the crops. Four paragraphs relate to the king's family, including his grandparents and father; and the third paragraph has an invocation of the **gods** of the grandfather's palace. Mountains and rivers are normally linked to a particular territory, for example the **Lower Land**. Though the **Marrasantiya** is named once, rivers are normally anonymous, mountains being named more often. This is scarcely remarkable, since they were di-rectly associated with the Storm-God.

Most of the above cult centers lay within the Hittite lands proper. Clearly not all were of great importance; but they serve to demonstrate the breadth and pervasiveness of the cults, as well as the readiness of Muwatalli II to invoke not only the state gods and goddesses but those closer to the hearts of the majority of their sub-jects, continuing their devotion to divinities of the natural world, whose cults long preceded the advent of the Hittite state with its re-ligious centralization. Many rituals and paraphernalia are found spread across different cults.

CULT INVENTORIES. Without these the long-lasting local cults in the Hittite lands would be little understood. These inventories were compiled by officials sent out by **Tudhaliya IV**, as part of his pro-gram of religious reform and reorganization at the behest of his mother, **Puduhepa**. The officials had to collect evidence on the condition of local shrines. Some of these reports are no more than lists of **temple** furniture, sometimes including recent royal dona-tions. Others, more thorough, include descriptions of the local reli-gious **festivals**.

In most of these shrines the deity had been represented only by a symbol or by a **stela** (Hittite: *huwasi* stone). The **Storm-God** (Weather-God), however, was usually represented by a bull, both before and after enrichment of the shrines by Tudhaliya IV, under whom for the first time appeared cult images in human form. The reliefs at **Alaca Höyük** give a well-known example of the Weather-God worshiped as a bull.

In provincial centers it seems the **statues** were only small, no bigger than statuettes, measured by the unit *sekan*, probably about 22 centimeters. On this basis the statuettes measure 22 to 44 centimeters in height. Unfortunately no inventories have been found for the temples of **Hattusa**, though the stone bases in the sanctuaries of the excavated temples must have been designed for full-size statues, as mentioned in a prayer of Puduhepa for her ailing husband, **Hattusili III**.

CULTS. *See* **ANATOLIAN RELIGION: EARTH AND WATER; ANCESTOR CULT; ARINNA; CULT CENTERS; CULT INVENTORIES; FESTIVALS; HEARTH (CULT OF); NERIK; STATUES; STELAE; TEMPLES.**

CUNEIFORM. This Mesopotamian script was originally adapted from Sumerian to Akkadian writing in the land of its birth and only much later was it used for texts in the **Hittite language**, with adaptations required of the students undergoing the lengthy, laborious process of learning the syllabic script and the craft of incising the signs in clay. Students perforce were recruited very young, forming a privileged and valued caste, the **scribes**.

The dating of Hittite **tablets** is by no means always clear from their content, as for example where two kings of widely different date share the same name. Now some texts can be ascribed to an earlier date than before, on the basis of their script and, secondarily, on grammatical details. These criteria can be used to test the hypothesis that, until the destruction of **Mitanni** by **Suppiluliuma I**, scribal borrowings by the Hittites from Assyria and Babylonia could occur only through **Hurrian** intermediaries. In **Hattusa** it was diplomatic texts in the Akkadian language which were the first to be susceptible to changes introduced from Mesopotamia, gradually appearing only later in the style of cuneiform script used for Hittite texts.

In the earlier stages of cuneiform writing in Anatolia, the script used for the cuneiform tablets of the Old Assyrian period, notably in **Kültepe-Kanes**, is markedly different in the shapes and values of signs from that used in tablets of the earliest Hittite kings, including **Hattusili I**. Therefore the Hittite Old Kingdom cannot have derived its script from the former Assyrian colonies, but rather, in the 17th century BC, from a scribal center in Syria, very possibly from **Ebla**. The script more closely resembles that of the earlier Old Akkadian period rather than those of contemporary Assyria and Babylonia.

During the Hittite Empire abundant and varied literary imports from Mesopotamia have been found at Hattusa, among them many Sumerian-Akkadian bilingual texts. Imported Mesopotamian texts occur both in Middle Babylonian script and in a Hittite hand, indicating the employment of both foreign and local scribes. Among **Hurrian** imports are the Gilgamesh epic and the myths of the **Kumarbi** cycle. Direct contact between Hatti and Mesopotamia must have begun before the mid-14th century BC on quite a regular basis, and certainly was reflected in the development of the Late Hittite cuneiform script under the Empire.

Similarities between the Middle Hittite script and the script of the cuneiform tablets recovered from **Tell el-Amarna (Akhetaten)** suggests it may well have been Hittites who taught Egyptian scribes to write cuneiform. This is certainly an attractive theory. An exchange of letters in Hittite between the Pharaoh and a ruler of **Arzawa** named **Tarhundaradu** demonstrates the ability of Egyptian scribes to master the writing of Hittite. It is noteworthy that these exchanges occurred in the **Middle Kingdom**, certainly before ca.1380 BC. Such contacts did not have to await the time of military expansion of Hittite power under Suppululiuma I.

CURTIUS, LUDWIG (1874–1954). German archaeologist, who took part in the early excavations at **Boğazköy** as assistant to **Hugo Winckler**. He kept a detailed diary, though not publishing this till decades afterward. While very critical of the methods used for extracting **tablets**, with no record of their findspots, he was too diplomatic and too junior to be in a position to speak out. He did also witness the more methodical work of **Otto Puchstein**.

CYCLOPEAN MASONRY. This style of construction used large rectangular and polygonal blocks up to one and a half meters long, carefully though not exactly fitted together, their mass providing structural stability. Best known in the defenses of **Boğazköy: Upper City**, as on either side of the King's Gate, cyclopean masonry can be seen also in the Mycenaean world, at Mycenae and Tiryns. There is no reason to suggest a western influence on the **architects** of **Hattusa**. It may, however, be relevant to note that traces of similar masonry, not known to be of Phrygian workmanship, survive in a few of the *kales* in the area of Midas City in Phrygia. Strongholds of **Arzawa** or its allies could have preceded the monuments of Phrygia built in the first millennium BC.

- D -

DELAPORTE, LOUIS (1875–1944). French Assyriologist and Hittitologist, who led the first expedition to carry out excavations at **Malatya (Arslantepe)**, revealing both **sculptures** of the Neo-Hittite period and prehistoric occupation levels, yielding painted **pottery** not of Hittite date as he suggested but of the late third millennium BC.

DENDROCHRONOLOGY. A dating technique through counting of tree rings, correlated to demonstrate a sequence spanning many centuries, in Anatolia and elsewhere. This is a valuable aid to establishing **absolute chronology**, and is normally more accurate than any other method. This technique has been advanced, extended and publicized by Peter Kuniholm (Cornell University). Dendrochronology can also be applied to research into **climatic change**: the greater the precipitation for a given year, the wider its tree ring, and the converse.

DEPORTATION AND RESETTLEMENT. This policy was pursued consistently by successive Hittite kings at least from the time of **Tudhaliya I/II**, in whose reign the only recorded rebellion of deportees occurred. Perhaps learning from this, subsequent Hittite kings suffered no such confrontation. Nevertheless, the transportation of such large numbers, sometimes whole communities, of conquered enemies or rebellious vassals must have presented practical problems: living off the land would have been a necessity, as indeed for the **army** on campaign. Yet this seems to have been an even more prominent aspect of regular royal policy for the Hittites as for the later Assyrians.

    Prisoners of war either went to serve the king, becoming his property and thus effectively in a state of **slavery**, or they might be assigned to the estates of his senior officers. Alternative duties might be in the service of a **temple** or in a frontier garrison. In this last function they would be among those sent to resettle the depopulated areas along the frontiers, especially those bordering the **Kaska** lands.

Persistent importations of prisoners of war made for an ethnically mixed population, increasingly so as the generations passed. It is very possible that this was a factor contributing to the abrupt downfall of the Empire.

DIPLOMACY. This required trained civil servants to act as envoys or intermediaries, especially when negotiations were in progress between Hatti and one of the other great powers. A common topic was dynastic **marriage**, with which was associated **gift exchange** as a routine element in the proceedings. Records survive giving the names of individual diplomats as well as foreigners of lower status visiting or residing at the Hittite court in **Hattusa**.

One of the best known diplomatic negotiations, destined to end in tragedy, involved the urgent request of **Ankhesenamun** to **Suppululiuma I**. A Hittite envoy named Hattusa-ziti was dispatched to Egypt, returning to the Hittite court the following spring together with Hani, a special emissary of the widowed Egyptian queen. He was clearly a highly experienced, sophisticated diplomat, who by his conciliatory tone succeeded in winning the aggrieved Suppululiuma over to consenting to the proposed royal marriage. Hani was active in Egyptian–Hittite relations over some years. The personal link counted for as much as it does today.

The names of two Babylonian ambassadors and one Assyrian accredited to the court of **Hattusili III** are known. A regular exchange of messengers, specialists and information among the leading powers of the Near East in the Late Bronze Age is exemplified by a long letter in which Hattusili III rebukes the king of Babylon, Kadashman-Enlil, for breaking off regular diplomatic contacts. The excuse was unrest caused by seminomadic tribes, the Ahlamu, associated in the Assyrian **annals** with the Aramaeans. The only states whose rulers were recognized by the Hittite kings as "brothers," thus of equal standing, throughout the period of the Hittite Empire were Egypt and Babylon, dealings with the latter being rather intermittent. The status of **Mitanni** fell and that of Assyria rose as time passed. Relations with **Ahhiyawa** were for most years remote.

International relations had been well established even before the rise of the Hittite Empire, as demonstrated by developments in the **cuneiform** script in Hattusa, beginning in the reign of **Hattusili I.**

DIVINATION. Three professions practiced this art of interpreting **omens**: the "diviner," the "bird operator" and the "Old Woman." The first was expert in reading the omens from liver and entrails, by **extispicy**; the second in interpreting the flight of birds; and the third was involved with an enigmatic type of **oracle** termed the KIN. This last was manifested in symbols representing divinity, human beings and positive and negative entities. One **tablet** from **Boğazköy: Büyükkale** IVb confirms the Anatolian origin of the KIN system of divination, being written in archaic language, and thus a unique oracular text of the Hittite Old Kingdom. When the diviners practiced **magic**, this was commonly done by foreigners. It seems that the diviners were apt at times to dabble in magic without official permission, this being outside their remit. **Hattusili I** recorded his strong disapproval of such activities by the Old Women, suggesting that they wielded excessive influence over the ordinary Hittite population. A college of divination was established in **Hattusa**, where it was well developed and frequently practiced.

DOMUZTEPE. A companion fortress to **Karatepe,** on the farther side of the River Ceyhan, dated to the ninth century BC and perhaps the original location of the earlier reliefs found at Karatepe, to which they would have been removed. (This site is not to be confused with the large mound of the Halaf period dating to the fifth millennium BC and situated near Kahramanmaraş.)

DRESS. Many representations, notably on reliefs, tend to depict ritual dress of king, **queen** or deity rather than everyday clothing and accessories. Small caps crowned the head, allowing thick hair to fall from beneath. Horns appearing on these caps indicate divinity, following Mesopotamian style. Short-sleeved shirts or tunics and short kilts, worn above the knee, were typical, practical attire, originating at least as early as the **Kültepe-*karum*** IB period. This is the style depicted on **Sarruma** and many of the other deities of Chamber A at **Yazılıkaya**; on the god and king at **Fraktin**; on the huntsmen on the **Alaca Höyük** reliefs; by the presumably princely figures on the **Imamkulu, Hanyeri-Gezbel** and **Hemite** rock reliefs; and by the glyptic art of **Hattusa** and **Maşat Höyük, seal** impressions and a seal respectively.

　　Boot-shaped terracotta (pottery) drinking-cups from Kültepe-

karum II indicate forerunners of the highly distinctive "winkle-picker" footwear with exaggerated pointed toes—boots rather than shoes—found in the Hittite Old Kingdom and common under the Empire. Presumably these were made of animal hide.

For ordinary purposes belts would have been made of leather or possibly of woven string. More decorative belts, such as those on the bowl from **Kinik**, were of metal. Stitch holes occur elsewhere on some excavated examples, for attachment of a backing of leather or hide, a style recurring in the splendid bronze belts from **Urartu**.

The roughest garment was the simple shepherd's cloak, even donned by the king during certain **festivals**.

DUMANLI. As the result of an archaeological survey of Çankiri province, northeast of Ankara, by Roger Matthews, then director of the British Institute of Archaeology at Ankara (1995–2001), many settlement sites of the Late Bronze Age have been found, Dumanlı having especially well-preserved **fortifications**. Many of these sites have stone-built defenses and access ramps, and clearly were tactically sited to serve as centers of local control and links in a system of in-depth border defenses in the repeated confrontations of the Hittites with their **Kaska** neighbors to the north.

In the Iron Age, in common with most of the Anatolian plateau, there emerged new categories of site—hilltop forts, tumuli and rock-cut tombs—continuing into the Hellenistic period.

DÜNDARTEPE. A short distance east of Samsun, this was the most important of three settlement sites—with Tekkeköy and Kavak-Kaledoruğu—excavated by Kiliç Kökten with **Tahsin Özgüç** and **Nimet Özgüç** (1940–1941). All three sites, including Dündartepe III, revealed Middle Bronze Age occupation, preceded by Early Bronze Age levels with characteristic dark burnished handmade **pottery**.

- E -

EARLY TRANSCAUCASIAN (ETC) CULTURAL ZONE. A vast territory extending from the **Malatya**-Elaziğ region in the west eastward to the Caucasus and the Urmia basin of northwestern Iran. It is readily distinguishable by its pottery, much of it with relief or incised decoration, and by its buildings, rectangular or round. There was an ubiquitous **hearth cult**. This cultural tradition spanned ca.3500–2000 BC, with three subperiods (ETC I–III). By the ETC III period, in the later third millennium BC, the unity of this zone had broken down: in the Malatya-Elazığ region a painted pottery developed. This cultural zone impinges on Hittite history, as having in all probability been the homeland of the **Hurrians** before their southward and westward expansion in the second millennium BC.

ECONOMY. *See* **DEPORTATION AND RESETTLEMENT; GRANARIES;** *KARUM***; PRICES; STORE CITIES; TAXES; TEXTILES; TRADE.**

EFLATUN PINAR. A spring near Lake Beyşehir—the most easterly of the lakes that lie along the north side of the Taurus range—that had its area increased to make a pool of 30 by 35 meters, by the construction of a small dam of two rows of orthostats with rubble filling and a sluice. Here was the site chosen for a remarkable spring sanctuary, with masonry forming a façade on the north side, in the absence of a natural rock face, the sanctuary facing south. The blocks of the relief-decorated façade are seven meters long. The masonry has carefully drafted edges, and is of the highest quality, surely indicating a date in the later 13th century, very probably in the reign of that great builder, **Tudhaliya IV**.

Across the top of the façade stretches a badly worn winged sun disk, supported at either end by two hybrid demons, one standing on the shoulders of the other. Beneath the great winged disc are two lesser winged sun disks, side by side, supported by six demons in superimposed pairs. The lesser suns crown two seated deities: to the left a **god** with a peaked cap, to the right a goddess with the disk of Hathor. One interpretation describes these as a mountain god and goddess of the spring, respectively. Recently the pool has been drained, with excavations taking place nearby. While this has removed some of the visual impression of this sanctuary, no longer as immediately appealing to the eye, it has exposed a whole lower section of the façade, comprising five identical figures resembling mountain gods, depicted with tall headdress, hands clasped and scaly lower half. The surface of the pool must therefore have been lower than in modern times, silt indeed being required to be removed by the excavators. The most likely reconstruction puts two colossal **statues** crowning the façade, on the left a god and on the right a goddess, the former most probably being represented by the great monolithic statue lying on the ground at **Fasillar**, some 50 kilometers away, evidently awaiting transportation. The fact that this never took place is a hint that by then the Hittite Empire was approaching its downfall. An alternative reconstruction would have two statues which would have been larger versions of those on the façade below.

There is no proof that Eflatun Pınar was the work of any Hittite king or provincial ruler, the character of the masonry being perhaps the strongest clue in this direction. Yet it could well have been erected by a local ruler much influenced by Hittite art, for the absence of any inscription distinguishes it from the monuments of Tudhaliya IV—**Yazılıkaya, Karakuyu, Emirgazi** and **Yalburt**—all inscribed with his name. There can be not the slightest doubt that spring sanctuaries in Anatolia were not a Hittite innovation; and indeed they persisted after the end of the Empire. Eflatun Pınar may be compared with **Mount Sipylus**.

The deities represented on the façade of Eflatun Pınar are generally agreed to be related to the **Hattian,** non-Indo-European mainstream tradition in early religion in Anatolia. One may follow the suggestion that the god and goddess were intended to be seen as rising out of the waters of the pool, to symbolize its importance as the source of all life. They are thus depicted not in their Indo-European transformation as **Storm-God** and **Sun-Goddess** but in their primary non-Indo-European characters as god of streams and the **Underworld** and goddess of fertility and the earth. There is a strong argument for ascribing a dominant role in **Anatolian religion** to earth and water.

An archaeological field survey suggests Tolca Höyük, on the northeast shore of Lake Beyşehir, as the probable administrative center of the district, with the main second-millennium BC sites in the Beyşehir area located at the north end of the lake. Recent research into Hittite and related **historical geography** points to **Hapalla** as the land in which Eflatun Pınar was constructed. Seeing that this was a frontier area, sometimes under the rule of **Arzawa** but whenever circumstances allowed under Hittite control, as it was in the period to which this sanctuary can be ascribed, Eflatun Pınar owed its existence at least to a concept inspired by Tudhaliya IV, even if not directly designed by his orders.

ELECTRUM. *See* **GOLD.**

EMAR (TELL MESKENE KHADIME). Excavations conducted by

a French expedition (1972–1976). This city, on the right (west) bank of the Euphrates by the great bend where the river turns southeast into Mesopotamia, was a major trading center and river port in the early second millennium BC, attested by references in the **archives** of **Mari**. In one letter Zimri-Lim, the last king of Mari, refers to the control then exercised over Emar by the kingdom of Yamhad **(Aleppo)** and his prohibition of the sale of any corn bought or sold in Emar to Mari. The circuitous route of the mission, swift but brief, from Larsa in southern Mesopotamia to Emar recorded on this tablet may best be explained by the interposition of a hostile or obstructive power in the Euphrates valley. Which more likely than Mari itself, and what better background to the eventual conquest of Zimri-Lim by Hammurabi (ca.1757 BC)? Later, in the 15th century BC, Emar appears in the inscription of Idri-Mi from **Alalakh**, as his mother's birthplace and the city whither he fled into exile. The site of Emar in these years has not been located: it was presumably not far from the new foundation.

This new city was built under Hittite supervision and inaugurated by **Mursili II**: there is no trace of earlier building levels. This new kingdom, under Hittite overlordship, stretched from the borders of **Carchemish** in the north to those of **Aleppo** in the west, both Hittite **viceroyalties**. Indeed, Emar came under the direct jurisdiction of the viceroy in Carchemish, administrative powers being divided between him and a local king, backed by a body of elders with power to curb his authority. Thus government was more complex than in other vassal states.

The Hittite authorities did not interfere in business or **trade** in Emar, but were closely concerned with the administration of justice and anxious to be seen as being fair to local interests.

It was not the official or royal **cults** which dominated the lives of the majority of the population, but rather the domestic (or family) cult. The principal sources of **tablets** documenting this cult are from the site of Nuzi, in the kingdom of Arrapha, some 13 kilometers southwest of modern Kirkuk, but also from Emar. From these it is clear that cultic traditions differed widely from those of Babylonia. Emar and the other cities of **Astata** have yielded data on the domestic cult comparable with the textual evidence from Nuzi to the east. There seem to have been five formulae, the most significant reading thus: "The **gods** belong to the main house. The main house is the portion of my eldest son." This goes far to explaining the other formulae, two of which read: "The gods belong to the main house." The status of chief heir—normally but not quite invariably the eldest son—carried with it the responsibility of looking after the gods, whose cult had to be maintained without interruption, being clearly associated with the main house. This was the cult of "the gods and the dead," thus directly attached to the family's **ancestors**. It had no connection with priesthoods or **temples**. This was a funerary cult: hence the references to "honoring" the dead, "offering" and providing them with **food**. The close connections between family gods and family house may explain the popularity of baked clay models of houses and towers at Emar, providing interesting architectural details.

Hurrian society in Astata was saved from excessive rigidity by the frequent necessity for younger children, after division of the family property, to set up homes elsewhere for themselves and their families. The overriding consideration was the strength and survival of each family, centered round the "main house," the dwelling of the head of the family and the household gods in the form of statuettes, groups of which were housed in the homes of leading families in Nuzi and elsewhere. The implication of the texts is that minor houses were grouped around the main building, thus often accommodating large extended families. The archaeological evidence does not corroborate this conclusion, but neither does it disprove it. There was a code of conduct to be observed: thus, when an elder son behaved unacceptably, as by insulting his father, he might in effect be disinherited, an adopted son or even a family friend being chosen in his stead.

The position of **women** in Hurrian society was stronger than might be expected. A widow, when head of the family, was customarily given the legal status of father; and a father without sons might make his daughters legally sons, while making his will in their favor. This has bearing on the prominent role of women in a rather earlier period, in the Old Assyrian **trade** with Anatolia.

Families passed down from father to son their *ilanu*, statuettes of the so-called gods, in fact quite evidently the ancestors, and as such the focus of the domestic cult. All the family had the right to attend the ceremonies and to see the statuettes personifying their forebears. There is no evidence revealing how far back in time this domestic cult was practiced among the Hurrian people, though it is not too fanciful to imagine their introducing it to the middle Euphrates valley from their highland home in eastern Anatolia. If so, this would have come about during or immediately after the Early Transcaucasian III period, around the end of the third millennium BC. Distinctively Hurrian as this domestic cult appears to have been, it can hardly have originated in cities such as Emar.

EMIRGAZI. Located 46 kilometers north-northwest of Ereğli and 50 kilometers south-southwest of Aksaray, in the Konya Plain, Eskikişla being the findspot of six stone blocks, four of which are more probably altars rather than **stelae**, with **hieroglyphic** inscriptions written on the orders of **Tudhaliya IV**, setting out highly detailed rules and regulations for offerings and the use of the original sanctuary.

Almost all the remains were discovered by W. M. Ramsay in 1904 and 1908. **Bedrich Hrozny**, the first to study the inscriptions, labeled the four altars A, B, C and D. Later E. Masson labeled the better preserved rectangular block V. The inscription includes the words: "I made the divine mountain throne; (and) I placed (these) victory monuments; and I placed for myself this altar in front."

The inscription continues with injunctions to honor the altar and the sacrificial offerings, specifically sheep, with dire threats of divine punishment for those scorning or flouting these regulations. Implied is the common curse formula against anyone destroying or obliterating the inscription, such as occurs repeatedly, for example, in the later inscriptions of Assyria and **Urartu**.

The inscription on the two rectangular blocks is closely related in content to part of the **Yalburt** annalistic text, and can thus also be connected to the campaign of Tudhaliya IV in the **Lukka** Lands (Lycia), of which he was inordinately proud. In Emirgazi V the place-names Pinata and Awarna occur, indicating a campaign not in the Konya Plain but in the Xanthos valley of Lycia, as demonstrated by the references in the Yalburt text to Awarna, Pinata, Patar and Talwa, whose Lycian equivalents are Arnna, Pinale, Pttara and Tlawa.

With the agreement that the Emirgazi remains comprise four round stone altars and two rectangular blocks of uncertain function, the reference to the "divine mountain throne" could conceivably signify the mountain whereon the altars were placed; but more probably it signifies the sanctuary in which they were erected.

ERGANI MADEN. The major source of **copper** to this day in Turkey, halfway between Diyarbakir and Elaziğ in the uppermost Tigris basin. Copper has been mined here for millennia. It was readily accessible to the merchants of the cities of Mesopotamia, an alternative supply whenever access to Oman was barred.

ESKIYAPAR. Heavily fortified in the second millennium BC, this site—situated 25 kilometers northeast of **Boğazköy** and 20 kilometers southeast of **Alaca Höyük**—was excavated by Raci Temizer (1968–1983). It was occupied from the Early Bronze Age until the Roman period.

In the Late Bronze Age it was a town devoted in part, doubtless like many other communities, to production of **pottery**. Two round kilns in an open courtyard were 1.5 meters in diameter: the firing chamber was supported by a central pier and radiating struts. The clay was mixed with water from terracotta pipes. Wasters, unfired and misfired, illustrate the use of these kilns.

Already in the third millennium BC the Early Bronze Age settlement had an urban character. From the very last phase of this era (Early Bronze III.3) came two treasure hoards, buried each in a container in pits under the floor of the same room. These were definitely not grave-goods, but were buried before the house was abandoned after a fire. **Silver** goblets and a ceremonial **ax of electrum** were in the larger hoard, the other one being entirely of jewellery, including pins, earrings, bracelets and beads. Significantly, the parallels for these finds are with the west, especially **Troy** and Poliochni in the Aegean island of Lemnos, including shell-shaped earrings and basket-shaped beads, the latter occurring in central Anatolia only at Eskiyapar. The closest correlations with Alaca Höyük are with the later Early Bronze tombs, of Level 5 rather than Level 6. A dating for these hoards to ca.2200-2000 BC seems plausible.

EXTISPICY. "Reading" the entrails of animals sacrificed for purposes of **divination**. This was practiced commonly both in Mesopotamia and in Anatolia.

- F -

FALCONRY. Whereas this was unknown in Mesopotamia, there is varied evidence for the practice of this skill in Anatolia, primarily in depictions of the equipment peculiar to this sport. This activity has engendered a considerable literature over the centuries until the present day, although no work surpasses the treatise written in Latin on falconry (*De Arte Venandi cum Avibus*) by the emperor Frederick II Hohenstaufen (1194–1250). Falconry demands immense knowledge, skill and patience on the part of the falconer in training a bird. The relevant equipment comprises jess (short strap around the leg of the falcon or hawk), leash, neck band, glove, curve-ended stick for flushing game and perhaps a lure.

Suitable for falconry are: goshawks, sparrow hawks, a few falcons other than peregrines and golden eagles. Though in English usage "falcon" and "hawk" are generally synonymous, in fact these birds belong to different genus, family and species. They differ in appearance, flight, diet and habitat, as well as their nesting habits. In Anatolia it was probably the short-winged goshawk that was used in falconry. While the falcon is represented in ancient Egypt as the god Horus, with large black eyes distinct from the smaller eyes of the goshawk, only two examples are known for sure in Anatolia, both in Egyptianizing style, an ivory falcon from **Acemhöyük** and a bone inlay from **Alaca Höyük**.

The bones of a hare, golden eagle and kestrel (a kind of falcon) were found in subsidiary chamber C at **Yazılıkaya**, with traces of burning and repeated cleaning, in an unburnt level among bones of cattle, sheep and dog.

Falconry is depicted from the mid–third millennium BC, with a representation of a falconer holding up his dead prey from Tell Chuera in Syria; and one of the "standards" from Alaca Höyük has birds of prey perched along the top, two with a small animal in its beak. In the Old Assyrian Colony period, potters fashioned raptors perching menacingly on rims or handles. Stamp **seals** of the time of *karum* IB show hawks hovering over hares and gazelles. Some of these birds have neck bands. A highly unusual sealing of Mursili (probably **Mursili II**) shows a **god** brandishing a **lituus**, while he mounts a chariot in the form of a hawk, drawn by divine bulls. A mountain god with falcon or mace appears on two sealings of the time of **Arnuwanda III**. Falconry continues to be depicted either directly or by representations of the lituus in the Iron Age, at **Malatya**, **Zincirli**, **Guzanu**, **Carchemish** and **Karatepe**. In the Iron Age the falconer might often be depicted as lion-headed: thus at Carchemish a lion-headed figure with short stick and prey is shown on the right jamb of the King's Gate. At Karatepe is a relief of a hunter with spear and prey, here a lion, dangling from his left arm; and close to his left shoulder is a falcon facing outward, wings raised and with a hare in his talons. Equally vivid, if on a different scale, are numerous much earlier sealings showing a raptor on someone's hand or lap or in front of the human figure on a table, these dating to the period of *Karum* II of **Kanes.**

FAMINE. This became a recurrent problem for the Hittite lands from the time of **Hattusili III** onward, when **Puduhepa** refers to a shortage of grain in a letter to **Ramesses II**. Even if a serious and prolonged famine did not occur till the reign of **Tudhaliya IV**, Hatti seems to have become dependent on shipments of grain from Egypt and Syria on a regular basis. During the reign of Hattusili III a Hittite prince was sent to Egypt to organize a shipment of grain. The onset of serious famine was more the result of the decline of Hittite power and prestige, inhibiting regular imports of grain, than of any **climatic change**. Repeated demands from the **army** for recruits and a reduction in the manpower available from the policy of **deportation** will have depleted the agricultural labor force. **Plague** would at times likewise have diminished the labor force.

FASILLAR. Near Lake Beyşehir, west of Konya, is a large unfinished **stela** 7.30 meters tall, lying on a hillside. A deity wearing a conical cap stands on the head of a mountain god. This was very probably intended to be set up at the spring shrine of **Eflatun Pınar**. A replica is now standing in the garden of the Museum of Anatolian Civilizations in Ankara.

FERZANT. Thirty-five kilometers northeast of Çorum, plundered Hittite cemeteries at Ferzant-Buget, dating to the period of **Kültepe-karum** IB and the Old Kingdom.

FESTIVALS. These were the major religious celebrations, both royal and public, in the Hittite lands and the subject of the largest category of texts surviving from **Hattusa**. No complete record of any festival has yet been recovered.

The principal festivals were associated with spring or autumn and directly related to the agricultural cycle. The "crocus" and the *purulli* festivals were observed in the spring and the "festival of haste" (whatever the precise significance of its title) in the autumn, probably also the season of the briefer "gate-house" festival. The duration of a festival might extend over hours, days or even weeks. Most were celebrated annually. As many as 165 festivals featured in the official calendar of religious functions, representing the state cults. Numerous smaller local festivals were not reckoned in this number. Some were associated with particular activities, such as the grape harvest.

The prime purpose of the religious festivals was to keep the deities contented and satisfied with the deeds and dutiful demeanor of the king and **queen**. This was achieved by precise observance of the ceremonies, down to the most minute detail: hence the complex regulations preserved in the texts, which were instruction manuals for those controlling the proceedings on behalf of the king and queen. Any error or omission might bring disaster. Moreover, the **gods** would not necessarily reveal what had displeased them! The offerings of **food** and drink of the finest quality were likewise essential, the deities being particularly partial to fat.

The king and queen, as high priest and high priestess, held the religious leadership of their realm. No human beings took precedence over them. Yet they were obliged to humble themselves, at times almost abjectly, before the god or goddess. They wore special robes, the color distinctive of each festival. The king could even wear a rough shepherd's mantle, with **gold** earrings and skull cap. In some festivals he would remove his ceremonial robes and don military attire, symbolizing his role as war leader, along with the **spear** he could be given. Both king and queen had had to undergo the most thorough ablutions before donning their festal attire, to ensure ritual purity. This insistence on cleanliness extended to the strict hygiene demanded for the food offerings for the gods.

Royal duties related to the major religious festivals were stringent. While for many celebrations these functions could be delegated, the major festivals required the presence of the king, even if it meant his breaking off a campaign. **Suppiluliuma I** allegedly neglected some of his religious duties, the explanation for the various misfortunes of his own and his successors' reigns, so **Mursili II** claimed. This may explain that king's outstanding piety, comparable only with the assiduous attention to festivals by **Puduhepa**, sometimes deputizing for her ailing husband **Hattusili III**. It has been asked how the Hittite kings found time for all their religious obligations. There can be little doubt that the man-hours, material and consumable resources required made an inordinate drain on the wealth of the state, an economic factor in the end contributing to its downfall.

The festivals, though centered around the king and queen, were also the major public events of the year for the majority of the population. Only at this time was the **statue** of the god or goddess—itself representing the very person of the deity—brought out of its seclusion in the innermost sanctuary of the **temple**. According to the texts, this statue would have been sheathed in gold with rich encrustations; and it might be transported to the site of the public celebrations in a heavy ox-drawn wagon.

After the solemnity of the most sacred rituals, the festival became the occasion for public feasting and for entertainments by tumblers, jugglers, dancers, musicians, acrobats and athletes. These last might include wrestlers, whose contests were especially popular with king and people alike. The reliefs at **Alaca Höyük** may well depict a festival, with a hunting ritual.

The routes taken by some festival processions ranged from short distances to a nearby cultic site, with its *huwasi* stone, to routes extending over several days. Among these was the procession for the *purulli* spring festival, stopping after one day from **Hattusa** at **Arinna**, and continuing north to **Nerik**, until that **cult center** was overrun by the **Kaska** tribesmen. This is the leading example of a non-Hittite origin: the very name of the *purulli* festival derived from the **Hattic** word for "earth," while its deities— **Telipinu**, the **Storm-God** and Inar(a)—were **Hattian**.

FOOD. Except in times of **famine**, the population of the Hittite lands was probably adequately fed. In Anatolia there was enough fertile land to provide a good variety of cereals, vegetables and fruit, with extensive arable areas, orchards, gardens and **vineyards**. The vegetables were comparable with those found today, ranging from peas, beans and lentils to root vegetables, cucumber and parsley. Garlic and herbs such as coriander gave extra flavor to meals; and olives were everywhere available. Farmers of moderate wealth possessed an orchard, often serving also as a vineyard, and producing crops of apples, pears, figs, apricots, pomegranates and, of course, grapes. Dairy produce and honey from beehives were abundant.

Bread must have been a staple food, the cultivation of four strains of wheat and two or three of barley, the latter perhaps largely for brewing, suggesting several varieties of loaf. Grain was an important source of revenue for the state through **taxes**.

Livestock—cattle, sheep, pigs, goats and poultry—provided a varied meat component in the Hittite diet, supplemented by duck and partridge.

Naturally modern dietary fads were not found, fat being especially prized, by gods as well as men. The Hittite words for "**oil**," "fat," "lard," "tallow" or "grease" are commonly concealed behind Sumerian logograms, a usual phenomenon in the Hittite texts. Oil and fat from animal or vegetable sources were signified by the same word. The essential role of oil and fats in diet is illustrated by injunctions to show liberality to the poor by meeting their basic needs for oil. Such generosity must also be shown to the **gods**, as demonstrated by a passage in a recently discovered Hurro-Hittite bilingual text, where **Tesub** is said to be in need of food, clothing and oil from the other gods and goddesses.

In a Hittite Old Kingdom text a list of foodstuffs begins with "high-grade lard"—pig or sheep fat—followed by cheeses, rennet, wheat flour and bread. Such was the value of lard that it was legally permitted to kill a dog eating this very solid substance, to slit open its stomach and to recover the lard!

The gods delighted not only in fat and oil but in a variety of foods, presumably of the highest quality available. Butter and honey especially pleased the god **Telipinu**. Olives, figs and grapes are often mentioned together in relation to rituals.

FORRER, EMIL (1894-1986). Swiss philologist, who published a ground-breaking article entitled "The eight languages of the Boghazkoy inscriptions" (1919). Later, he published preliminary decipherments of the so-called Hittite **hieroglyphs**, now recognized as **Luwian**. He was one of a new generation attempting to overcome the considerable difficulties in this field.

FORTIFICATIONS. Anatolian fortifications attained a higher standard than before in the Middle Bronze Age, with earlier defenses built most notably at **Troy**. The objective was, of course, to make the greatest possible difficulties for any besieging force. Weak points such as corners, gateways, wall footings or the crowning parapets had to be reinforced as far as practicable; and indirect access through the city gates was highly desirable. The glacis—a sloping surface at the foot of the main defensive wall—achieved the dual purpose of preventing undermining by battering rams and exposing attackers to a shower of missiles from the wall above. This was never a device to thwart **chariotry**, anyhow not suitable for direct assault on a fortified stronghold.

Apart from those of **Boğazköy**, Troy, **Alaca Höyük** and **Alışar Höyük**, fortifications were built at **Eskiyapar, Beycesultan,** Kusura (near Afyon), **Porsuk, Meydancık, Mersin, Norşuntepe** and **Korucutepe**. Hittite influence is also apparent in Syria, at **Alalakh** and **Ugarit**.

There are some specialists who doubt the strictly military or defensive function of the great circuit enclosing **Boğazköy: Upper City**. While it is true that it would have required an extremely large garrison adequately to man the five kilometers' perimeter, any suggestion of a purely symbolic purpose behind this vast construction project exceeds the bounds of credibility. The earth rampart itself, 70 meters wide at the base, must have required a very large labor force; and masons were needed for facing with dressed stone some stretches of the glacis. The main city wall above the rampart was of double casemate construction, with outer and inner masonry skins and rubble filling in the compartments. On top of this stone wall ran a mudbrick wall, presumably with battlements, like those depicted on a baked clay model from the excavations. Rectangular towers projected from the wall at intervals of 30.5 meters or so, with an additional apron wall in front of vulnerable stretches of the main wall, as well as bastions midway between the towers.

The main gateways were flanked by massive towers. The bronze-plated gates were set some distance back from the façades of these towers; secondary gates were flush with the inner faces of the gate towers. Steep ramps parallel with the city wall gave access to the gates, exposing the flanks of an attacking force. A paved street, well preserved by the Sphinx Gate (Yerkapi) in the Upper City, allowed rapid deployment by a garrison, wherever it might come. There were fortifications within the city of Hattusa, notably around **Boğazköy: Büyükkale**, making defense of the different sectors of the city possible, even if the main wall was breached.

Strong fortifications, enclosing an oval area, were built to defend Alışar Höyük (Level II), including towers, gates and bastions. The masonry was of limestone blocks up to 0.50 meter wide, carefully set. There was also a perimeter wall enclosing the Lower Fortress, covering a terrace beneath the citadel mound. A later system of defenses at Alışar Höyük can be securely dated to the Iron Age: this settlement, smaller than its Middle Bronze Age predecessor, fell to a **siege** and was completely destroyed, after the gateway had been blocked.

FRAKTIN. Rock relief located 18 kilometers southeast of Develi and thus 50 kilometers south-southeast of Kayseri, on a signposted road, yet requiring local guidance, as with so many ancient sites in Anatolia. It has been equated with the Classical town of Dastarcum, mentioned by the geographer Strabo. This relief is near the Yenice River, the ancient Carmalas: it is carved on the face of a low rock escarpment beside a modern irrigation channel, being largely obscured by a plantation.

This is the most westerly, and arguably the most important, of a series of four rock reliefs, the others being at **Taşcı, Imamkulu** and **Hanyeri-Gezbel**. It is doubtful whether the Yenice River is wide enough to be termed a river frontier. Rather, this was a significant natural highway, clearly regarded as such at this period, during and just after the reign of **Hattusili III**.

This is a double relief, having a male group on the left and a female group on the right, each group comprising three elements— deity, altar and worshiper. Whereas the male group is finished, depicting Hattusili III pouring a libation on an altar, as the **Storm-God** approaches, and with accompanying **hieroglyphic** inscription, the sculptor abandoned his task before finishing the female group, of **Puduhepa** pouring a libation on an altar before a seated goddess, identifiable as **Hebat** or the **Sun Goddess** of **Arinna**. It cannot be said why this part was abandoned in an unfinished if recognizable state. There are stylistic traits leading to identification of a "Fraktin Master" responsible for the early work at **Yazılıkaya**. He was very probably dispatched to Fraktin from the court at **Hattusa,** whither he may have been urgently recalled. Already, though less so than at Yazılıkaya, the influence of the royal **seal** cutters on the relief sculptors is detectable at Fraktin.

A fairly close dating for the Fraktin relief is suggested by the representation of Hattusili III as divine, necessarily indicating that this work was not carried out until after his death, since no Hittite king claimed divinity during his lifetime. Was there perhaps a conundrum facing the court and its sculptors, in that the **queen**, destined in fact to live on for many long years, could not, strictly speaking, share her dead husband's divine status? This could explain the rather blurred representation of Puduhepa, in its unfinished state: no definitive answer to this problem is ever likely to emerge.

The figures stand 1.30 meters tall, over half life size, the treatment of the garments being characteristic of the so-called Fraktin Master. The male figures are depicted frontally instead of in profile, as at Yazılıkaya, where a new fashion in feminine headgear is to be seen in the form of the polos, in contrast to the conical crown worn by the goddess at Fraktin. Here the outlines of the figures are emphasized by grooves, probably intended to guide the semiskilled craftsmen whose task it was to grind or rub down the rock surface, as required.

Nearby is a settlement site excavated by **Tahsin** and **Nimet Özgüç** (1947 and 1954), where a Mycenaean IIIC stirrup jar and **sword** were found in the burnt destruction of the final Hittite level. This settlement stands 1,800 meters east of the Hittite reliefs. Beneath Roman and Iron Age levels, the later Hittite level yielded many finds, including bronze **axes**, **spearheads**, arrowheads and bracelets. The **pottery** is typical of the Empire, different from that found in the earlier Hittite level, also burnt, which contained walls of mud-plastered **cyclopean masonry**. This level dates either to the Old Kingdom or to the early Empire. *See also* **SCULPTURE**.

- G -

GARSTANG, JOHN (1876–1956). Though he read Maths at Jesus College, Oxford, he then turned to archaeology, at the age of 23 joining Flinders Petrie in Egypt. Then he worked in Anatolia (1904–1909), excavating **Sakçegözü**, near Gaziantep, with a later final season (1911). He traveled extensively across the Anatolian plateau, often by oxcart on the rough roads of the time, acquiring a knowledge of the lie of the land which was later—after the first deciphered Hittite texts became known outside Germany after World War I—to be of fundamental value in his work on Hittite **historical geography**. At this time Garstang suffered the major disappointment of seeing the concession for excavating the Hittite capital of **Boğazköy (Hattusa)**, which he had had reason to believe might be granted to him, given instead to **Hugo Winckler**. This did not damp his enthusiasm for all things Hittite, however, and in 1910 appeared his widely read and unforeseeably influential book *The Land of the Hittites*.

Garstang had already (1902) been appointed Honorary Reader in Egyptian Archaeology at the University of Liverpool, five years later becoming professor of the Methods and Practice of Archaeology, continuing at Liverpool until his retirement (1941). He was founding director of the British School of Archaeology in Jerusalem (1920) and of the Department of Antiquities of Palestine (1920–1926), drafting the first antiquities laws. He was later founding director of the British Institute of Archaeology at Ankara (1947), it being his decision to site it in the new capital of the Turkish Republic rather than in Istanbul, where the other archaeological institutes were based.

Garstang worked at the great cemetery of Beni Hasan in Middle Egypt. He also conducted excavations in the Sudan at Meroe (1909–1914) and in Palestine at Jericho (1930–1936), finally returning to Turkey to direct excavations at Yumuktepe, **Mersin**, not far from **Tarsus** (1937–1939 and 1947). This project was published in quasi-narrative form as *Prehistoric Mersin* (1953).

GAVURKALESI. Situated about 50 kilometers south-southwest of Ankara, on the road to Haymana, short of that town by 14 kilometers and close to the village of Dereköy, being accessible by car. This site comprises a small plateau 36.5 meters square, fortified with **cyclopean** walls and crowned by a later enclosure of Iron Age date. A stone-built chamber on the summit is commonly described as a tomb, dating to the main period of occupation, of the Hittite imperial period, probably 13th century BC: it may alternatively have served as a shrine. The dating to the 13th century BC depends solely on the style of the rock relief just below the fortress. It depicts two gods advancing toward a seated goddess, and has been compared in its general composition with the processions of Chamber A of **Yazılıkaya,** though less refined in execution. One god carries a **sword,** probably of western or Aegean type. Attribution to the reign of **Hattusili III** seems plausible, making it contemporary with the relief at **Fraktin.**

GIFT EXCHANGE. In his *Apology,* **Hattusili III** claims that diplomatic relations continued unbroken after his seizure of the throne; and that gifts were still being sent to **Hattusa.** The exchange of gifts was a prerequisite for sound international relations, almost as important as recognition of relative status and fundamental to the smooth operation of **trade** in the second millennium BC in and around the Near East and likewise for arranging a royal **marriage.**

Among the best known records of gift exchange were those of Akhenaten in his new capital of **Tell el-Amarna (Akhetaten)** and Tusratta, king of **Mitanni,** who openly demanded more **gold.** There were few inhibitions regarding dissatisfaction with a gift! *See also* **DIPLOMACY; HATTUSILI III: THE *APOLOGY.***

GLYPTIC ART. This was the craft of the **seal**-cutter, recognized from Sumerian times onward in Mesopotamia, at **Kultepe-Kanes** and elsewhere in the ancient Near East.

The tools used depended on the hardness of the material, mainly limestone, shell and haematite successively in Mesopotamia. For shell and bone seals a graver was used, while the drill was essential for seals of stone. The greater the pressure of the drill, the higher the relief, in "blobs," in a seal impression.

The term "glyptic" is often employed as shorthand for the various styles and subject matter displayed by seals. *See also* ***BULLAE*; SEALS.**

GODS AND GODDESSES. *See* ALALU; ANU; HEBAT; ISHTAR; KUBABA; KUMARBI; LELWANI; NERGAL; PANTHEON (HITTITE); PANTHEON (YAZILIKAYA); SARRUMA; SAUSGA; STORM-GOD; SUN-GODDESS; TELIPINU; TESUB; TETESHAPI; THEOGONY; WURUSEMU.

GOLD. It is not surprising that no records survive of the precise location of sources of this most precious of metals, prized for its rarity, appearance, malleability and incorruptibility. Ancient miners kept their trade secrets. Hints, however, may be gleaned from scattered clues.

In the **Kestel** mining area, the center of known Anatolian production of **tin**, gold is one of the many minerals found in the alluvial deposits in the nearby stream. It was certainly among the metals extracted in the third and second millennia BC from the Taurus Mountains, although that region was better known as the principal source in the ancient Near East of **silver**. Just one example of what must surely have been many places where gold was found and worked is the north slope of Bakirtepe, even though this Turkish name signifies "**copper** hill": this is situated 20 kilometers east of Kangal and 80 kilometers southeast of the provincial capital Sivas, in east central Anatolia, in the vicinity of Çetinkaya. Here were found indications of mining activity with large stone mortars, inside some of which were traces of gold. This site has been linked with **Hahhum**, whence, according to Mesopotamian written records, gold was being brought to Mesopotamia in the second millennium BC. Regrettably, however, the lack of dating evidence means that, in common with so many metallurgical sites, Bakirtepe cannot be fixed in any period with certainty.

The wealth of finds from Early Bronze Age cemeteries, notably **Alaca Höyük** and **Troy**, provides clear proof of the availability of gold through the third millennium BC in central and western Anatolia; and there were sources, too, in eastern Anatolia. The rarity of such burial goods in later periods, in part the result of recycling, in no way implies a decline in the popularity of gold: the Hittite kings, with their known exploitation of **iron**, are hardly likely to have lacked other metals.

Much of prehistoric gold contained a high proportion, in some examples over 30 percent, of silver, being thus the natural alloy of gold and silver known as **electrum**. There is a strong argument to support the view that little distinction was made between gold and electrum in the centuries before the first introduction of coinage, so that the technology required for separating the gold from the silver content of electrum may not have been developed before the reign of Croesus king of Lydia (561–547 BC).

That notoriously opulent ruler, not content with the electrum coins first produced by his predecessors in the seventh century BC, decided to issue coins of pure gold and pure silver. Archaeological investigation and experimentation have revealed the processes involved, starting with alluvial electrum from the Pactolus River beside the city of Sardis and recycled electrum coins. This material was beaten into wafer-thin foils and packed in salt in porous earthenware cooking pots, which were then heated, probably for several days, to a temperature between 600 and 800 degrees Celsius. The chlorine gas released from the salt removed the silver in the electrum foils as silver chloride vapor, thus absorbed into the wall of pot and hearth. This raised the gold content of the foil from 70 percent by weight to the coinage alloy of more than 99 percent purity. The silver was mostly recovered by crushing the silver-impregnated pots and furnace linings and smelting them with lead. The silver-bearing lead was then converted into molten lead oxide, from which the molten metallic silver would separate at about 1,000 degrees Celsius. If pure gold was thus obtained at earlier dates than the reign of Croesus of Lydia, it must surely have been by this process: the evidence is so far lacking. Its absence elsewhere in the Near East, including Egypt, is discouraging.

The largest quantities of gold in the Early and Middle Bronze Age (mid–fourth till mid–second millennium BC approximately) have in fact been found not in the Near East proper but in the Circum-Pontic region and in Trans-Caucasia, in many burial mounds (kurgans). The legend of the Golden Fleece in Colchis may reflect the long-standing wealth of Trans-Caucasia, dating back long before the first millennium BC. It is against this background that the rich tombs of Alaca Höyük may be set.

Any doubt about the value put on gold compared with silver, tin and copper is dispelled by scrutiny of the relevant written records. At Ebla, in north Syria in the late third millennium BC, one shekel of gold was priced at seven or eight shekels of silver, while one shekel of silver was priced at eight to 10 shekels of tin, gold thus having 60 to 80 times the value of tin. A little later, in the Old Assyrian trade with central Anatolia, the price of gold could vary slightly, usually from seven to nine shekels of silver. When differing grades of gold were used, some containing copper and thus meriting the term orichalchum, the price could drop as low as four shekels of silver. *See also* **METALWORK**.

GÖLLÜDAĞ. An Iron Age city in the province of Niğde, on a hilltop 2,143 meters high with a crater lake. Its area of three square kilometers, wall with three surviving gates, regularly laid out buildings and streets and central complex with twin-headed lion **statues** at the entrance, sphinxes on the inner portal and column bases with four lions all indicate its importance. It must be placed within the general Neo-Hittite cultural zone. The burning of Göllüdağ in the eighth century BC is possibly to be associated with Phrygian expansion eastward.

GORDION. The capital of the kingdom of Phrygia, at its zenith in the eighth century BC, it has been the site of limited earlier excavations, followed by an ongoing campaign of fieldwork directed by Rodney S. Young for the University of Philadelphia from 1950 until his accidental death in 1974, the excavations being currently under the direction of Mary Voigt. While the emphasis was at first largely on the tumuli, yielding remarkably rich and well-preserved finds, including the **timber** burial chambers and many wooden artifacts, work has increasingly been concentrated on the remains of the Phrygian and later levels of the great city, sited on the Sakarya River west of Ankara. Though there are some examples of Neo-Hittite **sculpture**, no strong cultural legacy from the Hittite Empire is apparent, either in architecture or artifacts, including **pottery**.

The city mound of Gordion (Yassi Höyük) has yielded a stratigraphic sequence of occupation levels from medieval times back to the Middle Bronze Age and earlier. Preceding medieval, Roman and Hellenistic levels (from 330 BC) were Late, Middle and Early Phrygian phases (4–6), dated ca.950–330 BC. The Early Iron Age (ca.1100–950 BC) marks the first occupation by the incoming Phrygians, though if correctly identified with the **Muski** they were present in Anatolia during the 12th century BC. Before then there was a hiatus in occupation, perhaps no more than a century. Dates from **dendrochronology** have ignited a current debate concerning the **absolute chronology** of Gordion during the Phrygian period. The Late Bronze Age (phases 8–9) was contemporary with the Hittite Empire and the Middle Bronze Age (phase 10) can be dated ca.1600–1400 BC, thus contemporary with the Old and "Middle Hittite" periods.

There is a suggestion that Gordion was the site of the major Hittite **cult center** of **Sallapa**, though a more southerly location is conceivable. Hittite stamp impressions are inconclusive. A Hittite Old Kingdom cemetery comprises inhumations exclusively.

The pottery of Late Bronze Age Gordion provides ample evidence of specialist production, though more notable for its standardization and quantity, more than could have been required at Gordion alone, rather than any aesthetic merit. In this respect it is typical of the **Late Bronze Age pottery** of much of Anatolia. All the principal ceramic forms found at Gordion occur also at **Hattusa**; but the converse does not apply.

GOVERNMENT AND ADMINISTRATION. *See AGRIG*; **ASSEMBLY; HITTITE LAWS; KINGSHIP; QUEENS; SCRIBES; TABLETS; TAXES; VICEROYALTIES.**

GRANARIES. These played an essential role in the government of the Hittite Empire, for here was stored the vast quantity of grain, mainly barley but with some einkorn wheat, required for the population of **Hattusa** and the surrounding region. Numerous silos have been excavated in recent seasons at **Boğazköy** by the German expedition under **Jürgen Seeher**, including some 11 on **Büyükkaya**, and other large granaries in **Boğazköy: Lower City**—behind the postern wall, halfway between Kizlar Kaya and **Büyükkale**. These were constructed in a complex of the 14th century BC (early Empire) 118 meters long by 35 to 40 meters wide, orientated northwest to southeast and with two rows of 16 chambers, each being 6 meters wide by 13 to 16 meters long. The building was mostly underground, as indicated by clay packing used as insulation on the outer walls. Silos were designed to be airtight with a thick straw layer then a one-meter-thick layer of clayey earth.

Several hundred tons of semi carbonized grain were found here, the largest quantity anywhere in the ancient Near East. The silo complex could have stored up to 7,000 to 9,000 cubic meters of grain, enough for a year for as many as 30,000 people. Clearly this was not for the city of Hattusa alone. It could be said that this represented part of the basis of royal power in the Hittite Empire.

GURGUM. Neo-Hittite kingdom centered on Kahramanmaraş.

GURNEY, OLIVER ROBERT (1911–2001). The leading British Hittitologist of his generation, also becoming a specialist in Assyriology, which he taught during his academic tenure at the University of Oxford (1945–1978). He had undergone an initial training in Hittite in Berlin (1935–1936), then the center of Hittite scholarship.

At Oxford he published many **cuneiform tablets**, including those excavated by **Seton Lloyd** at Sultantepe, near Urfa. Training several young scholars, he helped to raise the standing of his subject. His main scholarly contributions were in Hittite, beginning with his doctorate "The Hittite Prayers of Mursili II." With his uncle, **John Garstang**, he published *The Geography of the Hittite Empire* (1959). Though quite largely superseded by more recent discoveries, it remains remarkably prescient and unsurpassed in its comprehensive coverage of a notoriously contentious subject. His monograph *The Hittites* (1952, revised 1990) remains a masterly, concise work, more comprehensive than some lengthier publications and designed for a wide readership.

Associated with the British Institute of Archaeology at Ankara from its foundation (1947), he was for 40 years the efficient and scholarly editor of its journal, *Anatolian Studies.*

GÜTERBOCK, HANS GUSTAV (1908–2000). A leading Hittitologist of his generation, the political vicissitudes of the 20th century led to his becoming the apostle of this scholarly discipline in North America. Combining a formidable intellect with friendly support for younger scholars seeking his guidance, his major achievement in Chicago was the establishment of the *Chicago Hittite Dictionary*, work on which continues. His record over many decades of publication and commentary on Hittite texts was remarkable.

He studied in his native Germany at Berlin, Marburg and Leipzig (1926–1934), from 1930 publishing volumes of texts from **Boğazköy** and invited by **Kurt Bittel** to become the Hittitologist on the staff of the Boğazköy excavations. In 1936—excluded by the Nazi regime from academic appointments in Germany—he moved to Turkey, where several scholarly opponents of the Third Reich gathered in Ankara. There he joined the new Faculty of Languages, History and Geography established in the University of Ankara on the initiative of Atatürk: here he helped to train the first Turkish academics in this discipline. He was also responsible for organizing the display of reliefs from **Alaca Höyük**, **Malatya** and **Carchemish** in the newly restored Bedestan building on the citadel of Ankara, as the centerpiece of the new museum. With other academics he left Ankara in 1948, being appointed in 1949 to the chair of Hittitology in the Oriental Institute of the University of Chicago. He remained active long after retirement in 1976.

GUZANU (TELL HALAF). This site, excavated by Max Freiherr von Oppenheim, is well known for its prehistoric painted **pottery** termed Halaf ware, found over a wide zone from the Mediterranean to the Zagros Mountains. In the first millennium BC this was the city of Guzanu (biblical Gozan), on the Khabur River. The population was largely **Hurrian**, though ruled by the Aramaean dynasty of Bahiani, Kapara being the best-known ruler.

Seeing that the Aramaeans were virtually illiterate, even though gradually achieving the spread of their alphabetic script, Kapara had his inscriptions carved in Assyrian **cuneiform**. Assurnasirpal II (884–859 BC) and Adad-Nirari III (810–783 BC) were among the Assyrian kings who campaigned through or against Guzanu (Bit-Bahiani), the latter in 808 BC, from which date the city came firmly under Assyrian control.

Hittite traditions were retained in the relief **sculptures**, in a flamboyant version of Neo-Hittite art at its easternmost center, with Mesopotamian elements more evident than elsewhere and with greater variety of repertoire. The palace, badly denuded, is the greatest *bit hilani* so far excavated, approached by the Scorpion Gate and decorated along the façade of the supporting terrace with reliefs in alternating basalt and reddish limestone, a style reminiscent of the Heralds' Wall at **Carchemish**. A **statue**-base or altar in front of the palace portico was decorated in green, yellow and white glazed bricks. The description of this building as a palace rather than a **temple** is supported by its similarity of plan to others elsewhere and by inscriptions.

The most memorable works of the sculptors of Guzanu are the three statues supporting the architrave of the *bit hilani* portico: they lack the usual horned headdress of deities, and may represent members of the Kapara dynasty. Above these figures were conical elements, not accurately to be termed capitals. The statues themselves were nearly three meters high, two standing on a lion and the middle one on a bull, each animal being one and a half meters high. Such statues are unique in Neo-Hittite **architecture**.

-H-

HABIRU. A term occurring frequently in the records of the ancient Near East, especially Syria, it was understandably equated with the Hebrews by earlier Old Testament scholars. In fact, however, it can now be seen that this was not a simple ethnic name. Rather, it described under one heading various groups of rootless people and refugees who survived as itinerant laborers, mercenaries or even vagabonds. As such they seem to have been widely despised or feared, often raiding settlements near the edge of cultivated land. They probably originated from the economic and environmental changes beginning in the late third millennium BC, and might be officially reckoned as dependent personnel, as in a long list from the kingdom of **Tikunani** in the 17th century BC. They came into contact with the Hittite state in its involvement in Syria.

HAHHUM (HAHHA). An important staging point, where *datum* payments could be made, on the Old Assyrian route from Assur to **Kanes**, this was a major commercial center with a *karum* and a producer of **textiles** from pre–Old Assyrian times. Several scholars located it in the Elbistan plain or (less plausibly) northeast of **Malatya.** Another opinion placed Hahhum in a north Syrian rather than an Anatolian milieu, and this will fit with its identification with the excavated site of Lidar Höyük, on the Euphrates upstream from **Carchemish**. This town (Level 8) was thoroughly destroyed, almost certainly by **Hattusili I**. Thus ended the prosperity of Hahhum (Hahha in the Hittite records).

HAKPISSA (HAKMISSA). When **Muwatalli II** assigned a wide stretch of the northern borderlands to his brother, **Hattusili (III)**, he also made him "king of Hakpissa" and priest of the **Storm-God** of **Nerik**, symbolizing the military and religious duties respectively now assigned to him. Hakpissa was essentially a garrison town, making a good administrative base and located on the strategic route running northeastward from **Hattusa** to Nerik and on into **Kaska** territory. Late in his reign, Hattusili III appointed his son **Tudhaliya (IV)** as chief of the Bodyguards at Hakpissa, a very high-ranking office to which he himself had been appointed at the start of his career.

HAMA (HAMATH). Significant alike for its historical role and for the results of the excavations before World War II by the Danish expedition funded by the Carlsberg Foundation, this was the site of a settlement mound originating in the seventh millennium BC (Period M) and continuing with successive cultural periods, those of the Iron Age (Periods F and E) covering the time–span from ca.1190 to 720 BC, when Hama was annexed to the Assyrian Empire. The architectural monuments date to Period E (ca.900–720 BC), while four phases of **cremation** cemeteries, outside the area of the citadel but underlying the modern city, span Periods F–E. It is the **"Stones of Hamath,"** highly significant in the story of the decipherment of the "Hittite" **hieroglyphs**, which provide the strongest justification for classifying Hama as a Neo-Hittite city, in spite of its pronounced Aramaean character.

The steep sides of the ancient mound of Hama, whereon stood the citadel, have deterred settlement in the Christian era, though the present-day city closely surrounds the citadel mound. In Hellenistic times and later, however, the summit of the mound was honeycombed with pits, the bane of the archaeologist. The excavators were nevertheless able to expose impressive buildings in the southeast sector of the citadel.

The most important structure, Building II, was clearly a palace, found in fairly ruinous state, though in some parts with the walls standing 3.5 meters high. The plan indicates that the ground floor comprised almost exclusively storerooms. The living quarters were in the upper story, evidence of which was found in the burnt debris lying over the remains of the ground-floor rooms, including an important clue for reconstructing the height of this building, in the form of 48 courses' height of brickwork, fallen from above. Significantly, the buttressed façade of this palace has no columned porch, so that—as the report observes—it cannot in any sense be described as a *bit hilani*. Thus Hama stood to some degree apart from the mainstream Neo-Hittite civilization of north Syria and southeast Anatolia in the centuries following the fall of the Hittite Empire. Here it was the Aramaean rather than the Hittite element that was uppermost politically, though culturally it was less tangible than the Hittite legacy. There are only hints of the upper story, which must have been richly decorated, as traces of **gold** leaf and fragments of red, blue and white plaster indicate. Ten coats of plaster were found in part of the upper story. A basalt throne and window grille, found in the central square, probably came from the upper floor of the palace. A staircase had two flights, providing evidence that the total height of the façade, looking on to the central square, was 14.40 meters, with seven meters as the height of the upper story. Five rooms were found full of rows of storage jars, covered with lids. Corbeling was used for at least some of the doorways, which had wooden door frames, wood also being very extensively employed as a reinforcement for the brickwork of the walls, as in Anatolia and north Syria. This imposing palace had nothing in common with the design of Assyrian palaces, which were on one floor, but bore a fortuitous resemblance to some of the citadels of **Urartu**. Two red polished bricks were found lying in the square, bearing the inscription in Aramaic "Adanlaram, Governor of the King's House." This palace was constructed in the ninth century BC, with restorations in the eighth, largely during the reign of Eni-Ilu (743–732 BC).

One reason for describing Building III, on the east side of the square, as a **temple** is that one room seems to have served as the **archive**, containing fragmentary **tablets**, mostly **omens** and magical and religious texts. Building III has its walls orientated to the cardinal points. Over the stone-paved threshold was the antechamber, whence one entered an open courtyard, giving access to the archive room on the south side, with another room on the north. Here there may possibly have stood a **statue** of a deity; and comparison has been suggested with a hieroglyphic inscription on the "Great Stone" of Hama ("Urhilina, king of Hamath, eldest son of E-tas, erects a seat for the goddess Ba'alatas of Hamath, in the anteroom (?) of the temple"). Remains of the preceding phase (Period F1), on the same general alignment, were found beneath most of the rooms. A reused, rather worn **stele**, presumably of the earlier phase, was found set in the threshold between the anteroom and the temple court: it depicts a seated figure at table with another facing, and with the crescent moon, emblem of the god Sin, above. The presence of the cult of the Moon-God at Hama is scarcely surprising, given his prominence in Aramaean religion, with Hadad (identified with Ba'al and **Tesub**) as the chief deity. Here was essentially an agglomeration of the beliefs of the older population of the regions overrun by the Aramaean tribes.

Building IV was a gateway giving access to a higher part of the citadel, of simple construction and evidently the earliest of the excavated buildings of the citadel. There is some similarity to the south gate of the palace at **Guzanu (Tell Halaf)**. About 50 meters northwest of Building IV stood Building V, from the wealth of its contents evidently a palace, earlier in construction than Building II. This was only partially excavated in 1938 at the end of the campaign.

The main gate into the citadel was Building I, with a long staircase and a landing on the threshold, but with a simpler plan than in other Neo-Hittite cities, such as **Carchemish**. Although there is the same use of orthostats, they are plain, the work of the sculptors at Hama being almost confined to the provision of guardian lions. Moreover, there are no guardrooms on either side, though there are flanking towers.

One curious fact is that the central axes of Buildings I–IV converge on one point in the central court, whose surface was in part covered with a layer of hard white plaster.

The fragmentary contents of Building V give a tantalizing glimpse of the riches of one of the wealthiest cities of Syria, which, among other crafts, was probably a major center for ivory carving. Carved bone plaques, pieces of gold leaf and numerous **iron** arrowheads occur. **Pottery**, plain and painted, from Period E, mostly found near the west end of the palace (Building II), is paralleled in the fourth and last phase of the cremation cemeteries outside the citadel mound, and only in that phase. This is to be expected, seeing that pottery found in a building which ended its days in destruction inevitably belongs almost entirely to its last decade or two.

Apart from two on the outside of the main gateway (Building I), clearly reused and older, the guardian lions are all of comparable style and can be attributed with confidence to the ninth century BC, those of the eighth being altogether more savage and feline, as evident at **Tell Tayanat** and **Sakçegözü**.

The cemeteries naturally provide abundant funerary evidence, with no inconsistency seen in providing certain grave goods with the cremations, discussed elsewhere. The general character of the grave goods shows continuity from the Late Bronze Age, but in the fourth phase (eighth century BC) no weapons were included. The decline in the richness of grave goods from the first to the fourth phase may well have been owing to a fall in social standing, when the burials of the rich must have been at some other, unexcavated cemetery.

Significant historical detail is provided by the famous "Stones of Hamath," which hold a special place in the colorful story of early travelers in the Near East. Irkhuleni of Hamath, the ruler recorded by Shalmaneser III of Assyria as one of his opponents at the battle of Qarqar (853 BC), is clearly identifiable with the "Urhilina, son of Paritas, Hamathite king" of the largest of the "Stones of Hamath," who, with other inscriptions, is revealed as an active builder. Very similarly worded are the three other "Stones of Hamath" and two more recently discovered inscriptions, all of the son of Urhilina, named Uratamis, otherwise unattested but necessarily dating to late in the reign of Shalmaneser III. They refer to the building of "this fortress," maybe the citadel of Hama itself.

This Assyrian king records the contribution by the city of Hamath of no fewer than 700 **chariots**, 700 cavalry and 10,000 or perhaps 20,000 soldiers to the anti-Assyrian alliance which fought at Qarqar.

HANHANA. The location of this town cannot be precisely fixed: it was closely associated with **Nerik**. A governor is mentioned in a **land grant** text from **Inandik** of the Old Kingdom, though it is unlikely to be identifiable with that site. Hanhana was one of the towns under the jurisdiction of Hattusili as appointed to control the **Kaska** borderlands in the reign of his brother **Muwatalli II**. One text early in the reign of **Tudhaliya IV** refers to it as a land.

HANIGALBAT. *See* **ADAD-NIRARI I; MITANNI.**

HANTILI I. Coming to the throne by the assassination of his brother-in-law, the illustrious **Mursili I**, he did so with the help of his son-in-law **Zidanta I**, years later to murder one of his sons and his grandsons, to secure the throne for himself. Hantili himself proved to be a survivor, living to old age.

Initially active in the field, he campaigned to **Carchemish**. On his return march to **Hattusa** he came to **Tegarama**, probably to be identified with modern Gürün near Sivas, where, according to the *Proclamation* of **Telipinu**, the **gods** sought revenge for the blood of Mursili. No one dramatic disaster seems to have occurred then, but this moment may mark the beginning of the long decline of Hittite power.

HANTILI II (mid–15th century BC). Son of Aluwamna. In his reign the **Kaska** people made their first recorded appearance in Hittite history, capturing **Nerik** and **Tiliura**. He claimed to have built **fortifications** for **Hattusa** and other cities. He seems, like his successor Zidanta II, to have maintained close diplomatic relations with **Kizzuwadna**.

HANYERI-GEZBEL. Hittite rock relief situated southeast of Kayseri and 65 kilometers east-southeast of Develi, immediately beside the road and between the Gezbel and Küçük Gezbel passes. Though very accessible, this relief is so badly worn that it can be distinguished properly only at first light. A figure, probably a prince, carries bow and lance, and faces two mountain gods standing on bulls. The relief is in three parts. A bull or calf has its front hooves resting on a mountain god, while the mountain is named in a **hi- eroglyphic** inscription. Facing the bull's head can be read the words: "King of the mountain **Sarruma**."

HAPALLA. This territory comprised the districts around Lake Beyşe- hir and westward to Lake Eğridir. It adjoined **Pedassa** to the north- east and **Kuwaliya** to the west, but was separated from them by the Sultan and Karakuş mountain ranges.

Hapalla was the territory of **Arzawa** closest to the Hittite realm, and accordingly came under Hittite rule as often as the power of **Hattusa** allowed, notably under **Tudhaliya I/II** in the early 14th century BC. It lay between Arzawa proper and the **Lower Land.** It is recorded in the *Deeds* of **Suppiluliuma I (1344–1322 BC)** as being reconquered by the Hittite general Han- nutti, marching southwestward from the Lower Land, who carried off the inhabitants, their cattle and sheep to **Hattusa.** This was to become a usual Hittite policy, both subjugating enemies and add- ing to the population of the Hittite homeland. Hapalla joined the rebellion against the young king **Mursili II** on his accession. On the victorious outcome of his two years' campaign against Arzawa, however, he brought Hapalla once again firmly under Hittite rule. The vassal ruler, Targasnalli, was reinstated, Mursili II enforcing an oath of submission on Hapalla. It was to cause no more trouble to Hatti, although this land was almost certainly included within the territories forming **Tarhuntassa,** as established by **Muwatalli II.** Later, very probably after the rebellion by **Kurunta,** it was to be restored to direct rule from Hattusa.

HASANLU. The major settlement mound in the Solduz plain, immedi- ately south of the Urmia basin in northwestern Iran. Here stood an imposing citadel of the Iron II period (ca.1100–800 BC) with a group of public buildings with columned halls, all looted and burned, almost certainly by an Urartian force (ca.800 BC). The fa- mous **gold** bowl was found crushed beneath the body of a looter, killed by a falling roof. The motifs include a procession of **chariots,** the leading one manned by a **god,** plausibly though not necessarily to be identified as **Tesub,** and drawn by a bull.

Cultural links with regions to the west are less surprising against the background of **Hurrian** mythology, especially the tale of the god **Kumarbi,** demonstrating parallels with Greek myths. The reliefs of Neo-Hittite date at **Malatya (Arslantepe)** include a chariot closely comparable with those on the Hasanlu gold bowl, suggesting a date in the 11th or .10th century BC.

HATIP. Quite recently discovered Hittite rock relief located 15 kilometers southwest of Konya. The inscription of **Kurunta** gives himself the titles of "Great King, Hero, son of **Muwatalli**, Great King, Hero." Far-reaching political implications are possibly discernible.

HATTENA. One of the towns or lands in the **viceroyalty** of Hattusili in the **Kaska** borderlands.

HATTIANS. According to conventional wisdom, these formed the indigenous population of central Anatolia before the irruption of Indo-Europeans, comprising Hittites, **Luwians** and Palaites (see **Pala**) How long they had inhabited the land will probably never be known. They may well, however, have arrived later than the first Indo-Europeans, but seem to have been the first permanently settled population in central Anatolia.

The conquering Hittites were in due course to dominate in the fields associated with **government and administration**, as is apparent in historical, administrative, legal and diplomatic texts. The Hattian impact remained prevalent, however, until well into the New Kingdom in **cult**, mythology and art. These were the fields in which the older population group, subjugated as they may have been in political terms, could still exercise a profound influence over rulers all too susceptible to fear of divine wrath and the need to satisfy the demands of the **gods**. These demands were conveyed through the mediation of native Hattian priests and priestesses presiding over the local cults. Moreover, the **festival** rituals continued to be conducted in **Hattic**.

Hattian myths were written down early in the Hittite Old Kingdom, in the 17th century BC, often on **tablets** in the form of bilinguals, with a **Hittite (Nesite)** text in the column to the right of the Hattic transcription. In other examples the only written record was a Hittite translation of the Hattic original.

A tablet pre dating **Suppiluliuma I**—the *Protocol of the Gateman*—lists the Hattic titles, with translation into Hittite, of certain personnel housed in the palace, that is **Boğazköy: Büyükkale**. These include cup bearers, waiters, couriers, cooks, jesters, singers, marshals, scouts and "tentmen," none of them (it seems) of the highest status in society. Another bilingual text includes the Hattic word for "smith."

The emphasis on **religion** notwithstanding, Hattian influence on the Hittite Old Kingdom was pervasive. Nearly all the Hittite kings from **Hattusili I** until **Suppiluliuma II** bore Hattian throne names. Thus Hattusili, **Mursili** and **Hantili** all show the Hattic suffomative *il*, to which a Nesite (Hittite) theme vowel *i* has been added. The stem of these names was probably a toponym, clearly so with Hattus plus *-il*. The dynastic titles of the king (**Labarna** or **Tabarna**) and **queen** (Tawannana) are non-Indo-European.

The chief deities in the state religion until well into the New Kingdom were Hattian, comprising the following, whose precise order or ranking varies to some extent: a **Storm-God** (Taru); his consort, the **Sun-Goddess** of **Arinna (Wurusemu)**; their daughter and granddaughter, Mezzulla and Zintuhi; another daughter of the Storm-God and the genius or special guardian of **Hattusa** (Inara); a son of the Storm-God, probably less a god of vegetation than related to the weather-gods (**Telipinu**, originally Talipinu in Hattic form); a Moon-God (Kasku) and a Sun-God (Estan); the throne-goddess (Halmasuit); and the War-God (Wurunkatte), appearing in **treaty** lists under the logographic form Zababa.

Deities associated with death and destiny comprised: Siwat, "The Lucky Day," a euphemism for "Day of Death," especially frequent in the funerary rituals; **Lelwani**, associated with the **Underworld**, at first a god though later a goddess; similarly associated, Sulinkatte, equivalent to the Babylonian **Nergal**; Istustaya and Papaya, who spin the threads of fate.

Pirwa, Ilali, Tarawa and Assiyat were included among the "gods of **Kanes**," their names recurring in the Old Assyrian colonies, these later being addressed in Luwian. Zithariya was a god represented by a **shield** borne in procession. Kait was goddess of grain. Hapantalli, the Sun-God's shepherd, was among deities occurring in the Hattian myth of *The Moon That Fell From Heaven*. The god Hasammeli may have been a smith, god of **metalworkers**.

HATTIC. Formerly considered to be the indigenous, pre-Hittite language of the people living in central Anatolia. Indeed of non-Indo-European affinity, this language is now widely judged to belong to the West Caucasian branch of the North Caucasian linguistic family, and to have become established in central Anatolia as the result of migration from the northeast. The **Hattians** certainly exerted a profound and lasting cultural influence on the Hittites, but seemingly as an intrusive element, arriving later than the Indo-European groups, including the Hittites.

HATTUSA. The Hittite capital, at the site of **Boğazköy** (Boğazkale being the modern name of the Turkish village promoted to the status of district center), in hilly country near Sungurlu, some 200 kilometers east of Ankara. The ongoing **Boğazköy excavations** have been conducted by the German expedition since 1906, with long interruptions caused by World War I and II.

In **Boğazköy: Lower City** there was a trading colony (*karum*) contemporary with **Kültepe-Kanes** IB. **Anitta** of **Kussara** destroyed the city, leveled the remains and laid a curse upon the site. In spite of this it was rebuilt by **Hattusili I**, who made it his capital. Nearly two centuries later, at a time of weakness for the kingdom, Hattusa was fortified by **Hantili II**, he claimed for the first time. It was destroyed by **Kaska** and other invaders in the troubled reign of **Tudhaliya III**, but rebuilt once it had been recovered soon afterward. The **Upper City** was first fortified in the 14th century BC, when construction began.

When **Muwatalli II** transferred the capital to **Tarhuntassa** in the south, the administration of Hattusa was entrusted to **Mittannamuwa**. Widespread damage to **temples** and other buildings occurred during the brief seizure of power by **Kurunta** from his cousin **Tudhaliya IV**; and the **tablet archives** in **Boğazköy: Büyükkale** were disordered. The city as recovered by the excavators is largely the work of Tudhaliya, when the archives were reorganized and an extensive building program undertaken, continued under **Suppiluliuma II** and not completed at the downfall of the Empire.

HATTUSILI I (ca.1650–1620 BC). Acceded to the throne of Hatti ca.1650 BC, reigning for some 30 years. He was probably the grandson of **Labarna I**, founder of the Hittite kingdom, and described himself as nephew of Tawananna, the earliest recorded occurrence of this title, subsequently as a rule associated with Hittite **queens**.

Hattusili I was in many respects the greatest of the Hittite kings, in that his reign witnessed formative developments in political, economic and cultural terms. Inheriting a legacy of conquest in central Anatolia under Labarna I, rebellions, in Sanahuitta and elsewhere, had to be suppressed before he could restore his grandfather's realm. Having achieved this objective, his next act was to establish a new seat of government on the ruins of **Hattusa**, destroyed by **Anitta**, whose curse upon the site he chose to ignore: this is an argument against any familial descent of Hattusili I from

Anitta. This new foundation was very probably made as a measure against the growing threat from the north, notably from the **Kaska**. Defensively strong, Hattusa was strategically badly sited by comparison with **Kussara**, for purposes of access to north Syria and Mesopotamia. It seems that Hattusili took his name from his new capital.

The ideology of **kingship** was ever a driving motive in the ancient Near East, not least for the Hittite kings. Hattusili I was conscious of his roots, styling himself as "man of Kussara" and as "Great King **Tabarna**, Hattusili the Great King, king of the land of Hatti." He, alone among Hittite kings, identified himself as a matter of policy with the image of the lion, presumably to reinforce his political power. Moreover, the most plausible explanation for his Syrian campaigns was a desire to surpass his predecessor's achievements, limited as they had been to the Anatolian plateau. Military prowess and ruthlessness were the accepted marks of successful kingship, though at times mercy could properly be shown to an enemy submitting: any backsliding from surrender to the Hittite king would be punishable by death.

Hattusili I seems likely to have planned his first Syrian campaign right from the beginning of his reign, since the preparations began the very year following the suppression of the rebellion centered on Sanahuitta and **Zalpa**. He could not contemplate a direct attack on **Aleppo**, a formidable power for several generations and the center of the kingdom of Yamhad. He did, however, attack and destroy **Alalakh**—in archaeological parlance Tell Atchana Level VII—to whose rescue Aleppo failed to come. Possibly Alalakh had rebelled against the suzerain power and declared its independence. Having achieved this preliminary success, Hattusili set off on the homeward march, attacking a number of towns lying west of the River Euphrates and north of **Carchemish**, including **Ursu (Warsuwa)**. The **siege** of this stronghold lasted six months, as described in a later legendary text giving vivid detail of the king's anger at the incompetence of his commanders and his ordering a battering ram "in the **Hurrian** manner." Enemy personnel were evidently able to enter and leave Ursu despite the siege; and the Hittite army sustained heavy casualties. Eventually Hattusili arrived back at Hattusa. The tangible benefits from this bold venture, taking the Hittite army well beyond its range up to that time, were perhaps minimal, though an economic motive, a desire to secure the **trade** in **tin** from the east, may well have been significant, even though not recorded.

In the year following this first Syrian campaign, Hattusili marched west against **Arzawa,** mentioned for the first time in the Hittite texts, and is recorded simply as taking cattle and sheep. It is possible that a serious campaign was undertaken later in his reign, but the records have not survived. Meanwhile, a crisis threatening the whole kingdom arose in his rear: from the east and southeast the Hurrians overran the land, only Hattusa holding out. Though the Hurrians withdrew on the approach of the Hittite army, more than a year passed before Hattusili was able fully to restore his authority. This crisis was to be repeated throughout Hittite history, a frequent occurrence when the king was away on campaign for a prolonged period, far from the homeland. This time the threat seems to have been external, possibly a sequel to the sack of Ursu; but on many other occasions dissension had arisen within the royal family.

The second Syrian campaign of Hattusili I was marked by significant victories, notably the destruction of Hassuwa and **Hahhum (Hahha)**: the latter, mentioned in Old Assyrian, Old Hittite and Mari texts, is probably to be identified as Level 8 of Lidar Höyük, in which a great burning has been found, and from which four wagon loads of **silver** were removed to Hattusa. The king himself took particular pride in his crossing of the Euphrates, emulating the earlier achievement of **Sargon of Agade**, and thus placing himself in the ranks of the most renowned rulers of the ancient Near East. He claimed to have crossed the river with dry feet, presumably by some sort of pontoon bridge. He had good reason for pride, seeing that by his sixth campaign he had won control of all lands from the Black Sea through eastern Anatolia to the borders of western Mesopotamia.

The reign of Hattusili I ended with his death in circumstances not altogether clear. On the one hand, he gathered around him the leading men of the kingdom, constituting the **assembly** (*panku*), to inform them of his decision on the succession—not to consult, merely to inform. Perhaps significantly, they met not at Hattusa but at his ancestral headquarters, Kussara. Commentaries on this assembly generally state that the king was ill, indeed on his deathbed; but this could be an overstatement. What is certain is that first his sons and then his nephew had betrayed him or proved inadequate as heir to the throne, among those conspiring against him being his daughter. The claim of his family to the dynastic succession seems to have been undisputed: it was the recurrent curse of the Hittite state, the ambitions of royal princes, which created the political difficulties. Hattusili declared his achievements, stressing the punishment meted out to the numerous rebels who had at one time or another opposed his rule. Where were they now (he asked)? It is not hard to imagine the tension as men waited for the decision of Hattusili, who announced that the heir to his throne would be a minor, **Mursili**, his grandson, whose upbringing he entrusted to the leading men of the realm. On the other hand, Hattusili may have died as a result of a late campaign against Aleppo, of which little record survives, for his successor states that he marched against Aleppo to avenge his grandfather's death.

Hattusili I may probably be credited with establishing the Hittite tradition of **historiography**, manifested in his **annals**, covering a period of six years early in the reign, discovered at Hattusa in 1957 and emphasizing his military achievements. Domestic politics were recorded in the *Testament* (or Bilingual Succession Edict) concerning the assembly at Kussara. Both survive in Hittite and Akkadian **cuneiform** versions. The *Proclamation*, or Edict, of King **Telipinu** is preserved only in late copies: this includes a long historical preamble down to his succession (ca.1525 BC), covering the reign of Hattusili I and filling in gaps in the more contemporary records, though less reliably. The colorful legendary text covering the siege of Ursu dates from the Hittite Empire.

Stylistic parallels between the annals of Hattusili I and the Anitta text suggest a thread of continuity between the earlier text and Hittite annalistic language. This could perhaps throw doubt on the general acceptance of a lapse into illiteracy following the end of the Old Assyrian trading colonies. If this did indeed occur, it was under Hattusili I that cuneiform **scribes** once again became active in Anatolia. These came not so much from Aleppo, the enemy of Hatti, as from Ebla, known for its scribal school. There is no evidence to indicate whether the king was personally responsible for this development; but it seems fair to suggest that Hattusili I considered not merely the territorial aggrandizement of his realm but also its constitutional, economic and cultural well-being. His memory was indeed respected by successors over the generations.

HATTUSILI III (1267–1237 BC). During his reign the Hittite Empire enjoyed a period of peace and stability in some respects comparable with that earlier enjoyed in Egypt under Amenhotep III (1390–1352 BC), though not on so extravagant a scale. In both reigns **diplomacy** took precedence over military enterprises. With Hattusili III this was probably in a large degree owing to his advanced age: he may have been 50 by the time he seized the throne from his nephew **Urhi-Tesub,** an act he sought to justify in his *Apology.* That would give an age at death of 80: a sickly child, he suffered bouts of ill health throughout his life, to the consternation of **Puduhepa.**

Hattusili claimed that, while acknowledging his nephew's legitimate claim to the throne of **Muwatalli II,** he had deposed him owing to injustices he himself had suffered and to grounds for questioning his fitness for the crown. **Gifts** were exchanged and correspondence conducted, especially with Egypt and Babylon and to a lesser degree with Assyria. In military terms his main successes had been in the **Kaska** borderlands, before ascending the throne. His subsequent ventures in western Anatolia, when king, proved less successful; and he recognized the practical limits of Hittite power in that zone.

The fullest light on international diplomacy in this reign shines on Hittite relations with Egypt, then under the long rule of **Ramesses II (1279–1213 BC).** Early contacts were unfriendly, as a result of the suspicion of Hattusili III that Ramesses II had been harboring his exiled nephew, an accusation rebutted by the pharaoh. It took some 14 years, halfway through the reign of Hattusili III, for mutual self-interest to dictate an end to friction along the border between these great powers in Syria. This **treaty** was to endure some 75 years. Relations are illuminated by lengthy correspondence between Ramesses II and Puduhepa, largely concerning royal **marriages,** especially of a Hittite princess with Ramesses II himself. An invitation for Hattusili III to visit Egypt—without precedent in the ancient Near East—was not taken up, perhaps owing to residual reservations on the part of the Hittite king. The tone adopted by Ramessses could at times be patronizing to the point of arrogance.

Hattusili III had from the start of his reign sought to improve relations not only with Egypt but also with Assyria. With **Adadnirari I (1295–1264 BC)** he tried to mend fences after the brisk rebuff from Urhi-Tesub to his claim to brotherhood, thus equal status with the Hittite king. Hattusili wrote off **Hanigalbat,** the remnant of the kingdom of **Mitanni,** and ignored appeals for help from Sattuara in his vain rebellion against Assyria under **Shalmaneser I (1263–1234 BC).** The Assyrian king nevertheless claimed a great victory, that he had "slaughtered like sheep the armies of the Hittites and Ahlamu, his allies," but this was certainly a gross exaggeration. Some years later a second Hittite princess was sent to marry Ramesses II, perhaps after the death of Hattusili III.

By then Ramesses may have been 70 years of age. Ramesses enumerated the splendid dowry—doubtless jewelry and **textiles** but also livestock—dispatched from Hatti.

Hattusili was much concerned in his later years with the succession and the very real possibility of conflict arising from the rival claims of different royal lines. One aspect was the presence of children of an earlier marriage, before that to Puduhepa. The Empire could not any longer have survived unharmed in the hands of an elderly king. *See also* **HATTUSILI III: THE *APOLOGY*.**

HATTUSILI III: THE *APOLOGY*. The main source for the life and reign of Hattusili III is the so-called *Apology* (or *Autobiography*). In addition, there are an abbreviated version and an edict for **Mittannamuwa**. There has been much debate concerning the reliability of the *Apology* as a historical source: some authorities dismiss it as essentially a piece of propaganda, as such to be disregarded as a record of fact; others assert, perhaps more reasonably, that it contains historical events recorded with a degree of accuracy, although none can deny the largely propagandist intent. The simple truth is that it is the only source surviving for much of the story it relates.

Hattusili had an active and honorable career as soldier and administrator during the reign of his elder brother **Muwatalli II**, who clearly relied on him as his leading adviser and supporter. While preparations were being undertaken for the campaign which was to culminate in the confrontation with **Ramesses II** of Egypt at **Kadesh**, he was dispatched to the north, to deal with the threat on that front from the old enemy, the people of the **Kaska** lands. The king showed his partiality by removing a successful governor from office in the **Upper Land** and replacing him with Hattusili, who had (he claims) reconquered this territory against an enemy with superior numbers. Hattusili's seizure of **Nerik** from the Kaska people was among his outstanding achievements, with its reconstruction as the final stage in the reorganization of the whole Upper Land. During the earlier New Kingdom, with Nerik in enemy control, its **cult** was moved to **Hakpissa**; and it declined in favor of the **Weather-God** of **Zippalanda**.

The *Apology* of Hattusili III takes the form of a decree ordering the establishment of a sacred foundation for the goddess **Ishtar** of the city of **Samuha**: she was goddess not of love but of war, introduced by the **Hurrians** irrupting into Anatolia; and Samuha was the center from which the restoration of Hittite rule had been organized by **Tudhaliya III**. Moreover, it lay in the Upper Land. Thither

Hattusili, after visiting **Lawazantiya** on his return north from the Egyptian campaign, brought his young bride **Puduhepa**, who thus was to gain experience of high status before becoming **queen**, and to exercise a profound and enduring influence on her husband and on affairs of state.

Justification of his seizure of the throne was the leading motive underlying the *Apology*. Hattusili claims to have suffered slander and the effects of hostile **magic** at the instigation of his nephew **Urhi-Tesub**. Some scholars have found in the reign of his brother Muwatalli II evidence of long plotting and planning to seize the throne from his nephew, the dissensions within the royal family being largely owing to the ambitions of his stepmother Tanuhepa.

Initial difficulties, return to action, war and achievements in a peaceful context are all to be found in the *Apology*, which thus follows a certain established pattern. Hattusili had a difficult childhood, dogged by ill-health which he was not expected to survive; then came fighting in the north and against Egypt, with the trial of Arma-Tarhunda, the ousted governor of the Upper Land. On a happier note, there came his **marriage**, which seems to have been a love match, his nomination to the viceregal throne of Hakpis, the final condemnation of Arma-Tarhunda followed by his reprieve, and the restoration of Nerik. Urhi-Tesup was then installed as king after his father's death. His enmity toward his uncle Hattusili, claims the *Apology*, led to civil war. There eventually ensued the uncle's victory, the exile of the deposed king and the accession of Hattusili as the third ruler of that name. Prosperity and peace prevailed throughout the realm, and other kings paid homage to Hattusili III, who in gratitude created a new foundation for the goddess Ishtar, the patron to whom he attributed his good fortune throughout his long life. Thus the *Apology* ended on a note of self-satisfaction.

HAVUZKÖY. Situated 60 kilometers south of Sivas and 23 kilometers west of Kangal, on the northern edge of a high plateau, the Üzün Yayla ("Long Plateau"), in modern times known as a breeding ground for **horses**. The site lies some distance up a valley to the south of a village of this name, not far from the old Ottoman road to **Aleppo**. It was first noticed, in one of his journeys by car in the inter-war period, by **Hans Henning von der Osten,** although he seems not to have ventured beyond the valley. Thus he observed the sculptured stone gate lions in Neo-Hittite style, now removed to the Museum in Ankara, but did not discover the very extensive site above.

Up on the plateau a citadel can be seen, the stone walls, both external and internal, being clearly discernible above the present-day surface. The quality of the masonry, and especially of the glacis of dressed stone, at first suggested a dating to the imperial Hittite period. But this was plainly negated by the surface **pottery** of unmistakably Iron Age type, in line with the style of the gate lions. Outside the citadel but also on the edge of the plateau lies an extensive cemetery of cairn burials. One suggestion is that Havuzköy was constructed by the rulers of **Malatya** or **Tabal**, more probably the former, against attacks by the Cimmerians in the late eighth century BC. This seems improbable, however, in view of the time required to build such a citadel.

HAWKINS, JOHN DAVID (1940–). Professor of Anatolian Languages in the School of Oriental and African Studies, University of London. His major achievement has been the decipherment of the **Luwian hieroglyphs**, on which he recently published his definitive work. He has demonstrated how a number of false trails have been followed over the years by various scholars, ever since the days of **Bedrich Hrozny**. As he is the first to admit, he has owed much to the work of such scholars as **Emmanuel Laroche** and **Piero Meriggi**, with the more recent contributions of Massimo Poeto and Sargon Erdem. He has published studies of the **Kululu** lead strips and the badly weathered inscription of **Boğazköy: Nişantaş**, working on the latter in collaboration with the German expedition, then under **Peter Neve**.

HAYASA. *See* **AZZI (HAYASA).**

HEARTH, CULT OF. For all ancient peoples, particularly in lands with cold winters, the hearth was the focus of the family house, and understandably so. This applied to the Hittites, who naturally had to survive the harsh cold of the Anatolian plateau. A foundation ritual embraces each of the four corners of the building, the four pillars, the hearth and the door: purification and blessing also protected the windows and altar. The ritual of the hearth became in part absorbed into **Hattian** mythology. One foundation ritual survives in a Hattian-Hittite bilingual version. Then in a mythical session the goddess Kamrusepa used a hearth of **iron.**

The cults of hearth and fire, largely interlinked, can be traced across central Asia into Iran and Anatolia, demonstrating that these are not exclusively Indo-European in their context. The family hearth had its essential function through the cold, windswept winters of the open plains of central Asia. In the equally cold, if more sheltered, winters of eastern Anatolia and the Caucasus—the **Early Trans-Caucasian cultural zone** and the homeland of the **Hurrians** in the later fourth and third millennia BC—the domestic hearth had a comparable significance. This is indicated by ornately decorated portable hearths.

For the Indo-Iranian tribes, further east, there persisted a strong devotion to fire centered around the family. The flame was lit when the man first set up house, transported in a pot during nomadic journeys over great distances or shorter movements of seasonal transhumance and reestablished in each new home, however transitory. It was extinguished only on the death of the head of the family, in a strictly patriarchal society. This may have been a natural concept for people lacking the assurance provided by fixed landmarks such as **temples**.

HEBAT. Chief goddess of the western **Hurrian** pantheon, she was the spouse of **Tesub**, a position held in more easterly lands by **Ishtar**. In the 13th century BC in Hatti she was syncretized with the **Sun-Goddess** of **Arinna**, largely on the initiative of **Puduhepa**, in whose time the sanctuary of **Yazılıkaya** was designed. Here Hebat leads the procession of goddesses meeting the gods, led by Tesub.

HELMETS. Best known from the figure in the King's Gate but also from an incised drawing on a fragmentary **pottery** bowl dated ca.1400 BC, likewise from **Hattusa**. This shows a horn, crest and flowing ribbons, and may be of Aegean origin, perhaps depicting a soldier of **Arzawa**. Cheek flaps and neck flaps appear in both representations. A more formal design appears in the Iron Age in the crested helmets of soldiers on the Long Wall of **Carchemish**, later worn by Assyrian soldiers.

HEMITE (HAMIDE). One of a number of Hittite rock reliefs—along with **Sirkeli, Hanyeri-Gezbel** and **Karabel**—whose locations indicate their demarcation of boundaries, conceivably inspired by the slightly earlier boundary **stelae** of **Tell el-Amarna (Akhetaten)** in Egypt. The miniature depiction of a bull on the headgear of the brother of **Tesub** at **Yazılıkaya**, virtually as a badge, is paralleled at Hemite. This site is located 75 kilometers northwest of Adana on the right bank of the Ceyhan River in the Cilician plain (**Kizzuwadna**).

HIEROGLYPHS. From the discovery of the **"Stones of Hamath"** onward scholarly interest in the distinctive script carved on stone blocks or statues grew steadily, led initially by **Archibald Sayce**, his quest helped by the **seal** known as "Tarkondemos," in fact the **silver** plating of a hemispherical seal, with an inscription not (strictly speaking) bilingual but digraphic, that is, in the same language but written in two different scripts, with one line of **cuneiform** around the circumference and hieroglyphs in the middle. Sayce was able to recognize the signs for "king" and "country."

The first advance in understanding the hieroglyphs came with the decipherment of the cuneiform Hittite **tablets** from **Boğazköy-Hattusa**, the work of **Bedrich Hrozny** in the years following 1915. The number of hieroglyphic inscriptions had meanwhile almost doubled through the British Museum excavations at **Carchemish**, cut short by the outbreak of war in 1914. This accretion of inscriptions enabled five leading scholars from different countries, working independently, to reach broad agreement on the values of most of the signs as used phonetically and on the structure of the language.

In 1947 a new stage in the decipherment came with the discovery of a long bilingual inscription, in Phoenician and hieroglyphic, at **Karatepe** in the former land of **Kizzuwadna**, giving vital data on the many ideograms. Soon afterward, digraphic seal impressions from **Ugarit**, with hieroglyphic inscriptions transcribed into cuneiform, confirmed earlier readings and provided additional ones.

The modern phase of research into the hieroglyphs began when **David Hawkins** (School of Oriental and African Studies, University of London) began to address the possibility of amassing a corpus of all hieroglyphic inscriptions with a view to publication, a most ambitious and onerous undertaking only quite recently completed for the Iron Age. In visiting the sites and museums with these inscriptions, he soon began to find a number of deficiencies in the published copies. Further discoveries provided help, notably in the indications of measures scratched on storage jars excavated at **Altıntepe** in the Erzincan plain, near the northwest frontier of the kingdom of **Urartu**: these are not in Urartian but "Hittite" hieroglyphs, and moreover they match cuneiform inscriptions of the same measures on storage jars at other sites. Later came new **archives** of digraphic seal impressions from the Hittite new foundation at **Emar** in Syria on the middle Euphrates. A highly significant advance was made with the identification of the negative *na* in the hieroglyphs, found from close examination of the **stela** from Sheizar, now in two parts, one in the museum in Hama and the other in that in Beirut.

Hawkins has classified the great majority of the inscriptions forming his *Corpus* into 10 groups according to provenance. These groups are: Cilicia [former Kizzuwadna]; Carchemish; Tell Ahmar (Til-Barsip); Maraş; **Malatya**; Commagene (**Kummuhu**); Amuq; **Aleppo**; **Hama**; and **Tabal**.

The beginnings of the use of the hieroglyphic script by the Hittite kings seem to have come five generations earlier than previously supposed, with an inscription recording a military feat by a king named **Tudhaliya**, almost certainly the first king of that name rather than the fourth. The end of the story of the hieroglyphs comes with the bilingual inscription of Karatepe, of the early seventh century BC.

There are indisputable arguments for identifying the **language** of the hieroglyphs, at first termed Hittite, as in fact the related Indo-European language of **Luwian**. It seems very likely that many records were written in this script but have perished, having been inscribed on tablets of wood, to which there are textual references, as well as to **"scribes** in wood". The carving of the signs on basalt, as with many of the inscriptions, must have been a laborious task.

There are steady additions to the total of inscriptions carved in hieroglyphs, reinforcing the data for their thorough comprehension.

HISSASHAPA. One of the towns or districts in the **viceroyalty** of Hattusili in the **Kaska** borderlands.

HISTORICAL GEOGRAPHY. The identification of geographical names simply and solely on the basis of their sounding like later names, sometimes nicknamed the "cling-clang" method, is not a sound approach to solving the difficult problems of historical geography in Hittite Anatolia and surrounding lands. Yet there are exceptions, where a number of names can be correlated with later versions, usually in Greco-Roman times. Not isolated but clustered similarities can build up a convincing case. Among such names are the **Lukka** Lands, **Millawanda** and perhaps **Wilusa**. With other names and the locations of certain inscriptions, such as **Karabel,** a general westward shift of geographical names relating to the Hittite world has become inevitable for the regions west of the homeland in central Anatolia. One of the difficulties has been the enormous fluctuations in the territories controlled by the leading and most persistent opponent of Hatti in the west, **Arzawa**.

From the **Lower Land** eastward there has been less change in the interpretation of historical geography, the location of such lands as **Kizzuwadna** and **Isuwa** remaining fixed. The eastern zone of the Hittite Empire is illuminated not exclusively by Hittite texts but also by the **annals** of its often hostile and expanding neighbor Assyria, in the years of **Adad-nirari I (1295–1264 BC)**, **Shalmaneser I (1263–1234 BC)** and **Tukulti-Ninurta I (1233–1197 BC)**. These Assyrian annals are particularly relevant to lands near the middle and upper Euphrates—**Hanigalbat,** Isuwa and **Carchemish.** The reconstruction of Hittite historical geography proposed by **John Garstang** and his nephew **Oliver Gurney** in *The Geography of the Hittite Empire* (1959) in the end requires fewer modifications than had until recently appeared necessary.

HISTORIOGRAPHY. If the aim of the ruler ordering his **scribe** to record his deeds is that knowledge of them, and thereby his fame, should be spread far and wide among his subjects, then not every monarch in the ancient Near East achieved this. The Egyptian pharaohs were most obviously successful in the New Kingdom, notably in the **temple** reliefs and inscriptions of Seti I, **Ramesses II** and Ramesses III. In contrast, the Hittite kings almost always recorded their military and other achievements on clay **tablets**, historical records being destined for their **archives** in **Hattusa**, hardly the most effective method of making their contents known among the general population. One can only conclude that this was never their intention. Perhaps it is significant that the one important exception to this rule came in the reign of the last Hittite king, **Suppiluliuma II**, when events were conspiring against the Hittite Empire, and when it is conceivable that some doubts had crept in concerning the efficacy of divine protection for the king and his realm. The reality of events was to be proclaimed with strict adherence to factual accuracy, if we are to believe the inscription of **Boğazköy: Nişantaş**, in the Upper City of Hattusa.

A historical preamble was to become the norm for many major royal texts, from the time of **Hattusili I** onward, although Hittite historiography could be said to date back to the time of **Anitta**, in which period a legendary element might be incorporated, itself including a kernel of fact, as with the story of the **queen** of **Kanes** and **Zalpa**. In the Hittite Old Kingdom the main objective seems to have been the straightforward glorification of the king on the battlefield, in celebrating the religious **festivals**, in enriching the realm through his wars and in showing implacable ferocity to the recalci-trant enemy, balanced by justice and mercy for those who willingly submitted. Strength, wisdom, enlightenment and a sense of right conduct were the qualities to be stressed in the historical accounts by the Hittite king of his own reign. **Warfare**, hunting, commis-sioning of new buildings, worship and presiding at cultic festivals were the royal activities most clearly highlighted in historical ac-counts of the deeds of the king.

Unfortunately it is impossible to assign a precise findspot to all known tablets, including historical texts, from the excavations at **Boğazköy-Hattusa.** In the early seasons, under the direction of **Hugo Winckler**, recording was not up to the standard of the later years, from the seasons under **Kurt Bittel** onward. It is apparent that many tablets were missed, being found later on excavation of dumps from early seasons, especially near **Temple 1** and the House on the Slope. In such ways have missing fragments of his-torical records been recovered and painstakingly joined to pieces already excavated. It is important to stress the incomplete condition of many major texts. In the early years of work at Hattusa a con-siderable number of tablets found their way, perhaps inevitably, into the antiquities market.

The surviving texts can of course only provide an individual viewpoint, often from someone with an ax to grind, a propagandist message to record. This is particularly evident when the author is a usurper, and is seeking to legitimize his position as de facto king: **Telipinu** in the later Old Kingdom and **Hattusili III** in the 13th century BC both fall into this category. In each case—in the *Proc-lamation* of Telipinu and the *Apology* of Hattusili III—there is a very lengthy historical preamble, designed to demonstrate how events had led up to their inevitable conclusion, the accession of the rightful king destined to save his realm from all its enemies. There had been in the duration of over two centuries between these two reigns, however, a marked change of emphasis. In the Old Kingdom, notably under Hattusili I, all attention is centered on the king, with no reference to the **gods**: indeed, it might be said that a spirit almost of humanism prevailed. Well before Hattusili III that had radically changed: now the gods were the constant protectors of the king and his people, **Ishtar**, in Anatolia goddess of war rather than love, being the patroness of that king. The all-pervasive influence of the **Hurrians** in the New Kingdom or Empire, not least within the royal family, being of that ethnicity, may well have been a dominant factor behind this change compared with the Old

Kingdom.

Hittite texts of royal **annals**, in one form or another, from Hattusili I to Hattusili III were normally written in the first person, while Akkadian versions tended to be in the third person. Nevertheless, it took generations for the development of Hittite historiographic technique to reach maturity in the reign of **Mursili II**. The major texts from his reign are the Ten-Year Annals, the Detailed Annals covering events at least through his 21st year and the *Deeds* of Suppiluliuma. Of these the most relevant for study of Hittite historiographic technique are the Ten-Year Annals, since this text alone has survived virtually complete, the existence of serious gaps making stylistic analysis far harder in the other texts. In the Ten-Year Annals of Mursili II a prologue is followed by a longer central section and a concluding epilogue, picking up the points in the prologue. In the central section are included terse reports of campaigns in the north against the **Kaska**, little better than stereotyped formulae; but the lengthy war against **Arzawa** and other affairs of state are dealt with in a more literary style with more detailed description and extensive use of speeches, letters, accounts of simultaneous actions in separate locations and even speculations about hypothetical moves by the king or his adversary. A hint that this must be a shortened, edited version culled from a larger range of records which have not survived or which—conceivably but rather improbably—may have been deliberately destroyed is afforded by a passage in the epilogue stating that "the enemy lands which the king's sons and the lords conquered are not included here."

Historical prologues to state **treaties** survive for the reigns of **Suppiluliuma I**, Mursili II, Hattusili III, **Tudhaliya IV** and Suppiluliuma II. These seek to justify Hittite imperial foreign policy, and as such are thoroughly tendentious in tone. Given the incompleteness of surviving historical texts, however, these cannot be ignored.

In his annals Mursili II shows himself frequently on the defensive, rebutting accusations of immaturity on his accession, Uhhaziti, ruler of Arzawa, describing him as a mere child: "You have continually called me a child and have belittled me," wrote Mursili. It was an age when personal prestige and indeed *amour propre* counted for much in international relations, as well as affecting the king's image among his own subjects. The king's ego was also threatened when he suffered speech loss, the result either of aphasia or perhaps more probably of the milder dysphasia. As discernible in his Plague Prayers, Mursili II sought in the sins of his father the causes of the **plague** which afflicted Hatti for 20 years.

Causality was scarcely understood by the Hittite historians, though frequent reference was made to past events by way of precedents for the future. The Hittite kings believed to some degree in fate, a belief strengthened as time passed, and divine intervention was given greater prominence. A stereotyped wording for divine help given to the Hittite king on the battlefield first appears in the annals of Mursili II, the formula in his Ten-Year Annals reading thus: "The **Sun Goddess** of **Arinna**, my lady, the mighty **Storm God**, my lord, Mezzulla and all the gods ran before me, so that I defeated. . . ."

A variant was the formula in the Detailed Annals of the same reign: "The mighty Storm God, my lord, the Sun Goddess of Arinna, my lady, the Storm God of Hatti, the tutelary god of Hatti, the storm god of the army, Ishtar of the (battle-) field and all the gods ran before me, so that. . . ."

Mursili II sometimes recounts startling divine intervention, on one occasion the hurling of a bolt of lightning against the foe. More prosaically, he is the first to describe the terrain of some of his battlefields:"Now the city of **Ura**, which was the first border fortress of the land of **Azzi**, was situated in a very inaccessible place. Let whosoever hears these tablets [read aloud] send and look at that city of Ura, how it was fortified!"

The reference by implication to the reading aloud of tablets may suggest some qualification of the earlier comment about the lack of public dissemination of royal annals. Is it too far-fetched to visualize a messenger returning hotfoot to Hattusa with news of a great victory far from the homeland?

While Mursili II should perhaps be given the greatest credit for the development of Hittite historiography from its earlier manifestations, the reign of Hattusili III, his younger son, is likewise marked by outstanding historical texts, of which his *Apology* (or Autobiography) is the best known. Its long historical prologue covers all but the last two paragraphs, and it is clearly a piece of propaganda, designed to defame the deposed **Urhi-Tesub**, his nephew, as well as his supporters, and correspondingly to exalt his own legitimacy and his past achievements. Unlike most other Hittite texts, no human causation is recorded here: direct divine intervention is claimed for every major event, instigated by the patroness of Hattusili III, the goddess Ishtar of Samuha, exercising "divine justice," as the usual translation goes. *See* **HATTUSILI**

III: THE *APOLOGY*

There survive also from the reign of Hattusili III large fragments, constituting an attempted historical review unparalleled since the time of Telipinu and spanning the reigns of Suppiluliuma I, **Arnuwanda I**, Mursili II, **Muwatalli II**, Urhi-Tesub and of course Hattusili III, who attributes his predecessors' successes entirely to his own patron goddess, ignoring their respective patron deities!

It is fair to claim that the Hittites were in the forefront of historiography in the ancient Near East, probably providing some of the inspiration for the better-known annals of their Assyrian successors, and including human touches seldom found in Assyria at least before Sennacherib (705-681 BC). Yet the annals were not the sole source of historical record in the Hittite state: royal prayers often include historical reviews at some length, while court records contain much detail on the lives of all ranks of civil servants. It is well to remember that less than 10 percent of the total of tablets recovered contain historical data. By far the largest proportion of tablets concerns rituals and **festivals**.

HITTITE (NESITE). This is one of the Anatolian group of Indo-European **languages**, at first associated with the city of **Nesa (Kanes)**, whence the term Nesite (*Nesili*). Two other languages, **Luwian** and **Palaic,** are noteworthy in the second millennium BC, with Lycian, Milian, Lydian and Carian appearing in the first millennium BC. For the non linguist two examples may serve to underline the Indo-European identity of Hittite, namely *water*, meaning "water," while the Hittite word for "fire" is *pahhur*, clearly related to the Greek *pur* and to the English "pyre," "pyrotechnic," and so on. As many as four stages of development have been distinguished for the Hittite language from the Old Kingdom to the fall of Hatti, equivalent to the three main periods, with a fourth stage in the final decades.

The **cuneiform** adopted from the 17th century BC by the Hittite state was the Old Babylonian variant, not surprising in view of the campaigns of **Hattusili I** and his successor **Mursili I** and the economic interest of Hatti in expansion southeastward. Royal names can be written either phonetically or ideographically.

By the New Kingdom Hittite had become confined to the ruling class as a spoken language, with the majority of the population speaking Luwian. It would, however, be going too far to suggest that by this time Hittite had ceased to be a spoken language, for there is linguistic evidence demonstrating ongoing changes indicative of a spoken tongue. The **Hittite Laws** have the same passages surviving in different styles of script, the outcome of the scribal habit of partially updating texts they were copying: this makes distinguishing the developmental stages of Hittite much harder.

HITTITE LAWS. These differ markedly from the better-known Code of Hammurabi of Babylon (1792–1750 BC), not only in content but also in the form in which they have survived. Whereas the laws of Hammurabi are inscribed on a **stela** found by the French expedition in Susa, southwestern Iran, the Hittite laws have been transliterated, translated and edited from hundreds of fragments of clay **tablets** excavated in **Hattusa**, for the most part in **Büyükkale**. Inevitably many such pieces duplicate larger fragments; but gaps in the texts have been filled from elsewhere, such is the number of fragments recovered by the German expedition.

The Hittite Laws have been published in successive editions in French, English, German, Italian and most recently again in English, beginning with the pioneer publication by **Bedrich Hrozny** (1922). Johannes Friedrich used contemporary grammatical and lexical research to produce an updated German edition (1959); and Fiorella Imparati's Italian edition (1964) built on the work of Friedrich. Since then the late **Annelies Kammenhuber**, in due course in collaboration with Inge Hoffmann, developed the work of Friedrich (1975–). Now the *Hittite Dictionary* of the Oriental Institute of the University of Chicago is under the sole command of **Harry Hoffner**, following the death in 2000 of **Hans Güterbock**. American scholarship has indeed played an increasing role in Hittite studies over the past two decades. These details serve to exemplify the international character of research into the civilizations of the ancient Near East, unimpeded by claims for patents!

There is agreement among specialists that there was a code of laws divided into two series, each numbering 100, and accordingly numbered 1–200B in the modern literature. The laws were each worded beginning with a conditional clause ("if a man. . . .," "if a vineyard. . . ."), the first series concerned mainly with persons and the second largely with property, although the order of subject-matter is by no means entirely logical. This suggests additions made from time to time, without redrafting the entire code. The matters covered by the Hittite Laws are remarkably wide-ranging, more so than the Babylonian code. It is worth listing these: homicide, justifiable or not, or by pushing a man into a fire; assault and battery; ownership of **slaves**; sanitation; **marriage** procedure, in exceptional cases or where irregularity has been alleged; feudal duties in the context of land tenure, and conditions of land tenure; hiring for a campaign; accidents at a ford; magical contamination; finding property; offenses related to cattle; theft; arson; offenses related to vineyards and orchards; theft and damage to various types of property; irregularities in sale and purchase; rates of pay for various services; offenses connected with canals, and with cattle; religious ordinances related to agriculture; sorcery; disinheritance by a mother; compensation for maintenance during **famine**; refusal to comply with a legal sentence; an obscure offense (bestiality?) connected with a bull; list of **prices**; sexual offenses; the standard fee for instruction of an apprentice.

The wide range of the Hittite Laws gives a clear indication of the complexity of the state. Unfortunately there is only the most meager evidence concerning the Hittite courts and legal tribunals, largely owing to the total absence of private lawsuits, in marked contrast with Babylonia, though textual references do occur. The specific coverage of some of the laws indicates their basis in case law, in decisions over the years by the courts. The king was the fount of all law, and his decisions are frequently recorded, often in the context of changing a penalty *formerly* in force to one *now* decreed, usually less severe. This is one of the indications that Hittite law was always evolving, without excessive respect for the precise regulations of the past. Indeed, it seems to have come into force only as the need arose, custom presumably governing such fields as inheritance and contract, not included in the Hittite Laws.

It has been claimed with some reason that the laws of the Hittite state were more humane than those of Babylon and Assyria. This claim rests primarily on the more sparing application of the death penalty, the Hittite courts often imposing fines instead: as with the Germanic (including Anglo-Saxon) *wergeld*, payment depended on the status of the victim. Capital punishment was reserved for only a few crimes, comprising bestiality, incest, sorcery by a slave against a free man and stealing a bronze weapon from the King's Gate. This last—reminiscent of the English law against setting fire to the king's docks—is a hint of fears for the security of the state. It could also of course be an indication of the value attached to the products of the bronzesmiths.

While there is no doubt of the evolving character of the main law code, never as rigid as the word "code" may imply, another factor probably limited its remit. This was the likelihood that the law was not uniform throughout the Hittite Empire, and that this was an accepted fact, with tolerance of local customs. At one point garrison commanders were ordered to apply the death penalty wherever this was customary for certain crimes; but elsewhere banishment was to continue as the appropriate penalty.

HOFFNER, HARRY. Leading American Hittitologist, who has published prolifically on Hittite civilization. Long-serving assistant to the late **Hans Güterbock** in working on *The Hittite Dictionary* in Chicago, of which he is now in charge. *See also* **HITTITE LAWS.**

HOGARTH, DAVID GEORGE (1862–1927). Early in his career he took part in excavations in Cyprus, Melos and Crete and briefly in Egypt at Asyut. He was the excavator of the Artemision at Ephesus and first excavator of **Carchemish**, whither he brought on his staff **T. E. Lawrence**. Hogarth was a fluent Arabist, heading the Arab Bureau in Cairo in World War I, afterward becoming director of the Ashmolean Museum in Oxford. He published a seminal work on Hittite **seals** (1920), over 30 books and many articles.

HORSES. Whether or not they were from the first domesticated, which seems improbable, horses formed a regular part of the diet in the steppes west of the Urals, along with cattle and sheep, from as early as the sixth millennium BC. That these animals were valued by the population is indicated by the occurrences of their heads in clearly ritual contexts from the same period, with horse extremities likewise. Carved bone figurines of horses were deposited above human graves, in pits stained with ochre, a tradition surviving from the Old Stone Age (Upper Palaeolithic) times. Horses long continued to be prized beyond their economic functions.

The early story of the horse cannot be considered in isolation. Rather is it linked with the controversial problem of the *Urheimat* (homeland) of the **Proto-Indo-Europeans** as well as with the question of the origins of **wheeled vehicles**. Until recently the Dnieper basin in the fifth millennium BC was regarded as the likeliest home of the first domesticated horses; but now a wider geographical perspective is called for, most recently as the outcome of mitochondrial DNA analyses. It is often hard to be sure of the domesticated status of prehistoric horses, which were clearly hunted as a source of meat: they may conceivably have also been rounded up for other purposes.

The crucial developments occurred, it seems, in the later half of the fourth millennium BC, when the most striking evidence that horses were being bitted and ridden, probably to hunt wild horses, comes from the site of Botai, east of the Urals, where horses account, remarkably, for 99.9 percent of 300,000 identified animal bones. Contrary to the misconception that early steppe horses were the size of donkeys, the horses of Botai were big enough to ride comfortably: wear on their teeth proves use of the bit.

The economic importance of horseback riding in the steppes was at least as great as the military role of horses. Grassland herding benefited in efficiency and scale from riding. Ethnographic data suggest that one herdsman with a well-trained sheepdog could manage up to 200 sheep on foot, but 500 sheep on horseback. With a horse and wagon, for which oxen were the draught animals, the steppe herdsman could live with the herd and his family for months at a time. The wagon's ability to move the herdsman's household to distant summer pastures greatly expanded the potential scale of grassland grazing, with even larger herds thus possible. The combination of these three elements—grazing stock, horses and wagons—in the later fourth millennium BC radically changed society on the Eurasian steppes. With the disappearance of settlements across the western steppes, a far more mobile pastoral or semi pastoral economy emerged.

It took time for the horse to be introduced from the Eurasian steppes throughout the Near East. Horse bones occur in the Altınova, in fourth-millennium BC context, in the Elazığ region of eastern Anatolia just east of the upper Euphrates, in Hittite imperial times the land of **Isuwa.** Human remains of Early Dynastic I date, of the early third millennium BC, in Mesopotamia suggest bow-legged individuals accustomed to horse riding. The most vivid illustration of adaptation to horse riding comes from the archives of **Mari,** the great city on the middle Euphrates, now just within the territory of Syria. Bahdi-Lim, vizier of the last ruler of Mari, Zimri-Lim, writes to his master to urge him to remember that he is king of the city dwellers as well as of the semipastoralist folk living around Mari; that he may with perfect propriety be seen riding in a **chariot** through the city; but that it is distinctly not the done thing for him to be seen in public riding on horseback! This dates to the early 18th century BC, before the sack of Mari by Hammurabi of Babylon (1757 BC). It was not until about 1700 BC that the horse was introduced to Egypt, along with the chariot, by the Hyksos invaders ("Rulers of Foreign Lands").

The Hittites inherited the traditions of horsemanship associated with the ancestral Indo-European lands. Yet the most illuminating single piece of evidence on horsemanship in Hittite imperial times, though found on a **tablet** from the royal archives of **Hattusa,** is related to **Mitanni,** where one named **Kikkuli** was a horse trainer, concerned with the details of horse racing, such as the length of the course. The Indo-Aryan words used have long attracted scholarly attention. The archaeological record from sites of Hittite date in Anatolia is not abundant. A stable with mangers, tethering posts, grooms' quarters and straw was excavated at **Beycesultan** II, approximately contemporary with the final days of the Hittite Empire. At **Tarsus** a house built on a slope had a semibasement room with a manger. A slight link with the ritual practices of the steppes may be suggested by the horses' heads found with **cremations** at Osmankayasi, **Boğazköy.**

As to written records relating to horses, apart from the Kikkuli training manual, they were of course the constant unsung heroes of military engagements involving chariots; and the Hittite **army** probably used them for messengers and for reconnaissance. Earlier, during **Kültepe (Kanes)** II, around 2000 BC, **seal** impressions reveal religious iconography, with the **Storm-God** paramount but an important status accorded a **god** named Pirwa, having close links with the horse. It could be argued that this provides a hint of Indo-European affinities, evident in other forms at this site.

Horses were imported from **Arzawa**, where there was a tradition of horse training. The enemies of the Hittite kings—notably **Kaska,** Arzawa and **Ahhiyawa**—had significant chariotry, as likewise the city of **Ugarit** in Syria, one of the major vassals of Hatti. In Neo-Hittite times, horses were employed for chariotry, notably at **Carchemish,** though it could be that the most skilled horsemen were then to be found further east, in the kingdom of **Urartu** (Van). Cavalry was generally introduced some time after chariotry, in Assyria not until the early ninth century BC.

HROZNY, BEDRICH (1879–1952). Czech nationalist, Assyriologist and Hittitologist. During World War I, he was allowed to spend his time on academic research rather than active service in the Austro-Hungarian army. He published a decipherment of the Hittite texts and a study of the Indo-European affinities of the **language** (1915). He conducted excavations at **Kültepe (Kanes)**, in the hope of finding **tablets** in situ, following the appearance of such on the antiquities market. In this he failed until the divulgence of the area of the *karum* by a discontented villager. It is rather for his work as a philologist that he deserves to be remembered.

HULAYA RIVER LAND. Probably located immediately south of the Salt Lake, or alternatively along the Çarşamba River southwest of Konya: in either case it formed part of the **Lower Land**, and was a frontier district of importance. It was added to the already extensive territories of **Tarhuntassa** by **Hattusili III**. In due course he waived the levy of **chariotry** and troops required for a Hittite campaign, implying a fertile, well populated area. It lay in the line of march for many westward campaigns starting from **Hattusa**.

HUPISNA. Securely located at modern Ereğli (in Classical times the city of Cybistra within the region of Tyanitis) on the southeastern fringe of the Konya Plain, this city is associated in the Hittite records with **Tuwanuwa** (Bor). It is listed among the conquests of **Labarna**, founder of the Hittite kingdom; and nine centuries later it is a component of the Iron Age confederacy of **Tabal**.

HURRIAN. This **language** was first encountered in modern times on a large clay **tablet** from the **cuneiform archive** accidentally recovered from **Tell-el Amarna (Akhetaten)** in Middle Egypt: the short introduction, written in Akkadian, revealed that this was a letter from Tusratta, king of **Mitanni**, to the pharaoh Amenhotep III. It is thus not surprising that this newly discovered language was at first termed "Mitannian." Later, the term "Subarian" came into vogue, signifying the language of Subartu or the North, one of the Four Quarters of the Sumerian world, recognized as being non-Indo-European.

Hurrian is an agglutinative language, suffixes and associated particles being added to the word root, to express attribution, tense and case. As for the original homeland of the Hurrians, a clue may be found in the very term *hurri-le,* signifying "easterners" or "northeasterners." This fits with the description of Hurrian as a North Caucasian language of the eastern branch, and therefore not unrelated to **Hattic** of the western branch. The Hurrian moon-god Kushuh has been associated with the proto-Hattian moon-god Kasku, suggesting very early linguistic contacts between **Hurrians** and **Hattians,** and thus between central and eastern Anatolia. These may well have come about at some stage in the fourth millennium BC. The principal sources of Hurrian texts and for knowledge of the Hurrian language have been recovered from **Ugarit**,

Hattusa, Emar and Tell el-Amarna, the Hurrians of the northern east Tigris region at Nuzi writing in an early Middle Babylonian dialect. Bilingual and even quadrilingual vocabularies (Akkadian, Sumerian, Hurrian and Ugaritic), as well as literary and religious fragments and musical texts, have been found at Ugarit. At Hattusa was found a large, still not entirely understood, corpus of religious and ritual texts, usually accompanied by a **Hittite** version. From Emar have come a few lexical, medical and **omen** texts. The long, carefully written and perfectly preserved Hurrian letter from Tusratta of Mitanni to Amenhotep III of Egypt, from Tell-el Amarna, is still the basis of most knowledge of Hurrian grammar.

HURRIANS. Hurrian words and names have been recognized in documents of the Akkadian period from the Khabur basin, from Gasur (later Nuzi) and from Nippur, though suggesting no more than a limited infiltration at this early stage. While a Hurrian presence in northern Mesopotamia and Syria during the later third millennium BC is perforce agreed, there remains a reluctance to concede the case for a Hurrian homeland coterminous with the extensive **Early Trans-Caucasian (ETC) cultural zone**. There is, however, now some qualified support for this theory and a willingness to postulate a Proto-Hurrian homeland. This nomenclature is logical, given the wide agreement that **Hurrian** and Urartian were linguistically related through common Proto-Hurro-Urartian ancestry, with possible East Caucasian affinities. To attempt any solution to the problem of the original Hurrian homeland, it is essential to look back at the very least to the fourth millennium BC. This assertion runs counter to traditional historical opinion, based on the **cuneiform** sources.

Unfortunately for its ready recognition, the Hurrian contribution to the cultural landscape of the Near East became obscured by acculturation: the Hurrians became in effect the apostles of Sumero-Akkadian learning in the lands to the west and northwest of Mesopotamia, culminating in their role in the civilization of the Hittite Empire. Ardent warriors as they were, the more peaceful accomplishments of the Hurrians—in literature, **music** and their religious manifestations—have long been recognized, from central Anatolia to upper Mesopotamia. These were the Hurrians of the diaspora, who had undergone a long process of acculturation: those who remained behind in the ETC cultural zone stayed largely untouched by the urban world of the southern plains. It seems likely that there was a gradual and largely peaceful settlement of Hurrian groups in Anatolia west of the upper Euphrates, before the unification of north Syrian principalities into the kingdom of **Mitanni**. Such groups were willing to accept Hittite rule for much of the time, but proved susceptible to the ambitions of successive kings of Mitanni in times of Hittite weakness.

The rate of Hurrian settlement in Anatolia is uncertain, though only some individuals had reached **Kanes** in the time of the *karum*. It must be assumed that penetration of the lowlands of Mesopotamia and north Syria continued steadily through the centuries following the first arrival of Hurrians. By the later 17th century BC, in the time of **Hattusili I** and **Mursili I**, a large percentage of the population of **Alalakh** was Hurrian, judging by their personal names (**onomastica**). Few such, however, occur in the Old Assyrian colony of Kanes. Hurrians attacked the Hittite lands while Hattusili I was campaigning in the west, and subsequently harried the army of Mursili I during its withdrawal from the raid on Babylon (1595 BC), the earliest recorded military confrontations between Hittites and Hurrians. Later texts from Alalakh mention **Tesub** and **Hebat,** the leading members of the Hurrian pantheon.

Hurrian proficiency in **warfare** was recognized at an early stage by the Hittites, as shown by Hattusili I's reference to battering rams in the Hurrian style at the **siege** of **Ursu**. A word for "watch soldier" or "sentry"—possibly of Hurrian origin as well as Urartian, though found also in Late Akkadian, Ugaritic and especially in Assyrian—is *huradi*. This may be associated with the stem *hur*, related to the vocabulary of war. In **chariotry** in the lands which became Mitanni Hurrian dominance is beyond doubt.

The undoubted manifestations of the Hurrian presence over a wide zone of the Near East in the early second millennium BC and indeed rather earlier should not be allowed to obstruct investigation into earlier origins. The theory of an ETC Hurrian homeland—extending from **Malatya** in the west to Lake Urmia in the east and to the Caucasus in the northeast—cannot be dismissed out of hand, even though it cannot be proved on present evidence. It may be objected that the later fourth and third millennia BC are simply too early, seeing that written references do not antedate the Akkadian dynasty (2334–2154 BC). Admittedly, the highland zone of eastern Anatolia was occupied by a preliterate population with a culture altogether less sophisticated than that of the Mesopotamian and north Syrian lowlands, with their urban communities. Yet these Early Trans-Caucasian people showed adaptability to change when coming into contact with southern communities, especially in the latest of three sub periods distinguished largely on ceramic evidence (ETC III). This is most apparent in the upper Euphrates region near Malatya and Elazığ, where a distinctive handmade painted pottery developed, retaining some earlier forms but with lighter-colored wares, the painted decoration possibly in part derived from that of Alalakh XVI–VIII to the south. Faint hints of early Hurrians lurk in linguistic data: thus the Sumerian word *talibira* ("**copper** worker") can with certainty be attributed to a Hurrian derivation. Copper working in the Malatya-Elazığ region dates back well before the ETC III period, especially at **Norşuntepe** but also at Tepecik and **Malatya (Arslantepe).**

The Sumerian presence in merchant colonies and along the upper Euphrates valley and influence as far upstream as Arslantepe suggest, with the metallurgical evidence, a favorable cultural climate for the first entry of the Hurrian highlanders from their ETC homeland into the lowlands. Therefore, economic stimuli would have predominated, well before the military factors of **chariotry** and cavalry of the period of **Mitanni**. Thus may be explained the distinctive character of the ETC III culture of the Malatya-Elazığ region, a constant factor being the nearby abundant source of copper in **Ergani Maden**. Hurrians may well have penetrated widely through northern Syria and Mesopotamia by virtue of their skills as coppersmiths and very probably also as traders. Thus a favorable climate was created, with appropriate incentives, for the later mass movements of Hurrians into the lowlands. What then of the Hurrian homeland in the ETC zone? This seems far more plausible than the location of the **Proto-Indo-European** *Urheimat* in the same territory, leaving to one side the **Indo-Hittite** hypothesis.

Precisely when this population group arrived from beyond the eastern Caucasus remains to be determined. Archaeological indications of the Hurrian impact on the lowlands have long been associated with the emergence of the kingdom of Mitanni, first expanding toward the Mediterranean under its king Parattarna, who came to control the whole territory from **Kizzuwadna** and Alalakh in the west to Nuzi in the east. The excavations at Tell Brak, in the Khabur basin, remove any possibility that the Hurrian presence there was culturally negligible. On top of the ruins of the major **temple** was built a palace, whose private quarters were reached by staircases to an upper story, as at Alalakh, a departure from previous design. Traces of inlaid glass, with the historical record, indicate a date close to 1500 BC, Parattarna being contemporary with the Hittite king **Zidanta II**. The desecration of the temple and secularization of its site surely mark an alien intrusion on a massive scale. The kingdom of Mitanni was correctly described as Hurrian in the Hittite records, for the Indo-Aryan impact has been exaggerated.

Among the periods of Hurrian menace threatening the survival of the Hittite kingdom, the most dramatic came in the reign of **Tudhaliya III**, when there seems to have been some sort of concerted alliance against him. Whenever a Hittite king was in the field, especially in the west against **Arzawa**, the Hurrians seized their opportunity, support often coming indirectly from Mitanni or directly, as with rebellions by **Isuwa**. When the throne of Hatti was disputed, as occurred with the murder of the last ruler of the Old Kingdom, **Muwatalli I**, Hurrians came to the aid unsuccessfully of a supporter of the dead king.

The high point of Hurrian influence in the Hittite Empire came with the **marriage** of **Hattusili III** to **Puduhepa**, who imported many Hurrians, including priests, to **Hattusa.** With them came the Hurrian pantheon, magnificently displayed on the rock faces of **Yazılıkaya**. Before this the royal family in the Empire were of Hurrian ancestry, but felt it desirable or essential to assume a Hittite name on accession to the throne. Nikkalmati, the **queen** of **Tudhaliya I**, and her daughter-in-law Asmunikal, had names incorporating the Hurrian goddess who was wife of the Moon-God and derived from the Sumerian Ningal. The Hurrian antecedents of these two queens, at the beginning of the New Kingdom (Empire), seem to have had an abiding influence on the dynasty. Was it pure coincidence that the one king who did not use a Hittite throne name, though adopting that of **Muwatalli (III)**, was the ill-fated **Urhi-Tesub**?

A Hurrian legacy to Near Eastern **sculpture** and **glyptic art** is discernable in **gods and goddesses** standing on the back of an animal such as Tesub on a bull, seen at Yazılıkaya.

HUSEYINDEDE. An Old Hittite **cult center** about 30 kilometers north of Çorum, with excavations from 1998. Large rectangular stone wall footings with smaller stonework above display typically Old Hittite building techniques. The walls of the apparent cult room are thickly plastered. Parallels are drawn with **Alaca Höyük** IIIa and **Boğazköy: Büyükkale** IVc. A large relief-decorated **pottery** vessel is comparable with that found at **Inandiktepe**. The excavators suggest that this was a **cult center** for the **Storm-God**.

- I -

IKIZTEPE. In spite of its Turkish name ("twin mounds"), no fewer than four mounds make up this settlement and cemetery site, situated just west of the mouth of the Kızıl Irmak (**Marrassantiya**), where excavations were conducted by the late Bahadir Alkim and then by Önder Bilgi. Ikiztepe seems to have thrived on **trade** across the Black Sea and trans-Anatolian land trade linking with regions to the south through the territory which became the nucleus of the Hittite state. This prosperity was well established in the third millennium BC: figurines and weapons came from a rich Early Bronze III cemetery on Mound III, though most finds came from the settlement, including items of bronze, lead and **gold**. On Mound I was found an Early Bronze II–III cemetery. **Pottery** was in the handmade tradition of the era.

Ikiztepe provides an unbroken stratified sequence of occupation deposits from the Late Chalcolithic period (fourth millennium BC) to the middle of the Middle Bronze Age, followed by a long desertion until the Late Iron Age. In the Middle Bronze Age Mound I has Level 1, and contemporary occupation on Mound III—a hilltop promontory site east of the delta of the Marrassantiya —falls in a succession of 11 building levels. The traditional **building methods**, using wood and clay, continued, but buildings had become larger. Pottery is now wheelmade and hard-fired.

It can only be a matter for speculation whether the Middle Bronze Age folk of Ikiztepe were **Kaska**, abandoning their coastal homes for lands nearer the Hittite realm, or whether they were expelled by Kaska newcomers. Whatever the facts, this Pontic coastal region has yielded data of relevance to the Hittite background.

ILUYANKA. Mythical serpentine dragon, depicted in one of the early Neo-Hittite reliefs at **Malatya (Arslantepe)**. The slaying of this monster was the theme of one of the best-known **Hattian** and Hittite myths, of which two accounts have been preserved. This myth may perhaps be interpreted as handling the universal theme of the struggle between good and evil, in which the triumph of the good is achieved only after initial defeat and grievous hurt.

One version has the **Storm-God**, the adversary of Iluyanka, at first defeated but then victorious by guile, after the dragon and his children were tempted out of the safety of their hole in the ground to partake of a great feast: incapacitated by their gluttony, they were slain. Another version has the Storm-God deprived of his eyes and heart: he has to bide his time, begetting a son by a poor woman. This son then marries a daughter of Iluyanka, and has his father's missing parts willingly restored. The Storm-God then departs to fight a battle at sea, in which he is victorious over the dragon. The whole myth belongs to primitive folklore, without literary or theological embellishment.

IMAMKULU. One of the series of Hittite rock reliefs extending from **Fraktin** eastward to **Hanyeri-Gezbel**, this is carved on a large boulder located near the Yenice River, 70 kilometers southeast of Kayseri. The iconography is rather enigmatic. The likeliest description has a prince—possibly **Muwatalli II**, though the inscription is too worn for this to be certain—on the left side; in the middle is the **Storm-God** in a wagon drawn by bulls, supported by mountain-gods standing on mythical creatures; on the right stands a goddess, possibly **Ishtar**, wearing an open white robe.

IMUKUŞAĞI. Excavations at this settlement site on the east bank of the Euphrates were directed by Veli Sevin, then of the University of Istanbul. A long sequence of occupation levels from the Middle Ages back to the Middle Bronze Age was revealed (Levels 1–13). Imukuşaği probably had its most prosperous period in the Middle Bronze Age, on the evidence of a public building preserved to a height of three meters and **fortifications** including a large tower at the south gate.

　　Pottery demonstrates links with the region using Khabur Ware (Level 12); parallels with **Kanes (*Karum* IB)** and types typical of the Hittite Old Kingdom (Levels 11–10); some painted pottery (Levels 9–8); and coarse wheelmade pottery typical of the Hittite Empire (Level 7). After Late Bronze II, with the fall of the Hittite Empire, there is a complete change in pottery. In the Iron Age Imukuşaği was fortified with a double wall.

INANDIKTEPE. An excavated site about 40 kilometers south of Çankiri and northeast of Ankara. The principal building was a Hittite Old Kingdom shrine, associated with a **cult center**. Here was found a polychrome relief-decorated jar in the same genre as that of **Bitik**, a tradition continuing under the Empire, though in fragmentary monochrome examples, quite numerous at **Boğazköy** and earlier at **Alışar Höyük**. A **tablet** recording a **land grant** mentions a governor of **Hanhana**.

INDO-HITTITE. The ancestor of all the Indo-European **languages** of Anatolia.

IRON. Although the most widespread of metals in use by man, iron is not the easiest to place in its ancient contexts in Anatolia, where many sources are post-Hittite, among these being Divriği in Sivas province (Roman) and a number of sites south of Lake Van (mostly medieval or later). Along the southeastern shore of the Black Sea are black sands rich in iron. **Kizzuwadna** was an important source of iron for the Hittite kings.

Among iron artifacts of the third millennium BC is a hilted dagger from **Alaca Höyük**, containing a percentage of nickel but not therefore automatically to be termed meteoric. Smelting iron with arsenic or antimony usually results in an intermediate product containing such metals as iron, nickel and **copper** with arsenic or antimony. There is one pitfall related to the earliest reported examples of iron artifacts in Anatolia and indeed to later pieces too. Many are badly corroded, little better than lumps of rust, often being thrown out by earlier excavators: others, including some from Alaca Höyük, have been wrongly identified as iron.

The **trade** in iron was clearly on a significant scale in the time of the Old Assyrian merchant colonies, significant in its value if not in the quantities involved. It was to be many centuries before iron became a bulk commodity. At first it was used largely for ornaments. According to one text from **Kültepe-Kaneš**, iron (*amutum*) was exchanged for precious metals, **gold** and **silver**, but not for copper. At that moment eight shekels of gold was not enough to buy one shekel of iron; but that must have been a brief episode. Other texts imply that iron was 40 times more valuable than silver and that there was close control over the iron trade.

In the following Hittite period, it was long believed, there was probably a state monopoly of iron and its associated craft secrets. This theory, now discredited, was seemingly supported by a well-known letter from **Hattusili III**, probably addressed to the Assyrian king, and including the following passage:

> Concerning the good iron which you mentioned in your letter, the store in Kizzuwadna has run out of good iron. I wrote to you that it is not a suitable time to produce iron. They will produce iron, but they have not finished yet. When they have finished, I will send it to you. . . .Now I am sending you an iron (**sword**/dagger) point

The distinction between "good iron" and other iron in this letter has led to the suggestion that it refers to the production of steel, a theory indirectly supported by the distinction between a "steel dagger" and an "iron dagger" in the list of gifts recorded in one of the letters from Tusratta of **Mitanni** to Amenhotep III of Egypt. A more plausible interpretation, however, connects the passage of the letter from Hattusili III with the rather haphazard control of the iron smelting processes in Hittite times, producing a large percentage of material unfit for working into artifacts.

Iron was much more available under the Hittite Old Kingdom and thereafter than beforehand, and was now used not simply for ornaments but also for tools and weapons. Its distribution may have been largely in the hands of itinerant smiths, guarding the secrets of their craft, the forerunners of the Chalybes of the Pontic and Erzurum regions. Significantly, iron was no longer weighed like gold and silver, by the shekel, but like copper, by the mina. Ironsmiths and other metalworkers are listed in records related to religious **festivals**. While *amutum* had been the term for iron in the Old Assyrian colonies, the Hittites later used the Sumerian term AN.BAR, employed in the 18th century BC at **Alalakh (Tell Atchana)** for 400 weapons, possibly **spears**. One famous early Hittite text of the 16th century BC mentions an iron (AN.BAR) throne and a scepter of great size and weight. It does seem that the word "iron" had royal associations. Another reference to iron furniture occurs in a myth in a **Luwian** purification associated with a ritual of the substitute king: "The Sun-God and the goddess Kamrusepa are combing sheep. They are vying with each other and wrangling. Then Kamrusepa placed an iron chair, and put on it a wool-comb of lead. They combed a pure kid."

The biblical reference to Og the king of Bashan (Deuteronomy 3:11) variously has him possessing an iron bedstead (Authorized Version) or a basalt sarcophagus (New English Bible).

By the addition of carbon to iron in the process of smelting, a development which could well have occurred accidentally in the heat of the smithy, the technique of carburization produced steel, first occurring in the Levant in the 12th century BC. With this can be associated the general proliferation of iron working in the east Mediterranean zone before the end of the second millennium BC. In spite of the efficiency of the Assyrian civil service and war machine, iron was less widely in use in Assyria until the eighth century BC, iron arrowheads being a telltale sign of the abundance of the metal. Unfortunately the dearth of documentation for the Anatolian plateau for four centuries after the fall of Hatti makes it impossible to be sure about the development of iron working there at that time.

There are numerous references to iron in the lists of tribute which feature prominently in the royal annals of Assyria from the ninth to the seventh century BC. Noteworthy is the record of 250 talents (about seven and a half tons) of iron given by the king of **Carchemish** to Assurnasirpal II, demonstrating the ready access to sources of iron by that city.

IRON AGE GRAY WARE. This is the ubiquitous **pottery** of western Anatolia from the northwest to the Konya Plain during the early first millennium BC. At **Gordion**, the capital of the Phrygian kingdom, it is overshadowed by "palace wares" with a magnificent variety of maeander and other motifs in painted decoration and numerous imitations of metal prototypes. But outside the large cities gray ware was in general use, sharing some forms with the contemporary **Alışar IV ware** of central Anatolia, found in the lands controlled by **Tabal** and Milid (**Malatya**). With heavy rim and channel along the inside of the rim, the deep bowls of *krater* form are especially typical of the instantly recognizable Iron Age gray ware, a hallmark of its period wherever found. In the Konya Plain, for example, it occurs in Iron Age building levels crowning a long succession of earlier strata in steep-sided mounds.

ISHTAR. Goddess of love and war, never seen as mutually incompatible in the ancient Near East, she was an established member of the Mesopotamian pantheon, her **cult** extending thence far and wide. In Canaan and the Phoenician cities she was worshiped as Astarte, appearing in the **Bible** as epitomizing the evils of paganism over and against the cult of Yahweh.

Ishtar appears in Anatolia through her guise as Ishtar of Nineveh, often though by no means invariably known as **Sausga**. In the Hittite context she appears in the reign of **Arnuwanda I**, in the early 14th century BC, in a list of divine witnesses to a **treaty** with the **Kaska**; but already a **statue** of the goddess had been translated from **Kizzuwadna** to the major eastern Hittite city of **Samuha**. She continued to be venerated in Kizzuwadna, in the city of **Kummanni**.

Ishtar of Nineveh was popular in **Hattusa** in the period of the Empire, and she may have had a **temple** or at least a cult room there. Monthly **festivals** and seasonal rites in winter, spring and autumn were held in her honor. In the imperial cult, however, Ishtar had lost precedence in favor of the Syrian goddess **Hebat** and also **Tesub** and **Sarruma**.

As with many deities, there were numerous different local varieties of Ishtar, some 25 being recorded in the Hattusa **archives**, usually named after towns or mountains, mostly in north Syria or southeastern Anatolia. Significantly, none is named after the early Hittite **cult centers**. Ishtar of Samuha and Ishtar of Nineveh are the most frequently mentioned. Yet Ishtar as such, followed by Ishtar of the Battlefield, is usually put before Ishtar of Nineveh in lists of divine witnesses, as for treaties, of the Hittite Empire.

ISUWA. This region was centered on the fertile Altınova ("plain of **gold**") east of the modern provincial capital of Elazığ, and in the time of the Hittite Empire constituted its firmest base to the east of the Euphrates River. Nevertheless, it had an identity of its own, outliving the Empire: Shalmaneser III of Assyria, in the mid–ninth century BC, refers to "Enzite of the land of Ishua," whose settlements he duly devastated. Its allegiance fluctuated between Hatti and **Mitanni**, notably in the reign of **Tudhaliya I**, who was able to restore Hittite control, though not permanently: Isuwa was then essentially pro-Mitannian in loyalty, having a **Hurrian** population. In the disasters afflicting Hatti after the accession of **Tudhaliya III**, forces from Isuwa penetrated as far west as the land of **Tegarama** in the area of modern Gürün.

After his seizure of the throne **Suppiluliuma I** was free to turn his attention to the southeast. After an initial setback, in the fourth or fifth year of his rule he marched against the heart of Mitanni, the power behind Isuwa, which he conquered en route, to the border with the kingdom of **Alse**. Isuwa had long benefited from its geographical position, athwart a natural **trade** route from upper Mesopotamia into Anatolia, for centuries before the imposition of Hittite rule, and from access to natural resources, notably the **copper** of **Ergani Maden**, factors which must have been of some benefit to the Hittite Empire.

The importance which continued to be attached to Isuwa by the kings in **Hattusa** was demonstrated by the giving by **Hattusili III** of a daughter or perhaps sister of **Puduhepa** in **marriage** to the vassal king of Isuwa. Vassals, however, were by the nature of things fickle: when Assyria had for some time been a growing threat to Hittite rule east of the Euphrates, Isuwa failed to answer the urgent request by **Tudhaliya IV** for troops to join his army in its ill-fated march to **Nihriya**. Only the involvement of **Tu-kulti-Ninurta I (1233–1197 BC)** in Babylonia preserved the Hittite hold on Isuwa.

The archaeological data indicate—through the number, size and density of settlement mounds especially in Altınova—a populous and wealthy region, very different from many of the lands neighboring and often threatening the Hittite realm. Moreover, the **pottery** from excavated sites and surface collection includes unmistakable central Anatolian wares attributable to the Late Bronze Age, for which the sequence of stratified deposits at **Korucutepe** has permitted a subdivision into Late Bronze I (Phase I: ca.1600–1400 BC) and Late Bronze II (Phase J: ca.1400–1200 BC), with Level III at **Norşuntepe** contemporary. The parallels with Hittite central Anatolia in the mass-produced buff ware bowl and platter sherds found widely distributed in this region were immediately obvious to the writer on his field survey (1956), and were confirmed in the subsequent rescue excavations before the flooding by the Keban dam. It is not that common for political developments to be directly reflected in the archaeological record.

IVRIZ. One of the best preserved Anatolian rock reliefs, the Ivriz monument may well owe its survival to a widespread regard for springs of clear, cold water: into this one today many coins have been thrown. This relief, till recently (it seems) relatively inaccessible, lies near the village of Kaydikent at the foot of the Taurus Mountains, about 20 kilometers south of the town of Ereğli. The relief is carved on a rock face directly above the powerful spring, which waters extensive gardens below, before flowing into the plain.

The **hieroglyphic** inscription records that this was set up by Warpalawas, king of Tyana, the former Hittite city of **Tuwanuwa**, located at modern Bor. It is thus firmly dated not simply within the Iron Age (Neo-Hittite) period but more precisely to ca.740 BC, in the reign of Tiglath-Pileser III of Assyria, since Warpalawas appears in a long list of rulers, including eight from Anatolia, through compulsion or prudence sending tribute to Assyria. He is named in the **annals** of Tiglath-Pileser III (745–727 BC), sadly incomplete, as Urballa of Tyana.

On the left of the relief, facing right, stands the sturdy figure of the **god** of vegetation, Tarhundas, whose name indicates a **Luwian** origin. He wears the horned headdress of divinity, and holds in his left hand ears of corn and in his right a bunch of grapes. His muscular legs and style of **dress** reveal clear descent from the Hittite artistic tradition of the imperial age. The figure of Warpalawas, on the right, is much smaller, and stands in the humble attitude of prayer. His headgear and dress are quite different in style from those of the god, betraying direct Assyrian influence in the decoration of his fringed robe, very possibly with brocade design of **textile**, probably woolen. This robe is fastened with a brooch of fibula type, equivalent to a safety pin, for which the Ivriz relief provides secure dating.

The juxtaposition of these two very different cultural traditions in the same relief, at a site on the Anatolian plateau, is highly significant. It shows that at the beginning of the revival and expansion of the Assyrian state, which started with the seizure of the throne in Nimrud by Tiglath-Pileser III (745 BC), Assyrian cultural influence was already permeating the Neo-Hittite lands. The Hittite legacy to the principalities of the first millennium BC was about to go into decline.

IYAYA. A local Mother-Goddess, worshiped in the Anatolian towns of Lapana and Tiura, neither definitely located. Her chief interest lies in the description of her **statue** as seated and one cubit high (i.e. 50 centimeters), plated with **gold** and **tin**, with the latter used for plating also two wooden mountain sheep and one eagle. Two **copper** staves and two bronze goblets served as the cultic equipment. This description no doubt would have applied to many other statuettes of local divinities, not in the first rank but much revered by the populace.

IZGIN. Findspot, five kilometers southwest of **Karahöyük (Elbistan)**, of a **stela** to be dated to the 11th century BC: discovered ca.1880, it probably came from Karahöyük. The name of the author of this **hieroglyphic** inscription is uncertain, but he was ruler of **Malatya**. His predecessors had already left inscriptions recording building works during the 12th century BC, at Gürün, Kötükale, Ispekçur and Darende.

- K -

KADESH, BATTLE OF. This is the best known of all major military engagements in the second millennium BC, entirely owing to the flamboyant record left by one of the antagonists, **Ramesses II,**

Pharaoh of the 19th Dynasty of Egypt. On one point all are agreed, that it took place in the fifth year of his long reign of 67 years. The battle is recorded in large-scale reliefs and hieroglyphic inscriptions on the walls of five **temples** in Upper Egypt, including the Ramesseum (the king's mortuary temple) on the west bank and Karnak and Luxor on the east bank of Thebes. In the normal Egyptian fashion, the reliefs give the picture of the overwhelming strength of the Pharaoh, depicted on a superhuman scale. The absence of any counter comment from the Hittite side, led by their king **Muwatalli II,** is partly explicable by subsequent events in Hatti. But it makes it difficult, if not impossible, to determine the precise outcome of the battle. This is one of the points of disagreement among specialists, the other being centered on the conundrums of **absolute chronology.** On the latter, a choice has to be made and consistency maintained. There is a difference of 30 years between the highest and lowest dates proposed for the accession of Ramesses II, between 1304 and 1274 BC. The highest date is no longer widely supported. There is still strong support for 1279 as the date of this king's accession, putting the battle in 1274 BC, the date followed in this work.

As to the outcome, one authoritative suggestion is that this was merely a skirmish, in which the two sides had taken up positions at an expected location, though there are objections to this theory. Not only Ramesses but also Muwatalli seem to some degree to have been taken by surprise, though Ramesses more seriously so, having been credulous enough to believe the report by two Bedouin sent by Muwatalli, to the effect that he had retreated to or lingered in the land of **Aleppo**, in fear of the Egyptians! The Hittite clearly grasped a weak point in his enemy, susceptibility to flattery. Imagine Ramesses' surprise when he discovered his mistake, on learning that the Hittite forces were lurking behind the walled city of Kadesh, standing on its mound (Tell Nebi Mend), while he, having crossed the Orontes River, was setting up his headquarters to the northwest of the city! Thus it would seem that only for the Hittites was Kadesh the spot chosen for the test of strength between the two rivals for control of the lands of Syria.

With other threats to face, Muwatalli was willing to give Ramesses some rope. He even half chided him for the severity of his treatment of those soldiers of Re, the second of his four brigades in line of march on Kadesh, who had panicked under the unexpected attack of a detachment of the Hittite forces dispatched across the river to surprise and harass the enemy.

Perhaps asking who was the victor of Kadesh is the wrong question, if indeed the battle was inconclusive, never completed, with the majority of troops on both sides never engaged. Ramesses was indeed more courageous than thoughtful, not ensuring that his full forces were brought to the battlefield in time, like an inexperienced chess player who fails to deploy all his pieces. One reconstruction of events has some 4,000 Hittite "chariots" of the heavy, ox-drawn, solid-wheeled variety—as depicted on the reliefs of the successful attack by Seti I, father of Ramesses II, on the city of Kadesh—in effect kept in reserve. These vehicles would have served simply as troop carriers, transporting some of the infantry to the front line but not maneuverable like true **chariots**. Here we are up against a problem of terminology, with "chariot" being far too loosely employed as a term for certain **wheeled vehicles**.

Ramesses II had four "brigades" (Amun, Re, Ptah and Sutekh, in that order of march on Kadesh from the south). They may have been at about a day's march apart or rather less. While only the first two were heavily engaged in the fighting, the fourth brigade, Sutekh, arrived just in time to save the day. While the first three brigades, or divisions, had been recruited in major centers in Egypt—Thebes, Heliopolis and Memphis—the fourth brigade, Sutekh, appears to have comprised auxiliaries from the land of **Amurru** in southern Syria, a key region in the power struggle between Egypt and Hatti. Indeed, these troops were described as "the Ne'arin of Pharaoh from the land of Amor." Already the Egyptian army was dependent on foreign soldiers to make up its strength, as discernible under Ramesses II and III in the recruitment of Sherden (Shardana) mercenaries, distinguishable by their bronze horned **helmets**.

The Hittite king seems to have relied overwhelmingly on his chariotry, forming his shock troops: his **army** comprised Hittite regulars, forces from the vassal states and mercenaries, probably only the first being altogether reliable. The chariots would have been most effective in an open plain rather than crossing a river such as the Orontes. Ramesses II refers to his confronting 2,500 Hittite chariots, a force comprising 7,500 men and 5,000 **horses**. This is significant as an assessment of the overall strength of the Hittite army, though virtually certain to be a gross exaggeration of the number of the enemy directly facing Ramesses in hand-to-hand fighting, in which he undoubtedly displayed courage in compensation for his lack of generalship. It would have taken too long a time to bring thousands of horses across the river.

The sources for the battle comprise the *Literary Record/Poem* and the *Pictorial Record*, consisting of the *Bulletin* and *Reliefs.* These last have generally been credited as more reliable as accounts of events than the *Literary Record*, whose propagandist character makes it suspect. Though by far the fullest record of any battle in Egyptian history, this was not displayed until some years after the event, making any directly political intent less probable. Of course, few of Ramesses II's subjects could read. One motive might conceivably have been to ward off opposition within Egypt, where the fairly new northern 19th Dynasty was unpopular in the south (Thebes). While there is a considerable element of vainglorious boasting, Ramesses does not try to present this as an overwhelming Egyptian victory.

Seeing that it was the Hittites who remained in the field after this battle or confrontation, to them must surely be awarded the victor's palm. The more is the pity that we lack their side of the story!

KALE. Turkish word meaning "castle," "fortress" or "citadel," normally on a steep hill and naturally defensible. Sometimes *kale* refers simply to a steep-sided hill. Compare Büyükkale ("great/large castle/citadel") at **Hattusa**.

KAMAN-KALEHÖYÜK. This large settlement mound lies about 80 kilometers southeast of Ankara and 35 kilometers northeast of the north end of the Salt Lake, in the province of Kırşehir. A Japanese expedition led by Sachihiro Omura has continued excavations annually since 1987.

The earliest occupation (Kaman V) dates to the final phase of the Early Bronze Age. Contemporary with the Assyrian merchant colonies is Kaman IIIC, the settlement suffering the destruction inflicted on so many other sites of the period: skeletons in some rooms had bronze **weapons** beside the graves similar to some from **Kültepe-*Karum*** IB. A massacre may have occurred. Contemporary with the Hittite Old Kingdom is a **food** store (Kaman IIIB), when the site may have been partially deserted. In a thick ash layer were found **bullae** of the 15th and early 14th centuries BC, Kaman IIIA dating to the Hittite Empire.

A long sequence of 18 levels spans the Iron Age, in which some objects show close cultural links between the Neo-Hittite zone and Phrygia.

KAMMENHUBER, ANNELIES (1922–1995). Among her under-graduate studies were Indology, ancient **languages** and Indo-European studies. From 1950 she began work on **Hittite** grammar. She became the editor of *Munich Studies in Linguistics.* For a decade she worked in collaboration with E. Benveniste and **Emmanuel Laroche** (1959–1969). She was then appointed professor of Hittitology in Munich. In 1973 she embarked on *Materials for a Hittite Dictionary*: the first fascicle of this, her *magnum opus,* appeared in 1975.

KANES. See **KARUM**; **KULTEPE**

KARABEL. The most westerly Hittite rock relief, this attracted attention in the 19th century, being readily accessible from Izmir. It stands some 40 kilometers inland from that city, in a pass across the Tmolos range between Ephesus and Sardis. Originally four in number (Karabel A, B and C1–2), all but Karabel A were destroyed a generation ago, though not before several records had been made.

The royal figure here standing represents Tarkasnawa, king of **Mira**. He holds a bow and **spear**, and wears a **sword** with crescentic pommel and a tall peaked headdress stylistically comparable with other **sculptures** of the reign of the last powerful king of Hatti, **Tudhaliya IV**. Parallels have been drawn with the reliefs of **Mount Sipylus**, **Gavurkalesi**, **Yazılıkaya**, **Fraktin** and **Sirkeli**. As recently as 1997 **David Hawkins** was first able to read the inscription, in **hieroglyphs**, of Karabel A, thus removing uncertainties, attributing this relief to Tarkasnawa, king of Mira, who mentions also his father and grandfather. Their names cannot yet be deciphered.

The stylistic evidence agrees with the textual, in ascribing the Karabel relief to the time of Tudhaliya IV.

KARABURUN. An Iron Age stronghold overlooking the Kızıl Irmak (**Marrassantiya**) between Hacıbektaş and Gülşehir. The fortified citadel is approached by a road up the side of the hill through a gateway. Just outside this is a three-line rock inscription in **hieroglyphs**, being an agreement between the local ruler and his collaborator to respect the contribution made by each to the building of the fortress, dateable to the eighth century BC.

KARADAĞ-KIZILDAĞ. In the southeast Konya Plain, 25 kilometers north of Karaman, stands a group of **hieroglyphic** inscriptions, two on the mountaintop sanctuary of Karadağ and five from the city site of Kızıldağ. These were written at the command of the "Great King" Hartapu, son of Muwatalli, and can be dated to the years immediately after the fall of the Hittite Empire. If earlier in date, the title "Great King" would hardly have been used while kings were still reigning in **Hattusa**.

Muwatalli, the "Great King" and father of Hartapu, may have been none other than **Urhi-Tesub (Muwatalli III)**. Hartapu would thus have been of the same generation as **Suppiluliuma II**, his second cousin, and could have outlived him. These inscriptions are indeed similar in style to those of the last Hittite king. An alternative possibility is that Hartapu and his father descended from **Kurunta** of **Tarhuntassa**, perhaps the center of a south Anatolian kingdom under Hartapu, the immediate heir of the Hittite Empire.

A figure in relief, next to the Kızıldağ I inscription, has been dated on stylistic criteria to the eighth century BC, and probably represents Wasusarma (Uassurme), king of the united confederacy of **Tabal**, centered at **Kululu**, near Kayseri.

KARAHÖYÜK (ELBISTAN). Excavations were directed by **Tahsin Özgüç** and **Nimet Özgüç** (1947), revealing Late Bronze and Iron Age occupation of a settlement which must have been located, from the 12th century BC, in the kingdom of Milid (**Malatya**), near the border with **Tabal**. A **stela** was set up here by one named Armanani, describing himself as "Lord of the *Pithos*-Men." This inscription recounts the arrival of one claiming the title "Great King," who found the city devastated. The palaeographical style fits a date between the late Hittite Empire and the Neo-Hittite cities, and the event could well fall around 1150 BC, a generation after the sack of **Hattusa**, this ruler having connections with **Tarhuntassa**.

KARAHÖYÜK (KONYA). This large settlement mound, with an area of about 600 by 450 meters, has been excavated intermittently since 1953 by Sedat Alp of the University of Ankara. Its greatest period coincided with the Old Assyrian merchant colonies and their immediate sequel (Middle Bronze Age), though the settlement was established much earlier. Among the major buildings is a large palace; residential quarters with streets have also been excavated. This is one of a number of Anatolian cities with substantial casemate walls as **fortifications**, as at **Alışar Höyük**.

Though the absence of an **archive** means that the name of this city is unknown, Karahöyük has an outstanding wealth of **bullae**, **seals** and seal impressions, particularly of the native Anatolian style. Seal impressions are found on some loom weights, a hint of the importance to the local economy of **textiles**. Among artifacts are baked clay and lead figurines. **Pottery** includes forms familiar at **Kanes** and elsewhere in this period, such as grape-cluster bowls and the ubiquitous beak-spouted jugs. **Burial customs** are diversified, with both intramural graves and **cremations**.

KARAKUYU. A dam of Hittite date in the district of Pınarbaşı in the province of Kayseri: excavations were carried out by Kutlu Emre.

KARATEPE. On a hilltop overlooking the River Ceyhan, now dammed to form a reservoir, this site was found by **Helmuth T. Bossert** (1946), excavations beginning in 1947. It is situated near Kadirli, some 100 kilometers northeast of Adana, with a twin citadel of **Domuztepe** on the opposite bank, also on a hilltop. The natural route through Karatepe leads up from the Cilician plain (**Kizzuwadna** in the Late Bronze Age) towards the foothills of the Taurus to the north, and one inscription states that the citadel was built to protect this route; the Amanus forms a mountain barrier to easy communications with the long rift valley leading from Kahramanmaraş (Neo-Hittite **Gurgum**) southward to the Amuq plain, so that contact with the city of **Zincirli (Sam'al)**, though only 32 kilometers distant, was much less easy than with Adana and the Mediterranean coast. Culturally, Karatepe was almost as much Phoenician as Neo-Hittite. The archaeological evidence provided by the citadel and its relief **sculptures**, the historical content of the inscriptions and the important additions and clarifications to knowledge of the **hieroglyphs** are all aspects of Karatepe making it a site of primary significance, even if it must be admitted that the quality of the reliefs is provincial if not barbaric and the historical content of the inscription set up by the local ruler Azatiwada (ztwd) rather limited. The fortified area of 400 by 200 meters is enclosed by a wall about one kilometer in circumference, with two monumental gates, the lower part of each having orthostats and lengthy inscription in hieroglyphs, paraphrased on the side facing in Phoenician.

The reliefs make up in liveliness and variety of theme for what they lack in artistry and technical skill. Undoubtedly some reliefs are unfinished, suggesting a rather brief duration for this citadel and providing evidence of the methods used by the stone masons, whom it would flatter to call sculptors. First the scene was incised in outline; then the background had a layer of stone removed by chiseling, the chisels probably being of **iron** by this period, early in the seventh century BC. This crude technique rather strongly suggests that the craftsmen of Karatepe were more accustomed to wood carving than working in stone, and that the hieroglyphs, **Luwian** in origin, were first carved on wooden **tablets**, **scribes** in wood being recorded at **Hattusa** under the Empire. At the very least two craftsmen are indicated by the wide variation in standard and style of different relief-carved orthostats. The juxtaposition of different styles shows how style and date can by no means always be regarded as equivalent, Phoenician art being par excellence eclectic. Assyrian influence is also apparent, notably in the genius with bird's head and four wings, supporting the sun disk, and in a maritime scene, very possibly depicting Cilician ships. The tone of the reliefs is secular, depicting the ruler at ease, enjoying a sumptuous banquet and **music** provided by lyres. The **food** is varied, including bread, hare and other meats, as well as fruit and drink. Birds of prey peck at a hare, a monkey squats beneath the table, and bears perform a dance. The Monkey-God Bes, originating from the Sudan (ancient Kush) and associated with good luck in childbirth, has two monkeys on his shoulders. Warriors and a mother suckling her infant also appear.

There has been considerable debate over the date of Karatepe, some of the reliefs being earlier in style than those associated with Phoenician elements and possibly transported over the river from Domuztepe. These would date to the ninth century BC. The proud boast of the ruler, Azatiwada, that he was the vassal of Urikki is agreed to signify Urik of Que, lord of the fertile plain of Adana, the "cotton plain" of modern Turkey. He is listed with many other rulers in the inscriptions of Tiglath-Pileser III (745–727 BC) of Assyria. Such was the prestige of Urikki that his name was recorded by Azatiwada some years after his death, his descendants also being mentioned. Indeed, Azatiwada claims to have kept them in power. Urikki is named in the Phoenician text as 'wrk mlk *Dnnym*, "king of the Danunians." Azatiwada may well have built on the remains of an earlier citadel. The inscriptions must date to a time when the Assyrian presence was weak or absent in the plain of Adana.

Following his policy of turning vassal territories into directly administered provinces of the resurgent Assyrian Empire, Sargon

II (722–705 BC) made Que into a province. His death in battle in the Taurus region, however, was followed inevitably by widespread revolts, extending through **Tabal** and **Malatya** (Melid); and his successor, Sennacherib, was engaged elsewhere, eventually marching into Que. It remained for his son, Esarhaddon (681–669 BC) to subdue Que and neighboring areas. His campaign against Tabal (679 BC) implies safe passage through Que. Subsequently, Sanduarri, king of Kundu and Sussu, northeast of the plain of Adana, allied with the Phoenician city of Sidon against Assyria, but was captured and beheaded. Thereafter, Que remained an Assyrian province until the fall of the Empire. The suggested identification of Sanduarri with Azatiwada seems plausible, giving a historical setting for the inscriptions of Karatepe, never the seat of a major power, but an exemplar of the cosmopolitan character of much of the Near East by that time.

KARUM. This Akkadian term, widely current in Mesopotamia as well as in the contemporary Old Assyrian merchant colonies in Anatolia in the early second millennium BC, has been variously translated, the most common meaning being that of "merchant colony"; an alternative is "quay"; but "bank" is less probable. The *karum* in many cities in Mesopotamia as well as in Anatolia was in essence a settlement of foreigners living side by side but separately from the local townspeople, comprising living quarters and business offices as well as depots.

It was the *bit karim*, or "house of the quay," which centralized the business activities of the Assyrian merchants. It had control of the **trade** in **copper**, but tin, **textiles** and skins were also stored in the depots. Merchants could draw copper from the large stocks held by the various *karum* centers, not only that of Kanes.

All the operations of the *bit karim* required periodic accounting, as much to satisfy the regulations imposed by "the City" (Assur) as the demands of the native Anatolian authorities. Problems concerning the **taxes** levied by the *karum* are very complex, depending on the precise interpretation of various terms. The *karum* of Kanes had to dispatch or pay over dues to the central treasury of Assur in northern Mesopotamia (Assyria). The *nibum*, most probably the Kaneshite representative at Assur, wrote in one letter:

> The City has fixed at ten minas of **silver** your contribution
> for the **fortifications**. A messenger has been chosen, who
> must be sent to you in this connection. Yet we have made

the following request to the Elders: 'Don't send a messenger, to avoid burdening the *karum*. . . . Please send ten minas of silver by the first messenger. Moreover, following
the regulations of the City [Assur], write to the other *karu*,
and make them pay the silver."

The term *karum* indeed originated in Mesopotamia, where
ships loaded and unloaded their cargoes beside the levees built up
along rivers and canal-side settlements, whence the meaning
"quay" or "dam embankment." The Anatolian trade was of course
by land caravans, so that these early meanings of *karum* did not
apply in any literal sense. Those administrative bodies, judicial and
commercial, responsible for regulating the business of the merchants could themselves be termed the *karum*.

The related term *wabartum* signifies an officially constituted
form of settlement with legal jurisdiction over the Assyrian merchants: it may derive from *ubaru*, meaning "resident alien," "emi-
grant" or "neighbor," and thus a community of such.

The role of the merchant in the early second millennium BC
reflects a subtle change in Mesopotamian society not closely paralleled in Anatolia, largely because there was no such theocratic tradition, with government centered on the **temples**, as had prevailed
in earlier times in the cities of Sumer and Akkad. After the Third
Dynasty of Ur, whose Empire collapsed shortly before 2000 BC,
economic power shifted to the great merchant families, also by
then dominant in Assyria and destined to initiate and as widely as
politically practicable to control the Old Assyrian trading network
in Anatolia. An essentially secular, profit-orientated ethos came to
prevail.

The *karum* did not reemerge as an institution after the collapse
of the Old Assyrian network; and trade was centered on the local
palace or seat of administration in the days of the Hittite state. No
sophisticated mercantile class survived. To some degree the great
Hittite protectorate under the Empire, the city and port of **Ugarit**,
maintained the tradition of welcoming communities of foreign
traders, such as the Mycenaeans, to a city noted for its diversity of
cultural traditions with their attendant **cults**. There is, however, no
such record of tightly organized mercantile enclaves as there is of
those in the Old Assyrian period. Maritime trade brought with it a
freer spirit of enterprise, extending across the eastern Mediterranean. As for the craft guilds of Nineveh in the Late Assyrian period, they were restricted to their own city.

KASKA (KASKU). The evidence gathered from **historical geography** through textual records and from field archaeology, including intensive surveys, combines to indicate the Kaska homeland as having covered the modern provinces of Samsun with Sinop to the west and Ordu to the east. Through this coastal Pontic region settlements were deserted around 1750 BC and not reoccupied until well into the Iron Age; but the inland central Pontic region, equivalent to modern Amasya province, has settlements continuing during the Hittite Old Kingdom. A number of sites here are of the right date to have served as part of a Hittite buffer zone against repeated Kaska incursions.

Some 2,000 places of varying size are documented in the Hittite texts; but only a modest percentage has been recorded on the ground. This is largely owing to vegetation cover and the use of **timber construction** for buildings. The nature of the terrain, moreover, made any enduring successes by the Hittite **army** impossible: the ground was totally unsuitable for **chariotry**.

The Kaska tribes may have come from across the Black Sea in the early second millennium BC; and their arrival could have triggered ethnic movements leading to the widespread destructions at the end of the Assyrian colonies in central Anatolia.

One difficulty the Hittite kings, including **Mursili II**, faced was the absence of any coherent political system among the Kaska people, in contrast with the **Arzawa** lands. The Kaska first definitely irrupted on the Hittite scene in the reign of **Hantili II**, capturing and holding **Nerik**. They attacked again while **Tudhaliya I/II** was campaigning in the west; but he quickly expelled them from the Hittite homeland. A very serious invasion of the northern territories occurred under **Arnuwanda I** and his **queen** Asmunikal, whose prayers concerning the destruction of Hittite **cult centers** and scattering of their priests reveal real anguish.

In the reign of **Tudhaliya III** the Kaskans invaded as far as **Nenassa**, sacking **Hattusa**. When the Hittite counter-attack began, led by the young **Suppiluliuma I**, repeated assaults on the Kaska marked the first phase, with the capture of many prisoners. The first two years of Mursili II were occupied with campaigning in the Kaska lands, to which he had to return in his fifth year, with more devastating effect. A tribal chief named Pihhuniya caused particular concern, not only because he had taken and annexed the **Upper Land** but also owing to his political ambitions, succinctly outlined by Mursili: "Pihhuniya did not rule in the Kaskan manner. But suddenly, where in the Kaskan town the rule of a single man was not customary, Pihhuniya ruled in the manner of a king."

With the appointment of his brother Hattusili as virtual **viceroy** of the troublesome Kaska borderlands, **Muwatalli II** inaugurated the final pacification of these persistent enemies of Hatti. **Ramesses II** records the inclusion of the rich booty of Keshkesh (Kaska) among the gifts dispatched as **marriage** dowry by **Hattusili III**. Kaska remained an occasional threat, however, with **Tudhaliya IV** campaigning vigorously there in his youth, before his accession.

Texts from **Tabal** and the Assyrian **annals** mention the Kasku, clearly Kaskan descendants and neighbors of Tabal in the early first millennium BC.

KASTAMA. This was a city in the north, one of those pillaged by invading **Kaska** tribesmen in the reign of **Arnuwanda I**, whose **cult center** was destroyed. A text concerning the palace (*e-gal*) of Kastama reveals the grip held by the administration on the agricultural land, with issues of seed corn for sowing from the palace stores, with quantities specified, and with the enforcement of the corvée for sowing and reaping, from which none was exempt. First, however, the property of the crown in each village was listed. Here was a bureaucratic machinery as intensive as that deployed for the Domesday Book survey in England (1086). It is at this level that the sophistication of Hittite state control becomes most evident. A palace such as that of Kastama would have ranked below the "houses of the seal" described as the administrative framework of the state by **Telipinu**, in relation to his wide-ranging governmental reforms.

KATAPA. One of the lands in the **viceroyalty** of Hattusili in the **Kaska** borderlands.

KESLIK YAYLASI. Quarry and sculptors' yard northwest of Niğde, with scatter of **stelae** bases and uninscribed stelae. The carvings relate to the cult of **Kubaba** and other deities, with dating to the later eighth century BC, just after the reign of Warpalawas of Tyana. There is a rock-cut road for transportation of the blocks.

KESTEL. An Early Bronze Age **tin** mine and associated mining areas are located near the small town of Camardi, 30 kilometers east-southeast of the city of Niğde and above several rivers flowing through the Niğde Massif. The mine was cut into a slope composed of granite, marble, gneiss and quartzite, with a number of shafts and galleries: in the beginning (ca.3000 BC) it had been an opencast operation. Workshops were built outside the entrance to the mine. The evidence from Kestel indicates a remarkable mastery of the geology of metal ores and the chemistry of tin, the local ore being cassiterite. Clearly, the Kestel mining areas must be related to those in the Bolkardağ region a little distance to the south. Moreover, Kestel, Göltepe and the other centers of tin mining seem to have controlled resources, production and long-distance **trade** in tin in the generations before **Sargon of Agade** initiated Mesopotamian involvement in Anatolian trade (from ca.2370 BC). A hint of this economic power is provided by the growth of Göltepe, close to Kestel, into a considerable walled town, with workshops for processing tin.

KIKKULI. Four **tablets** excavated at **Hattusa** comprise a detailed treatise on the training and acclimatization of **horses**, ascribed to a horse trainer named Kikkuli coming from **Mitanni**, presumably in order to instruct the Hittite **chariotry** in the most up-to-date methods. Long after the first Hittite contacts with Mitannian forces, the Hittite **army** was not too proud to learn from the kingdom most advanced in several aspects of warfare.

The training of the horses—for pulling chariots, not for riding—was a lengthy affair, and this treatise includes a number of technical terms in the Indic language, akin to Sanskrit, notably relating to the number of turns on the course, of which two examples may suffice: first, *tera-wartanna* ("three turns"), compared with Sanskrit *tri vatana-m*; second, *satta-wartanna* ("seven turns"), compared with Sanskrit *sapta vartana-m*. Such skills in turning were essential for chariotry.

KILISE TEPE. Settlement site with occupation from the third millennium BC until the Byzantine period, located about 45 kilometers northwest of Silifke, above the left bank of the Göksu near where the river leaves the Mut basin to drop down between cliffs to the Mediterranean. Excavations began in 1994 under the direction of Nicholas Postgate (Cambridge). Stable conditions under the Hittite Empire (Level III) are accompanied by the standard **Late Bronze Age pottery**. A date of 1380 BC was obtained by **dendrochronology**.

Dating of the later levels is not precise, until close links with Cypriot pottery can be dated ca.750–650 BC. Four short-lived phases (IIa–d) seem to cover only 50 years (ca.1200–1150 BC), suggesting unsettled conditions.

KINET HÖYÜK. Excavations have been carried out at this settlement mound, ancient Issos on the Mediterranean coast near Iskenderun, since 1992 under the direction of Marie-Henriette Gates (Bilkent University, Ankara). This was a major port, with occupation from the Middle Bronze Age until the Iron Age. Medieval occupation ensued after a hiatus.

A large public building of Middle Bronze II (Kinet V) stood on the east terrace of the mound: an original structural phase was followed by a careless rebuilding, though storage jars indicate continued prosperity. To the original phase belong many containers holding liquids and perishable goods, in the southern rooms, while in the five northern rooms in the later phase cereals and **oil** were stored. In the west wing, with a large open court, was found evidence of **metallurgy**, including crucibles.

Painted **pottery** of earlier Middle Bronze II originating from Cilicia (**Kizzuwadna**) and imports from **Alasiya (Cyprus)** occur. Calibrated radiocarbon dates for the two building phases span from the late 18th until the mid–15th century BC. This building, perhaps a palace, was destroyed by earthquake and buried under gravel and marine shell deposits. The east terrace was not reoccupied until the Hellenistic period.

Three Late Bronze II building levels were uncovered on the west slope, demonstrating the integration of this harbor town into the Hittite Empire. The earliest level (Period 15) has stone foundations of a major building, with three separate stages until its abandonment. The pottery is similar to central Anatolian wares of the early Empire (14th century BC), with highly burnished jugs as well as bowls and coarser plates and platters of typically central Anatolian or "Hittite" forms, with occasional pot marks. Storage jars, however, are of "Canaanite" type. After this building was abandoned, its brick superstructure was razed and sealed by two levels of domestic houses, dating to the 13th century BC (Periods 14–13/Kinet IV:1). Both levels were violently burned. **Spearheads** and other **weapons** in the destruction debris of Period 14 indicate an attack; but it is difficult to relate this to the historical record of an essentially peaceful century. Could this conceivably have occurred in the aftermath of the battle of **Kadesh**, when Hittite vassals were restive? Kinet had a considerable economic role as a sea-trading community. Canaanite jars and a few Cypriot imports supplement the mainly "Hittite" fabrics and forms.

The abrupt end of Late Bronze Age occupation at Kinet Höyük was followed by radical changes at the opening of the Iron Age (Period 12/Kinet III:3). A new land-loving population, unfamiliar with the sea, turned away from the Late Bronze reliance on fish to a meat diet of sheep, goat and pig. So much for the term **"Sea Peoples."**

On the east slope, pottery kilns of the eighth to sixth centuries BC were found. *See also* **TRADE**.

KINGSHIP, KINGS. The most ancient title of the Hittite kings was Labarna (Tabarna in **Luwian** and Akkadian), while under the Empire "My Sun" came additionally into use. While this has been seen as a manifestation of an "orientalizing" tendency, the adoption of traditions of government native to Syria and Mesopotamia and the abandonment of older Indo-European institutions, more probably it expresses the devotion of the king to the **Sun-Goddess** of **Arinna** and to the Sun-God. Admittedly, from the reign of **Suppiluliuma I** the winged sun disk came into regular use in royal iconography, persisting through the Neo-Hittite period: of its Egyptian derivation there can be no possible doubt.

The ethos of the kingship was more strongly theocratic in the time of the Empire than in the Old Kingdom, largely through growing **Hurrian** influence. **Mursili II** was notably pious, interrupting campaigns in order to preside at major **festivals**. In large part this was owing to his urge to appease the **gods** for the **plague**, beginning in the time of Suppiluliuma I, who died from it, and lasting 20 years.

The king was servant or steward of the gods, especially the **Storm-God** and the Sun-Goddess.. He was not deified in his lifetime, in spite of references to his filial relationship to various divinities, to be regarded as mere figures of speech. Scattered allusions alone cast light on the question of the divinity of the Hittite kings. Ritual purity was nevertheless an essential attribute of the Hittite kings. For example, the finding of a hair in his washing bowl was a capital offense! This has to be understood in the context of the properties of hair in the realm of **magic**.

Few texts set out anything approaching a philosophy of kingship, one such being a ritual for building a new palace:

> To me, the king, have the gods, the Sun-God and the
> Weather-God, entrusted the land and my house. I, the king,

will protect the land and my house. . . . To me, the king,
have the gods granted many years. To these years there is
no limit.

There is no full surviving record of the coronation ceremony.
Hattusili III complained—in a letter to the king of Assyria—that
on his accession he had not sent him the customary gifts, such as
"the royal vestments and fragrant **oil** for the coronation." Perhaps
he was sensitive, after usurping the throne from his nephew **Urhi-
Tesub**? The succession normally depended on an act of nomination by the ruling king, clearly not given in this case.

Mursili II came before the gods in humble prayer for the
whole realm, not simply for his own health, in contrast with the
prayers of **Puduhepa** for her ailing spouse Hattusili III. The role of
the king as pastor of his people was thus emphasized in the plague
prayers of Mursili II.

It is well documented that the Hittite king was leader in war,
supreme judge and chief priest of the national **cults**, in this last
function aided by the **queen**. The largest category by far of **tablets**
in the royal **archives** of **Hattusa** deals with the king's priestly duties; but most are fragmentary and thus hard to interpret in detail.
The ceremonies described are normally termed **festivals**.

Each king tended to have a patron divinity to whom he was
especially devoted, as with the devotion of Hattusili III to **Ishtar** of
Samuha; of **Tudhaliya IV** to **Sarruma**; of Mursili II to **Telipinu**;
of **Muwatalli II** to the "Weather-God *pihassassis*."

KINIK (KASTAMONU).   Metal vessels of definitely Hittite style
from the area of Kinik in the Devrekani district, where a dam was
under construction, were brought to the museum in the provincial
center of Kastamonu—north-northeast of Ankara and 92 kilometers south of the Black Sea coast at Inebolu—in November 1990, at
much the same time as a statuette of Hittite style was acquired by
the Metropolitan Museum of New York.

It would seem curious that this hoard comprises almost exclusively vessels of varied forms and quality, lacking items found in
groups of **metalwork** housed in private collections on either side
of the Atlantic. Though proof is lacking, it seems very likely that
the hoard brought to the Kastamonu Museum had been stripped of
those artifacts expected to bring the highest price. This was an operation carried out by professionals.

What were these vessels? The most plausible answer is that

they were from a local **cult center**, part of the equipment of a **temple**. The geographical location places this hoard in the Pontic hills for generations under the control of the **Kaska** tribes, but largely reclaimed by the Hittite state in the early years of **Hattusili (III)**. His brother **Muwatalli II** had made him semi-independent ruler of a broad swathe of territory forming the northern borderlands of Hatti, when he recovered the long revered shrine of **Nerik**. The decorative style of the finest vessel in the Kinik hoard suggests a date in or close to the reign of **Tudhaliya IV**. A hint of the wealth of the region is provided and by implication of the resources so long at the disposal of the Kaska enemies of **Hattusa**.

Outstanding in the Kinik hoard are three bull rhytons and a bowl inscribed in **hieroglyphs** and decorated with registers of "typical Hittite figures." On this small bowl are depicted floral and figurative motifs in the repoussé technique. The longest frieze, just below the shoulder of the bowl, depicts a hunt involving the hunter and many deer and ibexes. A sacred tree flanked by two griffins appears in the lowermost register. The hunt is a characteristic theme of Hittite art, as for example on the reliefs of **Alaca Höyük**. This is a small vessel, the largest register being only 3.3 centimeters high.

KIZZUWADNA. Commonly equated with Classical Cilicia, the territorial limits of Kizzuwadna fluctuated considerably over the generations, largely depending on power politics, specifically the extent of Hittite control over north Syria and the strength or weakness of the kingdom of **Mitanni**.

During the Hittite Old Kingdom the later Kizzuwadna was a part of Hatti named the province of Adaniya (Adana), centered in the fertile plain now called Pamukova (Cotton Plain), one of the most prosperous areas of modern Turkey. It may already have been under Hittite rule in the time of **Hattusili I**, the first objective of whose Syrian campaign was **Alalakh**.

It was in the disordered reign of **Ammuna** that Adaniya seems to have rebelled, in the mid–16th century BC, becoming the independent kingdom of Kizzuwadna. The leader of this revolt and first king may have been one named Pariyawatri, though this cannot be proved. His son was Isputahsu, whose **seal** found at **Tarsus** is inscribed with the title Great King. He made a **treaty** on the basis of equality with the Hittite king **Telipinu** (ca.1525–1500 BC). A later king of Kizzuwadna, Pilliya, concluded a treaty with the Hittite king **Zidanta II**: in this reign the city of **Lawazantiya** is first mentioned as lying within Kizzuwadna. At some stage after the treaty with Pilliya, Hatti appears to have suffered a breach of its relations with Kizzuwadna, for Sunassura, presumably then king of Kizzuwadna, appears in a position of vassalage to the **Hurrian** power of Mitanni, ruled then by Saustatar.

The independence of Kizzuwadna seems to have persisted through the time when a treaty between this same Sunassura of Kizzuwadna and the Hittite king of the day was drawn up. This king, formerly supposed to have been **Suppiluliuma I**, now seems almost certainly to have been **Tudhaliya I/II**. In the text of this treaty, preserved at **Hattusa**, can be seen his viewpoint on events past and present:

> Formerly, in the time of my grandfather, Kizzuwadna was on the side of Hatti. Later, Kizzuwadna released itself from Hatti and turned toward Hurri. . . . Now Kizzuwadna is on the side of Hatti. . . . Now the people of the Land of Kizzuwadna are Hittite cattle and chose their stable. From the Hurrian they separated and shifted allegiance to My Sun. The Hurrian sinned against the Land of Hatti, but against the Land of Kizzuwadna he sinned particularly. The Land of Kizzuwadna rejoices very much indeed over its liberation. Now the Land of Hatti and the Land of Kizzuwadna are free from their obligations. Now I, My Sun, have restored the Land of Kizzuwadna to its independence.

This treaty provides an insight into international relations, with Kizzuwadna as a buffer between Hatti and Mitanni, whose enmity is clearly stated. The unusual feature is the emphasis on the oppressive character of Mitannian rule.

At some later date, possibly still in the reign of Tudhaliya I/II, Kizzuwadna was annexed, coming under direct Hittite rule, as it remained thereafter. Certainly it was not independent under **Suppiluliuma I**, for he appointed one of his sons, Telipinu, as "priest of Kizzuwadna," by a decree resembling a vassal treaty with its obligations. This same son later led forces in support of the Hittite **army** in Syria, with which no king of Kizzuwadna is mentioned.

Although Kizzuwadna had ceased to play a role in international relations, being a territory vital for Hittite access to Syria, its cultural influence on the Hittite monarchy seems to have grown, reaching its apogee with the **marriage** of **Hattusili III**, before he seized the throne, to **Puduhepa**, daughter of a priest of Lawazantiya in the Anti-Taurus of northeastern Kizzuwadna. Mitanni had long vanished from the political map. At least in the sphere of **cult** and ritual, however, the once hated **Hurrian** had in a sense triumphed.

KORUCUTEPE. A settlement mound situated 30 kilometers east of Elaziğ, in the Altınova, near the village of Aşaği Içme, its height was 16 meters and diameter about 190 meters. From 1968 three seasons of excavations were carried out under the direction of Maurits N. van Loon, sponsored by the University of Chicago and other institutions. A long sequence of stratified occupation levels through the Chalcolithic period, Bronze Age and Early Iron Age, with some medieval remains, was subdivided into 12 phases. These comprised no less than 140 strata, extending over a time span from ca.4500 until ca.800 BC, with occupation in a final phase, ca.1200–1400 AD.

Korucutepe, along with the whole Altınova, was occupied from the mid–fourth millennium BC by people whose material culture has been termed **Early Trans-Caucasian**, with good reason, though without conclusive proof associated with the **Hurrians.** Certainly they formed the population of **Isuwa** before the advent of Hittite rule. By the Middle Bronze II period (Phase H: ca.1800–1600 BC) Korucutepe was defended by a strong stone-built city wall. Probably it was at the opening of the Late Bronze II period (ca.1400 BC) that a corbeled stone **postern** tunnel on L-shaped plan was built. Could this have occurred in the reign of **Tudhaliya I/II?** If so, it would have been designed for a threatened **siege** by the forces of **Mitanni**. This postern antedates the better-known example at **Hattusa**: that at **Ugarit** suggests influence from Syria, consistent with other evidence of cultural contacts from the west.

Central Anatolian connections become very evident in the **pottery** from Phase H at Korucutepe, contemporary with the earlier Hittite Old Kingdom and showing beforehand parallels with **Kültepe-*Karum*** IB and also with the first half of **Boğazköy: Büyükkale** IVc and with early Late Bronze I at **Tarsus**. Such connections cannot have been entirely divorced from the **Old Assyrian caravan routes** in their late period of use or from the expansion of Hittite power under **Hattusili I** and **Mursili I**. Hittite power was by and large weaker during the Late Bronze I period at Korucutepe (Phase I: ca.1600–1400 BC), when ceramic parallels with central Anatolia and Tarsus continue, especially in orange and red burnished, slipped and smoothed wares. In Late Bronze II (Phase J: ca.1400–1200 BC), when Hittite power was dominant in

Isuwa, these wares were displaced by orange wheelmarked ware and drab unburnished buff ware, shallow bowls or platters demonstrating the marked decline in quality of much of the Phase J pottery, in line with the Hittite dominions as a whole. Pottery had declined in status, becoming almost mass-produced. Nearby excavations at **Norşuntepe** III and Tepecik have yielded the same pottery. Further afield parallels occur in **Kizzuwadna** at Late Bronze II Tarsus and **Mersin** V; at Hattusa in **Boğazköy:Lower City** I (ca.1300–1200 BC); and at **Beycesultan** I.

The prevalence of central Anatolian pottery in Isuwa could imply deliberate transplantation of people from the Hittite heartland, to counterbalance the pro-Mitannian sentiments of the local Hurrian population.

KOŞAY, HAMIT ZUBEYR (1897–1984). A man of wide learning in ethnography as well as archaeology, his outstanding achievement was the foundation of the Ethnography Museum in Ankara, of which he was the first director (1927-1931). He was born in Russia, studied in Budapest and became (1924) one of the Turks coming to the new Republic from abroad.

Atatürk saw Hamit Koşay as the leading archaeologist in his new state, whom he encouraged to carry out fieldwork around the new capital Ankara, at a time when communications were not easy with the more outlying areas of Turkey. The most important of his projects was the excavation of **Alaca Höyük** (1935-1948, 1963-1967), but he excavated at least nine other sites mainly in central and eastern Anatolia. Koşay published over 35 books and 150 articles on ancient Anatolia.

KÖYÜTLÜ. A dam of earth construction with masonry footings, making it clearly of Hittite date, it is 900 meters long and 25 to 30 meters high. It lies near the hill fort of Bulacan (Zaferiye), close to the ancient and modern route from Konya to Akşehir. This fortified site was, from the surface **pottery**, occupied both in the second millennium BC and in the Classical period. Beneath the fort stretches a lower fortified town, whose limestone **cyclopean** walls are in the tradition of monumental Hittite masonry apparent at **Gavurkalesi**, **Eflatun Pınar** and **Sirkeli**, similar to the extensive stronghold of **Yaraşlı**.

KUBABA. Anatolian Mother-Goddess, identifiable with Kybele/Cybele in Phrygia and elsewhere in the first millennium BC.

She was the patron divinity of **Carchemish**, and can be set within the long tradition of the Mother-Goddess cult which can be traced back at least to the seventh millennium BC.

KÜLTEPE (KANES). This large settlement mound (*höyük*), originally named Karahöyük in common with many other ancient mounds in Turkey, lies 20 kilometers northeast of the city of Kayseri (Roman Caesarea) in Cappadocia, a short distance southeast of the Kızıl Irmak (Red River), in Hittite times **Marrassantiya** and in Greco-Roman times Halys. One of the most important excavated sites in Anatolia, Kültepe is of special relevance for this dictionary, owing to its certain identification as the city of **Nesa**, which in its turn can be equated with **Kanes**, after **Kussara,** the first center of Hittite political and military power on the Anatolian plateau. Excavated since 1948 by an expedition directed by **Tahsin Özgüç**, of the University of Ankara, and sponsored by the Turkish Historical Foundation, it had been the site of earlier excavations between World Wars I and II under **Bedrich Hrozny** of Prague.

As happens all too often in the Near East, it was through the appearance of antiquities in the markets of Constantinople (Istanbul) and further afield, as well as locally, that scholarly attention was first drawn to south central Anatolia, Cappadocia in Greco-Roman times. Both ·inscribed clay **tablets** and distinctive painted **pottery** surfaced in considerable quantities, some 3,000 tablets in all, both categories being described as "Cappadocian." This Cappadocian ware is now commonly termed **Alışar III ware**, having been found in that excavated mound in stratified context. This pottery and these tablets have found their way into a number of museums and private collections around the world, unlike the material from the official excavations at Kültepe, now displayed in Ankara and among the major attractions of the museum.

Hrozny, a brilliant philologist, had been led to believe that this was the source of the Cappadocian tablets, though as a field archaeologist he found himself out of his depth. During his campaign of excavations at Kültepe ("ash mound") he eventually unearthed some 600 tablets, among them finding references which proved he had located the ancient city of Kanes, whose full importance was not yet realized. It was, however, some time before he stumbled upon the major feature of this large site, the presence at the foot of the main mound of an extensive low platform, not immediately recognizable as an outer, lower area of the town. He might not have located it when he did, had it not been for a disgruntled villager who came to Hrozny and divulged the secret of the area whence his fellow villagers were extracting clay tablets for sale in the markets. This was to prove to be the site of the greatest Old Assyrian trading community (**karum**), from which some 15,000 tablets and innumerable other finds have subsequently been recovered by the Turkish expedition.

There is a very long sequence of occupation levels in the main mound, or citadel, of Kültepe, from the Chalcolithic period (fourth millennium BC) down into the Iron Age (first millennium BC). For our purposes the strata from the later Early Bronze Age till the end of the Late Bronze Age are especially significant, the Iron Age also being not without interest.

It is apparent that the *karum* of Kanes was first built and inhabited before the arrival of the Assyrian merchants and the organization of the Old Assyrian **trade**, for the earliest levels (*Karum* IV–III) are completely devoid of clay tablets. One theory is that tablets of wood, mentioned in later Hittite texts, may have been in use: if so, this would tend to add weight to the suggestion of an Anatolian, more specifically **Luwian**, presence here. But without further evidence this remains a matter of enlightened guesswork.

The city of Kültepe-Kanes, contemporary with Level II of the *karum* and thus dating ca.2050–1950 BC or a little later, was protected by two defensive lines, the inner wall being built on large unhewn stones, reused in the later defenses of Kanes IB attributable to **Anitta**, son of Pithana. Among the buildings excavated in the city is a likely palace, with residential quarters and a large paved open square. A palace and five **temples** are mentioned in the tablets. The entire city and the *karum* outside the walls were burnt in a violent destruction, conceivably the result of a Hittite attack, although Anitta's association with Kanes IB and the intervening phase of Kanes IC make it chronologically unlikely to have been attributable to Pithana. The stratigraphy of the city, however, does not indicate any desertion of the site between Kanes II and IB, in spite of the destruction of Kanes II. The palace containing tablets of Warsama, king of Kanes, however, most probably belongs to a phase (IC) when the *karum* was abandoned, and the merchants had withdrawn within the walls of the Anatolian city, if they had not indeed retreated to Assur. A bronze **spearhead** with typically Anatolian bent tang bearing the inscription "Palace of Anitta the king" was recovered from a public building within the city in Kanes IB context, adding weight to the claims made in the Anitta Text.

In the *karum* of Kanes the orientation of streets and many

buildings remained essentially the same from Level II through IB–IA. The buildings all have andesite footings up to floor level only, with mud-brick walls above, though the stonework was in some places carried higher, as behind kitchen ovens. The whole character of the buildings was Anatolian, with no trace of influence from Assyria, the houses being plastered and whitewashed. There is no evidence of gabled roofs. Details such as door jambs, charred remains of wooden door frames and pivot stones demonstrate the access to buildings. Stone paving was used where water was much in use.

The majority of houses in Level II of the *karum* either have two rooms and a rectangular plan or two rooms opening on to a large main room or many rooms off a corridor. Houses were extended as required, presumably with the growth of the household, often with walls set at irregular angles. The population was evidently increasing.

Five districts have been identified in the areas occupied by the merchants' houses, with varying yields of tablets, while other houses excavated 1.5 kilometers to the south contained none. The significance of this can only be surmised. The makeup of the population of each district can be estimated from its tablets. Most of the Assyrians lived in the first and second districts, being in the majority in the third and fifth districts, alongside native Anatolian merchants. Only the fourth district was perhaps exclusively Anatolian, and the native houses yielded notably fewer tablets. The major archives were housed in the north, northeast and central areas of the *karum*.

Another area was devoted to workshops and supporting services in the southeast part of the *karum*, where native householders mostly dwelt. Workshops occur in widely separated parts of the *karum*, not grouped all together, though no **bit karim** has been found, this being known only from the tablets. Much evidence remains to be uncovered in the form of more workshops as well as in the thousands of as yet unpublished tablets, which must include references to **copper**, **gold** and **silver** artifacts. Tools, **weapons** and decorative items of metal, stone and terracotta were manufactured by the craftsmen, no doubt following traditional practices dating back well before the arrival of the Assyrian merchants. One workshop of the later period (IB) yielded portable and large fixed molds, crucibles, blow-pipes and pot-bellows, indicating **metallurgy** on an organized footing.

It would be mistaken to suggest that it was solely owing to the

arrival of the foreign traders from Assur that the level of sophistication in the economy of central Anatolia was attained. More
probably a network of trade routes had evolved through the activities of native Anatolian merchants, with the Assyrian newcomers
being adept at profiting from established business networks. Kanes
had a long history of urban life, the growth of trade in Anatolia
emerging during the Early Bronze III period, whose beginning in
the mid–third millennium BC could be said to mark a cultural wa-
tershed not repeated until the advent of the Iron Age in the 12th
century BC. The characteristic Alışar III (Cappadocian) ware appears at Kültepe in the levels termed Early and Middle Cappadocian, continuing through the Late Cappadocian phase, which includes the first two levels (IV–III) of the *karum* of Kanes. This
painted **pottery** underwent three phases of development conform-
ing with the sequence of levels at Kanes. It is noteworthy that it
was in the Early Cappadocian phase, long before the arrival of Assyrian merchants, that the Anatolian city contained a public building of *megaron* plan, either a temple or a palace, suggesting western influence on central Anatolia. Could this have been an outcome
of the Luwian migrations?

The vicissitudes of Anatolian society, with growing conflicts
between the various minor kingdoms perhaps in part stimulated by
competition to enjoy the benefits accruing from the presence of
foreign merchants able to pay tolls to allow safe passage of their
caravans, had driven the Assyrian inhabitants of the *karum* of
Kanes away. The perimeter wall surrounding the *karum* of Kanes
IB suggests the necessity of effective protection for the merchants
returning to Kanes and in fact extending their trade to other merchant colonies. How much significance is to be attached to the
smaller number of tablets found in *karum* IB compared with *karum*
II is not entirely clear. What is evident is that the second period of
Assyrian activity at Kanes lasted a shorter time, on the evidence of
limmu names on the tablets, than the first period (*karum* II). After
the first destruction the period of desertion of the *karum* (IC)
probably lasted not less than 50 years, seeing that graves of this
time dug into the ruins of *karum* II were evidently unknown to the
inhabitants of the reoccupied colony (*karum* IB), not being robbed
of their contents.

Though there are fewer tablets to reveal details of the Old Assyrian trade in the time of *karum* IB, it would be mistaken to conclude that this trade had shrunk in volume or variety. Two factors
indicate the contrary: first, the expansion of the area of the *karum*

of Kanes to a diameter of over one kilometer, within a wall built on a footing of massive andesite blocks, at the same time as the native Anatolian city grew in size; second, the establishment of other trading posts or colonies, each a *karum*, at **Alışar** II, **Boğazköy (Hattusa)** and **Acemhöyük (Burushattum)**.

The **relative chronology** of Kültepe-Kanes is greatly clarified by *limmu* names synchronizing Kültepe IB, Alışar II and Tell Chagar Bazar in the Khabur valley with the reign of Samsi-Adad I of Assyria (1813–1781 BC), overlapping with that of Hammurabi of Babylon (1792–1750 BC). The following **absolute chronology** for the successive periods of the *karum* of Kültepe-Kanes therefore seems plausible: Kültepe II, ca.2050/2000–1900 BC; Kültepe IC, ca.1900–1850 BC; Kültepe IB, ca.1850–1800 BC or slightly later; Kültepe IA, ending ca.1750 BC.

The final phase of the *karum* (IA) was but a pale reflection of what had gone before. It was undoubtedly owing to growing unrest and insecurity for the caravans with discord among the Anatolian kingdoms, rather than any economic changes in Assyria, that the Old Assyrian trade finally came to an end. A brief dark age descended upon the Anatolian plateau, to be lifted a century later under **Hattusili I**. Never again, however, was such a sophisticated commercial network to flourish in the lands destined to come under Hittite rule. The state would step in where the great merchant family firms had once ruled.

KULULU. This site lies 18 kilometers east of Sultanhanı, which stands on the Kayseri-Sivas road 30 kilometers northeast of **Kültepe (Kanes)**. It was occupied during the third and second millennia BC, first on the citadel. Relief-carved orthostats and fragments of **statues** show two styles of Iron Age date (ca.850/800–700 BC).

Kululu is best known for its inscribed lead strips, the **hieroglyphs** being examined first by **Emmanuel Laroche** and then by **J. David Hawkins**. They were unearthed by villagers, who used them in part to make lead shot, and were acquired by purchase (ca.1967). Though of little historical significance, they have contributed to decipherment of the hieroglyphs. Two of these inscriptions mention Tuwatis and Wasusarma, both well-known "great kings" of **Tabal**, as well as three other rulers, hitherto unknown. These lead strips list personal names, commodities (including sheep) and towns.

Such lead strips seem to have become the common medium from the eighth century BC for writing letters, business documents and **treaties**. These underline the importance of Kululu at this time, very possibly as the capital of Tabal, if not located too near its periphery.

KUMARBI. The **Hurrian** god often termed "King of the Gods" and the central player in the best surviving compositions of Hittite-Hurrian mythology, he was the protagonist in dramatic events affecting the community of **gods**. The main source concerning Kumarbi comprises mythological texts from **Hattusa**, especially the fragmentary *Kingship in Heaven* and *The Song of Ullikummi*. He appears also in cultic texts from **Mari**, Nuzi and **Ugarit** as well as in the myth concerning **silver** connecting him with his special **cult center** at **Urkesh (Tell Mozan)** and on a first-millennium BC **hieroglyphic stela** from Tell Ahmar (Til-Barsip) on the Euphrates River.

The Hurrian **theogony** is set out in the *Kingship in Heaven* text, giving Kumarbi as the third in succession to celestial sovereignty, after **Alalu** and **Anu**. At times Kumarbi is equated with Enlil, king of the Sumerian gods, whose seat was at Nippur in central Mesopotamia. The reference in one passage to Kumarbi's going to Nippur reinforces this identification. There are indubitable western links, with Greek mythology as narrated by Hesiod, although the roots of Hurrian theogony lie in Mesopotamia.

The second myth of the Kumarbi cycle, *The Song of Ullikummi*, has Kumarbi begetting the stone monster Ullikummi for the purpose of regaining the throne of heaven from **Tesub**. Kumarbi, setting out from his town of Urkesh, arrives at a spot called Cool Pond, where a great Rock is lying. Kumarbi is then invited by the Sea-God to have his child by the Rock brought up there. In due course the Rock bears Kumarbi a child, who, according to the text, it was hoped would "hit Tesub and pound him like chaff." After a warning from the Sun-God about the diorite stone child, offspring of the Rock Ullikummi, Tesub and his brother Tasmisu go to reconnoiter, being joined by their sister **Ishtar** (Hurrian: **Sausga**). All three ascend Mount Hazzi, on the Mediterranean coast near Antioch: this is the classical Casius. Then we read of Tesub ordering Tasmisu to prepare his war **chariot** and the two sacred bulls to haul it into battle. In this first confrontation, even with the support of "70 gods," Tesub is unsuccessful against the Stone. In the great second battle Ullikummi boasts of the role his father Kumarbi has assigned him. Thereafter, though there is a complete break in the text, it can be assumed the outcome is the final triumph of Tesub, since he is the supreme god in historical times.

There is a particularly close parallel with the Hittite-Hurrian myth of Kumarbi in the Greek story of Typhon, a new rival to Zeus in Hesiod's *Theogony*. A first, unsuccessful battle is even located on Mount Casius (i.e. Mount Hazzi). Typhon was believed to originate from Cilicia, and in a **cuneiform** text a Mount Ullikummi occurs in a list of mountains of **Kizzuwadna**.

It is uncertain whether the Kumarbi cycle survives in a Hittite translation of a Hurrian original or as the work of a creative Hittite writer based on Hurrian tradition. In another, very fragmentary myth, Kumarbi, helped by the giant daughter of the Sea-God, creates a snake monster, Hedammu, who develops a measureless appetite. The wise god Ea, at a gathering of the gods, accuses Kumarbi of having harmed the gods by annihilating mankind, resulting in the loss of sacrifices. The gods were going to be obliged to gather their own **food**!

The Hurrian character of the theme of the dethroned king of the gods seeking restoration is undoubted. The theater of action, however, cannot have been within the ancestral Hurrian homeland in the highlands of eastern Anatolia. The reference to Mount Hazzi and other clues indicate a north Syrian setting. Ullikummi's child will thus have been growing out of the Gulf of Iskenderun, at the northeast corner of the Mediterranean Sea. The mythology of Ugarit has the Sea-God Yam allied with El (= Kumarbi) against the **Storm-God** Ba'al.

The inclusion of rivers in the domain of the Sea-God is paralleled in Ugaritic mythology, whereas in Hurrian **religion** the sea has no role, and rivers are always mentioned in association with mountains, characteristics of an inland people. The theme of birth from stone may just possibly have been brought by the Hurrians from their ancestral homeland in the **Early Trans-Caucasian cultural zone**.

Kumarbi was the Hurrian Grain-God, a role perhaps subordinate to his more prominent manifestations in the pantheon. A relief figure at **Yazılıkaya** of a god, 1.35 meters high, with an ear of corn in front of him seems to represent Kumarbi. His cult continued into the Neo-Hittite period, when he occurs sometimes under the name of Kuparma.

A remarkable artistic manifestation of the myth of Kumarbi can very possibly be associated with the elaborate and unique conglomeration of motifs on the **gold** bowl excavated by the University Museum of Philadelphia expedition under the direction of

Robert H. Dyson at **Hasanlu** in the Urmia basin of northwestern Iran in 1958. It is the privilege of the writer to have been the only person to draw this vessel at firsthand rather than from photographs. The focal point of the design shows a man with knuckledusters confronting a composite monster comprising a human figure emerging from a rock, from whose rear grows a scaly dragon with three heads. Tesub is depicted in a **chariot** drawn by a bull, his special animal, from whose mouth gushes a torrent of water, falling on the dragon below: behind him come two other chariots, drawn by **horses**. The date of the context from which this bowl was recovered is well attested by radiocarbon determinations around 800 BC. The period of its production is far less certain, though one suggested dating as high as the 13th century BC seems rather improbable. A valuable piece such as this would be unlikely to have survived more than three or four generations.

KUMMANNI. Though described as a city of **Kizzuwadna**, it lay in the extreme northeast of that land, and was generally reckoned in **Hattusa** to be a Hittite city. Identified with Classical Comana, it can be located north of Tutanbeyli, in the valley of the Sariz Su, one of the headwaters of the Seyhan River, flowing to the Mediterranean past Adana. This was a major **cult center**, listed in the prayer of **Muwatalli II**, with the **Storm-God**, **Hebat** of Kummanni and Ningal, wife of the Semitic Moon-God Sin, as the chief divinities worshiped there.

KURUNTA. The second son of **Muwatalli II** by a concubine and brother of **Urhi-Tesub**. His father entrusted his upbringing to his brother Hattusili (the future **Hattusili III**), who claimed to have treated him as his own son, alongside his younger cousin, the future **Tudhaliya IV**. There has been debate over the identity of **Ulmi-Tesub**, the prevailing opinion being that he was one and the same as Kurunta, who adopted his **Luwian** name on accession to the throne of **Tarhuntassa**. His birth name, like that of his brother, had been **Hurrian**.

Evidently on close personal terms with his cousin Tudhaliya, the theory of a coup d'état by Kurunta (1228–1227 BC), perhaps in the aftermath of the serious defeat suffered by the Hittite **army** in the east at **Nihriya**, appears at first sight implausible. He may of course have harbored resentment, as son of Muwatalli II, that his line of the royal family had been passed over in favor of the son and heir of Hattusili III. Yet Tudhaliya IV had caused a doctor to be sent from Egypt, with the consent of the Pharaoh **Ramesses II**, successfully to treat Kurunta for a serious illness.

The case for a coup d'état resulting in the seizure of the throne by Kurunta rests primarily on **bullae** found at **Hattusa**, bearing the inscription "Kurunta, Great King, **Labarna**, My Sun." By themselves these bullae do not provide absolute proof, only that he had come to claim a title not granted to him. There is, however, the circumstantial evidence of destruction at Hattusa—mainly along the walls and in the **temple** area—subsequently repaired as part of a wider building program directed by Tudhaliya IV. Civil strife seems indicated.

The fate of Kurunta following the regaining of his throne by Tudhaliya IV is unknown. If a deliberate policy of suppressing any record of an uprising was followed, it was all too successful. Kurunta is most unlikely to have been allowed to remain as ruler of Tarhuntassa.

The part played by Kurunta has become much clearer since the unearthing (1986) of a perfectly preserved bronze tablet under the pavement just inside the Sphinx Gate in **Boğazköy: Upper City**. The text, of 350 lines of **cuneiform Hittite**, is of a **treaty** drawn up between Tudhaliya IV and Kurunta. The preamble clarifies the role of Kurunta in the years following his uncle's usurpation of the throne from Urhi-Tesub, as well as providing welcome new data on **historical geography**.

KUŞAKLI. Located south of the provincial center Sivas, this is currently the site of excavations directed by Andreas Müller-Karpe. This has been identified with the Hittite Sarissa, listed by **Muwatalli II** in his long prayer invoking the Hittite **gods and goddesses** in relation to their respective **cult centers**. For this city the **Storm-God, Ishtar** and unnamed gods and goddesses are mentioned. Sarissa was associated with the widespread cult of a god of the countryside, whose symbol was a stag.

Kuşaklı has yielded Hittite building levels of both Old Kingdom and Empire. On the west slope three levels have been distinguished, the earliest of the Old Kingdom. The plans of houses of Empire date are similar to those found at **Alışar Höyük**: in domestic buildings continuity of design is unremarkable. There are both differences and similarities in **architecture** compared with **Boğazköy**. The design of the city gate of Kuşaklı is more akin to plans seen in Syria than at Boğazköy, where this plan is not found. Similarities to Boğazköy are the use of a causeway as access to the city gate and of drilled stone blocks, some filled with burnt wood. Temple II was a major structure, with at least 83 rooms, forming a single complex around a central court: there were two entrances, each three meters wide, one having a guardroom. This **temple** was possibly dedicated to the Storm-God, associated with a majority of Hittite cities. **Tablets** indicate the presence of **archives** in a major center not too far removed from **Maşat Höyük**.

KUSSARA. Earlier identification of this city with **Alışar** 10TB–C has been abandoned in favor of a more southerly location, probably in the Anti-Taurus region on one of the **trade** routes from Assyria, possibly near the Roman site of Commana Cappadociae.

Kussara attained its highest status during the later Colony period, ca.1900–1750 BC, when it was the seat of the dynasty of **Pithana** and his son **Anitta**, before shifting their center of power to **Nesa (Kanes)**. Hittite military and political power was first built up at Kussara, even if there was no blood line linking Anitta with **Hattusili I** and his successors. At his accession (ca.1650 BC) Hattusili I was based at Kussara, though soon establishing his new center of government on the ruins of **Hattusa**. Yet he must surely have retained a royal palace at Kussara, for it was there that he held a great **assembly** shortly before his death. It would seem a rather inexplicable move of the chief seat of government northward, away from a site relatively accessible to Syria and Mesopotamia, during the reign of the very king who initiated Hittite military and political involvement in the heartland of Near Eastern civilization. Awareness of the constant threat from the **Kaska** tribes to the north seems the likeliest explanation.

KUWALIYA. A land formerly located in the area around Lake Beyşehir, now identified as **Hapalla.** In accordance with the westward shift of a number of geographical names in Anatolia, Kuwaliya now seems likely to have included the upper Meander valley, in the modern province of Denizli, and thus the major site of **Beycesultan,** even though the Late Bronze buildings excavated there are not on the same scale as the Middle Bronze burnt palace of Beycesultan V. It lay along the Astarpa River (Akar Çay?), across from the frontier with Hatti. Kuwaliya would thus cover the route southwest to Dinar on one branch of the upper Maeander, and could well have included the other branch and thus the district of modern Çivril and Bronze Age Beycesultan. Alternatively, **Mira** may have extended far enough south from the area of Kütahya to include

Beycesultan.

KUZI-TESUB. He became known from publication in 1986 of **seal** impressions excavated at Lidar Höyük on the Euphrates River. He is styled "King of **Carchemish**, son of Talmi-Tesub." He was thus the fifth generation of **viceroys** descended from **Suppiluliuma I**. In 1987 Kuzi-Tesub was identified as the grandfather in the genealogies of two different kings of **Malatya** who were brothers, where—on their monumental **hieroglyphic** inscriptions—he has the titles of "Great King, Hero of Carchemish."

Kuzi-Tesub was in office in Carchemish when the downfall of **Hattusa** brought the end of the Hittite Empire. His claim to the status and title of Great King derived from his being the great-great-great-grandson of Suppiluliuma I: he presumably assumed this title after the end of the dynasty of Hattusa. He formed a link between the line of **viceroys** and a dynasty of at least four generations recorded at Malatya.

- L -

LABARNA (before 1650 BC). This king was regarded by his successors as the founder of the royal dynasty, and his name was assumed as a title by each king on his accession, though for his lifetime only, not after death. Clearly therefore his achievements must have been such as to command lasting respect; and it seems most improbable that he could have been confused with his grandson **Hattusili I**, even though their military feats are described in similar language by **Telipinu** in his *Proclamation*. Labarna was more likely to have been the grandfather than the uncle of Hattusili I, who recalled the rebellion against him as a warning against disunity in the kingdom.

Labarna was probably based at **Kussara**, previously the ancestral home of **Pithana** and **Anitta** and the likely focus of the early Hittite kingdom. There are no surviving records from his reign, the one major source being the later *Proclamation* of Telipinu, well over a century after his death. This included a historical prologue containing a message for posterity, namely, that only at times of unity in the royal family and stability in the Hittite homeland was military expansion possible. Had Labarna himself achieved this stability early in his reign, or did he inherit it? There is just a possibility that an earlier king, Huzziya, preceded him.

Labarna conquered far-flung regions as far south as the Mediterranean. Though there is no mention of campaigning in **Arzawa**, he did reach the Konya Plain. A suggestion that he may have been responsible for the burning of the palace of **Beycesultan** V is thus very doubtful. A later date, in the reign of Hattusili I, would fit the Hittite records. The *Proclamation* of Telipinu mentions the conquest of **Hupisna**, **Tuwanuwa**, **Nenassa**, **Landa**, Zallana, **Parsuhanta** and Lusa—assigned to his sons to govern, summing matters up thus: "Formerly Labarna was the Great King. Then were his sons, his brothers, his relations by marriage, his (blood) relations and his troops united. And the land was small."

The name of this king, like many in Hatti, was of **Hattic** origin and thus non-Indo-European, being written Labarna in **Hittite** but **Tabarna** in Akkadian and **Luwian**.

LALANDA. An area within the **Lower Land**, whose rulers prudently submitted to Hannutti, the general appointed by **Suppiluliuma I** to consolidate the recently reclaimed Hittite hold on the Lower Land, when they feared retribution from the Hittite **army**. Later, early in the reign of **Tudhaliya IV**, their rebellion is mentioned in a letter from the king to **Puduhepa**, his mother, when the people are described as "notorious troublemakers." This rebellion was suppressed.

LANDA. One of the conquered areas, in or near the **Lower Land**, assigned by **Labarna** to his sons to govern. It is listed between **Tuwanuwa** and **Nenassa** and between Zallara and Parsuhanta.

LAND GRANTS. These were probably given as early as the reign of **Hattusili I**, though surviving examples date to ca.1500–1300 BC, or late Old Kingdom and early Empire (the so-called **Middle Kingdom**). As reward for services rendered or to ensure their loyalty, Hittite officials were granted land in different localities: the king thus deliberately prevented concentration of wealth and power and the risk of sedition from a power base. Estates and landed property granted included not only open land but also gardens, woods and meadows and even the inhabitants dwelling there.

LANGUAGES. Anatolia was home to several languages whose antecedents can be traced back many generations before the first appearance of written records on the plateau shortly before the end of the third millennium BC, in the Old Assyrian *karum* of **Kanes**.

Just how many generations back remains uncertain, a matter of scholarly debate, since the rate of changes and development in language cannot be determined with any precision. Such is the orthodox view: exponents of glottochronology, who claim to know what sounds were produced by people speaking a given time span before the present day, set out formulae to support their arguments. It is fair, however, to state that few take them seriously. The principal spoken languages of the Bronze Age in Anatolia are **Hittite, Luwian, Hattic** and **Hurrian**, with **Palaic** only meagerly represented in surviving records. Hittite, Luwian and Palaic are undoubtedly Indo-European, a fact recognized for Hittite for the past century. Equally clear is the non-Indo-European character of Hurrian. Only Hattic presents a problem, discussed below. Akkadian was used, along with Hittite, for official documents, while Sumerian features in Sumero-Hittite vocabularies, being widely used in the training of **scribes**.

In the absence of genetic data such as are now available for prehistoric Europe, the ethnicity of the various attested population groups in Anatolia can be studied effectively only in the linguistic context. To grasp the salient factors in relation to the languages of prehistoric Anatolia, however, it is essential to go back several millennia, in an effort to determine their ancestry. This involves consideration of the so-called **Indo-Hittite** hypothesis, first published in a lecture by Edgar Sturtevant in the United States in 1938: at first largely overlooked, with the advent of World War II in Europe, it was then rejected by most specialists, for reasons not entirely academic. Less than 20 years ago opinion began to change, under the impact of fresh thinking in **Proto-Indo-European** (PIE) research, and now the Indo-Hittite theory has gained growing acceptance, though inevitably with wide divergences of application, and still rejected by many scholars. Until this line of inquiry was developed, it was very difficult to understand how Hittite could have been the direct ancestor of the majority of Indo-European languages, given its many idiosyncrasies.

Unlike other Indo-European languages, the Hittite verb is conjugated in only two moods, indicative and imperative, and in only two tenses, present-future and preterite. Moreover, it lacks the feminine gender, found in Proto-Indo-European languages. These lost certain elements retained in Hittite, while demonstrating innovations not found in Hittite or the other Anatolian languages. It is now generally, though not universally, accepted that there was a separation of **Proto-Anatolian (PA)** from the linguistic stem originating in one ancestral language termed alternatively Pre-PIE or Proto-Indo-Hittite (PIH). The two problems remaining unsolved are where and when this separation occurred: the more conservative view still attracting majority support would place this separation in the Pontic-Caspian region north and east of the Black Sea, on the basis of the likely location of the PIE homeland. This must imply a movement of population from the north into Anatolia, still impossible to date with any certainty, but perhaps in the late sixth or fifth millennium BC: the older opinion that such a movement did not occur till the fourth or even the third millennium BC can be discounted.

A radically different approach, first advocated in 1987 by Colin Renfrew, has attracted some support from archaeologists but much less from linguists: this would locate the earliest Pre-PIE or PIH homeland in south central Anatolia, including the Konya Plain, at a date as early as around 7000 BC. By this reconstruction of developments, the PA linguistic group would have remained on the Anatolian plateau, while the others, to be termed PIE-speakers, migrated north into the Pontic-Caspian region, whence they moved away in stages to form new Indo-European linguistic entities. Whichever theory is correct, the Anatolian languages evolving from their PA ancestor were destined eventually to die out, though only after several millennia, while the main body of Indo-European languages, from Sanskrit in the east to Celtic in the west, were to flourish indefinitely.

Efforts to reconstruct the PIH lexicon suggest an **economy** with no wheat or rye nor cattle. Words for "sheep" and "wool" have, however, been detected, but not for flax. The inclusion of wool in the PIH lexicon has aroused controversy, in the light of the absence of sheep with fleece suitable for spinning in the Near East before ca.4000 BC. This has caused linguists to question Renfrew's high dating for the separation of PA from PIE groups. An inland home for the PIH people has been suggested, since among terms for landscape there is none for "sea." Hardly remarkable is the absence of any word for metal. By this scenario the languages of the PA group would have begun to evolve at least during the sixth millennium BC or alternatively by the early fourth millennium, if they had come from a northern homeland.

Of the Indo-European languages spoken in Anatolia in the Bronze Age, Hittite is by far the best understood, because most richly preserved in the archives of **Hattusa** and elsewhere. Widespread as Luwian was as a spoken language, it is still only inadequately deciphered, though its dialect form, written in **hieroglyphs**, is now much better understood as a result of the long labors of **David Hawkins**, following earlier false starts. Another derived dialect form of Luwian was the language of **Lukka**, Lycian. The poorly represented Palaic, the language of **Pala** spoken in part of northern Anatolia and perhaps over a considerable territory northwest of the Hittite homeland in the bend of the **Marrassantiya River**, was probably closer to Hittite than to Luwian. Two major non-Indo-European languages were spoken by populations which arrived at different stages in Anatolia, both of which belonged to the North Caucasian linguistic family, the **Hattians** to its western and the **Hurrians** to its eastern branch. The latter gained a wide homeland in the highlands of eastern Anatolia from about the mid–fourth millennium BC, and then percolated slowly but surely into much of the Anatolian plateau west of the upper Euphrates, as well as into **Kizzuwadna** by the late third millennium BC. The Hattians appear to have settled earlier in central Anatolia, at least by some date in the fourth millennium BC. They constituted not a pre-Indo-European indigenous population, as long assumed, but rather an intrusive group supplanting the earlier inhabitants and presumably absorbing many of their traditions. Since that population was probably Hittite, it would be fair to claim that Hattian culture, in spite of its distinctive religious aspects and the affinities of Hattic, its language, became to a significant degree Indo-European.

While discussion of the different languages evolved in or introduced into Anatolia will tend to stress cultural differences, it would be mistaken to overstate these. By the second millennium BC much of the population of the Anatolian plateau was bilingual or polyglot. At the same time language was a channel for the perpetuation of ethnicity and cultural identity, in its written form most strongly represented in the **annals** compiled by some of the Hittite kings.

LAROCHE, EMMANUEL. The leading French Hittitologist, publishing seminal works on Hittite **language** and history, as well as contributions to the decipherment of the **Luwian hieroglyphs**. Professor at the Collège de France, formerly director of the French Institute in Istanbul and excavator of **Meydancık**, he published penetrating insights into the meaning of **Yazılıkaya**.

LATE BRONZE AGE POTTERY. A great number of sites have yielded an abundance of relevant **pottery**, published in excavation

Boğazköy (Upper City): Sarikale

Boğazköy (Upper City): Lion Gate

Boğazköy (Upper City): View north to Büyükkale (left background) and Temple 3 (center right)

Boğazköy (Upper City): Temples 3 (center) and 2 (right background)

Boğazköy (Upper City): Glacis (restored by Peter Neve) along main defenses

Boğazköy (Upper City): Exit from postern tunnel

Boğazköy (Upper City): King's Gate

Boğazköy (Upper City): King's Gate (inside end)

Boğazköy (Upper City): Chamber 2

Boğazköy (Upper City): Nişantaş inscription

Boğazköy: Büyükkale, general view from south

Boğazköy: Büyükkale

Boğazköy: Temple 1 (center) seen from Büyükkale

Boğazköy: Masonry of Temple 1

Yazılıkaya: Chamber A

Yazılıkaya: Meeting of processions led by Tesub (left) and Hebat

Yazılıkaya (Chamber B): Dagger god and (right) Sarruma embracing Tudhaliya IV

Yazılıkaya: Tudhaliya IV

Alaca Höyük: Sphinx Gate

Alaca Höyük: Two headed eagle

Alaca Höyük: Frieze including sword-swallower (replica)

Alaca Höyük: King worshipping at altar of Storm-God

Fraktin relief: Puduhepa in act of worship (Hattusili III far left)

Fraktin relief: Hattusili III as a "god," after his death

Imamkulu

Gavurkalesi: relief and citadel wall (right)

Ivriz relief in shade

Ivriz relief in sunshine

Eflatun Pınar (from the side)

Eflatun Pınar (from the front)

Fasıllar: colossal statue (close)

Fasıllar: colossal statue (distant)

reports including those on **Boğazköy**, **Maşat Höyük**, **Gordion**, **Porsuk Höyük**, **Kaman-Kalehöyük**, **Tarsus** and **Beycesultan**. In general, these sites demonstrate a decline in quality, aesthetic and technical, of the potter's craft from the Middle into the Late Bronze Age, especially in Late Bronze II (Hittite Empire). This is evident too in the land of **Isuwa**, notably at **Norşuntepe**. Beycesultan, located in the **Arzawa** lands, had an entirely different ceramic tradition until the final period (Beycesultan I), when Late Bronze Age pottery of central Anatolian types appears, perhaps marking a refugee movement from the Hittite Empire after the fall of **Hattusa**. Beycesultan was not finally deserted until around 1000 BC.

The pottery of Boğazköy reveals a considerable degree of continuity from **Büyükkale** IVd (contemporary with the Assyrian *karum* at the foot of the citadel) until the final period of the Empire (Büyükkale IIIa), beak-spouted jugs being especially prominent. There is also a range of handled vessels, flasks, bowls and platters. It is the finish of the pottery as a whole which displays a steady deterioration, pottery no longer carrying the status of earlier times, presumably supplanted in fashionable circles by metal vessels. One form distinctive of the last century or so of the Hittite Empire is a stumpy version of the beak-spouted jug, with thick stem and heavy ring base, the whole being smaller than the majority of beak-spouted jugs. As for surface treatment, a creamy white slip only very slightly burnished is distinctive of some Late Bronze Age wares in and well beyond the Hittite homeland. Many jugs have a round base, and lentoid flasks are common in the 13th century BC. Open bowls with round base and often with inverted rim are very common, and naturally well represented in surface collections of sherds from numerous sites. Many bowls have triangular handles, occurring from Büyükkale IVd at least down to the early Empire. Originality was hardly the mark of the Hittite potter.

The Late Bronze pottery from Gordion, after intensive study, has yielded technical and comparative data for the time of the Hittite Empire. Standardization of forms and rather careless finishing characterize the Gordion pottery. Painted pottery with unsophisticated linear decoration, very rare at Boğazköy, occurs also at Gordion. Color ranges from creamy white through buff to reddish orange or brown. Wheelmade and handmade pottery and vessels turned on a slow wheel are all found, the coil method often being employed for larger vessels such as *pithoi*. Simple surface smoothing was commoner than a slip. Small shallow bowls with rounded rim, about 17 centimeters in diameter and similar to examples from

Maşat Höyük and Boğazköy, are typical. Production techniques mirrored those found at Hattusa, though not every form found there occurs at provincial Gordion. Nevertheless, it seems plain that production of pottery here greatly exceeded possible local demand. Here, through **trade**, pottery was exchanged for raw materials in demand. Yet it is unlikely that the Gordion vessels were transported any great distances, since other centers of production would have made this inappropriate.

At the time of the excavations at Tarsus this was one of the most important sites for the study of Anatolian Late Bronze Age pottery, and remains so today. Plain monochrome ware came into general use in Late Bronze IIa (ca.1450–1180 BC), continuing in Late Bronze IIb (ca.1180–1100BC). Wet smoothing and more commonly burnishing in streaks are found in use. The sharply carinated bowls of Late Bronze I are replaced in Late Bronze IIa by thick-walled vessels, some with two handles. Shallow bowls and large flat platters, the ubiquitous hallmark of Hittite pottery, appear in Late Bronze IIa Tarsus, while high-pedestaled bowls had vanished. Jugs with round or pointed base outnumber those with flat or ring base and trefoil mouth, typical of the Hittite Old Kingdom (Late Bronze I) at Tarsus, pottery being generally wheelmade.

There was less ceramic continuity at Tarsus from Late Bronze I to Late Bronze IIa (Old Kingdom to Empire) than in the same periods at Boğazköy, where earlier slipped, highly burnished wares persisted under the Empire, suggesting more conservative potters. Imported pottery—from **Alasiya (Cyprus)** and Syria—was rare at Tarsus, where Mycenaean pottery of "Granary" style (Late Helladic IIIC) occurs only in the Late Bronze IIb levels, brought by the **Sea Peoples** after the sack of the public buildings of the time of the Empire.

Porsuk Höyük (Level V) has yielded abundant Late Bronze Age pottery, overwhelmingly plain, with a very few sherds with painted decoration. At **Kilise Tepe** there was strong ceramic continuity from Middle to Late Bronze Age, the most marked changes coming between Early Bronze III and Middle Bronze Age.

At Boğazköy flasks and bottles of coarse ware with rope impressions first appear with the reign of **Tudhaliya IV**; and these occur in small numbers in the final phase of Beycesultan II, whose pottery had developed from the rich variety of forms found already in Beycesultan III. Most distinctive is the "champagne glass," with shallow bowl and tall thin stem. Not only shapes but also wares are of metallic inspiration, with yellow, red and silvery mica in the clay imitating **gold, copper**/bronze and **silver** respectively.

With Beycesultan I, after the burning of the previous level, 24 new forms of pottery appear beside 27 preexisting forms. Diverse elements occur, including instantly recognizable central Anatolian Hittite forms, such as highly burnished red, orange or porcelain-colored flasks, lentoid bottles, hemispherical bowls with lids and coarse-ware platters and large dishes. The fine flasks occur in the 15th–14th century BC levels at Boğazköy, disappearing by the time that the other, less refined pottery appears there. At Beycesultan I, however, they occur together.

LAWAZANTIYA. Telipinu campaigned to the southeast against Lawazantiya, Zizzilippa and Hassuwa, the first two later recorded as belonging to **Kizzuwadna**, in its northeastern area. This city came into the limelight not long after the battle of **Kadesh**, when **Hattusili**, then serving his elder brother **Muwatalli II**, was permitted to return north. En route from Syria, he visited Lawazantiya, to perform rituals in honor of **Ishtar**, his divine protectress. There perhaps the most significant event of his life occurred, apart from his seizure of the throne, when he met and married **Puduhepa**, daughter of a priest of the goddess and herself a priestess. Hattusili declared his **marriage** to have been made in heaven, although it does seem to have been based on genuine affection. He could not linger in Lawazantiya, for serious troubles in his northern **viceroyalty** demanded his urgent attention.

LAWRENCE, THOMAS EDWARD (1888–1935). It is not universally realized that the man best known as Lawrence of Arabia and the author of *The Seven Pillars of Wisdom* began his career in archaeology, after leaving Oxford. He went to the Levant in order to study Crusader castles for his intended thesis. He was recruited by **D.G. Hogarth** for the British Museum excavations at **Carchemish**, where he continued to work until the advent of World War I, through the seasons of 1911–1914. He and **C. L. Woolley** were engaged in the spring of 1914 to carry out an archaeological survey of the Negev, at that time a sensitive frontier region within the Ottoman Turkish Empire, adjoining British-controlled Egypt and of interest to the authorities in Cairo at a time of growing international tension.

LAZPA(S). A dependency of the **Seha River Land** under Manapa-Tarhunda, it was attacked by Piyamaradu. Close to the land of

Wilusa, Lazpa can confidently be identified with the island of Lesbos. Less certain is the recent suggestion that it was the base from which Achilles and his forces landed near **Troy**, though probably some distance to the south of the city. It was the earliest Greek foothold off the north sector of the Aegean coast.

LELWANI. Hattian goddess of the **Underworld**, associated with the chthonic role of the **Sun-Goddess**. She attracted Hittite veneration ever since the Old Kingdom, when she had a sanctuary on **Boğazköy: Büyükkale**; but she did not attain her highest status until the reign of **Hattusili III**, when **Puduhepa** frequently prayed to Lelwani to cure her ailing husband, the king.

LIMMU. A uniquely Assyrian institution, the *limmu* was appointed for one year only, seemingly with no powers attached to the office but a certain honorific status. Normally an Assyrian king became *limmu* at his accession. Assyrian historical records tend to refer to the *limmu* for a particular year, sometimes an invaluable aid for **absolute chronology**.

LITUUS. Numerous examples on Hittite reliefs and **seals** long seemed to indicate a purely ritual or ceremonial function for this long staff, curving at its foot and ending in a spiral, so common in **sculpture** and **glyptic art** alike. The best known examples are perhaps at **Yazılıkaya**, in the figure of **Tudhaliya IV** in Chamber A and of the same king in the embrace of his protector **god Sarruma** in Chamber B. The lituus of Rome was used by the augur, and this Latin word is still in general usage among Hittite specialists, though the Hittite word is thought to be *kalmus*.

There is ample evidence, however, to assign a specific origin to the lituus, even if it often came to be ceremonial in character. This was the throwing stick, an essential item in the equipment for **falconry**, used to flush out game and in the hunting of hares: once flushed out, the game was chased, brought down and killed by the falcon or the hunter. In Anatolia, falconers long carried these throwing sticks, sometimes being depicted brandishing them.

Curved metal sheaths, 15 to 22 centimeters in length, in many of the Early Bronze II tombs of **Alaca Höyük** may well have belonged to the curved throwing sticks (litui) seen in the following period. These began to appear over the shoulders of falconers on Anatolian-style seal impressions, notably from **Kanes** and **Acemhöyük** in the time of *Karum* II. At **Fraktin Hattusili III** is depicted pouring a libation to a god shouldering the lituus. At **Yazılıkaya** the "stag god" Karzi (no. 32 in the male procession in Chamber A) may well be carrying a lituus. The **bullae** of **Kurunta** show a god on a stag brandishing a lituus behind him, presumably about to throw it.

The longer lituus seems to be the earlier form, surviving into the Iron Age at **Malatya**, carried by a king, and by a god on a lion at **Guzanu**. A very short lituus is carried by gods at Malatya, while the falconers with lituus at **Zincirli** appear to be off duty.

The falconers of Bronze Age and Iron Age Anatolia can justly be seen as the forerunners of those practicing this skilled sport in much later generations. The explanation of the lituus in Hittite art, otherwise having no obvious function, as the falconer's throwing stick poses the question why it seems to have assumed a regular significance in courtly ritual and monumental art. Hunting was ever a prime diversion for kings, princes and nobility from the tedium of affairs of state. But could this possibly represent a survival from times long passed, when hunting played a leading role in the **economy**? If so, royal prowess in this field—and nowhere more forcibly than in falconry—would have been a mark of leadership in **food** gathering, not merely in sport. This could hark back to the very first days of Hittite settlement in Anatolia, for which the evidence to date remains all too sparse.

LLOYD, SETON (1902–1996). After qualifying as an architect (1926), he began a distinguished archaeological career briefly in Egypt and then for nearly 20 years in Iraq, notably with the Chicago expedition to the Diyala valley north of Baghdad and at Eridu in the far south. In 1949 he came to Turkey to succeed the founder, **John Garstang**, as director of the British Institute of Archaeology at Ankara (1949–1961), subsequently holding the Chair of Western Asiatic Archaeology in the London Institute of Archaeology (1962–1969). While at Ankara he directed excavations successively at Sultantepe (Harran), Polatli, **Beycesultan** and (jointly with the author) at Kayalidere in **Urartu**. He brought with him the benefits of a training in **architecture**, in this respect unlike the majority of British and American archaeologists working in the Near East but in line with the German tradition. His disentangling of the heavily burned ruins of the Middle Bronze Age palace of Beycesultan V was an outstanding achievement.

Like **Leonard Woolley**, Seton Lloyd was a fluent writer, with a gift not shared by all his successors of being able to bring archaeology in the Near East to the general reading public. His *Foundations in the Dust* told the colorful tale of the pioneering days of archaeology in Mesopotamia. He was also the author of many excavation reports and articles.

LOWER LAND. This stretch of territory covered the Konya Plan and beyond to the southwest border of Hatti proper. Its possession was essential for the security of the Hittite homeland and for control of the main route south into **Kizzuwadna** and thence into north Syria.

The most critical phase in the history of the Lower Land, from the Hittite viewpoint, came with its fall to western invaders from **Arzawa** during the dark days of **Tudhaliya III**. It was here that his son had his first major confrontation with the Arzawan enemy, successfully expelling his forces from the Lower Land, though only after hard fighting. After his accession **Suppiluliuma I**, to end this threat to the Hittite homeland, appointed a seasoned commander, Hannutti, as governor. He was provided with infantry and **chariotry**, enabling him in due course to move against the Arzawan state of **Hapalla**.

Lalanda was an area which had come to heel at this time, but rebelled later, early in the reign of **Tudhaliya IV**, who feared for the security of Hittite rule in the whole Lower Land. Moreover, the secession of **Tarhuntassa**, obscure as the precise course of events remains, involved the southern areas of the Konya Plain, thus impinging on the Lower Land. This was **Luwian** territory, as demonstrated by the principalities of the early first millennium BC.

LUKKA. The region known by this name was the precursor of the Classical Lycia, extending over the southwestern corner of modern Turkey and increasingly popular with tourists. Though featuring quite frequently in the Hittite records, it was never one unified kingdom, and thus could not be brought under vassalage. Nor was its population at all consistent in loyalty to the kings in **Hattusa**, for there was often the contrary influence of **Arzawa**, the long-standing opponent of the Hittite state.

The men of the Lukka Lands had a long tradition of seafaring, which they put to good use through piracy in the eastern Mediterranean, at least from the **Amarna** period in the 14th century BC, with Greek historical sources revealing the depredations of Lycian pirates. In the Late Bronze Age they commanded the sea route from the Mycenaean world (**Ahhiyawa**) eastward to **Alasiya (Cyprus)** and **Ugarit**. Lycian was an Indo-European **language**, one of those derived from **Luwian**.

LUSCHAN, FELIX VON (1854–1924). Anthropologist and prehistorian, directing excavations at **Zincirli (Sam'al)** (1888, 1890–1891, 1894 and 1902).

LUWIAN. This **language** has been described as more vigorous than **Hittite** by as early as ca.2000 BC, with its **cuneiform** variety drawing on **Hurrian** and Akkadian scribal traditions and its separate, indigenous **hieroglyphic** variety. It is therefore rather surprising to find it so poorly deciphered compared with Hittite. One Russian specialist detected no fewer than 53 features distinguishing Luwian from Hittite; but his employment of the technique of glottochronology must put a question mark over his conclusions, which do not readily square with the **Indo-Hittite** hypothesis. Nevertheless, it is of interest to note his highlighting words connected with a number of aspects of everyday life and **religion**, which appear distinctive of Luwian and Hittite respectively, such as terms relating to **wheeled vehicles**, military matters and personnel, **women**, **wine** and vine, water and washing. As for religion, there are indications that evil was associated with the left side, and the right side with good luck. The Luwian language was ancestral to languages which evolved in western Anatolia—Lycian, Lydian and probably also Carian—in the early first millennium BC, the first of these being the language of Bronze Age **Lukka**.

The spread of Luwian eastward into **Kizzuwadna** may well, on the evidence of **pottery**, have initially come about by maritime links from the Lukka Lands and the Aegean region; but by the time of the Hittite Empire there was certainly a landward expansion of Luwian-speaking people, with their extensive penetration of the homeland of Hatti. This may, however, have occurred largely through the Hittite policy of **deportation**, deliberately increasing the population of the homeland for military and economic purposes. The original settlement of Kizzuwadna by Luwian immigrants may be associated with the appearance at **Tarsus** of pottery with parallels at **Troy** and elsewhere in the west, notably the "red cross" bowls of Troy V dating to late in the third millennium BC.

Luwian survived as a spoken language over the wide Neo-Hittite zone during the Iron Age, down to the destruction of the city-states by Assyria late in the eighth century BC. Ironically it was Hittite, in spite of being better represented in surviving records, which began to decline as a spoken language well before the fall of **Hattusa**, an event which brought about its disappearance from the linguistic map. The virility of the Luwian language is demonstrated by its manifestation in two scripts, cuneiform and hieroglyphic, the latter becoming the dominant medium of royal records by the reign of **Tudhaliya IV**. Grammatical divergences between cuneiform and hieroglyphic Luwian are exemplified by the absence of a genitive case from the former and its presence in the latter.

LUWIYA. A term applied by the Hittites to the greater part of western Anatolia in the Old Kingdom, in a general ethnic and geographical sense. This was supplanted by the name **Arzawa**, when political entities became more clearly defined, but it reveals the Luwian basis of the population.

- M -

MACQUEEN, JAMES G. A student of **Oliver Gurney**, he carried out an archaeological survey around the Salt Lake. Subsequently (until 1992) at the University of Bristol, he has contributed to the debate on **historical geography**, especially of western Anatolia, tending to accept the views of **James Mellaart**. He is the author of *The Hittites and Their Contemporaries in Asia Minor* (revised 1986).

MAGIC. No ancient Near Eastern people could cope with the hazards of life, not least with war and sickness, without the penetrating power of magic. In some sense it was the link between the more complex manifestations of **religion** and the unsophisticated beliefs and practices of the majority of the population, undirected by priest or **scribe**. Though the Hittites owed much to Mesopotamian and **Hurrian** traditions, their magical texts were a collection of individual prescriptions rather than official products of **temple** schools.

It was not so much the heartland as the outlying regions, notably **Kizzuwadna** and **Arzawa**, that supplied a large number of those skilled in the magical arts. Linked with these was the art of **divination**. Only when a **god or goddess** was involved were prayers and sacrifices necessarily incorporated to reinforce the rituals of magic.

Hittite magical texts are more illuminating than those of Mesopotamia and Egypt, for the name of the practitioner, his or her profession and sometimes also the nature of the emergency requiring attention are clearly described in the opening words and in the colophon at the end of the **tablet**. In Mesopotamia, however, the priest acted merely as the agent or intermediary of the god Ea, god of the waters, dictating instructions to his son, thus in the second person. In Egypt magical spells or rites were ascribed to Thoth, ibis-headed scribe of the gods. Early in the Old Testament Yahveh conveys ritual instructions to his subordinate Moses.

Most of those practicing magic were women, among whom the "Old Woman" or "Wise Woman" features most prominently. Rarer professions associated with magic were those of midwife, doctor, temple **slave** and temple singer. Male magicians were described either as a priest or, more often, as a type of diviner. One ritual is attributed to a king of Kizzuwadna, Palliya, thus antedating the annexation of this region to the Hittite Empire.

Animals were prominent in Hittite magical practice, ranging from bull to ram to goat to mouse. This last features in one of the simplest rituals:

> She (the Old Woman) wraps up a small piece of **tin** in a bowstring, and attaches it to the patients' right hands and feet; then she takes it off again, and attaches it to a mouse, saying: "I have taken the evil off you and attached it to this mouse. Let this mouse carry it on a long journey to the high mountains, hills and dales."

The technical word for such a scapegoat or animal carrier is *nakkussi*, revealed in a ritual of the city of **Samuha** in the **Upper Land**, designed to purge the king of any defilement caused by curses. Many creatures—human beings, animals and birds—could function as *nakkussi*. This was a Hurrian word, reaching Hatti, like most Hurrian terms, from Kizzuwadna. The idea of a living carrier to remove evil from the community appears in Syria as well as in Anatolia. One exception to the norm that the *nakkussi* was a living being was a boat, occurring in the ritual of Samuha: "They make little oaths and curses of **silver** and **gold**, and place them in the (silver- and gold-lined) boat."

The river was seen as bearing the uncleanness downstream. In common with the Hebrews of the Old Testament and other peoples of the ancient Near East, the concept of the scapegoat was fundamental to Hittite magical practice. The English word "scapegoat" clearly derives from the Old Testament (Leviticus 16), where Aaron is ordered to take two goats and to cast lots. One is to be offered to the Lord (Yahveh) for a sin offering; but the goat on which the lot falls is to be presented alive "for a scapegoat" (Authorized Version, 1611), surely as good a translation as any of the modern versions. This was to make atonement and to be released into the wilderness: "The goat shall carry all their iniquities upon itself into some barren waste, and the man shall let it go, there in the wilderness."

The concept of a moral dimension, or sin, in connection with the scapegoat was apparently unique to the Hebrews, with their incipient monotheism. For the Hittites and others the scapegoat was commonly employed to remove harm from the **army** before battle or from the royal family, **plague** and pestilence being a recurrent menace. The Hittites might lay a wreath of colored wool on a ram's head, then drive it toward the enemy, according to a prescription of one named Uhhamuwa, a magician from Arzawa in the west. The ritual of Pulisa requires a bull to be garlanded, the prescription ending thus:

> Whatever god of the enemy country has caused this pestilence, if it be a male god, I have given thee a lusty, decorated bull with earrings. Be thou content with it. This bull shall take the pestilence back to the enemy country.

And he does the same with a decorated ewe, if it be a female deity.

A more elaborate if similar prescription—that of Ashkella, a man of **Hapalla**—is inscribed on the same **tablet** as the ritual of Uhhanuwa mentioned above:

> Each army commander, the evening before battle, is to prepare a ram, twining a cord of white, red and green wool; a necklace, ring and chalcedony stone are to be hanged on the ram's neck and horns. At night they tie the rams in front of the tents and say: "Whatever deity has caused this pestilence, now I have tied up these rams for you, be appeased!" With each ram in the morning they take one jug of beer, one loaf and one cup of milk (?). Then in front of the king's tent he makes a finely dressed woman sit, and puts with her a jar of beer and three loaves. . . .The rams and the woman carry the loaves and the beer through the army, and they chase them out to the plain. And they go running on to the enemy's frontier without coming to any place of ours, and the people say: "Look! Whatever illness there was among men, oxen, sheep, **horses**, mules and donkeys in this camp,

these rams and this woman have carried it away from the
camp. And the country that finds them shall take over this
evil pestilence."

The animal in each case is offered to the enemy deity in lieu of
human flesh. Evidently there was a strong prophylactic basis to
much, if not most, of Hittite magic and its attendant rituals. The
appropriate ceremonies must have been seen as essential for the
morale of the army; ill fortune would immediately have been
blamed on any failure in this respect. It is hard, however, to avoid
the impression that the Hittite kings ensured that such rituals functioned in the higher interests of the state.

MAKRIDI, THEODOR. Conservator in the Imperial Ottoman Museum in Constantinople. He undertook excavations with **Hugo
Winckler** at **Boğazköy** (1906–1907 and 1911–1912), as well as
previously with him at Sidon in Phoenicia. At Boğazköy he has
been described as "companion, collaborator, government official
and executive head of the expedition all rolled into one." He had
no idea how to control the excavations, keeping hardly any records,
nor preventing robbery of **tablets** and other finds at **Hattusa**.

MALATYA (ARSLANTEPE). This site, now best known for its
fourth-millennium BC occupation, is one of three locations for this
settlement, situated in a very fertile, well-watered plain just west of
the upper Euphrates and commanding a major **trade** route from
north Syria and Mesopotamia into central Anatolia. The early town
is located at Arslantepe, a stratified settlement mound; then in the
Greco-Roman period it moved some kilometers to the site of Melitene, now called Eski (Old) Malatya; and finally it moved to the
present location of the burgeoning Turkish provincial capital, the
home ground of Atatürk's successor, Ismet Inönü.

Three expeditions have excavated at Arslantepe in the past 70
years. First was **Louis Delaporte** (1932–1939); then **Claude F. A.
Schaeffer** made some soundings, in the early 1950s, leaving a very
useful collection of **pottery** from successive levels from the fifth
millennium BC onward; but it has been the Italian expedition,
working here regularly since 1961, which has made the greatest
impact, in scale and quality of excavation alike. The first director
was **Piero Meriggi** (Pavia), followed successively by Salvatore
Puglisi and Alba Palmieri (both University of Rome). After the latter's untimely death (1990), the excavations have been directed by

Marcella Frangipane, whose major discoveries fall too early to be relevant here.

From ca.2700 BC emerged the local **Early Trans-Caucasian II–III** culture of the Elazığ-Malatya region, characterized by a distinctive handmade painted pottery (Arslantepe VIC–VID). During VID a walled town was well laid out to a plan, with large terraces around the mound. This local culture did not change radically in the ensuing Middle Bronze Age (ca.2000–1700 BC) (Arslantepe VA). The Italian expedition began its campaign of excavations in the northeast area of the site, near the buildings exposed by Delaporte: here the period of Hittite influence, during and after the Empire (ca.1500–900 BC), was distinguished by successive phases of town walls and gates. There does not appear to have been the resistance to Hittite rule implied by the destruction at **Korucutepe**, but that town lay within the enemy land of **Isuwa**.

The first historical reference to Malatya occurs in the context of a Hittite offensive not long before the beginning of the Empire, around 1400 BC. Immediately after the fall of the Hittite Empire and the sack of **Hattusa** which accompanied that catastrophe, **Kuzi-Tesub** was ruling **Carchemish** as successor to the imperial **viceroyalty**, his father Talmi-Tesub having been viceroy during the reign of **Suppiluliuma II**. The territory under his rule stretched along the west side of the Euphrates River, from Malatya in the north through Carchemish to **Emar** in the south, much reduced from the bounds of the imperial viceroyalty. Thus began the long history of Malatya as a Neo-Hittite center, lasting till the later eighth century BC.

Malatya is an example of the remarkable endurance of a place-name through many centuries, even millennia: to the Hittites it was Malidiya; to the Assyrians, Melid or Melidu; to the kings of **Urartu,** Meliteia; to Greeks, Romans and Byzantines, Melitene (Eski Malatya); and Malatya in Turkish times.

Malatya remained relatively peaceful until menaced by the Assyrian king Tiglath-Pileser I on his fourth campaign (1110 BC), having advanced through the land of **Hanigalbat** (originally the remnant of the kingdom of **Mitanni**) across the Euphrates, when he describes Malatya as being within "the great land of Hatti." That the territory was predominantly **Hurrian** is suggested by its earlier links with Mitanni and further by a **hieroglyphic** inscription from **Karahöyük (Elbistan)** mentioning Arhi-Tesub, king of Malatya.

After a period of weakness in Assyria, Assurnasirpal II (883–859 BC) summoned envoys from Malatya to the refoundation ceremonies at Nimrud (Kalhu). Shalmaneser III in his sixth campaign received tribute from Sangara of Carchemish and from Lalli, king of Malatya (853 BC), whose city was also among the objectives of his 15th and 23rd campaigns. Malatya was evidently considered necessary as a tributary state by the Assyrian kings: it was the decline of Assyria in the last years of the ninth century BC which left the way open to Urartian expansion westward under Menua (ca.810–786 BC). The next recorded king of Malatya was Suliehauali, mentioned in a rock inscription of Menua carved on the summit of a natural stronghold at Palu, near the Arsania (Murat) River. One section of the **annals** of Argishti I of Urartu (ca.786–764 BC) deals with campaigns in the west, mentioning Malatya and its king Hilaruada, though Urartian control in this region seems to have been firmly established by Menua. At some date after the accession of the next king of Urartu, Sarduri II (ca.764–735 BC), Sulamal succeeded Hilaruada as king of Malatya and joined the ill-starred alliance against Assyria, defeated at Halpa (Halfeti, not **Aleppo**) on the banks of the Euphrates and within the territory of Kummuhi, the Urartian Qumahi and Classical Commagene, lying south of the kingdom of Malatya. This victory by Tiglath-Pileser III (745–727 BC) began the process of final subjugation of the Neo-Hittite city-states and their annexation under direct Assyrian rule rather than as tributary states as hitherto. Sargon II (722–705 BC) completed this process, involving the destruction of Melidu (Malatya), which he "smashed like a pot." Its days as an independent entity were over.

The excavations under Delaporte revealed significant, if hardly sophisticated, examples of Neo-Hittite art in the form of reliefs of a period when Malatya was enjoying something of a renaissance of Hittite civilization from soon after the fall of the Empire. In due course, by the ninth to eighth centuries BC, cultural contacts with central Anatolia become evident in the occurrence of **Alışar IV ware**: the Euphrates formed a ceramic boundary, with scarcely any of this pottery to be found on the east side, in the western region of **Urartu**, which had its own wares.

The dating of the Malatya reliefs has been raised, so that they are now attributed to the 12th century BC and thereafter, making them the earliest examples of Neo-Hittite **sculpture**. In style they are forerunners of the Iron Age city of Carchemish, very much Hittite rather than Aramaean, with such details as the distinctive pointed footwear. Two of the most important reliefs, in the Lion Gate, are centered on the act of libation, portraying the king pouring a liquid offering to the gods, in each case into a handled vessel with ring base. In one scene the king faces four **gods**, headed by the **Storm-God**, grasping the telltale thunderbolts, with the second and fourth gods holding an **ax** over their left shoulder; the second god appears to be holding a lance. In the other scene the king faces left toward the Storm-God, and behind him is a related god riding a heavy **wheeled vehicle** drawn by a bull, the sculptor having failed to allow enough space on the block for a competent depiction. This last bears some similarity to one of the scenes on the **gold** bowl from **Hasanlu**, implying a shared **Hurrian** cultural heritage. Another relief demonstrates the memory in Malatya of the myths of its Hittite forebears: it shows the fight of the Storm-God against the dragon **Iluyanka**, depicted in multi-serpentine form. These reliefs can be attributed to the 12th and 11th centuries BC. Much later is a colossal **statue** of a king of Malatya in semi-Assyrianizing style and attributable to the eighth century BC.

MALPINAR. This village derives its modern name ("cattle spring") from an artificially enlarged cave whence a spring flows into the Göksu, a tributary of the Euphrates on its west bank and downstream from Samsat. The proximity of this spring may well have influenced the choice of location, 150 meters away, of a **hieroglyphic** rock inscription of Atayazas, largely dealing with offerings to his "**statue**." He styles himself "River-Lord of the cities Sarita and Sukita," with his overlord Hattusili being entitled "Ruler, King." The style is similar to the Boybeypınarı blocks, naming "Panamuwatis, wife of Suppiluliuma the Ruler. . . .mother of Hattusili." The Assyrian **annals** mention kings of Kummuh (Commagene) by the names of Qatazili and Ispululume (Hattusili and Suppiluliuma), recorded in the annals of Assurnasirpal II and Shalmaneser III (883–824 BC) and of Adad-nirari III and Shalmaneser IV (809–772 BC) respectively. It is clearly these who are named at Boybeypınari. By ca.750 BC another ruler, Kustaspi, was on the throne of Kummuhu, being the victim of an Urartian offensive recorded in the annals carved at Van of Sarduri II of **Urartu**.

MAMA. A kingdom flourishing only during the Old Assyrian period, it is best known from the letter written for Anum-hirbi, its king, and dispatched to Inar, then king of **Kanes**. Periodically at war, these kingdoms shared a common interest in protecting the profitable Old Assyrian **trade**, from which both benefited. While the precise location of Mama is uncertain, it probably was centered either at Göksün or in the Elbistan plain. If in the latter, its distance east of Kanes implies that, with their vassal territories, these two kingdoms commanded a wide territory controlling the route of the trade into Anatolia from Assur.

MARI. Major city on the right bank of the middle Euphrates, coming into indirect contact with the Hittite sphere through **Emar, Carchemish** and **Aleppo** in the early second millennium BC. Its prosperity always depended on transit **trade** between the cities of Mesopotamia and those of Anatolia and the Mediterranean coast, though it had workshops for **textiles** and other industries, flourishing at the same time as the Old Assyrian trade with **Kanes** and beyond.

The great palace of Mari, eventually comprising over 250 rooms and covering more than 34 hectares, was repeatedly enlarged over four centuries, until its destruction by Hammurabi of Babylon. The ruler of **Ugarit** asked Hammurabi to present his son to Zimri-Lim, last of the kings of Mari, to enable him to widen his education by visiting one of the recognized wonders of the world. This combined several functions, being the private residence of the royal family, the center of the civil service, the place of reception for foreign visitors and embassies and the depot for **taxes** and tribute received in the form of **food** and other commodities needing extensive storage space, a feature it had in common with all ancient Near Eastern palaces.

Some 25,000 **cuneiform** clay **tablets** were recovered by the French expedition under the late André Parrot in the inter war seasons, the work on the site having resumed after World War II. Of these 1,600 were found in one room, evidently an **archive**, within the civil service quarters and close to two rooms with benches and exercise tablets, the school rooms for the young trainee **scribes**.

One of the most interesting aspects of life in Mari, as revealed by its tablets, is the evidence for the relations of the settled urban population and agriculturalists with the pastoralists exploiting the less fertile land outside the limits of irrigation. If such a delicate balance of differing interests obtained also in the less fertile parts of Anatolia, as for instance the environs of **Acemhöyük**, there is no documentation yet found.

The removal of Mari, which never revived, from the international scene indirectly assisted the rise of the kingdom of **Mitanni** and eventually also the expansion of Assyria.

MARRASSANTIYA RIVER. The Hittite name of the river forming the natural but by no means impregnable frontier of the homeland of Hatti, from southeast to northwest. This was the Halys of Classical times and today the Kızıl Irmak (Red River), from the silt brought down each spring. This river is too shallow and swift-flowing to be suitable for navigation.

MARRIAGE. The Hittite attitude to marriage was down-to-earth and tolerant for the times. Naturally the economic aspects loomed large in the formalities leading up to official marriages, with substantial **gift exchange**, including the "bride-price" (*kusata*). While present-day thinking would not suggest a privileged position for married **women** in Hittite society compared with their husbands, the laws of property were by no means one-sided. A wife retained the dowry provided on marriage by her family, with the view of its eventual inheritance by her children: only if she predeceased her husband did he acquire the investment represented by his wife's dowry; and, if Babylonian practice was observed, this wealth might descend directly to the children. Nor were arrangements as straightforward as might be expected: if the wife went to become a member of her husband's family household, her dowry passed from the donors, her family, in a "patrilocal" marriage; but sometimes, for whatever reason, the young husband went to live with his wife's family, in a "matrilocal" marriage, when he surrendered his economic rights.

In some circumstances, such as marriage between a male **slave** and a free woman, her status might be at risk. Young persons were cautioned against this type of mixed marriage, but it was not forbidden. Incest—such as intercourse with a sister-in-law—was strictly forbidden, as for the same reason was homosexual intercourse within the family: this seems to have been intended more as a protection of health than a moral judgment. This was of course different from Mosaic Law, though Hittite custom happened to parallel Hebrew tradition, as stated in Deuteronomy 25: 5–6, positively enjoining the survivor of brothers to take his widowed sister-in-law as wife, with any offspring being given his dead brother's name. Thus was each branch of the family to be preserved.

With the notable exception of the king, who might take a number of wives through diplomatic alliances, monogamy was the norm in Hittite society, even for junior members of the royal family. Infighting might quite often have been averted if the king had been content with one wife and her children!

Rape, adultery and divorce all feature in the Hittite records. There was a genuine attempt to face the difficult question of consent in relation to rape: location, the laws decided, was the determining factor. If a man raped a married woman on the mountainside, he must die; if in her house, she must die. Adultery was a very serious offense in Hittite law. A husband committing a *crime passionel* by killing his wife and her lover if caught *in flagrante delicto* had committed no crime; but if he later sought recompense, he was obliged to go to court. His wife's fate would then depend largely on his decision: he might take her back and "veil" her, or he might demand her death, along with her lover's. The sentence then lay with the king or his judges. Sparing his wife meant, however, also sparing the life of her lover.

Marriages might be formal, with the *kusata* arrangement, or they might be simple cohabitation. In either type, divorce proceedings could be initiated by husband or wife, quite regardless of social status. Normally all but one child went with the wife after divorce, and property was equally divided. Occasionally divorce occurred in the highest circles, causing serious diplomatic repercussions, as happened with two kings of **Ugarit**, Ammistamru II and Ammurapi.

Hittite marriages could be affairs of the heart, as seems to have been true of at least two royal marriages, that of **Mursili II**, devastated by the untimely death of his first wife, and the famous union of **Hattusili III** with **Puduhepa**. In the latter case it is clear that the **queen** successfully combined conjugal and political roles.

MASA. A land difficult to locate with certainty, Masa seems to have shifted from a more northerly region, not too far east of **Wilusa**, southward toward **Lukka**, on the evidence of the Hittite records. One explanation could be that the people of Masa were seminomadic, and that the name represents a population group more than a well-defined territory.

A northerly location is indicated by most of the relevant Hittite records, from the campaign of **Suppiluliuma I** with his father **Tudhaliya III** against the lands of Masa and Kamalla through the capture of a disloyal vassal (Mashuiluwa) by **Mursili II** in his 12th year to the destruction of Masa by **Muwatalli II**. As recorded in his **treaty** with Alaksandu, he was coming to the aid of Wilusa. Later, Piyamaradu was causing trouble for **Hattusili III** in Masa and Karkiya.

In the reign of **Suppiluliuma II** Masa was among the targets of the first part of his western campaign, along with lands including Wiyanawanda and **Lukka**, as recorded in the **hieroglyphic Boğazköy: Südburg** inscription. A more southerly location for Masa is thus suggested, as likewise by the reference in the Tawagalawa letter. The inclusion of a mock battle in the rituals ordained by **Tudhaliya IV's religious reforms** hardly implies very friendly relations between the Hittite king and the men of Masa.

MAŞAT HÖYÜK. Attention was first drawn to this major Hittite site with the discovery of a **tablet** (1943). Excavations have been conducted by **Tahsin Özgüç**, of the University of Ankara (1973–1984). This site is located 116 kilometers northeast of **Hattusa**, 20 kilometers south-southwest of Zile and 312 kilometers east of Ankara, standing just west of the modern village of Maşat, and is almost certainly identifiable with the Hittite city of **Tapikka**. This was a major administrative center near the border with the **Kaska** lands, sharing the same material civilization with the **cult center** of **Arinna** (**Alaca Höyük**) and the seat of royal government (Hattusa).

The history of settlement here began in the third millennium BC, the Early Bronze Age ending with a burnt destruction. Maşat V likewise ended in violent burning, as did the contemporary settlements of **Kanes** (*karum* IB), **Boğazköy: Büyükkale** IVd and **Lower City** 4, Alaca Höyük 4, **Alışar Höyük** and **Acemhöyük**. Maşat IV was contemporary with early Büyükkale IVc (Hittite Old Kingdom).

Maşat III can be dated to the very early Empire (early 14th century BC), when Hittite control over the troublesome Kaska borderlands was briefly restored, after the setbacks under **Hantili II**. The **archive** of tablets, most being letters, may represent only a decade or so, in the reigns of **Tudhaliya I/II** and **Arnuwanda I**. Their "Middle Hittite" script is consistent with a dating ca.1400 BC. These tablets were found in the palace built on the citadel, with a contemporary **temple** in the lower city, both destroyed at the same time. The latter is very similar in plan to other Hittite temples, with paved central court, magazines and other rooms.

Very soon after the destruction of Maşat III, large new public buildings were constructed under **Suppiluliuma I**. Dating for Maşat II is provided by tablets, still in the "Middle Hittite" script, a seal impression and **seal** of Suppiluliuma found together in one major building. This building level was short-lived, destroyed probably in the reign of **Mursili II**, shortly before the second major

Kaska raid on the Hittite lands. Maşat II can be correlated with Boğazköy: Büyükkale IVb and Lower City 2. The city never fully recovered from this destruction.

Maşat I is likely to have been built directly after the previous destruction, very probably under the **viceroyalty** of Hattusili. A large building set on a high rock outcrop in the west sector of the citadel yielded tablets in the script of the Hittite Empire, attributable to **Hattusili III** and his successors. Many buildings were completely razed in the destruction of Maşat I at the fall of the Empire. There was some Iron Age occupation on the citadel.

The **pottery** from Maşat Höyük reveals a continuing tradition from the Middle Bronze Age until the destruction of Maşat II, with forms including teapots, goblets, beak-spouted jugs, "fruitstands," *pithoi* and braziers. Maşat I shows a complete break in ceramic continuity, with a range of vessels in the Hittite Empire style and its associated deterioration in quality. Most pottery has a buff, light red or gray slipped surface. Five Mycenaean IIIB vessels have been distinguished, hardly evidence of significant dealings with the Aegean world but demonstrating imports from **Alasiya (Cyprus)** via north Syria or **Kizzuwadna**.

Of the tablets 96, the largest number, are letters, sent by the king to his local officials; copies or drafts sent by officials to the king; and exchanges between officials, sometimes critical. One named Kassu, in command of regional defense and entitled "Overseer of the Military Heralds," was the most frequent addressee of royal letters. Next to him in rank stood Himuili, the local "Lord of the Watchtower" (*bel madgalti*). A Hittite text gives a detailed record of his responsibilities as district governor, especially important along the frontiers, where security was the prime requirement: fire and infiltration by hostile intruders mingling with the peasants returning in the evening from the fields were particular hazards. Another rank of official likewise answerable directly to the king was the *agrig*, in charge of the local government storehouse, the collection point for **taxes** and sometimes also an arsenal.

This was the first Hittite **archive** to be found outside Hattusa. Its tablets include **land grants**, inventories of goods and personnel and consultations with the **oracle**. The letters reveal the close attention to administration and security by the king, taking most decisions personally.

McEWAN, CALVIN W. He served in a senior capacity with the expedition of the Oriental Institute of the University of Chicago to the

Amuq plain (Plain of Antioch), where excavations were carried out
before the annexation of the Hatay by Turkey (1938). He subsequently directed excavations at **Tell Fakhariyah**, near **Guzanu
(Tell Halaf)** (1940).

MEDICINE. Among causes of sickness were reckoned sins of the fathers, a concept of course not peculiarly Hittite. Ritual acts, including speech, were highly relevant. Many **gods and goddesses** could
be healers, among them Ishara, **Sausga** and Kamushepa. It is not
known that any Hittite **temples** functioned as sanitoria, but prayers
and **divination** had their roles, as did female healers or diviners
and midwives, some having their own associations. External influences had a significant impact on Hittite medical theory and practice, **Luwian** and **Hurrian** traditions being incorporated. Already
in the Old Kingdom Hittite physicians are recorded, some probably
trained by Assyrian doctors, whose influence may have been
stimulated by the importation of the **cuneiform** script under **Hattusili I**. Professional healers were brought in from Mesopotamia
and Egypt during the Empire, on one occasion on the initiative of
Ramesses II. As for symptoms, disorders of eye, mouth, throat and
intestine are recorded.

In spite of the extended plague prayers of **Mursili II**, the epi-
demic which struck the Hittite realm with the arrival of Egyptian
prisoners of war at the end of the reign of **Suppiluliuma I**, and
which persisted for some 20 years, remains unidentified, for lack of
description of the symptoms.

Poor sanitation was a major cause of sickness, more so in the
towns than villages. Drain pipes have been found at **Boğazköy**,
Alaca Höyük and other Late Bronze Age centers, some wealthier
households at Boğazköy and elsewhere having toilets. Dysentry
must have been endemic, with dire effect on infant mortality. Pestilence was a recurrent fear for the **army** embarking on a battle, lest
it be contracted from the enemy. **Magic** was the most usual anti-
dote.

MELLAART, JAMES (1925–). He graduated in Egyptology (Leiden
and London). In 1951 he began his first archaeological survey, or
reconnaissance, continuing into 1953, across the southern regions
of the Anatolian plateau, from the Konya Plain westward. Assistant
director of **Beycesultan** excavations, with **Seton Lloyd** (1954–
1959), he excavated Hacilar and Çatal Höyük (1957–1965).

He has published excavation reports and numerous articles on pottery, **historical geography** and other aspects of Anatolian pre-history, including Indo-European migrations. While his work has largely centered on earlier periods, he has long participated in debates on Hittite matters. He has also distinguished the different cultural provinces of Anatolia, previously inadequately discerned.

MELLINK, MACHTELD. Professor and long-serving faculty member in Bryn Mawr. A widely renowned archaeologist many years active in Anatolia, where her fieldwork has included excavations at Karataş-Semayük, just southeast of Elmali, in the plain in the Taurus region. She has put every Anatolian archaeologist in her debt by her annual reports, published in *The American Journal of Archaeology*, with short contributions from excavators, usually within a year of their previous season.

MERIGGI, PIERO. Italian Hittitologist. He attempted decipherment of the **Luwian hieroglyphs**, although his work is now largely superseded. He led archaeological surveys in the areas between Sivas and **Malatya (Arslantepe)**, where he became the first director of the Italian excavations, succeeded by Salvatore Puglisi, Alba Palmieri and now Marcella Frangipane.

MERSIN (YUMUKTEPE). British excavations, directed by **John Garstang** before and after World War II, revealed a succession of occupation levels beginning in the Neolithic period (seventh millennium BC). While less informative than its neighbor **Tarsus** for the Bronze Age, the expansion of the Hittite Old Kingdom into **Kizzuwadna** was apparent in the design of its **fortifications**. Towers were built wherever the wall changed direction, and a street along the inside allowed movement of the garrison as required.

METALLURGY. The metalsmiths who served the requirements for peace and war of the Hittite state were highly skilled and in all probability well organized and able to guard the secrets of their trade; and it was in the interests of the Hittite kings that they should do so, for it protected their advantage over their international rivals, who did not possess the resources of the Anatolian highlands. The Hittite state inherited a metallurgical tradition extending back well into the third millennium BC and indeed even earlier. Only with the expansion of **iron** working beyond its early limited uses was that tradition seriously threatened. Hittite texts mention iron blooms, lumps of ore and hearths.

Hammering and casting were used largely for tools and **weapons** but also for a variety of nonutilitarian items such as figurines and personal ornaments. The exploitation of alloys was first developed late in the fourth millennium BC, the commonest in early Hittite Anatolia being arsenical **copper**, continuing the tradition evident at **Alaca Höyük** and elsewhere in the Early Bronze Age and outlasting the imports of **tin** in the Old Assyrian period. Alloys of copper with nickel, tin and lead occur under the Hittite Empire.

It was in remote, relatively inaccessible mountain sites that the laborious tasks of mining, extraction, smelting and refining were carried out, unfortunately not recorded in the Hittite texts. For such a record it is necessary to turn to the Assyrian **annals** of the first millennium BC. Modern mining activities are of limited use in efforts to pinpoint prehistoric metallurgical sites, since the smaller metal sources once exploited have no commercial value today. Archaeological science, however, includes the technique termed lead isotope analysis, now quite widely employed to determine sources of metals.

Sheet metal was produced and shaped, and jointing was achieved by casting or riveting. For decorative metalwork and personal ornaments the various techniques found as early as the mid–third millennium BC in the "Royal Cemetery" of Ur in southern Mesopotamia—chasing, cloisonné, filigree, granulation, gilding and repoussé—were practiced in Hittite Anatolia, with wire-drawing as an innovation. Repoussé was the technique used for the small-scale friezes on a bowl from the rich hoard of metal vessels from **Kinik** (Kastamonu).

METALS. *See* **COPPER; GOLD; IRON; KESTEL; METALLURGY; METALWORK; SILVER; TIN.**

METALWORK. The rich metal sources of the Anatolian plateau and mountains, contrasting with the metal-starved Tigris-Euphrates basin of Mesopotamia, might suggest that the Hittite state would have been wealthier than Assyria or Babylonia, not dependent on long-distance **trade** for these raw materials, essential in peace and war alike. Internal dissensions and a chronic shortage of manpower, however, reduced this natural advantage. The relative paucity of metal artifacts among the finds from excavations is nevertheless no reflection of the quantity and variety of metalwork manufactured by artisans under the Old Kingdom and Empire nor of the production and uses of **iron**, from early beginnings to the fuller exploitation of this metal in the first millennium BC.

Apart from some smaller tools and weapons, direct knowledge of metalwork derives overwhelmingly from burials and hoards rather than buildings, normally emptied on abandonment or looted at their destruction. This goes to explain the taste among archaeologists until fairly recent times for excavating cemeteries. Metalwork can be broadly classified into a few main categories, in the Hittite lands as elsewhere in the ancient Near East: tools for farming, construction purposes and fashioning objects of wood or bone; components for **wheeled vehicles**; items or parts of furniture; **weapons and military equipment**; jewelry and personal ornaments; and vessels of all sizes, utilitarian and decorative. Metal was also used for some **seals** and, uniquely, for the **cuneiform** text of a lengthy **treaty**, the other copies of which have not survived or at least remain to be found.

The survival of metalwork is indeed a matter of chance, most being melted down for reuse in antiquity, plundered after enemy attack or looted by grave robbers in modern times. The Turkish Republic has an uphill struggle to foil the efforts of those trying to satisfy the demands of the market for antiquities.

Relevant to the centuries of the Hittite state are assemblages of metalwork from central Anatolia excavated at **Boğazköy**, **Alaca Höyük** and **Maşat Höyük**, as well as recently published hoards from **Kinik**, near Kastamonu north of Ankara, and from the area of Bolu further west. The latter hoard includes a number of shaft-hole axheads and plain bowls. Though tools and weapons do survive, their disproportionately small numbers suggest that it was these which were most likely to be melted down rather than ritual objects offered to the **gods**.

Figurines and pins of bronze are common, but decorated vessels such as rhytons are rarer. **Swords** and **axes** could be decorated in relief against a smooth ground. The best known objects ascribed a ritual purpose are: the bronze **spearhead** inscribed "**Anitta** the king"; a sword dedicated to **Nergal**; a sword recording the victory of **Tudhaliya I/II** over **Assuwa**; and a spearhead inscribed *walwaziti* ("Great **Scribe**").

The evidence for metalwork of Hittite times does not stop at the surviving examples now in museums or private collections. There are three categories of data to be noted. First, the pictorial record, from **sculpture** and **seals**, including the so-called Dagger God at **Yazılıkaya** and, best known of all, the battle-ax held by the figure, almost certainly divine, in the "King's Gate" at **Hattusa**.

With its spiked butt it resembles axheads found widely in western Iran, especially in the cemeteries of Luristan, exemplifying the cosmopolitan character of the metalworkers' trade, recognizing no political frontiers. In the Neo-Hittite zone of the first millennium BC, a distinctive metal artifact was the crested **helmet**, as worn by the soldiers of ca.900 BC depicted on the Long Wall at **Carchemish**, and the precursor of the helmets of Classical times in Greece.

Almost the richest source of information on metalwork is derived from the Hittite texts, the Assyrian **annals** with their long lists of itemized plunder and tribute giving even more vivid detail for the early first millennium BC. Hittite state inventories list military equipment such as **chariots**, **horse** bits, arrows, axes and maces; sickles too are recorded. Luxury items also are listed, among them those associated with **dress**, for which **gold** and **silver** brocade and appliqués were clearly in fashion at court in Hattusa. Gold and silver necklaces as well as pins, pendants and beads contributed to rich trousseaux of personal adornments. Bathtubs of **copper**, cymbals and other musical instruments appear too. Metalwork might occur also among items presented as diplomatic **gift exchange** or as tribute or a straight gift to placate a possible antagonist: that this occurred at a very early stage is demonstrated by the gift of an iron throne to Anitta, king of **Kanes**. Such items as writing implements of gold have not been recovered, nor are ever likely to be. Cream, yellow, blue, gold and silver colors sparkled on ceremonial paraphernalia, inlaid with metals and stones and adorned with materials ranging from ivory to lapis lazuli and crystal. Human **statues** are recorded as being fashioned of wood or cast in iron, with gold, silver and **tin** inlays. Figures of lions and bulls made of iron were associated with the major divinities.

A third category of evidence on metalwork is less direct but very widespread, being related in essence to vessels of many forms and sizes. For some years students of Anatolian **pottery**, not exclusively that from the Hittite lands, have recognized the pervasive impact of metalwork on the potter, though this is more prominent on **Middle Bronze Age pottery** than on that of the Hittite Old Kingdom and Empire, when the quality of pottery by and large declined. Whether this was the result of a greater use of metal vessels is far from certain. There can be no disputing the *skeuomorphs* discernible on many pots, the imitations of rivets and handles, the long spouts and carinated, or sharply angled, profiles, represented in fired clay but more natural in metal: for example, a carinated profile strengthens a metal vessel but creates a potential line of fracture for a pot. High burnish may even be another indication of metallic origins. These are apparent at many sites, including **Kültepe (Kanes)** in the Middle Bronze Age and **Beycesultan**—in Hittite times in the **Arzawa** lands—from Early Bronze III to the end of the Late Bronze Age. Here a deliberate admixture of mica of different colors with the clay produced the effect of gold, silver and copper: forms, too, were largely of unmistakable metallic inspiration, including goblets with slender stem. In prehistoric Iran also there was clear metallic impact on pottery of the finer qualities. Indeed the plunder of clandestine excavators in Iran as well as the contents of certain private collections suggest that for every pottery form there exists a gold or silver prototype. *See also* **METALLURGY**.

MEYDANCIK KALESI. Fortified citadel in **Kizzuwadna** of Hittite Empire date, with later Persian, Hellenistic and Byzantine remains. Excavations were directed by **Emmanuel Laroche**, who erroneously believed that this might have been the royal residence in **Tarhuntassa** of **Muwatalli II**, whose name can be read in one of the **hieroglyphic** inscriptions at this site. On the corner of the monumental northeast entrance is the upper part of a relief of a royal figure, similar in style to the **Hanyeri-Gezbel** relief. The Hittite masonry is composed of regular courses, though of differing height and only roughly dressed, not to be termed **cyclopean**.

MIDDLE BRONZE AGE POTTERY. From excavations and surface surveys alike a marked change is evident in the **pottery** following the end of the Early Bronze Age throughout and indeed beyond central Anatolia. At the risk of oversimplification, it can be said that handmade dark burnished wares, fired at a low temperature, give way to wheelmade red and buff wares, fired at a high temperature and commonly highly burnished. Painted decoration is relatively rare. The influence of metal prototypes is certain, probably including the characteristic "teapot" jugs with long spout and pronounced carination, a hallmark of this period. It must be stressed, however, that it is primarily in the main centers that this radical change in pottery is to be seen. As in all periods, the villages and small towns of Anatolia remained conservative in material culture and in other respects, tending to cling to earlier styles. Ceramic changes of fashion were largely the effect of external contacts through **trade** and conquest, explaining the extraordinary variety of pottery from the excavations of **Kültepe (Kanes)**, where the native Anatolian population lived side by side with the Assyrian merchants, albeit in separate quarters.

In Kültepe *karum* II, no fewer than 20 forms, including the "teapot" with "basket" handles, were continuing earlier Anatolian types, though some altogether new vessels appear, among them "fruitstands" with eagles perching or antelopes sitting on the rim, jugs with quatrefoil mouth and vessels shaped like a bunch of grapes, a hint of the importance of **wine** for the economy. Painted designs are distinctive of *karum* II, though the popular "pot-hook" motif originated in **Alışar III ware**. Contacts with north Syria are evident, but there is no slavish ceramic imitation.

There are marked differences between the pottery of Level II and Level IB of the *karum* of Kanes: the typical Middle Bronze Age highly burnished, red-slipped ware gave place to wares simply wet-smoothed, leaving the color of the clay on the surface. Painted pottery was now less prominent, but comprised Anatolian products and the widespread Khabur ware at home in north Syria and upper Mesopotamia, where it persisted for some centuries. The distribution of Kültepe IB pottery was much wider in Anatolia than that of Kültepe II had been, indicating the expansion of the Old Assyrian trading network. Bronze vessels found in the graves of Kültepe-*karum* II and IB provided prototypes for many pottery forms, such as jars with "basket" handles and strainer funnels with short feet.

In the Kültepe IB period (later 19th century BC) pottery similar to that from Kanes has been found especially at **Alışar Höyük** and also at **Alaca Höyük**, **Boğazköy** and even **Gordion**.

In Alışar II, wrongly described by the excavator **Hans Henning von der Osten** as the "Period of the Hittite Empires," the pottery was wheelmade and predominantly plain and wet-smoothed, the grape-cluster jugs being of necessity handmade. Much of the pottery has slightly burnished buff slip or a yellowish to red slip, more highly burnished. The highest burnish occurs on vessels such as the "teapots." Many shallow bowls and small cups also occur, the latter echoing the painted examples in Alışar III Ware. Relief decoration representing animals in whole or part occurs especially on pots with spouts or handles.

MIDDLE KINGDOM. This term is sometimes applied to the period of decline and internal dissension around the royal house, approximating to the 15th century BC and spanning those reigns between the death of **Telipinu** and the beginning of the New Kingdom (Empire) with **Tudhaliya I/II**. In political terms this means little, but it represents the greater part of the time span in which the Middle Hittite script was in use, extending into the early Empire.

Aluwamna succeeded Telipinu. The throne was then seized by Tahurwaili, possibly one of the three assassins of Huzziya I. There followed the reigns of the kings **Hantili II**, Zidanta II, Huzziya II and **Muwatalli I.**

MILLAWANDA (MILAWATA). The identification of this with Classical Miletos, long the focus of fervent scholarly debate, is of crucial significance for the interpretation of the **historical geography** of Late Bronze Age western Anatolia. If it is placed much further north near the Sea of Marmora, in the area here identified as **Wilusa**, then a whole string of geographical locations has to follow. This did seem perfectly arguable, along with locations for a number of lands further east and closer to the Hittite homeland, before the discovery of new inscriptions of **Tudhaliya IV.** All these clarify points of geography, not least among these being the Bronze Tablet. Linguistically, there has been some doubt about the identification of Millawanda with the Greek form Miletos, owing to the disparity with the Late Bronze Greek (Mycenaean) form of the name. On the other hand, the Hittites, unfamiliar with this place-name, may well have given it a form more acceptable to them, by adding the suffix -*wanda*, occurring in some 50 names, while the prefix *mil-* is common in Hittite contexts. The weight of probability therefore now favors equating Millawanda and its alternative form Milawata with Miletos, fitting in with the archaeological evidence.

In the third year of **Mursili II**, Millawanda became in some way involved in an anti-Hittite alliance led by Uhhaziti, king of **Arzawa**, and by **Ahhiyawa**. Hittite commanders were dispatched against Millawanda. Though this may have been little more than a raid, the destruction of Level II at Miletos, revealed by excavations, could be connected with this Hittite intervention, lacking textual support. Miletos throve as a port, on the maritime **trade**, yet was geographically isolated from the Anatolian hinterland, explaining the evident inability of Mursili II to retain control of Millawanda-Miletos. The **pottery** of both **Troy** and Millawanda, however, shows changes in the phase termed by Mycenaean scholars Late Helladic IIIB which could reflect the destruction of greater Arzawa by Mursili II and its reduction to a number of vassal kingdoms.

A generation later **Hattusili III** marched down the Maeander valley to Iyalanda-Alinda. From the city of Iyalanda he attacked the land of that name, then advancing to the boundary of Milla-wanda, which probably extended across the isthmus of the peninsula on which Millawanda stood. There he negotiated the surrender of the renegade fugitive Piyamaradu. It is quite clear that Milla-wanda was now ruled by **Ahhiyawa**.

Although it might be thought that Millawanda was of major significance to the Hittite kings, it meant much more to the Mycenaean merchants and settlers from Ahhiyawa. In fact, Milla-wanda is mentioned in only three Hittite sources, the Extended Annals of Mursili II and the Tawagalawa and Milawata letters of Hattusili III and Tudhaliya IV respectively, in the latter commanding but three lines. The Hittite kings were more concerned with territories a little removed from the coast; and it seems that Tudhaliya IV, in addressing "my son," was writing to Tarkasnawa, king of **Mira**, who was holding the ruler of Wilusa, Walmu.

In the generations following the end of the Hittite Empire and of the Late Bronze Age world, many settlements in western Anatolia perished; but major communities, including Miletos, survived. Indeed they prospered, with the whole region, benefiting from the immigration of Aeolian and Ionian settlers from across the Aegean Sea.

MIRA. This kingdom is attested over four Hittite royal generations, from **Suppiluliuma I** to **Tudhaliya IV,** being most fully documented in the reign of **Mursili II.** Tarkasnawa (formerly read Tarkondemos) was probably the son of the third attested king of Mira, Alantalli, and contemporary with the later years of Tudhaliya IV. He seems to have been a major Hittite ally in the west, and as such to have helped to thwart the ambitions of **Ahhiyawa** in the region. Though his name is not preserved in the **"Milawata letter,"** he is the most likely recipient, the sender being almost certainly Tudhaliya IV.

The reference to Mira in the **Karabel** inscription of Tarkas-nawa clinches its general location in central western Anatolia rather than far inland on the plateau, although it surely did extend over the Kütahya area, some 250 kilometers from the Aegean coast. Mira shared a common frontier with the Hittite state through the area of Afyon, and was originally landlocked. Only with the collapse of **Arzawa** on its comprehensive defeat by Mursili II did territorial rule by the kings of Mira extend westward to the Aegean Sea, when the Karabel monument was carved. Mira had in effect become the vestigial Arzawa, its capital located at Apasa (Ephesus). The best natural road uniting this territory from plateau to coast ran down the Maeander (Menderes) valley.

Four cities in Mira were fortified and garrisoned on the orders of Mursili II. There may or may not have been a city named Mira, as the seat of government. Though far inland, the Byzantine name Meiros, located at Malatça Höyük, is a possible site.

MITANNI. A major power in the Near East from mid–16th to mid–14th century BC, centered in north Syria east of the Euphrates River. During that time it posed a recurrent threat to Hittite ambitions: this danger had first appeared with the harassment by **Hurrian** tribes of the Hittite **army** under **Mursili I**, during its withdrawal from the raid on Babylon (1595 BC). These were the precursors of Mitanni, which at its greatest extent controlled lands from its vassal **Kizzuwadna** in the west, thus cutting Hittite access to north Syria, to Arrapha (Kirkuk) in the east. It was probably just after Thutmose III's campaigns extending Egyptian power in Asia (ca.1458–1438 BC) that Saustatar, then king, reunited Mitanni after its setbacks against Egypt, defeated Assur and made the king of Arrapha his vassal. In the west he was suzerain of **Alalakh** and **Ugarit**. The kingdom of **Aleppo** had already been absorbed.

When a **treaty** was drawn up between Mitanni and Egypt under Amenhotep II (ca.1425–1398 BC), fixing for decades the frontier in Syria between the two powers and sealed by a diplomatic **marriage**, it seemed that Mitanni had entered upon a period of prosperity and peace. This was to end first with internal conflict within the royal house, a recurrent drain on Mitannian strength; and then through enemy attack, by the Hittite army under **Suppiluliuma I** (ca.1340/1339 BC), marching against Tusratta, who had been put on the Mitannian throne as a minor after the murder of the previous king. A further blow to Mitanni came with the failure of Akhenaten, then pharaoh (1352–1335 BC), to continue his gifts of **gold**, doubtless reflecting the declining prestige of Mitanni in the face of Hittite expansion.

Though its memory lingered on, Mitanni was effectively brought under Assyrian rule by **Shalmaneser I (1263–1234 BC)**, marking the end of **Hurrian** political power in the Near East.

The name of the kingdom derives from a personal name, Maitta, found at Nuzi, changed to a geographical name, Maittani and later Mitanni. The first reference is in an Egyptian tomb inscription at Thebes of Thutmose I (1504–1491 BC). Known to the

Hurrians as Hurri, the term applied by the Hittites, Mitanni was Naharina to the Egyptians. It was **Hanigalbat** to the Assyrians, a term continuing for some centuries, though shifting rather north-westward.

Much attention has been devoted to a non-Hurrian element in Mitanni, on linguistic evidence clearly Indo-Aryan. Highly influential as this group was, they were undoubtedly a small minority among their Hurrian subjects. They included, however, the royal house, whose names were all Indo-Aryan: among these Tusratta may mean "owner of terrible **chariots**," while Biridashwa means "possessing great **horses**." Mitra and Indra were among the divine witnesses to a **treaty** between Suppiluliuma I and Kurtiwaza of Mitanni. Theophoric names seem to be Indian rather than Iranian, many recalling Indo-Aryan proper names of later periods. Vedic deities have been identified, including Indra, Soma, Vaya (Wind), the Devas, Svar (Heaven) and Rta (Divine Law).

The backbone of state and society in Mitanni was the chariot-owning nobility or chivalry termed *mariyanna*, a word very possibly derived from the Old Indian *marya*, meaning "young man" or "warrior." These exerted a significant influence on Hittite military thinking, notably in the deployment of chariotry, the training of horses and the adoption of the composite bow (*see* **ARCHERY**). Mitanni was indeed a formidable force in battle; but it proved unable to curb the ambitions of rival contenders for the throne. As time passed, especially in western cities such as **Alalakh**, this knightly class came to abandon the hazards of the battlefield in favor of the prosperity to be gained from becoming major land-owners. A more conservative ethos seems to have prevailed in the east of Mitanni, where ownership and management of chariots remained a prerequisite of membership of this privileged caste, requiring considerable wealth.

MITTANNAMUWA. A high official who was promoted to the rank of "Great **Scribe**" under **Mursili II**. When his successor, **Muwatalli II**, decided to move the capital south to **Tarhuntassa**, he was appointed administrator of the city of **Hattusa**, the former capital, probably under the overriding authority of the king's brother, the future **Hattusili III**. Meanwhile, the son of Mittannamuwa was in turn appointed Great Scribe. His family, however, may have fallen out of royal favor, for at some future date, under **Urhi-Tesub**, this son is found no longer in office. The family fortunes were restored when Hattusili negotiated with his nephew, resulting in the appointment of another son of Mittannamuwa, now an old man, as Great Scribe. It is evident that Hattusili had close links with this family.

The Great or Chief Scribe held a highly respected governmental office, whose title can perhaps be compared with that of secretary of state in our own times. At **Emar**, on the middle Euphrates, the holder of this office was termed the "king's son."

MOUNT SIPYLUS. *See* **SIPYLUS, MOUNT.**

MUKIS. A territory lying north of **Aleppo** and from time to time under its rule, it was conquered in a rapid campaign by **Suppiluliuma I**, after his defeat of **Mitanni** and capture of its capital **Wassukanni**. When Mukis proved an unwilling vassal of Hatti, **Ugarit** was persuaded to join Suppiluliuma against **Nuhasse** and Mukis, whom he called his enemies. He gave much of Mukis to Niqmaddu II of Ugarit, increasing his realm almost fourfold. Suppiluliuma then extended the kingdom of **Carchemish** (under the **viceroy** Sarri-Kusuh) to the borders of Mukis, which was thus hemmed in by Carchemish and Ugarit.

MURSILI I (ca.1620–1590 BC). In spite of the outstanding victories of this reign, the surviving records are few, the most significant being the *Proclamation* of **Telipinu**. Almost certainly power must initially have been in the hands of a regent. In contrast with later reigns, the succession passed off without upheaval, at least in the central homeland, following the provisions set out by the new king's grandfather, **Hattusili I**, before the **assembly** at **Kussara**. Probably, however, Mursili had to reassert the control exercised by his grandfather over the peripheral territories, not least **Kizzuwadna**, lying astride the routes leading to **Aleppo**.

The kingdom of Iamhad, centered on Aleppo, must have been weakened by the campaigns of Hattusili I, perhaps explaining the fall of Aleppo to the Hittite **army**, leading to its destruction and the disappearance of Iamhad from the historical records. There remained, however, a constant threat from the **Hurrians** to Hittite ambitions in the southeast. An alliance with the Kassites, tribes settled in much of Mesopotamia during the 17th century BC, cannot be proved, but would fit the facts as known, for they were the lasting beneficiaries of the sack of Babylon by Mursili I, leading to the fall of the First Dynasty, whose most illustrious member had been Hammurabi (1792–1750 BC on the "middle" chronology). The

Kassites took over power as the next ruling dynasty in Mesopotamia, as they continued to be for four centuries. Indeed, it is hard to distinguish any tangible, enduring advantage gained by the Hittite state from a feat of arms which brought immense prestige at the time to Mursili I, a feat which sent shock waves through the Near East and which established him as a worthy successor to his grandfather but also to the great rulers in the past of Mesopotamia and Syria, from **Sargon of Agade** onward. Politics was above all centered on prestige, and this was essentially based on military prowess, the only path to immediate fame.

The raid on Babylon—dated on the middle chronology to 1595 BC—involved a march into territory altogether new to the Hittite army, 800 kilometers on from Aleppo across to and down the Euphrates. The dangers were underlined by the harassment of the Hittites by the Hurrians on their homeward progress, laden with the booty which had given extra point to the operation. No solution to the Hurrian menace was achieved by Mursili I nor by his successor.

Not more than five years later, Mursili I was assassinated by his brother-in-law **Hantili I**, presaging the long decline of Hittite power in the later years of the Old Kingdom. Fuller surviving records would accord Mursisli I the place he undoubtedly deserves in Hittite history.

MURSILI II (1321–1295 BC). By the chances of preservation of texts, even though his **annals** are missing for the later years of his reign, as an individual he is in many ways the best known of all the Hittite kings, save only his youngest son **Hattusili III**. He is remarkable not only for his own military achievements, supported by able commanders, but also for his contributions to Hittite **historiography**. In addition to the annals for his own reign, he ordered the compilation of the *Deeds* of his illustrious father, **Suppiluliuma I**.

He emerges as a vigorous ruler, too often on campaign to carry through to completion such policies as the resettlement of the depopulated **Kaska** borderlands, though he may well have contributed to building works in **Hattusa**. He could show mercy to defeated adversaries, as to Manapa-Tarhunda, king of the **Seha River Land**, even if there was an element of *Realpolitik* in this! He was exceptionally pious, his devotion to the **gods** equaled only perhaps by **Tudhaliya IV**. This piety was inspired by the necessity of calling upon the gods to relieve the realm of the scourge of the **plague**. He had to discover the causes of the gods' seemingly implacable wrath against the land of Hatti. His father's neglect of a certain **festival**, his alleged breaking of a frontier **treaty** with Egypt and—to modern eyes far the most serious—his slaying his elder brother to gain the throne were all cited as provoking the gods. Mursili could not understand why his offerings were not sufficient compensation, although he never denied that a father's guilt descended on his children.

When he came to the throne, Mursili II was mocked by his enemies as a mere child, though probably in his early twenties. This may have happened because he was the fifth and youngest son of Suppiluliuma I, his eldest brother, **Arnuwanda II**, having died of the plague and another brother, Zannanza, having been murdered on entering Egypt to marry **Ankhesenamun**. Yet it seems curious that two other brothers, **viceroys** of **Aleppo** and **Carchemish**, were willing to remain as such, allowing their younger brother to ascend the throne in **Hattusa**. It is noteworthy that during their lifetimes Mursili seems to have relied heavily on their support in maintaining his hold on his father's territorial gains in Syria.

Mursili was immediately to prove his enemies sorely mistaken in their estimate of him: his youth probably gave him an energy not always seen in kings of more mature years. The first major crisis of his reign was one experienced by most Hittite kings, whose enemies, sometimes seducing some of the Hittite vassals, saw the accession of a new king as an opportunity to strike out against their overlord or threatening neighbor. Vassalage anyhow implied a personal bond, which a royal Hittite successor could not assume automatically to inherit. The most unrelenting danger to the Hittite Empire came from the Kaska lands to the north; and the new reign began with two years' campaigning against these tribesmen, whom he never permanently subdued.

Mursili then turned his attention to the west, where he was to win his most significant successes, removing **Arzawa** from the map as a political and military threat and securing his triumph by the **deportation** of 65,000 to the Hittite homeland, along with livestock and military paraphernalia. He was to have no serious trouble in the west for the remainder of his reign, bar minor sedition, enabling him to concentrate on dangers in the northeast, the south and the southeast.

It was to the north and northeast—the Kaska lands, the **Upper Land** and **Azzi-Hayasa**—that Mursili constantly found his attention drawn, in the early years of his reign leaving Syria to the experienced hands of Telipinu in Aleppo and Sarri-Kusuh in Car-

chemish. Trouble with a rebellious vassal in **Nuhasse** was aggravated by Egyptian military involvement in the reign of Horemheb
(1323–1295 BC), an almost exact if older contemporary of Mursili.
Then in his ninth year Mursili was to suffer the grievous blow of
the deaths of both his brothers, each succeeded by a son as viceroy.
The death of Sarri-Kusuh encouraged Assyria to invade the kingdom of Carchemish, at least to the Euphrates. This was a serious
enough danger for Mursili himself to march into Syria, where he
successfully restored Hittite control over the viceroyalty of Carchemish, though not removing the future threat from that quarter.

It was in the same ninth year of his reign that Mursili II suffered the heaviest personal blow of his life, with the death of Gassulawiya, his first and dearly loved **queen**, from a mysterious illness. This he came to blame on his domineering stepmother
Tawananna, a Babylonian princess who imported foreign favorites
and customs to the Hittite court, to the chagrin of her stepsons. She
had assumed as her personal name the title given to the first wife of
the reigning king or, if still alive, to his mother or stepmother,
widow of the previous king. With the name of Gassulawiya appearing on the royal **seal** along with that of Mursili as "Great
Queen," jealousy for her status may well have provided a strong
motive for murder. Mursili certainly thought so, attributing it to
magic. He resisted advice to execute her, instead banishing her
from Hattusa, while giving her adequate provision for daily life.
This was a recurrent problem for the Hittite monarchy.

The king had another affliction, evidently a minor stroke,
which he ascribed to the shock of a thunderstorm, stating that "my
mouth went sideways." It cannot have been too severe, since he
was able fully to continue his responsibilities. It is a unique medical record for the time.

Mursili II died leaving the Empire rather stronger than at his
father's death, especially in the west, although a threat from Egypt
was soon to emerge for his successor.

MURSILI III. *See* **URHI-TESUB.**

MUSIC. Naturally scant evidence survives to illuminate the undoubted
musical accomplishments of the different peoples of the ancient
Near East. That the lyre and harp were played by Sumerian per-
formers in the third millennium BC has for decades been well
known from the discoveries by **Sir Leonard Woolley** in the so-
called Royal Cemetery of Ur. It was not the Sumerians but rather

the **Hurrians** who seem to have introduced musical instruments and skills to the Hittite court at **Hattusa**. These were imported probably directly through Hurrian penetration of the Hittite homeland in the days of the Empire; an alternative route would have been from **Ugarit**, once it had come under Hittite suzerainty in the reign of **Suppiluliuma I**. Here a small corpus of musical texts has been found.

Cultic texts quite often include instructions for choral or instrumental accompaniment, some Hurrian religious songs from Ugarit even giving the most ancient known musical notation. Though the long poems of Ugarit were recited, not sung, the tune of a Hurrian love song found at Ugarit on a clay **tablet** has been reconstructed.

Textual references make it clear that music played a significant role in the royal ritual of the Hittite **festivals**, though the only contemporary visual record is provided by relief blocks at **Alaca Höyük** depicting musicians playing the lute and bagpipes. A sculptured scene of Iron Age date at **Karatepe** depicts a dancer accompanied by players on the lyre, lute and tambourines: it seems almost certain that similar performances were given in the days of the Hittite Empire.

The instructions for the ritual of the royal festivals appear to have been fairly standardized, and include the following passage:

> The Master of Ceremonies goes outside to the courtyard and says to the verger, "Music, music!" The verger goes out to the gate and says to the singers, "Music, music!" The singers pick up the "Ishtar"-instruments. The verger walking in front, the singers bring the "Ishtar"-instruments in, and take up their position.

From this text the prominent role of the singers is plain. Whether bards played a role in the Hittite Empire comparable with their place in Iron Age society in many lands is uncertain: their propensity for satire might have been unwelcome at the Hittite court! In the Caucasus at least two Bronze Age burials in Georgia contained musical instruments, and there may well have been a tradition continuing into early Christian times, when the Armenian king Pap was murdered at a dinner (AD 374), while he was watching groups of minstrels performing to an accompaniment of drummers, pipers, lyre players and trumpeters. The deeds of ancient Armenian kings and heroes were handed down by the chants and popular songs of certain minstrels, in the absence of written histories. Such music indeed tends to flourish in less sophisticated and bureaucratic societies than the Hittite Empire, wherein the religious establishment had the upper hand.

MUSKI (MUSKU). Conventional opinion identifies the Muski with the Phrygians, and suggests their arrival in Anatolia from the Balkans with the body of invaders known as the **Sea Peoples**. They are not mentioned by Ramesses III nor in the **tablets** of **Ugarit**; but they irrupt on the historical scene in the late 12th century BC, in the accession year of Tiglath-Pileser I of Assyria (1114 BC), when in his **annals** the story is told:

> In the beginning of my reign, 20,000 men of the land of Muski and their five kings, who for 50 years had held the lands of Alzi (**Alse**) and Purukuzzi, which in former years paid tribute and **tax** to Assur my lord, and no king had vanquished them in battle—in their own strength they came down and seized the land of Kutmuhi. . . .I gathered my **chariots** and my troops. . . .Mount Kashiari, a difficult region, I traversed. With their 20,000 warriors and their five kings I fought in the land of Kutmuhi and I defeated them.

The Muski may well have been responsible for the destruction of **Carchemish** (ca.900 BC).

Mita of Musku, prominent in the annals of Sargon II of Assyria (722–705 BC), was surely the great Midas, whose capital was at **Gordion**. But Muski/Musku must have been a generic tribal name, used over a wide zone and for centuries in Anatolia. Only thus can its presence in the annals of Sargon II and rather later in the inscriptions of Rusa II of **Urartu** (ca.685–645 BC) be adequately explained.

MUWATALLI I (ca.1400 BC). An interloper on the throne of **Hattusa** and the last king of the Hittite Old Kingdom, he seized power from the royal dynasty which otherwise maintained its hold on the **kingship** more or less throughout the Old Kingdom and Empire. He may well have gained power with **Hurrian** support. After his assassination, his successor, **Tudhaliya I/II**, brought the legitimate dynasty back to power.

MUWATALLI II (1295–1272 BC). In many respects he inherited from his father, **Mursili II**, a strong kingdom, more secure than at the opening of previous reigns. Yet it was not long before a fresh challenge was to emerge and some old problems to resurface. Within the royal family a source of friction developed around the **queen** mother and stepmother of the king, Mursili's second wife Tanuhepa, probably of **Hurrian** background. Though, like the previous queen mother, she was put on trial, unlike her she was acquitted, a scenario destined to provide a simmering source of disaffection within the royal family.

The fresh challenge came from Egypt, where the new 19th Dynasty under Seti I (1294–1279 BC) was intent on reviving the glories of Tuthmose III (1479–1425 BC) in Asia. Seti I scored a considerable victory over the Hittite forces in Syria, recorded on the walls of the great temple at Karnak in Thebes: many prisoners were taken. That this was a genuine success rather than a mere propagandist boast is most clearly demonstrated by the recovery by the Egyptian king of the kingdoms of **Kadesh** and **Amurru**, brought under Hittite control by **Suppiluliuma I**. This in effect meant that Muwatalli was obliged to accept a division of Syria into two spheres, as he may have recognized diplomatically by **treaty** with Egypt. He could not, however, accept this as a permanence without endangering Hittite power throughout the rest of Syria. This was a threat which became all the more imminent with the accession of **Ramesses II (1279–1213 BC)**. In military terms the reign of Muwatalli II was principally devoted to preparations for a confrontation with Egypt, recognized as a power of equal status, and to facing the consequences of such large-scale mobilization. Without the difficulties he had to face in lands to the west and north of **Hattusa**, Muwatalli could well have marched south sooner.

In western Anatolia all might have been well but for the emergence of a renegade Hittite of aristocratic birth named Piyamaradu, destined to be a thorn in the side of the Hittite authorities in the west for many years, a clever schemer able to win military successes and then, faced with Hittite force, to melt into the background, escaping capture. Hittite power in the west had somewhat declined since the early years of Mursili II, with the transfer of **Millawanda** (Miletus) from Hittite suzerainty to that of **Ahhiyawa**, while the Mycenaean presence was beginning to become apparent. Piyamaradu arranged the **marriage** of a daughter of his to the Ahhiyawan vassal ruler of Millawanda. Piyamaradu became ever more ambitious, conquering **Wilusa** and defeating Manapa-Tarhunda, ruler of the **Seha River Land**, who had come to its aid. This was a rebellion not to be tolerated: Muwatalli dispatched

Gassu, one of his generals, whose success is to be presumed—given the fragmentary preservation of the record—from the recovery of Hittite control over Wilusa. Piyamaradu, however, eluded the Hittite **army**, not for the only time withdrawing to Ahhiyawa. Some time later, Muwatalli drew up a treaty with Alaksandu, the legitimate vassal ruler of Wilusa.

Muwatalli II seems to have decided the vital need was to secure his rear before marching against Egypt in Syria, recalling how his father and grandfather had each been distracted at times from operations in Syria by unrest in Anatolia, particularly along the border with **Kaska** territories. Such was the drain of military manpower for the campaign which culminated at Kadesh (1274 BC), with calls on vassals to provide soldiers for the great expedition, that there may not have been the *masse de manoevre* essential for any counter-attack against the northern tribes to be sure of success. Some steps were called for. The first crucial decision was to remove a substantial portion of the Empire from his own to his brother's administration, creating in effect a kingdom within a kingdom for the future **Hattusili III**, already experienced in war. This was not achieved without some unhappiness, notably for the displaced governor of the **Upper Land**. A major reason for this unprecedented step may well have been the necessity of resettling the depopulated northern borderlands, as a buffer against the ever restless Kaska tribes: the classic method was by **deportation**.

Even more radical was the decision of Muwatalli, around the middle of his reign, to move the seat of royal government from Hattusa to **Tarhuntassa**. The thinking behind this move was almost certainly the relative vulnerability of the old Hittite capital and the desirability of a more secure location, while the king's attention was elsewhere. There is no record to suggest that any return to Hattusa was planned in this reign. How much discontent the move to Tarhuntassa provoked is unknown: conceivably this was a factor behind his death (1272 BC), an assassination in obscure circumstances.

The outcome of the battle of Kadesh undoubtedly indicates a Hittite success, if not a stunning triumph, the principal prizes being the regaining of the vassal kingdoms of Amurru and Kadesh, thus permanently expelling Egypt from serious involvement in Syria and restricting Ramesses II to more southerly lands in Palestine and over the Jordan. There may have been some encouragement to those seeking to undermine Hittite rule in Syria; but the main threat now came from further east, and was to persist throughout the remaining century of the Hittite Empire. **Adad-nirari I (1295–1264 BC)** of Assyria had occupied **Hanigalbat**, the northwesterly remnant of **Mitanni**, making the bend of the River Euphrates the effective frontier between Assyria and Hatti. This was a greater threat than Egypt ever could be. It is therefore not remarkable that Muwatalli wished to return north soon after the battle.

While Muwatalli II may be reckoned a strong king, he bequeathed serious problems, not merely in the matter of his stepmother but also more fundamentally in the division of the kingdom through his moving the capital to Tarhuntassa and giving so much authority to his brother Hattusili. His successor, **Urhi-Tesub**, inherited a fractious climate within and around the royal family, leading in due course to internecine rivalry between the heirs of Muwatalli and his brother, a factor contributing to the ultimate downfall of the Empire.

- N -

NARAMSIN (2291–2254 BC). Grandson of **Sargon of Agade**, also intervening in Anatolia. In his reign the Akkadian Empire reached its zenith, but fell soon after.

NAUMANN, RUDOLF. For many years he was the architect with the German excavations at **Boğazköy**. Among his contributions were plans and reconstructions of the buildings of **Büyükkale**. He is the author of *Architektur Kleinasiens*.

NENASSA. A town with surrounding land on the southern reach of the **Marrassantiya River**, for which a local **cult** was established. It is twice mentioned with **Hupisna** and **Tuwanuwa**. It may have sunk into obscurity under the Empire, but lay on a major **trade** route from Assyria to **Burushattum** (**Acemhöyük**) in the period of the Old Assyrian colonies. It is mentioned in the *Proclamation* of **Telipinu** in connection with the deeds of **Labarna**, in a list of seven areas to which he dispatched one each of his sons as governor, setting a precedent for later Hittite practice.

NERGAL. Mesopotamian **god** of **plague**, **warfare** and the **Underworld**, identified with the **Hattian** War-God Sulunkatte. Probably depicted in **Yazılıkaya** Chamber B as the "dagger god," supporting the suggestion that this was a funerary shrine for **Tudhaliya IV**.

NERIK. A **Hattian cult center** subject to **Kaska** control from the reign of **Hantili II**. The role of Nerik was transferred to **Hakpissa**. It was recaptured with great pride before his seizure of the throne by **Hattusili III**, who, along with his dominant Hurrianizing policy, seems to have encouraged a revival of Hattian cultic traditions at Nerik. The chief god of Nerik was its **Storm-God**, identified with that of **Zippalanda**, another holy city, and also to some extent with the Hurrian **Sarruma**, as son of the Storm-God of Hatti. Others whose cults flourished at Nerik were the god of the **Underworld**, Sulinkatte (alias **Nergal**) and the War-God Wurunkatte. The god **Telipinu**, less a god of vegetation than one related to the weather-gods, was among the deities associated with **Kastama**, a place closely linked with the holy city Nerik.

No suggested site for Nerik has yielded evidence of Late Bronze Age occupation. It is certain that Nerik lay not too far from the lower reaches of the **Marrassantiya River**: possible locations are at Havza or at Oymaağaçtepe, northwest of Vezirköprü, or alternatively 70 kilometers west, on a bend of the Marrassantiya opposite the village of Kargi.

The *purulli* (spring **festival**) procession started out from **Hattusa**, stopping at **Arinna** and in due course ending at Nerik, one of the leading holy cities of the realm, along with Arinna, **Samuha** and Zippalanda. Two crown princes in their turn were appointed priest of the Storm-God of Nerik, after its recovery.

NESA/NESILI. Nesa was the original form of the city name **Kanes**, with which the earliest historically attested Hittite presence in Anatolia was associated. The application of the name to the **Hittite language**, as Nesili (Nesite), continued much longer.

NEVE, PETER (1929–   ). Having arrived aged 25 as a student of **architecture**—a classic German training for a Near Eastern archaeologist—at **Boğazköy** in 1954, he became an established expedition member, succeeding **Kurt Bittel** as the director of excavations at **Hattusa** (1963–1994) and as expedition director from 1977. While his predecessor had put the excavations on a sound modern basis, Neve's most distinctive contribution may be seen as his great efforts for conservation of the architectural remains, notably the defenses of **Boğazköy: Upper City**, and for the protection of the whole area, now classified as a United Nations Educational Scientific and Cultural Organization (UNESCO) World Heritage site.

Under Neve's leadership major extensions to the excavations were achieved, including exposure of many **temples** in the Upper City; of Hittite buildings around **Boğazköy: Nişantaş and environs**; of the area of **Boğazköy: Lower City** northwest of **Temple I**; of the large fortress wall round **Büyükkaya**; and of **Boğazköy: Südburg**. His most sensational artifactual find was the Bronze Tablet of **Tudhaliya IV** recording the **treaty** with **Tarhuntassa**, found on 20 July 1986 under paving just inside the perimeter defenses of the Upper City, near the Sphinx Gate.

NIHRIYA (NAIRI). Extending over the highlands north of Diyarbakir and eastward to the Van region, this territory had shifting boundaries consistent with the tribal character of the inhabitants, and sometimes paralleled by the name of Uruatri, the early form of **Urartu**. This was a region of more direct concern to Assyria than to the Hittites, mainly owing to closer geographical proximity. **Shalmaneser I** of Assyria (1263–1234 BC) had campaigned into Uruatri and further west toward the Euphrates River; and **Tudhaliya IV**, in a diplomatic overture to mend fences with Assyria on the accession of **Tukulti-Ninurta I** (1233–1197 BC), tacitly acknowledged the loss of **Hanigalbat**, the remnant of **Mitanni**, to Assyria in the reign of Shalmaneser I. Thus, in effect, all the conquests east of the Euphrates a century earlier by **Suppiluliuma I,** save only **Isuwa**, had been lost: this was one of the serious problems bequeathed by **Hattusili III**. Assyria had made the major economic gain of winning control of the most important **trade** routes across the Euphrates into Anatolia.

When Hittite patience was exhausted, Tudhaliya IV advanced boldly eastward into Nihriya, whence Tukulti-Ninurta I withdrew to a base at Surra, probably on the north slopes of the Tur Abdin range. The two armies met somewhere between Nihriya and Surra, between the Tur Abdin and the upper Tigris River. If the Hittite king had hoped to repeat the success of Suppiluliuma I in his descent on the Mitannian capital, he was to be sadly disappointed. The Hittite **army** had marched very far from its bases, and moreover the reinforcements on which they had been counting after crossing the Euphrates did not appear, as indicated by a bitterly reproachful letter from Tudhaliya IV, probably to the Hittite vassal ruler of Isuwa, written after the defeat. No details of the battle have survived.

Disastrous as this defeat was to the Hittite state, in the immediate aftermath demonstrated by an Assyrian overture to the Hittite vassal kingdom of **Ugarit,** things could have been far worse, had Tukulti-Ninurta I pressed home his advantage across the Euphrates. Though unquantifiable, these were probably factors contributing to the coup d'état a few years later by the king's cousin **Kurunta**.

NORŞUNTEPE. One of the most important excavations carried out under the Keban Dam Rescue Project in the 1970s, before the flooding of Altınova ("the golden plain") near Elaziğ by construction of a dam on the Euphrates River. This excavation was directed by Dr. Harald Hauptmann, director of the German Archaeological Institute in Istanbul.

The settled population in this fertile plain grew steadily through the third millennium BC, with "manor houses" appearing at **Korucutepe**, Norşuntepe, Tepecik and elsewhere. By the latest phase of Early Bronze III, a public building with storerooms in Norşuntepe VI seems to mark a concentration of resources in this local center, near the end of the long succession of 33 levels of the Early Bronze Age with 18 meters' depth of deposits of the total of 35 meters from top to virgin soil. Norşuntepe VI may mark the beginnings of the **trade** between Mesopotamia and Anatolia, standing on what was to become one of the **Old Assyrian caravan routes**. Local craftsmanship had earlier roots, demonstrated by the discovery in Norşuntepe XIX of a **copper** workshop, with slag, clay ladles for casting, nozzles for bellows and molds for shafthole **axes**, giving proof of active **metallurgy** in the third millennium BC in the region later known as the kingdom of **Isuwa**.

In the Hittite Old Kingdom Norşuntepe was defended by a well-built stone wall of casemate construction in the widespread manner of Anatolian **fortifications**. Norşuntepe was one of a number of Anatolian towns in the second millennium BC to display a degree of planning in the regular layout of streets, often with gravel surface and drainage channels. During the Empire the strongest archaeological indication of Hittite rule in Isuwa, from the conquest by **Suppiluliuma I** onward, is provided by the typically monotonous central Anatolian plain wares, especially open bowls and platters. These are clearly intrusive and characteristic of the mass-produced **pottery** of the Hittite Empire.

NUHASSE LANDS. These occupied the region between the rivers Euphrates and Orontes and between **Hama** and **Aleppo**, adjoining the kingdoms of **Mukis** and **Kadesh**. Though mentioned in the **ar-**

chives of **Mari** and **Alalakh** VII, Nuhasse was not a political entity until the campaigns of **Suppiluliuma I**. In his time there were several rulers within the Nuhasse Lands, minor chiefs who oscillated in their loyalties between Hatti and **Mitanni**.

In the reign of **Mursili II** Nuhasse again rebelled. The Hittite policy of indirect rule with reliance on compliant puppets failed to secure prolonged tranquillity. **Hattusili III** decided on the Nuhasse Lands as the place of exile of the deposed **Urhi-Tesub**, a serious mistake as it proved.

- O -

OIL. Fine oil was akin to perfume, and as such much prized, being used for anointing divine **statues** in the **temples** and during **festivals**, as well as the king himself in the accession ritual. The nobility certainly used it for their toilet. Fine oil was more than a cosmetic or cleanser, however, for it clearly brought good fortune: hence the anointing of the commanding officer before battle, together with his **horses**, his **chariots** and all his **weapons**. Cedar oil was especially valued. Fine oil could be stored in horns, or in some rituals mixed with **wine**. An Egyptian king, possibly Amenhotep III, in a letter written in Hittite to the king of **Arzawa** refers to the anointing with oil the head of the woman selected to be his wife.

Oil was extracted from a variety of vegetable sources, notably olive, sesame, cypress, juniper and nuts. It might be used along with resin, though that would be prized largely for its fragrance. It was also used regularly for lamps and torches and for the preparation of **food**, especially breads and pastries. Oil could be employed, with fat or grease, as a waterproofing agent.

That oil had its uses as a medicament, doubtless for aches and pains and strained muscles, is perhaps implied by the instruction to trainers, in the **Kikkuli** treatise, to massage their horses with fine oil on the fifth day, after daily washing during the preceding days.

There can be little doubt that for the majority of the population fine oil was a luxury they could ill afford. They were, after all, of inferior status compared with the horses of the elite chariotry! Animal fat must have been their standard medium for cooking and lighting.

OLD ASSYRIAN CARAVAN ROUTES. As with all problems involving **historical geography**, there is unlikely to be unanimity on the routes taken by the merchants traveling to and fro between Assur and the *karum* of **Kanes** or the other Anatolian merchant colonies. It seems that the total distance each way of the caravan route was about 1,200 kilometers; that the precise route varied according to external factors or individual choice; and that, after reaching the Euphrates River from Assur, the commonest route on to Kanes passed **Ursu** (west of Birecik) and **Hahhum**, with an alternative from Ursu via the more easterly **Mama**, likely to have lain in the Elbistan plain.

Sidelights on the caravan route occur in references to the **textile trade** en route from Assur to Anatolia. Several **tablets** mention textiles from the town of Talhad, near the upper Balikh River, a tributary of the Euphrates west of the Khabur River: belts and shawls were among the products of Talhad. Most such tablets are transport contracts, dealing with shipments from Anatolia to Assur.

References to the *datum*, or caravan toll, are highly relevant to the problems of the caravan route taken by the Old Assyrian merchants. Percentages of the *datum* payable at each town en route should correspond with the relative situations of these stations on the road, as indeed they appear to do. Such *datum* texts are often, though misleadingly, called itineraries.

OMENS. These, like **oracles**, were a means of discerning the future fate of individuals or of great operations, as when the **army** was about to march out on campaign. All Hittite omen texts are of Babylonian origin. Precedents were all-important; and dreams might be the vehicle for messages from the **gods**. Celestial omens were prominent, messages often coming from above by lightning, thunderstorms or eclipses. Other omens were noted at childbirth, for the infant's horoscope: the second and seventh months of the year were especially auspicious for a birth, the fifth and eighth months the most ill-omened.

ONOMASTICA. This, the classification and study of personal, geographical and divine names, can contribute toward the better understanding of the role of the various ethnic groups in and around the territories ruled in successive periods by the Hittite kings based in **Hattusa**. Inevitably names which are linguistically not **Hittite** but **Luwian**, **Palaic**, **Hattic**, **Hurrian** or otherwise are included, as occurring in the Hittite records. A seemingly primitive category of personal name is based purely on sound, with differing number of syllables, such as: Ta-a, Lala, Aba, Arara, Ananu, Walawala,

Kakariya, Kuzizi, Kuwa and Niya. Personal names related to the geographical origin of the bearer are of several types, some being formed with the suffix -*il*, for example Hattusili ("he of the city Hattus"). This suffix is found in Hittite and also in the non-Indo-European Hattic. The **storm-gods** of **Nerik** and **Zippalantiya** in Hattic texts carry the epithets Nerikil and Zippalantiel. The **Sun-Goddess of Arinna** bore the epithet Arunitti, the female toponymic suffix being -*itt*. Where toponyms form the nucleus of a personal name, the Hittite suffix is -*um(a)na*, its precursor being -*uman*, found in Old Assyrian texts from **Kanes**. One Hittite example is *purushandumna.* The equivalent Luwian suffix is -*wanni*. Recognition of different **languages** is discernible in the use of an additional suffix -*ili*, as in *kanisumnili* and *palaumnili,* "in the language of Kanes and **Pala**" respectively.

Names of **gods and goddesses** form the nucleus of many personal names, not only Hittite but also Hurrian, Hattic and Luwian. Such are the Luwian Sausga-ziti ("man of **Sausga**") and Hepa-muwa ("life-force of **Hepat**"). Among many other theophoric names are- Hattusa-Lamma ("patron-god of Hattusa"), Talmi-Sarruma ("**Sarruma** is great") and **Urhi-Tesub** ("**Tesub** is true"). A few personal names contain two divine elements, including Arma-Tarhunt ("Moon-God Storm-God"), or the name of an animal, such as Walwa-ziti ("lion-man"). Occasionally names linked to a profession, such as "gardener," occur. Personal names ending in -*ahsu* are purely Hittite (Nesite). Hattic remaining a poorly understood language, its divine names are little known, some being descriptive. One such is that of the War-God Wurunkatte ("king (*katte*) of the land (*wurun*)"). Hanwasuit, another Hattic divine name, signifies "throne dais." Some **cult centers** feature in certain Hattic and Hurrian divine names. Luwian names or epithets for deities include parts of the body, such as Genuwassa ("of the knees"): note the parallels with Latin *genus* and English "genuflect." The name of the Luwian **Storm-God** is a participle, Tarhunt, "the conquering one."

Among the more distinctive toponyms are those ending with the suffix *wanda* meaning "having," including Wiyana-wanda ("having **vineyards**"), Samlu-wanda ("having apple trees") and Sapagur-wanda ("having beards"). Many place-names in Hittite texts end in -*ha*, -*(i)ya*, -*ka*, -*la*, -*ma*, -*na* and so on.

Proper names can be quite revealing, even in modern times. One such in Turkish means "flower in the vineyard," though professions occur more commonly. A recently published inscription, described as the **Habiru** Prism of King Tunip-Tesub of **Tikunani**, is of real interest in relation to personal names and the ethnic composition of the population of the time, contemporary with **Hattusili I**. As many as 438 persons belonging to the Habiru class are listed, up to some 62 percent being Hurrian. Akkadian, Amorite or Kassite (Babylonian) names occur rarely, as well as one Elamite. A large percentage (122 persons) is described simply as "other non-Semitic." Not more than 26 Semitic names occur. There are no certain Indo-Aryan names. The Hurrian names are mostly similar to those from the royal **archives** of **Mari**.

As for the act of naming a human child, this is mentioned in both mythological and non mythological texts. In the myths the father names the child, whose name sometimes foreshadows its destiny. This did not, however, apply to non mythological texts. Family tradition and continuity could be reinforced by the giving of the same name in different generations, when a word for "former" or for "small" or "young" might be added. The only instance of names given to animals comes with the pair of divine bulls of Tesub, **Seri and Hurri** ("day" and "night").

ORACLES. Oracular texts record question and answer, from man and **god** respectively. These continue until a positive reply emerges, even if it means revealing intimate or guilty secrets! Experts in **divination** were employed to interpret the signs by which the god or goddess responded. Answers were a brief "yes" or "no."

Extispicy—examining the pulsing entrails of sheep just slaughtered—was expensive, the prerogative of the wealthy. For the poor there was interpretation of the patterns formed by drops of **oil** in water.

Lot- (*kin-*) oracles required a board with symbols of human life, interpreted by the "Old Women," perhaps by a throw of the dice. Snake-oracles were governed by a water-snake's movements through a basin divided into sections filled with water.

Bird oracles were performed by trained augurs, often **slaves**. Every detail of species and flight of birds coming within a demarcated area, frequently beside a river, was conscientiously recorded. The augurs had to have extra keen eyes and ears. This augury was employed before campaigns, with augurs accompanying the **army**: it was not unknown for a military venture to be delayed until a favorable oracle could be obtained.

ORTAKÖY-ÇORUM. Situated nearly 50 kilometers east of **Alaca**

Höyük, the numerous **tablets** excavated here make it possible to identify this site as the Hittite Sapinuwa. The excavations are directed by Aygül Suel. Two major structures, Building A and Building B, have been exposed. The former is 27 meters long with surrounding cobbled area, the walls being of fine masonry. Here some 3,500 tablets and fragments were recovered. Building A has been dated by **dendrochronology** to 1365 BC, and recent further samples confirm a dating in the 14th century BC. Building B includes a huge depot with 40 large jars (*pithoi*) in several storerooms. Tablets have been found, though badly burnt: these include **oracle** texts and letters comparable with those from Building A.

OSTEN, HANS HENNING ERIMAR von der (1899–1960). An energetic archaeologist active in Anatolia in the inter war years, one of his major achievements—using a Ford car over rough tracks and unmade roads—was to discover some 300 ancient sites in central Anatolia, his surveys being aimed especially at finding Hittite remains. He published a record of these surveys in his *Explorations in Hittite Asia Minor* (1927–1930). It is perhaps ironical that at **Alışar Höyük**, where he directed major excavations under the auspices of the Oriental Institute of the University of Chicago (1927–1932), in collaboration with **Erich Schmidt**, there was a hiatus in occupation of the site during the Late Bronze Age.

Forced by political circumstances to leave his studies of archaeology in Berlin (1923), von der Osten worked for a time as assistant curator in the Metropolitan Museum of Art in New York. Thereafter he worked for 10 years for the Oriental Institute, Chicago, not only at Alışar Höyük but also at Kerkenes Dağ (1928) and **Gavurkalesi** (1930). From 1936 to 1939 he was chairman of the Archaeological Department in Ankara University, when he worked at Ahlatlibel (1937), Van (1938) and the Roman baths in Ankara (1938–1939). It was during these years that he had frequent social contact with Atatürk, who clearly held his work in high regard.

Whatever the precise truth of the matter, von der Osten was accused of spying for the Third Reich, spending 10 years from 1940 in a Turkish gaol. Released in 1950, he was not received back in Chicago, being given instead a post in Uppsala University, Sweden. He excavated briefly in Syria and Iran, and was appointed director of the German Archaeological Institute in Tehran, shortly before his death (1960).

Historical topography and ancient Near Eastern **glyptic art** were his principal research interests. Von der Osten was by all accounts a likable man and certainly a vigorous pioneer of central Anatolian field archaeology, whose career was blighted in midstream, a setback from which he never fully recovered.

OTTEN, HEINRICH. German Hittitologist and professor at the University of Marburg. He worked for many seasons as epigraphist with the German expedition at **Boğazköy**, and has published numerous Hittite texts and historical studies throughout a long career.

OYMAAĞAÇ HÖYÜK. This settlement mound, known locally as Höyük Tepe, is located seven kilometers northwest of Vezirköprü: it is 20 meters high and has an area of approximately 200 by 180 meters. Surface **pottery** of several periods has been collected, from Early Bronze II to Late Iron Age, though not Late Bronze Age. Nevertheless, large basalt blocks from a major defensive wall and a **postern** suggest Late Bronze as well as Middle Bronze occupation. This is a possible location for **Nerik**.

ÖZGÜÇ, NIMET. Professor in the University of Ankara. In 1962 she began excavations at **Acemhöyük** near the Salt Lake and later, as part of the Euphrates Salvage Project, at Samsat (Samosata). Excavations were resumed at Acemhöyük in 1988; and in 1989 the direction of this major project was passed to Aliye Özten. Her numerous publications, many of them on the **glyptic art** of **Kültepe-Kanes** and Acemhöyük, as well as **Karahöyük (Konya)** and other sites, on which she is an internationally acknowledged authority, have made Nimet Özgüç one of the leading figures in Anatolian archaeology.

ÖZGÜÇ, TAHSIN (1913–). For many decades a leading light among Turkish archaeologists, beginning his career in the field in 1940. He was for some years Rector of the University of Ankara and has been a strong supporter of the Turkish Historical Foundation, established by Atatürk.

His excavation reports tell the story of a lifetime's fieldwork as well as his training of many archaeologists. While he is best known for his excavations at **Kültepe (Kanes)** since 1948, he has also excavated several other Bronze Age and Iron Age sites, comprising: **Dündartepe**, under Kiliç Kökten (1940–1941); **Karahöyük (Elbistan)** and **Fraktin Höyük** (1947); **Altıntepe** (1959–1964); **Kululu** (1967) and **Maşat Höyük** (1973–1984), also publishing a report on the excavations at **Inandiktepe**.

- P -

PALA. This district was located just west of the lower reaches of the **Marrassantiya River**. It is significant not for any political or military prominence but as the homeland of a population speaking **Palaic**, a distinct Indo-European language, which seems to have superseded a **Hattic** substratum.

Palaic texts are all too rare in the surviving records. **Emil Forrer** recognized Palaic (*palaumnili*) as one of the seven **languages**, in addition to **Hittite**, in the **archives** of Hattusa. One such text comprises a mythological tale followed by a hymn-like composition. The mythical theme is of **gods** attending a feast, where they can neither slake their thirst nor satisfy their hunger. The hymn mentions Zaparwa, the leading god of Pala, probably a **Storm-God**. There are similarities to the Hittite tales of the Vanished God. All elements can be traced back to Hattic origins. The town of Lihzina is mentioned.

Pala was of strategic importance for the defense of the northern borderlands of Hatti, and as such merited the appointment of a senior official as governor of Pala-Tummanna, an office held by Hutupiyanza, to whose aid **Mursili II** marched, after access to Pala had been cut by a **Kaska** attack. In the **Hittite Laws** Pala is mentioned as one of the foreign destinations of merchants; and there were severe fines for crimes against such traders.

PALAIC. One of the Indo-European **languages** derived through **Proto-Anatolian** from **Indo-Hittite** and spoken by a group which settled in part of northern Anatolia named **Pala**. It is closer to **Hittite** than to **Luwian**. Very few texts survive.

PANTHEON (HITTITE). Although even at the height of the Hittite Empire there was no single unified hierarchy of **gods and goddesses**, the order of deities became more or less fixed from the time of the **treaty** made by **Suppiluliuma I** with Hukkana, ruler of **Hayasa,** till the fall of the Empire. At the head stood male and female sun deities: first, the Sun-God of Heaven, King of the Lands, shepherd of mankind; and second, the **Sun-Goddess** of **Arinna**, Queen of the Lands. Then comes a long list of weather-gods, designated either by epithets or by **cult centers**. Local **cults** were increasingly brought in under the umbrella of the state.

The official cult, ever more complex, is most typically seen in the "Thousand Gods of Hatti," manifested in treaty lists, those agreements sworn with vassal rulers or foreign states. In some examples the **Storm-God** has his attendants as further witnesses, namely, the bulls **Seri and Hurri** and the mountains Namni and Hazzi. Some Babylonian divinities are then included, among them being Ea, god of fresh waters, and Marduk. Then follows the god **Telipinu**, followed by **Ishtar**; then come the Moon-God and the goddess Ishhara, both special guardians of the treaty oath; and the War-God (Zababa). Local deities follow, then a group associated with the **Underworld**; and then the "primeval gods," with whom Sumerian deities—including Anu, Enlil and Ninlil—are closely associated. The list ends with the mountains, rivers, springs, the Great Sea, heaven and earth, winds and clouds, all normally nameless. The prayer of **Muwatalli II** enumerates the Hittite pantheon in order of cult centers: **Hattusa, Nerik, Zippalanda,** Halap (**Aleppo**) and **Arinna** take leading places, as well as **Samuha**. Hattusa had its own pantheon, including the goddesses **Hebat** and **Kubaba**, Ishtar of Nineveh and especially the Storm/Weather-God.

PANTHEON (YAZILIKAYA). By far the best representation of the **gods and goddesses** revered at the Hittite court is to be seen in the rock reliefs of **Yazılıkaya**. It may be most accurate to describe this pantheon as Hittite-**Hurrian**, the former for its political context and the latter for its religious inspiration. It represents the refinements of successive generations, in the last stage of Hittite power. The two processions in the outer rock chamber, male and female, meet in the middle, the gods advancing from the left and the goddesses from the right. These are listed from back to head.

Male Procession

Pisaisaphi (**tablets**); **Nergal (Underworld)**; **Seri and Hurri**; Hesui; Pirinkir (?); "Stag God" (Karzi); Astabi, Simegi ("Sun-God of Heaven"), paired with Aya; Kusuh (Moon-God) paired with Nikkal; Ninatta and Kulitta (servants of **Sausga**); Sausga (goddess of War and Love); Ea (Water-God), paired with Tapkina; **Kumarbi** (Grain-God, equivalent to Dagan in the middle Euphrates valley); Tasmisu, brother of Tesub; then comes a gap, in the sense that six deities in the female procession have no opposite figures in this male procession; then comes "Calf of Tesub" (= **Sarruma**); at the head of the male procession stands **Tesub** (Storm-God), paired with **Hebat**.

Female Procession

Sausga; unknown; Aya (?), paired with Simegi; Nikkal (= Ningal), paired with Kusuh; Tapkina, paired with Ea; Salus-Bitinhi, paired with Kumarbi; Naparbi, paired with Tasmisu; Allatu; Hutena and Hutelluna (goddesses of Writing and Destiny); Darru-Dakitu (servants of Hebat); granddaughter of Tesub; Alanzu (daughter of Tesub and Hebat); Sarruma, son of Tesub and Hebat; Hebat (Sun-Goddess of **Arinna**).

PARSUNTA. *See* **BURUSHATTUM (PURUSHANDA).**

PITASSA (PEDASSA). This land lay northwest of the Konya Plain and some distance west of the Salt Lake, embracing much of the barren Axylon plain and the foothills of Sultan Dağ. The **historical geography** is based on the fourth of a series of **treaties** drawn up by **Hattusili III** with **Ulmi-Tesub**, alias **Kurunta**. Early in the reign of **Arnuwanda I**, during his incursions into Hittite territory, Madduwatta gained the support of the elders of Pitassa against their Hittite overlord. Later, **Mursili II** reckoned it to belong to the land of Hatti. In his **Kadesh** inscription **Ramesses II** listed Pitassa as one of the lands which had mustered to the Hittite **army**.

PITHANA. The ruler of **Kussara** around the mid-19th century BC, who may with some reason be regarded as the original founder of Hittite political power in central Anatolia, through the conquest of the city of **Kanes (Nesa)**. The ethnic origins of Pithana and his son and successor, **Anitta**, cannot be determined from their names alone, though it has tentatively been suggested that they could be **Hattian**. The predominant element in the population of Kanes, however, was certainly Indo-European.

The so-called Anitta Text is the one historical source for the reign of Pithana and his subjugation of Kanes, surviving in **cunei-form** clay copies, the earliest of which is from the Hittite Old Kingdom. The original was inscribed on a **stela** in the gateway of the royal city of Kanes. In spite of a curious sentence, there is nothing to indicate a consciously Indo-European policy by either Pithana or Anitta in their conquests. The crucial event in the reign of Pithana is succinctly related thus in the Anitta Text:

> The king of Kussara came down from the town in great
> force and took Nesa in the night by storm. He seized the
> king of Nesa, but inflicted no harm on the inhabitants of
> Nesa. Instead, he made them his mothers and fathers.

It is difficult to interpret the true significance of this final
phrase, which could indicate a blood relationship or equally well
simply a politic gesture of conciliation, in line with common Hittite
practice in later generations.

PLAGUE. The pestilence which struck the Hittite Empire after the
capture of Egyptian prisoners of war and their removal to Hatti
killed both **Suppiluliuma I** and his successor, **Arnuwanda II**. It
continued for some 20 years to ravage the land, provoking **Mursili
II** to enunciate his *Plague Prayers* in an effort to appease the **gods**.
Medicine was then bound up with prayer, propitiation and **magic**.
In the end, of course, it was simply natural processes whereby the
infection lost its strength which ended the plague. There is no clear
indication of its precise nature, though presumably it was one of
the numerous sicknesses still to be found in the waters of the Nile,
from which native Egyptians had probably acquired immunity.

Recurrent **famine** had not yet afflicted the Hittite population,
but any shortage of **food** must have weakened immune defenses.
Sanitation was far from perfect in the cities, though sewerage is
apparent in some areas of **Hattusa**.

PORADA, EDITH (1912–1994). She was taught by tutors in Vienna
and on the family estate at Hagengut in central Austria. She then
gained her doctorate in Vienna at the age of 23, on the **glyptic art**
of the Old Akkadian period. The study of ancient Near Eastern
seals was to be the focus of her lifetime of research and publication. With the German occupation of Austria she left for the United
States (1938), where she studied and published material from the
Metropolitan Museum of Art in New York and the Pierpont Mor-
gan Library. In due course (1958) she joined the faculty at Colum-
bia University. She wrote nine books, 130 articles and a similar
number of book reviews.

PORSUK HÖYÜK (ULUKIŞLA). Located 10 kilometers east of the
district town of Ulukişla in the province of Niğde, on the old road
from Ankara to Adana through the Cilician Gates (Gülek Boğazı)
some 50 kilometers distant. This site was thus open to contacts

with the Cilician plain (**Kizzuwadna**, later Que), reflected in the archaeological record. The mound stands on a conglomerate platform, covers a roughly triangular area (400 meters east-west and 150 meters north-south) and comprises up to 10 meters of deposits. The site was visited by William Ramsay, the Classical epigraphist (1891), surveyed by **Emil Forrer** (1926) and recorded by **James Mellaart** (1951) at the start of his extensive survey of the southern Anatolian plateau, when, from the surface **pottery**, he classed it as a major Early Bronze Age site. Later, a **hieroglyphic** inscription on a block was found. Then a French expedition under Olivier Pelon excavated for seven seasons (1968–1977).

The Late Bronze Age (Level V) settlement was strongly fortified, with a bastion and entrance ramp. The pottery was overwhelmingly of the plain wares associated with the Hittite homeland under the Empire. The violent burning marking the destruction of this level must be dated to the fall of the Empire.

If the dating of the Early Iron Age occupation (Level IV) is accepted, as beginning in the 11th century BC, there must have been at least a century when the site was deserted, no rare phenomenon in Anatolia at that time. There are a few other early Iron Age settlement sites in the area. Porsuk IV, like Porsuk V, was violently burned. The Middle to Late Iron Age (Porsuk III) is marked especially by massive **fortifications** of the eighth century BC, together with pottery with a slight preponderance of the distinctive **Alışar IV ware**, including handled vessels, so widespread in and beyond central Anatolia, with which the dominant cultural connections of Porsuk continued to lie. Level III did not end in violent destruction.

POSTERN TUNNELS. Designed for counter-attack during a **siege**, the best known example runs for 83 meters through the defenses of **Boğazköy: Upper City**, being constructed in effect by the corbeling technique and thus virtually indestructible. It was built before the great defensive rampart above. Another postern was built through the south wall of **Boğazköy: Lower City**. Posterns occur also at **Alaca Höyük**, **Alışar Höyük** and **Ugarit**, and in the Middle Bronze Age at **Korucutepe**.

POTTERY. *See* **ALIŞAR III WARE; ALIŞAR IV WARE; BEAD RIM BOWLS; IRON AGE GRAY WARE; MIDDLE BRONZE AGE POTTERY; LATE BRONZE AGE POTTERY; RELATIVE CHRONOLOGY.**

PRICES. These can be illuminating socially as well as economically, the principal sources of evidence being the **tablets** of the Old Assyrian colonies and the later **Hittite Laws**. **Gold** and **silver** were the basic media of exchange in the merchant colonies of central Anatolia, but quite often prices could be expressed in **copper** or **tin**, ruling out any rigid theory of "bimetallism." The finer quality of silver (*sarrupum*) was much in demand with the Assyrian merchants, whereas it never occurs in transactions between native Anatolians, who used either standard silver (*kapsum*) or else silver probably alloyed with a percentage of copper. Gold too could be of various qualities or grades, its price normally from seven to nine shekels of silver to one of gold. When the price fell as low as four shekels of silver, gold containing copper may have been used. For **textiles** of *kutanu* category the purchase price averaged four to five shekels of silver, the average sale price being at least 15 shekels. This represented gross profit, before payment of **taxes** and caravan expenses.

In the state-controlled world of the Hittite Empire it is the Hittite Laws which provide detailed records of prices, primarily for the products of the land but also for industrial products, textiles and **metals**. In many cases a price is given as in effect the level of fine to be levied on a wrongdoer as compensation to be paid to his victim. Clothing and textiles had different values, the finest set at 30 shekels per garment and blue garments at 20 shekels each, while a fine shirt was worth three and a large linen cloth five shekels. **Horses** varied from 14 shekels to 20 for draft use. A plow ox was worth 12 shekels. A cow was worth seven and a sheep one shekel, a lamb being priced at half a shekel. Animal skins ranged from one shekel for sheepskin with fleece to one-twentieth of a shekel for the skin of a lamb or a kid.

There is significant evidence of the land values decreed by the Hittite authorities, with one acre of irrigated land set at three shekels, land for dry farming at two shekels per acre and a vineyard, presumably the poorest land, at only one mina per acre, meaning that irrigated land was 120 times more valuable. It cost one shekel to hire a plow ox for one month but a mere half shekel for **women** laborers doing harvest work for one month!

The relative weights of the shekel and the mina in the Hittite Empire differed from those in Babylon, being 1:40 compared with 1:60 for the latter. Assuming the same weight of 8.4 grams for the shekel, the Hittite mina would have been much lighter than the Babylonian: this was certainly true of the "mina of **Carchemish**" much later. In spite of these detailed prices, however, the costs of commodities, livestock and land must in fact have been largely determined by local conditions independent of the central administration. The prices for commodities ranging from emmer wheat and **oil** to **wine** and cheese are set down in the Laws, but the value of the measures is yet to be determined.

Textual evidence reveals, in part from the late third millennium BC in Syria at Ebla, that, while one shekel of gold was worth seven or eight of silver, one shekel of silver was worth eight to ten of tin, making gold worth some 60 to 80 times the value of tin.

PROTO-ANATOLIAN. *See* **LANGUAGES.**

PROTO-INDO-EUROPEANS (PIE). These were the ancestors of all the branches of the extended family of the Indo-Europeans, who spread out over a vast zone stretching in the end from Siberia and India in the east to Spain and Ireland in the west. The Hittites formed one of these branches. An approximation for the time of their arrival on the Anatolian plateau can be gauged from the evidence for the diffusion of tribes from the PIE homeland: a date from ca.3000 BC seems reasonable.

It has to be admitted that there is no such thing as a PIE inscription, and that skepticism concerning the whole discipline of comparative linguistics, on which the reconstruction of the PIE proto-language depends, remains quite widespread, notably among archaeologists. Nevertheless, the study of the whole problem of the PIE **language** and homeland is no flash in the pan, no invention of one or two mavericks. Two centuries have passed since Sir William Jones' labors on Sanskrit, the foundation of Indo-European scholarship. Archaeologists are well advised, as many do, to avail themselves of a potentially invaluable research tool.

Reconstructed PIE terms relating to subsistence indicate a people comprising herders and cultivators, using the plow for growing cereals and having domesticated sheep, pigs and cattle. The linguistic evidence demonstrates strong parallels with, and early borrowings from, two other language groups, the Proto-Caucasian and Proto-Uralic.

This points to PIE as having been spoken in the open plains and steppes between the Caucasus and the Urals, rather than further west, the Dnieper River forming an apparent linguistic boundary in fourth-millennium BC Europe, with immigrant farmers to the west and indigenous stockbreeders to the east.

Alternative theories for the location of the PIE homeland (*Urheimat*)—in Trans-Caucasia, around the Konya Plain in Anatolia or in northern or southeastern Europe—are altogether less credible.

It seems likely that it was in the context of the Yamna (Pit-Grave) culture of the Pontic-Caspian zone, which endured from mid–fourth to mid–third millennium BC, that the PIE linguistic unity began to break down into the beginnings of distinct Indo-European languages.

PUCHSTEIN, OTTO (1856–1911). German archaeologist, directing the 1907 season of excavations at **Boğazköy**. The pioneer specialist in Hittite **architecture**, he excavated the **fortifications** of the **Upper City**. Confronting the view of **Hugo Winckler**, who was almost exclusively interested in inscriptions, Puchstein felt obliged to insist that the expedition should concentrate also on the architecture.

PUDUHEPA. The best known and most remarkable of the Hittite **queens**, she is one of the very few persons whose character can be envisaged at least to some degree from the surviving records. Her husband, **Hattusili III**, acceded to the throne at the age of about 50 having deposed his nephew **Urhi-Tesub,** and reigned 30 years, thus dying at about 80. She devoted continuing care for his fluctuating health, often in the form of lengthy prayers. Indeed, the prosperity of her husband's kingdom and his own good fortune were her overriding concerns throughout his reign, and she devoted the same loyal support to her son **Tudhaliya IV**.

The piety of Puduhepa and her ingrained attitudes originated in her early years in her native city of **Lawazantiya** in the land of **Kummanni**, the northeastern area of **Kizzuwadna**, as priestess and daughter of Pentipsarri, priest of **Ishtar**. This deity was, though female, a warrior. The future husband of Puduhepa, Hattusili III, had as his patroness Ishtar of the city of **Samuha,** depicted carrying **weapons** as a winged goddess. Puduhepa herself had her father's deity, Ishtar of Lawazantiya, as her patron, as was only to be expected.

Coming from the **Hurrian**-dominated territory of Kizzuwadna, with her husband the new king likewise looking to that region, Puduhepa seems to have played a decisive role in the importation of Hurrian elements into the state **cult** of **Hattusa**. This would not have been too difficult, given the Hurrian heredity of the royal dynasty at least from the 15th century BC. Various deities of

Hurrian origin gain marked promotion in the divine hierarchy: among these are **Sausga**, goddess of war; **Sarruma**, previously venerated only in the southeastern region under Hittite domination, including Kumanni and the city of Lawazantiya; and the great mother goddess **Hebat**, mother of Sarruma. It is recorded that Puduhepa brought **tablets** with lists of deities with her to Hattusa, suggesting a religious program planned in advance.

As a corollary of these cultic changes, it seems that the religious duties of both king and queen increased in burden and complexity, eventually imposing an economic drain, not to say a distraction from military and political affairs, which was to contribute to the downfall of the Hittite Empire. To what degree these religious routines were undertaken in straightforward piety, as an insurance policy or for reasons of state, to satisfy potentially discontented subjects, it is hardly possible even to guess on the available evidence. Genuine piety surely played a dominant role in the life and works of Puduhepa, aimed as it was at the well-being of her family. This great queen was involved, often in the leading role, in the many great religious **festivals**, one of which lasted 38 days, in which she acted as chief priestess. The vows made by Puduhepa to the goddess **Lelwani** included, the texts record, reference to her dreams.

The queen might remain behind in Hattusa to preside over the ceremonies of the "Great Gathering" while the king was away conducting ceremonies in **temples** elsewhere. Puduhepa at least was virtually coequal with the king, maintaining her exalted status after his death. Her role in affairs of state is nowhere more remarkably demonstrated than in her correspondence with Egypt, from the time of the **treaty** between the two great powers, 16 years after the battle of **Kadesh**. Fifteen letters survive, including four written to Puduhepa by **Ramesses II**, who evidently held her in great respect. Her authorship of letters is demonstrated in the customary manner, by use of her own **seal**. She was par excellence a royal matchmaker, when political alliances were thus secured. She corresponded with vassals of the Hittite king, such as the ruler of **Amurru**. She must also have been concerned for the wider welfare of the population, as evinced by requesting shipment of corn to the Hittite lands at a time when there was a recurrent shortage.

Though accidents of preservation have been favorable to the reputation of Puduhepa, one suspects that no other Hittite queen equaled her. *See also* **TUDHALIYA IV: RELIGIOUS REFORMS**.

- Q -

QUEENS. The office of queen (Tawananna) carried with it a higher
status and prestige than merely that of the king's consort; and it
continued to be held by the queen mother after the death of the
king, her husband, for the remainder of her life. Two outstanding
examples are Tawananna and **Puduhepa**, wives of **Suppiluliuma I**
and **Hattusili III** respectively. The former was a Babylonian princess, the second wife of Suppiluliuma I, who proved a dominating,
even domineering personality during and after her husband's reign:
she caused much grief to her stepsons, **Arnuwanda II** and **Mursili
II**, especially to the latter. He blamed her for the death, in his ninth
year of reign, of his much-loved queen, Gassulawiya. Though the
oracles declared her guilty of a capital crime, her life was spared.
Instead, she was put on trial, stripped of office and banished from
the palace. It seems evident that her status had been such that it
would have been impolitic to have her executed. In her heyday she
had played a major role in affairs of state, having her own royal
seal. By contrast, Puduhepa was a very different personality,
rightly respected over many years, while holding the same high position in the machinery of state.

The office of Tawananna has by some scholars been considered anomalous, given the patriarchal character of Hittite society,
with its Indo-European roots. It could indeed be seen as a survival
of non-Indo-European—doubtless specifically **Hattian**—traditions
involving matriarchy and the supremacy of the mother goddess. In
practical terms, the queen would often remain at the court while the
king was away for long periods on campaigns. With the heir to the
throne commonly a minor, she was the obvious repository of royal
authority in the king's absence, and normally behaved as such.

- R -

RAMESSES II (1279–1213 BC). Perhaps the best known of all the
pharaohs of Egypt, he does not deserve to be reckoned the greatest.
Two things ensure the abiding memory of this reign, its length of
67 years and the number of his inscriptions all over Egypt. Specialists touch upon Ramesses II in connection with the fine tuning of
absolute chronology, lowered by 25 years, or 30 years by some,
compared with the dating favored a generation ago.

In spite of very limited military successes and the setback at the battle of **Kadesh** (1274 BC), he maintained the status of Egypt as a power of the first rank, following the victorious reign of his father Seti I. His main architectural monuments are his mortuary **temple** at Thebes, the Ramesseum, and the unique rock temple of Abu Simbel, where the small scale of his **queens**, even Nefertari, compared with his own colossal figure symbolizes the return to strict Egyptian orthodoxy after the heresy of the **Amarna** period. Not content with his own building achievements and beset by a shortage of skilled labor, Ramesses carved his name on numerous monuments of his royal predecessors.

Ultimately coming to be aware of a common interest with the Hittite power to the north, then ruled by **Hattusili III**, a **treaty** was ratified by the two sovereigns in the 21st year of Ramesses II (1258 BC), and remained in force until the fall of the Hittite Empire some 80 years later. The common interest was a combination of acceptance of the status quo in Syria, following the battle of Kadesh, and fear of the rising power of Assyria.

Several documents survive which illustrate the personal aspects of the **diplomacy** governing relations between these two great powers. **Puduhepa** had been a co-signatory of the treaty with Ramesses, and was much involved in correspondence with him concerning the **marriage** to Ramesses of a daughter of Hattusili III and Puduhepa, to whom the Egyptian king wrote in the same terms as he used in correspondence with her husband. Ramesses responded to an urgent request for an Egyptian doctor to attend the sick Hattusili, but was less impressed by a request for medical help to assist the ageing sister of Hattusili to become pregnant past the normal age. Ramesses II himself must have needed medical attention as he approached 90 years of age, 24 years after the death of Hattusili III; and Egypt suffered from the debility of a geriatric ruler.

RELATIVE CHRONOLOGY. This can in a narrow sense be historical, where a king-list provides a firm succession of rulers, no exact dates but cross-references to dynasties in other lands.

Relative chronology can alternatively be constructed from archaeological data, not giving any precise dates, except where radiocarbon determinations are available. Comparative tables can be constructed on the evidence of stratigraphic sections of occupation levels, most commonly in a *tell* or *höyük* (settlement mound). For such, excavations are of course required. Similarities in material finds, most frequently **pottery**, from different sites afford insights into cultural relations between sites and areas often quite widely separated by geography. Changes in material culture, however, seldom proceeded identically.

Pottery is by far the most useful indicator, from its ubiquity and fragility alike. In a long-lived major building level the surviving pottery is likely to date to its final years. Much attention has been devoted to **seals**, but these have less chronological significance, since they are more durable and often handed down as family heirlooms from one generation to the next.

The longest continuous sequences of stratified occupation levels have been excavated outside the Hittite homeland, at **Mersin** (Yumuktepe) and **Beycesultan**, each covering several millennia. In Hatti, **Boğazköy** has occupation on one hilltop (**Büyükkaya**) of the sixth millennium BC, but the area was not continuously settled until the later third millennium BC. **Alışar Höyük** was occupied for more than three millennia, until Hellenistic times, but with a hiatus in the Late Bronze Age. **Alaca Höyük** too has a lengthy stratigraphy. **Gordion** had quite a long settlement history. **Kilise Tepe** was continuously occupied from Early Bronze II into the Iron Age. In Altınova, east of the Euphrates River, **Korucutepe** and **Norşuntepe** both provide lengthy sequences of occupation levels. *See also* **ABSOLUTE CHRONOLOGY**.

RELIGION. *See* **ANATOLIAN RELIGION; ANCESTOR CULT; DIVINATION; FESTIVALS; GODS AND GODDESSES; MAGIC; PANTHEON (HITTITE); PANTHEON (YAZILIKAYA); TEMPLES; THEOLOGY.**

RHYTONS. Zoomorphic drinking vessels, most commonly in form of a bull, were especially popular in the period of the Old Assyrian colonies, but continued thereafter. They occur at a number of sites, including **Alaca Höyük**, where two identical specimens were found. Textual references occur in the *bibru* inscriptions, from which three types of bull rhyton can be distinguished, one being a complete bull standing on its four feet. All the rhytons mentioned in the *bibru* texts seem to have been in precious metals, **gold** or **silver**, the latter especially valued for its ritual purity. Poorer folk could have afforded only the **pottery** rhytons, which imitated those of the wealthy.

ROYAL BODYGUARD. A small elite unit of spearmen, the *mesedi*, numbered only 12, and were responsible for the king's safety wherever he might go. They must have numbered more in total, enough to ensure that 12 could be on duty at all hours, guarding the palace gates and the king's person. Their commander, the *gal mesedi*, enjoyed immense prestige: it was to this post that **Muwatalli II** appointed his brother Hattusili. They were reinforced and perhaps monitored by another unit numbering 12, who doubled up on guard duties: these were the "golden spearmen." There can be little doubt that their prime duty was protection against assassination, so often the curse on the Hittite monarchy. They were also prominent during **festivals**.

ROYAL FUNERARY CUSTOMS. The death of the king or **queen** was a potential disaster for the realm: consequently it was essential that the requisite rituals be performed correctly to the last detail. Any omission or deviation would be an ill **omen**. These rituals continued for 14 days from the day of death, when the king or queen "became a god."

On the first day an ox is slaughtered and put at the feet of the deceased, while a libation of **wine** is poured and the drinking vessel smashed. **Food** and libations are offered the next day; and in the evening came the first step toward **cremation** with the laying of the body on the pyre, which is then lit. On the third morning the charred bones were collected and cleansed in **oil**. With the bones placed on the seat at the head, the funeral feast began, with three toasts drunk in honor of the deceased. Feasting continued with sacrificial rites during the following days.

On the sixth day the bones were taken to the *hekur*-house, the "stone house," where the royal bones were laid on a couch, with an oil lamp placed in front of it. Sacrifices of cattle, sheep, **horses** and asses continued.

This was to be the focus of veneration by members of the royal family through perpetuation of their **ancestor cult**. The *hekur*-house was an institution in its own right, served by its own priests—resembling medieval chantry priests—and generously endowed with land and the labor to work it.

Symbolizing the elysian fields where the sovereign is to abide, a sod of turf was cut and taken to the *hekur*-house; and with it were placed farming implements no longer for use in this life and therefore deliberately broken.

- S -

SAKÇEGÖZÜ (COBA HÖYÜK). This mound lies in the fertile plain east of Gaziantep in the Rift Valley, first attracting attention by the visibility of carved stone orthostats beside a spring at the base of the mound. The prehistoric site is often termed Coba Höyük, while Sakçegözü is applied to the Neo-Hittite occupation. **John Garstang** conducted excavations here (1908 and 1911), followed by Veronica Seton-Williams and John Waecher (1949). Prehistoric occupation extends from Late Neolithic times (seventh millennium BC) until the Uruk period (fourth millennium BC).

A Neo-Hittite enclosure of some 70 by 50 meters tops the conical mound, with a buttressed perimeter wall, having a single gateway decorated with reliefs showing a lion hunt. In the east corner of the enclosure was a *bit hilani* with relief-decorated portico and a column base with a pair of double human-headed sphinxes, the entrance flanked by lions. The relatively small reliefs of Sakçegözü betray a late Neo-Hittite Assyrianizing style, suggesting a date in the mid–eighth century BC. This minor citadel probably lay within the territory of the kingdom of **Zincirli** (Sam'al).

SALLAPA. Probably located near the Classical Pessinus, perhaps at Sıvrıhısar, in the light of the Hittite record that their **army** had first to cross the Sakarya River. It stood at the junction of two main routes into **Arzawa**, from Hatti and Syria, where the troops of **Mursili II** and his brother Sarri-Kusuh from **Carchemish** joined forces for their attack on Arzawa. Sallapa stood on a Hittite route west from the Ankara region (**Gavurkalesi**) as far as the Aegean region (**Karabel** and **Mount Sipylus**). It had earlier been the base for the counter-attack by **Arnuwanda I** against the forces of the rebel Madduwatta and the rulers of **Pitassa**, his allies.

SAMUHA. A major **cult center**, along with **Nerik, Arinna** and **Zippalanda**, also functioning as one of the **store cities** of the Hittite state, it was located in the upper valley of the **Marrassantiya**, in the **Upper Land**. While its site has not been identified, two possibilities are the citadel of Sivas, the modern provincial center, and the site of Tekkeköy, four kilometers south of Zara, upstream from Sivas and not far from the river. At the former, the second-millennium BC remains are buried under the Seljuk citadel, of medieval date. Tekkeköy, a site on a rock ridge, has surface pottery of Late Bronze and Iron Age wares, and by its area was clearly a town site.

Samuha was one of many cities regained by **Telipinu**, but played its most significant political role under **Tudhaliya III**, when it may have proved to be the one remaining center loyal to the Hittite king, when **Hattusa** and most of his other territories had fallen to the combined assault of enemies from west, north and east. Even Samuha fell for a time, when "the enemy from **Azzi** came and sacked all the Upper Land and made Samuha his frontier."

Samuha may have been the first major city to be recaptured and brought back to Hittite rule by Tudhaliya III, who may have established his court there, while Hattusa remained under enemy rule. It became the base for successive attacks northeastward against the tribes of **Kaska**, the menace which had to be confronted first, if only to liberate Hattusa. Tudhaliya III led these campaigns in person till near the end of his reign, when he lay sick at Samuha, command being handed over to his son, the future **Suppiluliuma I**. It seems that, despite the incursion from Azzi, Samuha by its location proved relatively secure from attack.

In the final act of his troubled reign, **Urhi-Tesub** marched against his uncle's strongholds in the Upper Land but failed to win support against **Hattusili (III)**. He reached Samuha, but was soundly defeated, being shut up in the city "like a pig in a sty," and eventually compelled to surrender. Hattusili attributed his success to the support of the goddess **Ishtar** of Samuha, to whom both he and his successor **Tudhaliya IV** were dedicated in their youth.

SAPINUWA. Located at **Ortaköy**, 50 kilometers southeast of Çorum. Turkish excavations in progress.

SARAGA HÖYÜK. On the west bank of the Euphrates River, five kilometers north of **Carchemish**. Excavated in 1999 as part of the Ilisu-Karkamis Dam Project and one of the first victims of the water. The settlement mound had an area of 200 by 150 meters. It was occupied from the later fourth millennium BC (Late Uruk period) through the Early, Middle and Late Bronze Age into the Iron Age.

The excavations were concentrated in the levels of the second millennium BC, with a monumental building found in the first Middle Bronze phase. **Pottery** of these levels followed the wares typical of the middle Euphrates valley. Pot- and inhumation-graves occur in a later Middle Bronze level overlying the remains of the major building. Obviously Saraga must have been little more than a satellite of Carchemish.

SARGON OF AGADE (2371–2315 BC). Founder of the Akkadian dynasty, unifying Mesopotamia and establishing the first Empire (2371–2230 BC). A later text, *The King of Battle*, records his ventures on to the Anatolian plateau, clearly for purposes of **trade**, centered in and around the leading city of central Anatolia, **Burushattum (Acemhöyük)**.

SARISSA. Located at **Kuşaklı**, 50 kilometers south-southwest of Sivas. German excavations in progress.

SARRUMA. This god (in Neo-Hittite times Sarma) is best known from his representation in Chamber B of the **Yazılıkaya** shrine as the protector of the Hittite king **Tudhaliya IV**, being depicted embracing the king with his arm around his neck. There are two other depictions of Sarruma at Yazılıkaya. He also appears on the badly weathered **Hanyeri-Gezbel** relief, as well as on the **seal** of Ini-Tesub, **viceroy** of **Carchemish,** from **Ugarit**. Though some written references to Sarruma can be dated, those from religious texts are difficult to attribute to any reign. In Neo-Hittite times the **god** Sarma was venerated. It seems significant that the **onomastica** reveal no longer **Hurrian** but rather **Luwian** roots. His name is recorded over a wide zone, from Sultanhan (near **Kültepe**) in the north to the Mediterranean coast (at Korykos) in the south; and from **Topada** and **Porsuk** in the west to **Malatya** in the east.

Sarruma was an ancient Anatolian divinity, not originally Hurrian but adopted into the Hurrian pantheon by the Hurro-**Mitannian** conquerors of **Kizzuwadna**, comprising lands from eastern Cilicia northeastward. It was as a consequence of the conquest of Kizzuwadna by **Suppiluliuma I** that the name of Sarruma, and by implication his **cult**, was spread abroad over a wide zone, with his name appearing as an onomastic suffix to the names of kings or princes of Carchemish, **Aleppo, Isuwa** and Ugarit; and likewise with certain Hittite princes, contemporaries of Suppiluliuma I and Tudhaliya IV, and Hismi-Sarruma, possibly the future Tudhaliya IV. Sarruma occurs as a suffix also for some names on seals, one in the royal lists and a number of **scribes**, one of the time of the end of the Empire, under **Suppiluliuma II**.

Sarruma originated as a provincial god, whose cult was centered in the highlands of the Anti-Taurus in northeastern Kizzu-wadna, around Comana/**Kummanni**. He was depicted as a sacred calf emerging from the mountains, destined in the imperial period to become the "son" of the **Storm-God**. It was probably in the 15th century BC that there emerged the divine triad of **Tesub, Hebat** and their son Sarruma, imposed by the ruling Hurrian dynasty on the capital itself, **Hattusa**, and on their domains to the east and south. It was, however, only under the so-called Kizzuwadnan kings, **Hattusili III** (with **Puduhepa**) and **Tudhaliya IV**, that Sarruma was accorded a precise status in the Hittite **pantheon**. He was not always shown as an imitation of his parents, Tesub and Hebat, with their attributes: he could be characterized by a deer or a hare, by a bow or **spear**, hinting perhaps at a warlike origin.

SAUSGA. A deity not unique in the Hittite world in being both male and female, variously associated with war, love and fertility, and related to the Semitic **Ishtar**, Sausga is best known from the Hittite texts and from the reliefs of **Yazılıkaya**. There, she is depicted among the male deities, wearing a tiara, distinctive hairstyle and kilt, giving a military appearance, but with her clothing pulled away to expose her lower torso. Sausga was especially venerated by **Hattusili III**, very probably owing to the **Hurrian** background of this deity, aligning with **Kizzuwadna**, the homeland of his **queen, Puduhepa**.

This was, however, a relatively late import into the Hittite royal pantheon, being almost unknown before the Middle Hittite period. The earliest reference occurs in association with Nineveh, where the cult of Ishtar took a distinct form from that found elsewhere in the Mesopotamian world. A lamb was offered to Sausa, later identified in a lexical list as "Ishtar of/in Subartu," that is, of the North, soon before 2000 BC, during the Third Dynasty of Ur.

It was the Hurrians who enthusiastically adopted the cult of this deity, renaming her Sausa or Sawuska. Widely though not prominently venerated, Ishtar/Sawuska was the chief divinity of Tusratta of **Mitanni**, who invokes her alongside Re, the Sun-God of Egypt. The increasing popularity of Sausga from the Middle Hittite period until the fall of Hatti is but one manifestation of the Hurrian impact on the court and kingdom.

This deity continues to be mentioned in the Iron Age in the **hieroglyphic Luwian** inscriptions, while the **cuneiform** sources mentioning Ishtar of Nineveh are exclusively Assyrian.

SAYCE, Rev. ARCHIBALD HENRY (1845–1930). A scholar in the Victorian English mold, he has fair claim to be regarded as the founder of Hittitology, in that he was the first to recognize the historical significance, homeland and distinct identity of the Hittites, though it was left to others to prove their Indo-European affinities. In 1880 he gave a lecture in London to the Society for Biblical Archaeology, asserting that all the enigmatic reliefs and inscriptions found recently in Asia Minor (Anatolia) and Syria must be attributed to the Hittites, hitherto dismissed as a people with a minor role in the Old Testament. He had already (1876) guessed the truth from his examination of the **"Stones of Hamath,"** finding the same **hieroglyphic** script at **Mount Sipylus** in western Anatolia (1879). He later spotted **tablets** from **Tell el-Amarna (Akhetaten)** on sale in Cairo, and reported them (1888). He published *The Hittites—the Story of a Forgotten Empire* (1888).

SCHAEFFER, CLAUDE-FREDERIC-ARMAND (1898–1982). After initial archaeological experience in Alsace, from 1929 he directed the excavations at Ras Shamra on the Syrian coast. In 1930 the newly discovered alphabetic **cuneiform** texts were deciphered; then in 1932 the site was identified as **Ugarit.** Schaeffer soon grasped the significance of its relations with Cyprus, beginning excavations at Enkomi, near Famagusta. In 1939 he began the series of monographs entitled *Ugaritica.* After service with the Free French in World War II, he resumed excavations at Ugarit and Enkomi. Schaeffer also excavated at **Malatya (Arslantepe)** (1946–1951), completing excavation of the palace begun by the late **Louis Delaporte**.

SCHLIEMANN, HEINRICH (1822–1890). Rightly regarded as one of the founders of Near Eastern and Aegean archaeology, he was responsible for the first excavations at Mycenae and Tiryns in Greece and **Troy** in Turkey. A successful businessman, he was driven by an obsessive interest in Homer. With the help of Wilhelm Dorpfeld he exposed a long sequence of building levels at the mound of Hissarlik (Troy). Schliemann earned the strong disapproval of the Ottoman Turkish authorities for breaking his promise that all objects of **gold** and **silver** should be handed over to the Turkish government: in the event, the great majority went abroad, finally to Berlin and in 1945 to the Soviet Union. This has had an abiding effect on Turkish official attitudes to foreign archaeologists seeking excavation permits.

SCHMIDT, ERICH F. Codirector with **Hans Henning von der Osten** of the excavations at **Alışar Höyük** (1927–1929), under the auspices of the Oriental Institute of the University of Chicago. He made a major contribution to fieldwork in Iran through aerial photography.

SCRIBES. In the earliest phase of writing, with the keeping of the first commercial and administrative records, the scribe was the linchpin of sophisticated government in the Sumerian cities of southern Mesopotamia. Only later was writing employed for literary purposes such as epic poetry or legends, and it was some centuries before the first efforts at **historiography** are manifested. In early periods in Mesopotamia scribes were trained and employed in the **temples**, the royal palace with its bureaucracy being a later phenomenon.

In all periods and regions of the ancient Near East learning by rote was the rule for the training of the young scribe, a method in accord with long-standing traditions and anyhow unavoidable when mastering such a complex script as Akkadian **cuneiform**. First came the copying of simple syllables, Akkadian and likewise Hittite being syllabic scripts. Lexical texts, among those imported to **Hattusa** from Mesopotamia, were then to be learned. Afterward came literary compositions.

The Hittite scribe or scholar needed the cuneiform script for his native Indo-European **language**, nevertheless having to copy texts in Akkadian. Though in a dead language, Sumerian compositions were highly respected and included in the curriculum, albeit often poorly understood. It was through the scribes that a whole cultural tradition was transmitted into the Hittite lands from Mesopotamia: their education therefore played a crucial role in the assimilation of much of the customs of the ancient Near East.

References to foreigners from Assyria and Babylonia present at Hattusa include at least three named scribes, one Babylonian and two Assyrian, though one of these has a Babylonian-sounding name (Nabu-nasar). **Diplomacy** is better represented, no doubt owing to the higher rank of an ambassador compared with a scribe; but the latter was every bit as indispensable for the smooth operation of **government**.

The corps of scribes at the Hittite court comprised for the most part natives of the kingdom, principally Hittites, with duties and responsibilities varying with their rank. At the bottom of the scale were those who spent their time copying texts, governmental, commercial or literary, for storage in the official **archives**. This tedious work had to be repeated at regular intervals, for the clay **tablets** were normally unbaked and by their material not indefinitely durable. Presumably not every scribe was competent in a language other than Hittite, though many tablets were copied in Akkadian.

Their mastery of languages contributed to the prestigious status of senior scribes in the Hittite kingdom; but their critical advantage lay simply in their literacy, for it seems virtually certain that the kings were illiterate. When it came to formulating new documents, notably **treaties**, the content naturally depended in the last resort on the will of the king; but the text would surely have been drafted by a high-ranking scribe, one who was well acquainted with the ways of government, the intricacies of foreign relations and the foibles of his royal master. These highest-ranking scribes were in effect government ministers, and they often inherited their post from father to son, helping to consolidate the grip of the aristocracy as the power behind the throne. **Mittannamuwa** was chief scribe in the reign of **Muwatalli II**, who appointed him as administrator of Hattusa on the transfer of the royal seat of government to **Tarhuntassa**.

While we lack personal details of individual scribes, they can sometimes be identified by postscripts to documents, added after formal approval by the king and commonly addressed to the recipient. Clearly the scribes at both ends of the line of communication shared a fellow feeling as professionals. Moreover, tablets can be attributed to the same scribe through close examination of the *ductus*, the degree of pressure applied through the stylus or pen on the wet clay.

A separate group of scribes specialized in writing not on clay but on wood, it seems largely for rather temporary records, the script used being not cuneiform but **hieroglyphic**, better known on rock inscriptions such as that of **Suppiluliuma II** at **Boğazköy: Nişantaş**. Not Hittite or Akkadian but **Luwian** was the language written in hieroglyphic script. *See also* **DIPLOMACY**.

SCULPTURE. Most Hittite sculpture can be categorized as single or multiple rock reliefs, widely scattered or in series, notably **Yazılıkaya**, or as architectural embellishment, rather earlier at **Alaca Höyük** and subsequently in the great gates of **Boğazköy: Upper City**. Royal patronage is strongly implied by the close similarity of the work of the **seal** cutters and even that of the **gold-**

smiths, evident as late as the Iron Age in **Carchemish**.

The question of the ultimate origin of Hittite sculpture centers on the role of Mesopotamian influence. A rock relief of **Naram-sin** of the Akkadian dynasty (23rd century BC) could be the earliest link in the long tradition of such carving in the Near East. One textual reference could suggest the introduction to Hattusa by **Hattusili III** of Kassite Babylonian sculptors. Yet Mesopotamia, with its lack of local stone, would seem an unlikely home for sculptors to instruct native Anatolian craftsmen. Guardian lions at gateways, however, were indeed of Mesopotamian derivation, having initially been fashioned not in stone but in fired clay. These were to become a standard feature of much of Neo-Hittite **architecture**, as at **Hama**, but were already well established under the Hittite Empire.

The art historian Robert Alexander has divided the Yazılıkaya reliefs into four groups, detecting two master sculptors each with an assistant. The cessation of work by one—the so-called **Fraktin** Master—was for reason unknown; but his older style did not die. There seems likely to have been a tradition of apprentices, presumably young, the requisite time for training being made easier by the inevitably slow pace of the work, pecking and rubbing the rock face.

Egyptian influence on Hittite sculpture and **glyptic art** was not new, for the motif of the sphinx occurs on **seals** of the time of the Assyrian trading colonies. When work began at Yazılıkaya, under Hattusili III, relations between Hatti and Egypt became quite close after the **treaty** with **Ramesses II** (1258 BC). Thus the importation of motifs from the latest of the monumental buildings of Egypt is not surprising. Such is the motif of the king in the embrace of his protector **god**. The clearest evidence of Egyptian artistic influence, however, is the winged sun disk, consistent with the adoption of the regal style "My Sun" and with the identification of the Hittite king with his Sun-God.

Hittite sculptors surely worked to a pattern book, very much on the same lines as those followed by seal cutters and goldsmiths alike. Originality was not an artistic trait of the Hittites. The artists were, after all, working to the orders of an essentially traditionalist court, except for the foreign elements introduced by Hattusili III and Puduhepa and followed till the fall of the Empire.

See also: **EFLATUN PINAR; FASILLAR; GAVUR-KALESI; HANYERI-GEZBEL; IMAMKULU; IVRIZ; KARABEL; SIPYLUS, MOUNT; SIRKELI; TAŞCI.**

SEALS (GLYPTIC ART). The field of study of what is commonly termed glyptic has occupied archaeologists and art historians of the ancient Near East for many decades, the pioneer being Henri Frankfort (ca.1900–1956). Philologists and historians are also concerned, especially with the contexts of the sealing of goods. Here, with but brief reference to earlier backgrounds, attention will be focused on the Old Assyrian colonies in Anatolia and on the Hittite Old Kingdom and Empire. Not every detail, notably material, can be given, simply because most of the examples of seals survive only in the form of impressions, often as **bullae**.

The two broad categories of seal are the stamp and the cylinder, with finger rings also often used as seals in the Old Assyrian colonies. Stamp seals first appear in Neolithic times, and continued as the principal form for seals of the native Anatolian tradition. Cylinder seals originated in southern Mesopotamia in the mid–fourth millennium BC, and predominated throughout Mesopotamian history, being disseminated widely through the Near East including Anatolia, normally in Mesopotamian styles. Stamp and cylinder seals were in use side by side in the Old Assyrian colonies.

The seals of **Kültepe-Kanes** and the other Assyrian colonies show much greater variety in their designs than those of the Hittite state afterward. This reflects the difference between communities based on private enterprise and the products of a closely structured state bureaucracy.

At Kanes there were separate workshops for stamp and cylinder seals, and there are hints of individual seal carvers, though no names survive. These were not so exclusively specialist craftsmen as not to engage in other trades: for example, unfinished cylinder seals were excavated in a workshop for bronze tools and **weapons**; and a stamp seal workshop flourished in a house with **tablets**. Some native Anatolian seals were doubtless home made and cheap, judging by their crudity and idiosyncrasies of style.

Iron oxide in the form of haematite was probably extracted from the volcanic areas of eastern Anatolia, and was the commonest material for seal cutters of the Assyrian colonies in central Anatolia ("Cappadocia") but also in Mesopotamia and Syria: there are textual references to its use, as well as to seals of lapis lazuli. Serpentine, steatite and bone, all softer, were used for cheaper, sometimes cruder, seals in Kanes, as well as lead, bronze and clay for stamp seals. Metal cylinder seals first appear in the later second millennium BC in southeastern Anatolia and north Syria. Wooden stamp seals have not survived, but very probably occurred, for use in stamping **textiles**. Steatite was used for some of the Hittite seals excavated at **Ugarit**.

It is the cylinder seals which display the skills of the cutter in design, the stamp seals being relatively simple and limited in repertoire. The Old Assyrian style probably derived from the glyptic art of the Third Dynasty of Ur in southern Mesopotamia (2113–2004 BC), specifically from the rule of Ur over Assur. Influences are discernible from the Syrian-style seals of the third millennium BC and from seals of the so-called Syro-Cappadocian style. Seals of the Old Assyrian style were presumably made both at Assur and in Anatolia. Lapis lazuli seals are textually recorded as being sent from Assur to Anatolia. Themes in this style include: standing figures; introduction to a seated deity, a dominant subject in Mesopotamia; supplication before a seated deity, those without inscription often having one of a rich variety of subsidiary subjects forming the end or terminal element of the design; processions of deities with thunderbolts and other symbols or weapons; a **god** in a **chariot**; the Water-God and scenes with the water hero; the nude goddess; combats; scenes in two registers. The basic scene of introduction or supplication forms the center of nearly all designs. Terminal elements in a design can combine serpents, bulls, lions, scorpions, crossed animals, and tiny human figures or deities, making for a rich repertoire in contrast with the stereotyped seals of contemporary Mesopotamia.

The cylinder seals of the Anatolian style are mostly of high quality, though some can be classed as crude. The origin of this style could lie in *karum* III–IV or in Syria or both. The cylinder seal must have been imported by the first Assyrian merchants, along with the **cuneiform** script, into central Anatolia. By the time of *karum* II at Kanes the cylinder seals in the Anatolian style had developed entirely original designs. Native Anatolian subjects, among them different forms of **Storm-God** or Weather-God, especially animals, are combined with Mesopotamian and other foreign themes, all fitted into crowded Anatolian designs, often on several levels though not in rigid registers. Hittite art was later to absorb elements of iconography and composition from Anatolian glyptic art of the Old Assyrian period. The classification of the subject matter of such crowded designs is difficult. They include: introduction, supplication and offering before a seated deity or ruler; deities and others standing before a seated deity or ruler; deities enthroned or in procession; scenes of animals with "heroes of the field" or showing whole animals or parts; animals in single or double files; and combats. Human beings and animals in the presence of a bull, along with ritual drinking, are among themes on cheap seals of bone, steatite and possibly also wood. It is tempting to see these as particularly popular with poorer folk.

Stamp seals were the dominant Anatolian form, few surviving at Kanes before *karum* IB. The motifs of the Kültepe stamp seals are only very broadly paralleled at **Karahöyük (Konya)** and at **Boğazköy**, such as simple floral designs or spirals within a round face. No parallels occur at these two sites for the stamp seals with human or animal faces or the single couchant animals of Kültepe *karum* II. Whereas stamps of all types were used on the Old Assyrian **tablets**, only geometric stamps were used in the sealing of bullae from bales and storage jars from the palace. Karahöyük (Konya) has yielded a far greater variety of stamp seals than has been excavated at Kanes or at the IB-period colonies at **Alışar Höyük** and **Hattusa**. Motifs at the latter include a stylized leaf or quatrefoil pattern and star, a variety of creatures (double eagle, eagle-demon, griffin, lion, tortoise, hare, stag and sheep), predators killing prey (eagle, double eagle, griffin and lion), a figure drinking with a straw from a vessel on a tripod, a cow's hoof, a foot and a duck.

In the Hittite Old Kingdom at Hattusa are found several glyptic designs on stamp seals: animal heads and **hieroglyphs**, among the early examples of this script; hieroglyphs surrounded by a decorative band, usually interlaced; figures flanked by decorative strips, some with a star in the center, and/or by hieroglyphs; and running spirals. Pictorial designs include a bull, lion, stag and god seated on a chair, all on square or rectangular stamp seals. Other themes are a god facing a nude goddess, each standing on a bull, and a worshiper standing before a seated god (?) with a small stand between, possibly an altar or offering table.

Seals of the later New Kingdom (Empire) include flat examples with rather concave face, giving a slightly convex impression; but biconvex seals with their concave impressions are more common, designed for the most part solely with hieroglyphs, occasionally with a horned goat or sheep. One design has a double eagle, ornaments and flowers. Ornamental motifs include flowers and animals. Hemispherical, discoid and conical seals occur; and a few stamp seals have a suspension loop, more frequent on seals of the Iron Age.

The royal stamp seals of **Ugarit** are centered on a hieroglyphic monogram surmounted by the winged sun disk and surrounded by **cuneiform** script of one, two or occasionally three lines. These seals begin with that of **Suppiluliuma I** and his queen, Tawananna, then those of **Mursili II** and **Hattusili III** with **Puduhepa**. The stamp seal of **Tudhaliya IV** shows a change of design, with the hieroglyphic monogram flanked by figures: on the right side looking left, the king embraced by **Sarruma**; on the left looking right, a goddess. Ini-Tesub, **viceroy** of **Carchemish**, has a god standing with scepter in his right hand and a sphinx standing on his outstretched arm, and is wearing the typical Hittite shoes with upturned toes. The cylinder seals of Carchemish also have standing figures, with cuneiform and/or hieroglyphic inscription. One cylinder used by "Du-Tesub the king" (of **Amurru**) was intended to impress on the inventory of his daughter's dowry for her **marriage** to Ammistamru, king of Ugarit. Although displaying an often rich variety in their designs, seals are not the best evidence for dating, seeing that they are durable and frequently handed down as heirlooms from one generation to the next, no doubt as much for practical business reasons favoring continuity as for any family piety.

SEA PEOPLES. These were groups of invaders of differing origin who came to the knowledge of modern scholars through the records of Ramesses III of Egypt for his eighth year (1177 BC), these being inscribed and depicted on the walls of his great mortuary **temple** of Medinet Habu, the last and best preserved of the royal mortuary temples on the west bank of Thebes in Upper Egypt. Ramesses III caused an account of dramatic events to be written in appropriate words:

> The foreign countries made a conspiracy in their islands. All at once the lands were removed and scattered in the fray. No land could stand before their arms, from **Hatti**, Qode, **Carchemish**, **Arzawa** and **Alasiya** on, being cut off at one time. A camp was set up in one place in **Amurru**. They desolated its people, and its land was like that which has never come into being. They were coming forward toward Egypt, while the flame was prepared before them. Their confederation was the Peleset, Tjeker, Shekelesh, Denyen and Weshesh, lands united. They laid their hands upon the land as far as the circuit of the earth, their hearts confident and trusting: "Our plans will succeed!"

Even allowing for the hyperbole characteristic of Egyptian inscriptions, with their intention of proclaiming the prowess of the Pharaoh, it is apparent that a violent disruption of the Hittite lands and of Syria had occurred, which has to be associated with the downfall of **Hattusa** and the end of the Hittite Empire. Precisely in which year this came about is still uncertain; but it must have occurred between ca.1180 and 1175 BC. The lowering of Egyptian **absolute chronology** has meant that the final end of Hatti has to be set a few years later than hitherto supposed.

The 19th-century Egyptologist Gaston Maspero first suggested a mass migration of northern barbarians into the Hittite lands and southward to the borders of Egypt, and the picture of military and naval confrontation was heightened by the later discovery of an **archive** of **tablets** at **Ugarit**, among them a letter from the last king of the city, Ammurapi, in reply to a call for help from the king of **Alasiya (Cyprus)**, a letter which spoke for itself:

> My father, behold, the enemy's ships came (here); my cities (?) were burned, and they did evil things in my country. Does not my father know that all my troops and **chariots** (?) are in the Land of Hatti and all my ships are in the Land of **Lukka**?. . . . Thus the country is abandoned to itself. May my father know it: the seven ships of the enemy that came here inflicted much damage upon us.

This tablet was with others in an oven where they had just been baked: they were never dispatched.

Who were the Sea Peoples? Not all the groups which disrupted Anatolia in the 12th century BC can be included under this overriding name, notably the **Muski**. Of those listed in the above-quoted inscription at Medinet Habu, the majority evidently came from Palestine (Peleset or Philistines), the Aegean region (Denyen) and Sicily (Shekelesh). One suggestion is that two other groups should be largely discounted, not being mentioned in most of the inscriptions: these are the Sherden or Shardana and the Teresh, the most westerly of the Sea Peoples, so-called. These must clearly be associated with Sardinia and with mainland Italy (Tyrenia). The Sherden first appear in the early 14th century BC in Egypt, in the reign of Amenhotep III, and were being employed as mercenaries by **Ramesses II**. In the Medinet Habu reliefs they appear fighting on both sides, distinguished by their bronze horned **helmets**: their association with Sardinia is based not merely on their name but also on bronze statuettes with horned helmets, found in the distinctive fortified towers of the island, the *nuraghi*.

It is apparent that a considerable naval force attacked the Nile Delta, with the aim of sacking the royal palace of Ramesses III, built on one of the mouths of the Nile, close to the site of the palace of his predecessor **Ramesses** II. Their repulse marked the end of any attempt to occupy Lower Egypt.

The theory of a mass migration had rested largely on the representations of women and children advancing in oxcarts: these, it was assumed, were the families of the invading land and sea forces. It is, however, far more likely that these were refugees from southern Palestine, fleeing the destruction and disorder caused by the intruders. The role of the sea force has perhaps been exaggerated, although the tablets found at Ugarit hardly support this suggestion. Probably the whole Mediterranean was subject to frequent piratical raids, sometimes mirrored on land. The Egyptian word translated as "islands" might more safely be rendered as "seacoasts," only the Shekelesh and Sherden being definitely islanders.

Yet, however the earlier view of the Sea Peoples has had to be modified, their role in the downfall of the Hittite power and in bringing the Bronze Age to an end in Anatolia and the Levant can scarcely be doubted. Many cities, notably Ugarit, were never rebuilt. Only Egypt survived relatively unscathed, troubled more by internal weakness and dissension.

SEEHER, JÜRGEN. Director of the **Boğazköy excavations** since 1994. He gained his doctorate at the Free University of Berlin (1983), with his thesis on the Neolithic, Chalcolithic and Early Bronze Age **pottery** from Demircihöyük, in northwestern Anatolia. He is thus a prehistorian by training. While assistant director at the German Institute of Archaeology in Istanbul (1989–1993), he excavated a Bronze Age cemetery at Demircihöyük-Sanket. His excavations in Boğazköy include work on **Büyükkaya** and the reservoirs in the **Upper City**.

SEHA RIVER LAND. The river was probably the Classical Caicos, which flows into the Aegean Sea not far north of the mouth of the Hermos River. This territory formed the northern part of the homeland of **Arzawa**, lying north and northeast of modern Izmir and immediately north of Sardis. It was fertile land, destined to become part of the central region of the kingdom of Lydia in the Iron Age.

The Seha River Land was in the anti-Hittite alliance defeated by **Tudhaliya I/II**. In the ensuing period of Hittite weakness, however, it inevitably gravitated again to Arzawa, as a result of which it was strongly attacked by **Mursili II**, following his defeat of Arzawa and the death of Uhhaziti, its king. Mursili unexpectedly showed clemency, when the mother of the ruler of the Seha River Land, Manapa-Tarhunda, came to plead for mercy. It almost smacks of chivalry! The land and its ruler—whose name betrays his **Luwian** affinities—were reduced to vassalage.

Later, in the reign of **Muwatalli II**, Piyamaradu defeated an expedition led against him in **Wilusa** by Manapa-Tarhunda. Muwatalli was compelled to act, sending a Hittite force under the command of Gassu, mainly to remove Piyamaradu from Wilusa. He wisely withdrew to the protection of **Ahhiyawa**. **Tudhaliya IV**, obliged to restore Hittite rule in the west after the relative weakness in his father's reign, attacked Arzawa Minor under Tarhunaradu, and placed a descendant of Muwawalwi, father of Manapa-Tarhunda, on the throne of the Seha River Land.

SERI AND HURRI. The bulls of the **Storm-God**, bearing names in **Hurrian** signifying "Day" and "Night," are agreed to be represented by two large baked clay statuettes 90 centimeters high, found in the 1963 excavations on **Boğazköy: Büyükkale** by **Kurt Bittel**. Attributed to Büyükkale IVb2, they can be dated to the beginning of the Hittite New Kingdom or Empire. With light-red to red highly burnished slip and patches of cream on shoulders, haunches, foreheads and horns, their eyes are white with black inlaid pupils, giving them a fierce look. They were found together in a cache; and their tails, hanging down the left and right leg respectively, demonstrate that they were a pair. Each bull has a funnel-shaped opening at the neck for pouring in liquids and two openings in the nostrils as outlets. These were thus **cult** vessels for rituals involving libations.

Textual evidence shows that these divine bulls acted as intermediaries, interceding for men before the **gods**, and may have been associated with the domestic cult. This is suggested by the occurrence of fragments of similar large baked clay statuettes in houses in **Hattusa**.

In one of the scholarly disagreements characteristic of a vigorous discipline, Bittel saw Seri and Hurri appearing in the reliefs of **Yazılıkaya**, whereas **Emmanuel Laroche** saw the "bull-calf of **Tesub**." The argument hung largely on the interpretation of one

hieroglyph, opinion now coming down on Laroche's side. Be that as it may, the function of Seri and Hurri was to draw the **chariot** of the **Storm-God**, a theme indirectly echoed later on the **gold** bowl of **Hasanlu** and the reliefs of **Malatya**.

SHALMANESER I (1263–1234 BC). He maintained an aggressive policy toward Hatti, though his claim to have slaughtered Hittite soldiers like sheep may be questioned. He constituted a threat, however, at the end of his reign to the new Hittite king, **Tudhaliya IV**, when Hatti was beginning to weaken.

SHIELDS. Hittite shields carried by the shield bearers in the **chariots** as depicted on the Egyptian reliefs of the battle of **Kadesh** are of figure-of-eight shape. They were evidently designed to protect the whole body of the driver during the charge. The round shield was brought to the Near East by the **Sea Peoples**, becoming standard issue for Neo-Hittite troops.

SIEGE WARFARE. The evidence suggests that siege operations did not usually rank among the most successful achievements of the Hittite **army**. Two sieges occurred under **Hattusili I**: the high-flown account of the siege of **Ursu** reveals weaknesses in the attacking Hittite force, while the city of **Hahha** on the Euphrates valiantly repulsed two Hittite attacks before finally succumbing. The siege of **Carchemish** by **Suppiluliuma I** was more of a triumph, the **Mitannian** stronghold falling to a direct assault on the eighth day.

Voluntary surrender was obviously the best outcome for the besieging force. An alternative would be to ravage the surrounding land belonging to the city under siege. In a direct assault, battering rams would be deployed against the main gate, where the garrison might be tempted to come out in a counter-attack, exposing themselves dangerously. For a lengthy siege of many months, towers and ramps of earth were required, to surmount the **fortifications**, and tunnels to penetrate beneath their foundations, a laborious operation demanding the skills of seasoned sappers. Starving the inhabitants was not as easy as it might appear, for it was far from simple to prevent all movement to and from the besieged city, as the siege of Ursu demonstrated. The besieging force would probably have to break off operations if not completed at the onset of the Anatolian winter.

Posterns were a favored device for the besieged garrison to mount a sally or counter-attack, most suitably at night.

SILVER. In some ways this was regarded in the ancient Near East as being as highly prized as **gold**, although its lower exchange rate belies this impression. In some excavated sites it is rare or non-existent, owing to the fact that, unlike gold, it corrodes badly in adverse soil conditions. As with gold, artifacts of silver are overwhelmingly recovered from burials, and then only from those not robbed.

In Anatolia the earliest major find of silver comprises personal ornaments from graves of the fourth millennium BC from **Korucutepe**, in the Keban area of the upper Euphrates valley, subsequently the land of **Isuwa**. Silver artifacts of the third millennium BC occur at **Alaca Höyük** and elsewhere in central Anatolia, at Mahmutlar, Horoztepe, **Eskiyapar** and **Alışar Höyük**, as well as at **Troy**.

The major evidence for silver comes from contemporary **tablets** and other inscriptions. It was in use in Mesopotamia from the mid–third millennium BC as the dominant medium of exchange in **trade**, in a society where something approaching a form of currency was required. Silver was employed in making purchases and arranging loans and deposits, as well as paying rents. It was, moreover, included in offerings to the **gods** and in items of tribute in peace and war, featuring prominently in the last capacity in the Late Assyrian royal **annals**. The most numerous textual references occur in the tablets from **Kültepe-Kanes**, when silver was one of the major exports from Anatolia, and when it appears in complex partnership and other deals.

Various hints can be found of the value attached to silver over and beyond the obvious commercial contexts. It was evidently regarded as the metal of special purity, mentioned in the context of Hittite **royal funerary customs**: a silver vessel was used by the women responsible for collecting the bones from a royal **cremation**, early on the second day of the funeral rites. Later, a kinsman of the dead cuts down a vine with a silver ax. In an early **Hurrian** myth preserved in a Hittite version, the young god Silver, living in the countryside with his mother, is told by her: "O Silver! The city you enquire about, I will describe to you. Your father is **Kumarbi**, the Father of the city **Urkesh**. He resides in Urkesh. . . ."

This story was originally set in the mountains where silver was mined, a region with which ethnic affiliation is claimed for the citizens of Urkesh. The Keban area is nearer the location of

Urkesh at **Tell Mozan** than the silver mines of the Taurus Mountains, and the population there would have been mainly Hurrian. A more economic use of silver, in a professional context, is apparent in a text from **Hattusa** describing the construction of a house, with the completion of the **timber** roof structure. At this point the **architect** is obliged to shin up a rope to the roof, three times on to the roof and down again, the third time cutting a sash hanging from a roof beam: in this sash are tied an **ax** and a knife of silver. After bowing to the owner of the house, the architect goes home, taking the ax and knife for himself, as his fee.

The principal Anatolian sources of silver were the Bolkardağ region of the Taurus Mountains, including Madenköy, and the Keban mine, until 1833 yielding up to five tons of silver annually. Silver is also found in western Anatolia, in the Çanakkale and Izmir areas, and in the Pontic highlands south of the Black Sea, where place-names—including Trabzon-Gümüşhane and Amasya-Gümüşhaciköy—are highly suggestive, *gümüş* being Turkish for "silver."

The extraction of silver was commonly associated with sulfide ores, particularly lead sulfide (galena), sources of lead thus being a strong pointer to silver too. Cupellation was the technique used for extracting silver from lead ores, evidence occurring in the Bolkardağ mining region. Native silver is rare today, though it may have been more common in antiquity.

SIPYLUS, MOUNT. A Hittite rock relief with **hieroglyphic** inscriptions, located near Akpınar in the province of Manisa, northeast of Izmir. Its stylistic similarities to the reliefs of nearby **Karabel** and more distant **Gavurkalesi**, **Yazılıkaya**, **Fraktin** and **Sirkeli** place it clearly in the early to mid–13th century BC. A recess contains a colossal figure in relief, most widely agreed to represent a seated goddess, probably the "Mother of the Gods," wearing a crown in the semblance of a walled city. Alternative interpretations postulate either an enthroned, bearded figure or a bearded Mountain-God, standing and wearing a horned crown. An inscription close to the goddess has its hieroglyphs carefully rendered in relief, whereas another inscription is unfinished, its signs incised and hard to distinguish, as so often depending on the angle of sunlight.

SIRKELI. Rock relief overlooking the Ceyhan River and the Yakapınar-Ceyhan road, 37 kilometers east of Adana and not far north of the modern east-west highway past Adana. This is one of a number of Hittite reliefs overlooking fresh water, in this example flowing water rather than a spring: it is generally agreed that this association with water has a religious significance.

This relief has an inscription identifying the single figure as the Hittite king **Muwatalli II.** It is thus the earliest dated Hittite relief, and the only one preceding the reign of **Hattusili III.** Given its location, near the line of march from the Hittite homeland to the battlefield of **Kadesh** in Syria, a date around the time of the battle seems plausible. This association with the great confrontation with Egypt has led to speculation, not unreasonable, on the possible influence of Egyptian on Hittite art, given the very long tradition of rock reliefs in Egypt. Hittite **sculpture** yields other evidence of Egyptian influence.

The Sirkeli relief exemplifies the predominant category, having one or only two or three figures, rather than the long processions seen at **Yazılıkaya**. Again it follows the majority of rock reliefs in being unframed, in contrast with most at Yazılıkaya. Though 30 years or more earlier than the **Fraktin** relief, it seems to represent the same artistic stage, perhaps a hint of overlapping among the sculptors employed, who were probably few, at least for the more experienced.

SLAVERY, SLAVES. An uncertain but undoubtedly large percentage of the population of the Hittite lands comprised slaves, in fact if not by legal definition in every case. The great majority were captives in war, most of whom were sent to form the labor force on the estates of senior officers of the **army**, on **temple** estates or to rural communities whose manpower was depleted by constant military service. Other slaves had been reduced to this status through debt, but stood a chance of regaining their freedom by repayment of the debt or by royal amnesty. A few murderers might be enslaved to the family of their victim, an example of the underlying principle of the **Hittite Laws**—in contrast to the Babylonian—that compensation took priority over retribution. A poor man had only his labor to give.

While attempts to flee and regain freedom were not rare, Hittite slaves did not suffer as severely as those in many other societies through history, and certainly not as those on the cotton plantations of the South before the American Civil War, still less the forced labor under the Third Reich. Indeed, under a benevolent, paternalist owner they would enjoy economic and personal security. Moreover, the legal attitude to a mixed **marriage** was tolerant, though allowing a slave to marry a free woman involved economic loss to the owner, since the children of such a marriage would be free, and thus would be lost to him for good. Slaves might own property, though those enslaved to a temple and thus to the **god or goddess** might enjoy fewer privileges.

Nevertheless, whatever benefits might accrue to many slaves of Hittite masters, they were bound to their owner for life; and he enjoyed absolute legal control over them, even to the extent of execution for causing acute anger. The capital penalty could legally be applied to the whole family of the offending slave, though the economic loss usually restrained an owner from reducing his labor force. There was the lesser yet brutal punishment of mutilation, originally applicable to free men also, though this was changed with the revision of the Hittite Laws, leaving it permitted only for slaves.

SPEARS. A long spear was especially employed in open battle, the socketed spearhead displacing the earlier form with bent tang and slots in the blade, in use from the later third millennium BC. The spear was balanced by a metal spike at the bottom end, for skewering an enemy or planting in the ground during pauses on the march. A spearman was put aboard the Hittite **chariot**, along with the driver and **shield** bearer.

STAMP SEALS. *See* **BULLA(E); GLYPTIC ART; SCULPTURE; SEALS.**

STATUES. **Gods** were usually represented in human form, as indeed they were conceived; and in the later Empire their statues, set up on stone bases in their **temple** sanctuaries, were life-size or larger. They were fashioned in **gold**, **silver**, **iron** (a valuable metal) or bronze; or carved out of wood plated with gold, silver or **tin**, and sometimes decorated with materials such as lapis lazuli, originating ultimately from Afghanistan.

Images of dead kings might also be found in temples. One offering for a cure from maladies and for long life was made by **Puduhepa** to the goddess **Lelwani** on behalf of her aging husband, **Hattusili III**, in the shape of a life-size silver statue.

STELAE (*HUWASI* STONES). Deities could be represented by a **cult** object rather than a **statue** as normally understood, in the form of a totem or stela, mentioned especially in **festival** texts and

cult inventories. The basic meaning of *huwasi* was a stone stela, sometimes relief-carved and set on an altar in the sanctuary of the **temple**. There it might be washed, anointed, clothed and given **food** and drink. A *huwasi* could be larger, a rough monolith, set up in open country and representing a separate deity, or one of a number marking off a sacred area. It thus seems that this manifests the indigenous, essentially chthonic cultic tradition of the Anatolian countryside, long pre-dating the Hittite state.

"STONES OF HAMATH." Johann Ludwig Burckhardt (1784–1817) describes in his *Travels in Syria and the Holy Land* (London, 1822) a stone he had seen embedded in the corner of a building in the bazaar at Hama—"A stone with a number of small figures and signs which appears to be a kind of **hieroglyphic** writing, though it does not resemble that of Egypt."

In the later 19th century two Americans, J. A. Johnson and Dr. Jessop, spotted Burckhardt's stone and three others. But the local inhabitants objected to their touching them, thinking they had curative properties. Soon afterward, another hieroglyphic stone was discovered—at **Aleppo**.

Then, a year later, **William Wright**, an Irish missionary in Damascus, had the opportunity to examine the stones, when Subhi Pasha, the new governor of Syria, gave his support, protection with soldiers and finally money for the locals, to permit removal of these stones to Constantinople. This was not, however, before repeated loud demonstrations by angry townsmen.

Meanwhile, discoveries of "Hittite" hieroglyphic stones widened to **Carchemish** and further afield to **Ivriz**, **Yazılıkaya** and elsewhere. **A. H. Sayce** was in the forefront of the quest for hieroglyphic inscriptions, a hunt which had been sparked by the discoveries at Hama.

STORE CITIES. Ten or more storehouses, sited in "store cities," are mentioned in the decree of **Telipinu**, among them being **Samuha**, **Kussara** and Parsuhanda. Fewer than the centers with an *agrig*, these were presumably more important. They comprised two categories: those in provincial towns and those belonging to the same town but located in **Hattusa**. Unlike the centers with an *agrig*, the store cities must have played a crucial role in the administration of the Hittite state, with their direct connections with the heart of **government** in Hattusa. Theirs was a fiscal and economic function, not simply linked to religious **festivals**. Like all the major polities of the ancient Near East, this was a storage economy, state-controlled rather than free enterprise.

STORM-GOD (WEATHER-GOD). The sovereign head of the hierarchic order determining the shape and destiny of the Hittite realm. The king held second place in this hierarchy, acknowledging that he was the slave of the Storm-God, to whom he owed his power. The ideogram for this god could represent different divinities, deriving from **language** and cultural context: the Hittite Tarhunt(a), the **Luwian** Datta, the **Hurrian Tesub**, the Akkadian Adad and even the Sumerian Iskur and the Northwest Semitic Ba'al. Understandably there were innumerable local manifestations of the Storm-God; and most **cult centers** gave him a place in their hierarchy to be worshiped.

SUGZIYA. A city located in the Euphrates region, probably north of **Ursu** and thus further north of **Carchemish**. It was lost in the reign of **Hantili I** (ca.1590–1560 BC), whose **queen** and sons were held captive and killed there. This was among territories regained by **Telipinu** and is one of a number of Hittite **store cities** listed in his reign.

SUN-GODDESS. While ostensibly to be regarded as an Indo-European sky deity, she was in fact of **Hattian** origin and chthonic rather than celestial in character. Her high status was especially revered in relation to the **cult center** of **Arinna**, only one day's journey from **Hattusa** and thus at the heart of the kingdom. Under the Empire, the native triad of the Sun-Goddess of Arinna, the **Storm-God** of Hatti and the Storm-God of **Nerik** was identified with the **Hurrian** divinities **Hebat**, **Tesub** and **Sarruma**.

SUPPILULIUMA I (1344–1322 BC). His is generally regarded as the most successful of the Hittite kings' reigns, although not without unsolved problems at his death. He was long supposed to have reigned for some 40 years; but this time-span has been shortened by almost a half, to 22 years. This does not, however, give a true impression of his life and achievements, for he had campaigned for many years under the authority of his father, **Tudhaliya III**, who may have been middle-aged when he acceded to the throne in **Hattusa**. Suppiluliuma himself may have been about 40 years old when he gained the throne: while no Hittite records survive to reveal the birth dates of successive kings, his second son, Telipinu, was appointed high priest in **Kizzuwadna** early in his reign (ca.1342 BC). His eldest son, Arnuwanda, was very probably born some 20 years earlier, when Suppiluliuma would have been about 20 years of age. His active life in serving and then ruling the state would thus have spanned at least 40 years.

He appears to have been equally responsible, with his father, for the counter-attacks against the enemies who had invaded the Hittite kingdom from all directions, with the loss of Hattusa and most of the Hittite lands. This concerted military recovery, mounted from headquarters at **Samuha**, was directed first northward and then to the west. By his accession Suppiluliuma had secured all the Anatolian territories lost in his father's early reign.

While no records survive, if they ever existed, to reveal explicit sidelights on the personalities of successive Hittite kings, aspects of which they would presumably not have wished to be exposed, their successors on occasions were more informative. Their evidence, however, has to be taken with caution, since they were apt to be seeking explanations for unwelcome events or excuses for their own setbacks. Thus **Mursili II**, in his prayers to the gods to end the **plague** afflicting his realm, identified possible reasons for their wrath, among them being the killing of Tudhaliya the Younger, elder brother of Suppiluliuma and ordained successor to Tudhaliya III, by Suppiluliuma, who had succeeded in gaining the support of most of the nobility and **army**, men who had just previously given their allegiance to his brother. This seizure of the throne, interpreted by Mursili as an act of impiety requiring atonement, displayed the ruthless side of Suppiluliuma, perhaps a prerequisite for the military and political triumphs of his reign. A similar attitude to his family was demonstrated by the apparent banishment of his first **queen**, Henti, probably the mother of all his five sons, when he saw the opportunity for a politically advantageous **marriage** to a Babylonian princess who assumed the name and style of Tawannana, following the Hittite royal custom. He was not to know what difficulties she would bring to his son and successor. **Seals** and inscriptions link three queens with Suppiluliuma during his reign, his mother Daduhepa and Henti and Tawannana successively.

On his gaining the throne, Suppiluliuma saw the principal threat to Hittite interests as lying in the east, where Hittite rule had not yet been fully restored. Behind all the rebellious princelings stood the great kingdom of **Mitanni**, which he correctly saw as the enemy to be overcome by direct confrontation in battle. A first attack proved abortive, Tusratta of Mitanni claiming a great victory and dispatching some of the booty to Amenhotep III in Egypt, as recorded in one of the **Amarna** letters addressed to this pharaoh. Since—on the currently proposed **absolute chronology**—there was a period of perhaps eight years between the death of Amenhotep III (1390–1352 BC) and the accession of Suppiluliuma I, either the chronology must be changed, with all the attendant side-effects, or it must be assumed that this action occurred under Suppiluliuma's inspiration but during the reign of his father. This seems far the more plausible explanation, and might be accounted for as a result of youthful inexperience.

Suppiluliuma had learned his lesson, not to underestimate Mitanni and also to prepare the ground diplomatically for his next assault. This shrewdness was to characterize all his subsequent enterprises in Syria, the most notable example of his choice of **diplomacy** being his dealings with the kingdom of **Ugarit**. Understanding its wealth and importance as a center of **trade**, he successfully weaned it away from allegiance to Egypt: it was to remain in the Hittite sphere until the fall of the Empire.

First, however, came his outstanding military success, commonly termed the Great Syrian War, an amazingly victorious campaign of one year (1340/1339 BC), of which the details survive not in the sadly damaged *Deeds* but in the preambles of two of this king's **treaties**, with Sattiwaza of Mitanni and the king of **Nuhasse**. Suppiluliuma must have been aware of the internal tensions within Mitanni, with Tusratta on the throne but not commanding universal support, and of the necessity of striking at the heart of his enemy's realm. Until this was achieved, there was no expectation of defeating the Mitannian vassals west of the Euphrates River, his major objective. After sacking **Wassukkanni**, Suppiluliuma was able to subdue a string of minor kingdoms from the Euphrates to the Mediterranean, over a region extending south to Aba (Damascus), bordering the Egyptian Empire: the most important of these were **Aleppo**, **Mukis** and Nuhasse. Swept up in this triumphal succession of conquests was the kingdom of **Kadesh** on the Orontes, earlier under Mitannian overlordship: it had been defeated and annexed by Tuthmose III of Egypt, and was later, by a treaty with Thutmose IV (1398–1390 BC), acknowledged by Mitanni to fall within the Egyptian sphere. Suppiluliuma had no desire for confrontation with Egypt, though having been provoked by the ruler of Kadesh. Egypt accepted this as a fait accompli, if reluctantly; but in the reign of Tutankhamun (1336–1327 BC) an attempt was made to recapture the city. At the end of the Great Syrian War west of the Euphrates only **Carchemish** remained under Mitannian control.

Hittite military and diplomatic involvement in Syria continued, with the eventual winning over of **Amurru**, under its devious ruler Aziru, from its allegiance to Egypt under Akhenaten (1352–1336 BC) to Hittite overlordship, to which he remained loyal until his death, having understood the weakness of Egypt in Syria. Meanwhile, Hittite forces were penetrating the land of Amka—the Biqa' valley between the Lebanon and Anti-Lebanon ranges— recognized hitherto as within the Egyptian sphere. At some point the king's son Telipinu was moved from his post in Kizzuwadna to appointment as king, in effect **viceroy**, in Aleppo, a nominal priest turned general. When his father returned to Anatolia, for punitive operations in the **Kaska** lands, Mitanni saw its chance for a final attempt to regain its lost territories west of the Euphrates; but Telipinu counter-attacked, establishing a winter camp near Carchemish and subduing the areas surrounding the city, though not the city itself. He was then summoned to meet Suppiluliuma in the **Lower Land**. Perhaps inevitably, Mitanni responded by laying siege to the Hittite camp near Carchemish.

A Hittite reaction was clearly demanded, and Suppiluliuma was not one to shrink from the challenge. Carchemish had to be taken. Thus opened the Second Syrian War, known otherwise as the Hurrian War, with operations extending over some six years. After a week's **siege**, a fierce battle the next day led to the fall of Carchemish, destined to remain in Hittite hands until the end of the Empire and indeed beyond. It was during the siege that Suppiluliuma was astonished by a message sent from **Ankhesenamun** in Egypt, following the death of her young husband, Tutankhamun, possibly murdered.

When Zannanza, fourth of the five sons of Suppiluliuma, was slain at the border of Egypt, war was inevitable, despite the denials of the next pharaoh, Ay, of complicity in the crime. Militarily successful as was this attack on Egyptian territory in Syria, there was one disastrous consequence: the thousands of prisoners of war brought with them into the Hittite realm a fatal **plague**, in due course killing both Suppiluliuma and his eldest son and successor.

Mitanni fell ever more deeply into internecine strife, continuing with the murder of Tusratta and dethronement of his son Sattiwaza, who sought the support of Suppiluliuma. Concerned at the threat to Hittite rule in north Syria from the growing power of Assyria under **Assur-uballit I (1353–1318 BC)**, he determined to act, sending a force eastward from Carchemish under its viceroy, his son Sarri-Kusuh, together with a Mitannian force under Sattiwaza. The Assyrian threat was warded off by the capture of the Mitannian capital, Wassukkanni; and for the remaining years of the reign Hittite rule in north Syria was secure, administered by the two viceroys, with their headquarters in Aleppo and Carchemish.

Great as the achievements of his reign undoubtedly had been, Suppiluliuma left ongoing problems for his successors in relations with Assyria and Egypt; and the widespread revolts after his death showed the fragility of Hittite control over Arzawa and the other lands of the west.

SUPPILULIUMA II (1207–ca.1180/1176 BC). The history of the last years of the Hittite Empire is now much better understood than it was around 1970. Initially this seemed far from the case, since refinements in Hittite palaeography led to the redating by general agreement of important historical texts from **Tudhaliya IV** and **Arnuwanda III** to **Tudhaliya I/II** and **Arnuwanda I**, six generations earlier. Newly discovered texts and reinterpretation of others longer known have been filling this gap in scholarly knowledge.

David Hawkins attributes the final decline of Hatti largely to the rise of **Tarhuntassa**, located by him in Rough Cilicia (Hilakku), signs of which are discernible in the concessions evident in the Bronze Tablet of Tudhaliya IV, compared with the **treaty** drawn up by **Hattusili III**. Tarhuntassa was accorded equality of status with **Carchemish**, the rulers of each ranking immediately after the crown prince in **Hattusa**. The **Sea Peoples** were stirring. Matters had gone badly in the east since the battle of **Nihriya**. Only in the west do affairs seem to have progressed more in favor of the Hittites.

Internal factors may well have been more significant in the downfall of the Hittite Empire, apart from the activities of the Sea Peoples. Recurrent **famine**, depletion of manpower for the **army** and internal dissensions in and around the royal family, these last originating as far back as the seizure of the throne by **Suppiluliuma I** or at least to the usurpation by Hattusili III—all these factors took their toll.

Supppiluliuma II records his western campaign in a **hieroglyphic** inscription of six lines within Chamber 2 beneath the Southern Citadel **(Boğazköy: Südburg)**, mentioning the conquest of Wiyawanda, Tamina, **Masa, Lukka** and Ikuna in a building inscription. This is a genre not found earlier in the Empire but quite common in the first-millennium BC **Luwian** hieroglyphic inscriptions. This is significant also in derivation from Middle Assyrian texts, where the genesis of historical **annals** can be detected. The conquest of Tarhuntassa is also mentioned. This western campaign may also have been directed against the homeland of some of the maritime marauders soon to join the Sea Peoples, and who were already a major threat to Hatti. The same enemy may well have been the target of the attack by Suppiluliuma II on **Alasiya (Cyprus)**, which can be deciphered in the very badly worn rock inscription of **Boğazköy: Nişantaş**, 11 lines of text and 8.5 meters long. Initially this was ascribed to Suppiluliuma I but then to Suppiluliuma II (strictly, Suppiluliama).

An indication of the tensions surrounding the throne comes from an oath taken by a **scribe**, with heavy emphasis on loyalty to the king and his immediate descendants. Such divisions inevitably weakened the king in the homeland, and tended to undermine the loyalty of vassals, including **Ugarit**.

SWORDS AND DAGGERS. The Hittite sword was not a rapier but was used for slashing. Its cutting edge was on the outside of the sickle-shaped blade, and it was fashioned of bronze. This weapon remained in use until the introduction, possibly from western Anatolia, of the straight sword—superior in design and in being forged of **iron**—by the **Sea Peoples** or in their time. Often only the pommel of stone, bone or metal has been recovered in excavations. Swords appear on the reliefs of **Karabel**, **Gavurkalesi** and **Yazılıkaya** and in the Iron Age at **Zincirli**. Hittite soldiers were also equipped with a short dagger, frequently to be seen on the reliefs, its hilt often crescentic. More elaborate hilts with animal heads appear on daggers clearly for ceremonial use. Blade and hilt were originally attached by rivets but later cast in one piece. Inlays of wood or bone could be attached by rivets and flanged edges.

- T -

TABAL. A confederation of some 12 principalities, initially independent, extending from the Kayseri region over the Konya Plain (the Hittite **Lower Land**) to the Taurus Mountains. In the ninth century BC these local rulers sent gifts to the Assyrian king, Shalmaneser III (859–824 BC), who had invaded Que (formerly **Kizzuwadna**):

he referred to "24 kings of Tabal," probably the political embodiment of the surviving **Luwian** population after the fall of the Hittite Empire, preserving much of its religious and artistic heritage.

Tabal was united into one kingdom in the eighth century BC under the dynasty of Birutas, whose most powerful ruler was Wasasarma, named in the **annals** of Tiglath-Pileser III of Assyria (745–727 BC) as Uassurme, a list of the local rulers being recorded (738 BC). One of his vassals was Warpalawas (Urballa) of **Tuwanuwa** (Tyana), whose domain also included Tunna (**Porsuk Höyük**) and **Hupisna**, in the region of Ereğli and Niğde. He is depicted on the rock relief of **Ivriz**. The governmental center of Tabal was probably at **Kululu**. The reputation of Tabal is hinted at by its mention in the Old Testament as Tubal. Its most prominent divinity was **Kubaba**, a later version of **Hebat**, implying that mixed in with the Luwian majority was a **Hurrian** element.

TABARNA. Royal title attached to the Hittite kings in Akkadian and **Luwian** texts, this was the equivalent of the title **Labarna** in texts written in **Hittite**.

TABLETS. At **Kanes** some tablets may have been baked in the merchants' hearths, but most were found by the excavators either unbaked or fired only by the destruction. There was no uniformity of size or type of tablet according to contents. Orthography also varied. All in all, the Old Assyrian merchants seem to have organized their businesses, including their tablets—**archives**, correspondence, contracts and so on.—on a "family firm" basis. The Cappadocian tablets are usually small, about five by four centimeters, and rectangular, probably in part owing to practicalities of transport and storage in private houses with limited space. But legal transcripts, *karum* statutes and some letters and memoranda were of necessity written on very large tablets. While the tablets of *karum* II were put into clay envelopes which were then sealed, in *karum* IB the **seal** was often impressed directly on the tablet.

The tablets from **Hattusa**—some 5,000 or more in some 30,000 fragments—are rectangular, with the whole obverse and reverse closely written in **cuneiform** script, each side divided into up to four vertical columns. The text was also divided into sections. They were not fired, except in the final conflagration. The contemporary tablets from **Ugarit** were, however, baked in ovens. The vast number of fragments has kept Hittitologists employed for almost a century, the discovery of a join often being greeted as a major advance.

jor advance.

Wooden tablets are textually recorded, along with "**scribes** in wood," but of course have not survived. These would have been written in **hieroglyphs** and in the **Luwian** language.

TAPIKKA. Located at **Maşat Höyük**, 116 kilometers northeast of **Hattusa**. Turkish excavations, 1973–1984.

TARHUNDARADU. A powerful king of **Arzawa**, with whom Amenhotep III of Egypt (1390–1352 BC) was in diplomatic contact, aware of the extreme weakness of Hatti in the time of crisis under **Tudhaliya III**.

TARHUNTASSA. This region, created a kingdom by **Muwatalli II**, played a crucial role in the last century of the Hittite Empire. It is of interest also in the context of **historical geography**, for there is good evidence, from a recent field reconnaissance (1998), that Tarhuntassa extended not only over "Rough Cilicia" (the Mediterranean littoral immediately west of **Kizzuwadna** as far west as the Ak Su, just east of modern Antalya) but also over lands immediately north of the Taurus range, from the southern part of the Konya Plain to Lake Beyşehir and Lake Eğridir, the frontier thence running south by the Ak Su valley to the Mediterranean. The Ak Su (*white water*) can be identified with the Kastaraya River, mentioned in the **treaty** inscribed on the Bronze Tablet found at **Hattusa**, and with the Kestros River of Classical times.

The restriction of the geographical extent of Tarhuntassa to the hilly country of Rough Cilicia alone seems justifiable for the reign of **Suppiluliuma II**, last of the Hittite kings ruling from Hattusa, with the challenges to his kingdom presented by the incoming **Sea Peoples**. Such a restriction does not, however, fit the data for the earlier years of Tarhuntassa.

The reasons behind the revolutionary decision of Muwatalli II to make what he clearly intended to be a permanent removal of the seat of royal government from Hattusa to the city of Tarhuntassa (formerly read as Datassa) in the land of that name have been much discussed. The intended finality of this transfer is indicated by the removal of the **gods** from their old seat at Hattusa: it is hardly surprising that such a decision aroused resentment in some quarters. No doubt priestly interests were affected.

The obvious factor behind this removal of the Hittite **government** to a more southerly Anatolian location was its greater suitability as a base for the campaign against **Ramesses II** of Egypt, culminating at **Kadesh** (1274 BC), and likewise for future Hittite involvement in and perhaps beyond Syria. Hattusa, moreover, was chronically exposed to depredations by the **Kaska** tribes from the north, whose thwarting had been one of the motives for the original choice long since of Hattusa as his governmental center by **Hattusili I**.

Muwatalli II had in effect partitioned his realm, assigning the northern territory, including much of Hatti, to his brother, the future **Hattusili III**. Tarhuntassa thus became the center of government for the Empire as a whole. The exact whereabouts of the city chosen as the new capital is unknown, though obviously it has to be a site with traces of occupation of the relevant period, presumably in the form of surface **pottery**. There is evidence which could support a location near Karaman, accessible to the route through the Cilician Gates, the pass leading to the lowlands of Kizzuwadna and thence into Syria. It must have been a major settlement before its selection by Muwatalli II.

Administration of Tarhuntassa was later entrusted by Hattusili III to the second son of Muwatalli II, his nephew **Kurunta**. This arrangement appears to have worked harmoniously over many years, beginning with the usurpation by Hattusili III. It was doubtless to assure his continued loyalty to Hattusa that Kurunta was given part or parts of the Hittite **Lower Land**, including especially the **Hulaya River Land**, clearly demonstrating the wide territorial expanse of Tarhuntassa at this stage.

Whatever the precise circumstances at the time (1228 BC) of the likely coup d'état by Kurunta, his subsequent fate is unknown. It seems very possible that Tarhuntassa was lost to Hittite control after **Tudhaliya IV** regained power in Hattusa, although an alternative theory would date its loss later, to an incursion by an advance wave of the Sea Peoples, rebuffed by Suppiluliuma II in his third campaign, when he recovered Tarhuntassa.

The separate identity of Tarhuntassa, from its establishment as virtually one of the Hittite **viceroyalties** by Hattusili III, may be partly explicable by demographic divergence from Hatti. The population was predominantly **Luwian** rather than Hittite. Herein lay its strength in the generations after the downfall of the Hittite Empire, when Iron Age kingdoms flourished in this region.

TARSUS (GÖZLÜ KULE). An American expedition directed by Hetty Goldman and supported by Princeton University, Bryn Mawr

College and other institutions carried out excavations before World War II (1934–1939) and on a more limited scale thereafter (1947–1948). The result has been to reveal a cultural sequence for the whole Bronze Age unsurpassed in the Cilician plain, **Kizzuwadna** in Hittite times. To some degree Tarsus provides evidence of cultural connections between north Syria and central Anatolia, as well as further west. It also affords a range of **pottery** contemporary with the Hittite Old Kingdom and Empire, Late Bronze I and Late Bronze IIa respectively in the Tarsus chronology.

Previously enjoying long-lasting relations with Syria, from the beginning of the Early Bronze Age Tarsus became dominated by Anatolian influence. With the Early Bronze III period newcomers arrived, evidently from northwestern Anatolia, bringing new types of pottery and the *megaron* plan of house, with one rectangular room having a central hearth and with a deep porch. In the following period (transitional Middle Bronze Age) the "red-cross bowl" typical of **Troy** V appears at Tarsus in the late third millennium BC. It seems very probable that these newcomers were **Luwians**.

With the Middle Bronze Age at Tarsus, from ca.2100 BC, a distinctive dark-on-light painted pottery arrives from the east. This has been associated with **Hurrian** newcomers, who came to dominate the region which became the kingdom of Kizzuwadna and later a Hittite province.

Then at Tarsus some pottery types of the plain monochrome ware associated with the time of the Hittite Empire appeared already in Late Bronze I (Hittite Old Kingdom), to which the **seal** of the ruler Isputahsu belongs, when Tarsus may perhaps have been the capital of the kingdom of Kizzuwadna.

The following period (Late Bronze IIa) coincided with the annexation of Kizzuwadna to direct Hittite rule, marked by the dominance of typical monochrome pottery, with less continuity from the previous period than is apparent at **Boğazköy**, where slipped and highly burnished pottery persisted in some quantities under the Empire. The Hittite presence is clearest, however, in a large building covering the whole top of the mound and comparable with the **temples** of **Hattusa**. The south and east edges of the summit were bounded by a wall three meters thick of **cyclopean masonry**, its construction similar to that of the walls around **Temple I** at Boğazköy: this acted as a retaining wall for the terrace.

A heavy burnt layer marks the violent destruction of the Hittite buildings, presumably by the **Sea Peoples** in approximately 1176 BC or a little earlier. In material culture there was no complete change, the ensuing period being termed Late Bronze IIb and dated until ca.1100 BC. There was, however, one significant innovation, the arrival of Mycenaean pottery of "granary" style (Late Helladic IIIC). Tarsus had been brought within the Aegean trading zone.

TAŞCI. Located between **Fraktin** and **Imamkulu** in a chain of Hittite rock reliefs, it is dated by the cartouche of **Hattusili III**. The compositions of this monument are sculpturally rather primitive, Taşcı I having a file of three praying figures and Taşcı II a single figure, both with **hieroglyphs**, merely incised with a sharp point. Sited immediately above the Yenice River, this is difficult to discern: the location is 36 kilometers southeast of Develi.

TAWANIYA. On textual evidence this was the **cult center** of the goddess **Teteshapi**, a deity of **Hattian** origin associated with animals, **music**, dancing and festivities. It has not been located, though one theory, not widely supported, would identify it with **Alaca Höyük**, more probably **Arinna**.

TAXES. Written records from the Old Assyrian trading colonies and the Hittite state alike attest the character and imposition of taxes in order to raise revenue. This applied to the small Anatolian principalities which dealt with the Assyrian merchants and later likewise to the provincial centers obliged to remit payments to **Hattusa**. The differences lay in the more far-flung range of the earlier **trade** and in the more equal weight of the parties involved compared with the centralized **government** of the Hittite Old Kingdom and Empire. No records of tax evasion through smuggling survive from Hittite sources, such as taking a caravan of donkeys over the hills to avoid a customs post, as occurred in the time of the Assyrian trade.

None of the **treaties** or "sworn oaths" between the Assyrian authorities and the local Anatolian rulers has survived. But recurrent themes, no doubt prominent in such treaties, were the import tax on **tin** and **textiles** and the "tithe." If prohibited goods, such as Anatolian textiles and meteoric **iron** (*amutum*), were traded, tax could be avoided. Textiles were the most profitable goods to smuggle, more so than tin, whose sources could more easily be controlled.

Under Hittite rule the major centers of the Old Assyrian period largely went into decline, with the shrinkage of long-distance trade and the concentration of Anatolian commerce on Hattusa. Nevertheless, the smaller centers and those not easily accessible from the capital retained economic independence. The basis of their wealth was inter city trade and local industry, including **metalwork** and textiles. The evidence for their **economy** rests, however, on the records kept in Hattusa of the payments in kind, or taxes, which they were obliged to send to the Hittite **treasury** in Hattusa. These payments might be made in currency in the form of **silver** bars, weighing up to 18 kilograms. More often they were in the form of **copper** artifacts or of raw wool or woven garments. Modest quantities of clothing, industrial products and **food** were sent, for example, from **Ankuwa**. Most such taxes in kind—whether tribute (*mandattu*) or gifts—were in small quantities from small communities; but in total they must have accounted for much if not most of the revenue received at Hattusa, over and above receipts from vassals outside the central homeland.

Not only the Palace but also the **temples** in the major **cult centers** received taxes in kind, though the precise bureaucratic machinery is unknown. Circulation of goods, however, continued independent of the palatial system controlled from Hattusa. *See also* **TREASURY INCOME.**

TEGARAMA. Probably centered on modern Gürün, on a tributary of the Euphrates River and on the route from **Hattusa** to **Carchemish**, whence it was reached by **Hantili I** (ca.1590–1560 BC) on his homeward march. Tegarama was sacked by enemy forces from **Isuwa** in the disastrous period early in the reign of **Tudhaliya III**. In his final decisive campaign against **Mitanni**, **Suppiluliuma I** halted at Tegarama, where he inspected his infantry and **chariotry**. He then sent an **army** under the command of his son, the future **Arnuwanda II**, with his brother Zida, chief of the **bodyguards**, to prepare for his own assault on Carchemish.

TELIPINU. The **god** of fertility and patron god of **Mursili II**, who may well have sought his special protection for the recovery of his land from the devastation caused by the great **plague**. Telipinu was son of the **Weather-God**, and in one text was credited with the foundation of the Hittite Kingdom.

He was the hero of the Myth of the Missing God, whose disappearance led to catastrophic impoverishment of the land, with failure of crops and sterility of livestock. After much ritual activity, the wrath of Telipinu was eventually appeased, and he set about restoring general fertility.

The well-being of the population as a whole and of the king and his family alike was directly dependent on the favor of the god of fertility, as in a prayer to be read daily by the **scribe** for Mursili II before his god Telipinu:

> To the king and the **queen**, the princes and the land of Hatti, grant life, health, strength, long years and enduring joy. Grant everlasting fertility to their crops, vines, fruit-trees, cattle, sheep, goats, pigs, mules and asses, together with the beasts of the field, and to their people. Let them flourish! Let the winds of prosperity pass over! Let the land of Hatti thrive and prosper.

TELIPINU (ca.1525–1500 BC). Having foiled a plot on his life, Telipinu seized the throne from the usurper Huzziya I, successor of **Ammuna**. Huzziya and his five brothers were sent into exile; but Telipinu ordered no further harm to them, wishing to end the chronic bloodshed among his predecessors.

Telipinu succeeded in regaining extensive territories lost to Hittite rule in the southeast and in the **Lower Land**, perhaps as far as the Mediterranean. **Samuha**, Marista, Hurma, **Sugziya**, Purushanda and the **Hulaya River Land** occur in a list of **store cities** restored to the Hittites at this time. The **Marrassantiya** basin was firmly under control again. Telipinu was obliged, however, to accept the independence of one former Hittite-controlled land, **Kizzuwadna**, making a **treaty** of alliance with Isputahsu, ruler of the then newly established kingdom. Telipinu may have wished to avert the possibility of Kizzuwadna joining a **Hurrian** alliance against Hatti.

Contrary to Telipinu's order, the deposed king Huzziya and his five brothers were secretly murdered. The three assassins, convicted by the **assembly** (*panku*), were spared and banished. He may have finally been spurred into action to end bloodshed after his own wife and son were murdered. He summoned the members of the assembly to hear his *Proclamation*, providing regulations for the succession to the throne. The assembly had been summoned simply to hear his decisions, not to debate them. Inheritance of royal power was now fixed on direct patrilineal succession. No formal criteria for determining the male successor to the throne had been established in or after the reign of **Hattusili I**. The arbitrary behavior of a king in choosing his successor or changing his choice was thus curtailed, though he did not have to choose the eldest eligible candidate.

The lengthy historical preamble to the *Proclamation* could serve as a warning of the effects of ignoring these regulations. Henceforth no member of the royal family could be immune from punishment for crimes committed. Enforcement was assigned to the assembly (*panku*). Under Telipinu this institution was revived, evidently comprising not the nobility but court personnel, from servants and **bodyguard** to cooks and stable boys, as well as the Captain of the Thousand. This body was probably convened only on an ad hoc basis.

Justice must be enforced, but not in secret: it had to be seen to be done. Only the offender was to be punished: even with a capital offense his property was not to be seized. The whole aim was to enforce the regulations with the minimum cause for wider resentment and potential conspiracy. This policy went along with the improvements in the bureaucracy which affected the king's subjects throughout the realm, not least in the countryside.

Telipinu apparently died without surviving male issue. His *Proclamation* was largely disregarded during the century or so following his death in relation to the royal succession, though it was not forgotten by later kings. His achievements outside the homeland, however, seem to have remained intact, as with relations with Kizzuwadna. The 15th century BC was a time of growth of the power of **Mitanni** and of Egyptian expansion in Syria, in the so-called Hittite **Middle Kingdom**.

TELL EL-AMARNA (AKHETATEN). This remarkable city, built on a virgin site in Middle Egypt on the orders of Akhenaten (1352–1336 BC), was the capital of Egypt for the pharaoh who had made a deliberate and drastic break with orthodox state religion and its cult of the god Amun-Re. The reasons for this radical step were probably political and economic more than theological: during successive reigns land had continued to be given to the **temples**, resulting in a progressive decline in royal resources. As long as the pharaohs of the 18th Dynasty were actively campaigning in Asia, tribute, plunder and manpower accrued to the royal treasury in Thebes, making up the deficit from gifts to the gods. With the accession of Amenhotep III (1390–1352 BC), however, there began a long period of inactivity in Asia, continuing under Akhenaten. The so-called "**Amarna** period" in fact began under Amenhotep III.

Some concern for Egyptian authority in Syria persisted, as became evident through a sensational discovery at Tell el-Amarna (1887). Thousands of clay **tablets** were accidentally unearthed, narrowly escaping destruction, with many soon surfacing in Cairo on the antiquities market and attracting scholarly attention. These were instantly recognized as being written in Akkadian, a Semitic tongue long since deciphered: their contents could therefore be quickly understood. Here was a wholly unexpected reinforcement for **A. H. Sayce** in his advocacy of the importance of the Hittites as a power in the ancient Near East. Among the numerous letters from Egyptian vassals in Palestine and Syria, requesting help or complaining of neglect by their overlord, were a smaller number of letters from foreign rulers, including one from **Suppiluliuma I**.

The city of Akhetaten, built by the heretic king, did not outlive his radical changes, being abandoned during the reign of the young Tutankhamun (1336–1327 BC). It was anyhow hurriedly if ambitiously constructed, eschewing solid masonry in favor of mud brick, plaster and wood, with colorful mural paintings. It was also a center of glassmaking, probably introduced rather earlier from Syria.

TELL FAKHARIYAH. Possibly the site of the capital of **Mitanni**, **Wassukkanni**, situated near the sources of the Khabur, south of Ras al-Ain and opposite **Guzanu (Tell Halaf)**. An inscription on a basalt **statue**, in Assyrian and Aramaic, declares that a ruler of Guzanu had set this up in honor of the god Adad of Sikan, a placename possibly identifiable with Wassukkanni. Dating to the later ninth century BC, this is the earliest known Aramaic inscription of any length.

One season of excavations by **Calvin McEwan** at Tell Fakhariyah in 1940 revealed medieval, Roman and Hellenistic occupation (Levels I–IV), preceded by a palace with *bit hilani* plan (Level V). Underlying this building was a rich level (VI) of the 13th century BC, yielding ivories in the Levantine tradition, **seal** impressions and Middle Assyrian **cuneiform** tablets. The next level (VII) yielded the highly distinctive painted **pottery** termed Nuzi ware, and is attributable to the period of the kingdom of Mitanni. The earliest level (VIII) yielded Khabur ware, of the period beginning with the later phase of the Old Assyrian trading colonies.

TELL MOZAN. *See* **URKESH.**

TELL TAYANAT. At this site in the Amuq plain the expedition sent to north Syria, as then delineated, by the Oriental Institute of Chicago in the 1930s carried out a limited area of excavation. This was largely in the hope of finding what they had been unable to discover at Tell Judeideh, their principal excavation in the plain, namely, monumental **architecture** and **sculpture** of the Neo-Hittite period.

The excavators were more fortunate at Tell Tayanat, where two adjacent buildings were uncovered, one a *bit hilani* and the other rather questionably termed a *megaron*, and as such out of place in north Syria: its description as a *megaron* ignores the fact that its focus was not in the large central room immediately inside the entrance porch but in the small sanctuary beyond. Henri Frankfort compared it with the Assyrian **temples** at Khorsabad, not much later in date, and with a temple built during the Assyrian occupation of **Guzanu (Tell Halaf)**, which began not later than 808 BC.

There can be little doubt that these buildings at Tell Tayanat date to the time of Tiglath-Pileser III (744–727 BC) and thus to the beginning of the final phase of Neo-Hittite civilization, for two reasons: first, the three basalt column bases of the porch of the *bit hilani* are the same as those of Building F/K, erected by Bar-Rekub at **Zincirli**; and second, because of the finding of relief slabs of the style of Tiglath-Pileser's reign, though provincial in quality—reliefs depicting a row of soldiers—reused as pavestones of a gate in the area. This reuse may well belong to the later rebuilding of the *bit hilani*. The suggestion of **Calvin McEwan**, the excavation director, that there was only a minor entrance to the ground-floor rooms of the *bit hilani* in the original plan seems improbable.

The double-lion column base, one of an original pair in the porch of the so-called *megaron*, must be reckoned one of the indigenous elements of Neo-Hittite architecture; and with this may be classed the double-sphinx base at Zincirli. Neo-Hittite sculpture, whether orthostats or column bases, was essentially part of the over-all architectural scheme. The inclusion in the design of gateways and porticoes of guardian lions was an idea of ultimately Mesopotamian origin, transmitted both to the Hittite capital at **Boğazköy-Hattusa** and to Late Bronze Age Palestine, exemplified at Hazor. Its lasting place in Neo-Hittite architecture can reasonably be ascribed to Hittite influence.

One invaluable piece of evidence from Tell Tayanat deserves mention: a fragment of a colossal **statue**, showing the top of a column with its capital, rather similar to the column base.

TEMPLE 1 (BOĞAZKÖY). This, the greatest single structure within the vast area of **Hattusa**, covers in all (reckoning the whole complex with its surrounding storerooms) an area of about 14,500 square meters. It is both elusive and informative in the light it casts on Hittite civilization. There is no dedicatory inscription, so that attribution of the building of this great shrine to any one king is difficult. **Hattusili III** (1267–1237 BC) had seemed a very probable candidate; but recent opinion in the German expedition has favored a dating to the 14th century BC, along with much of **Boğazköy: Upper City**, instead of attributing much of that to **Tudhaliya IV**. The area had been occupied almost continuously since ca.1800 BC. Its foundation terrace may well conceal remains of earlier major structures, very possibly antedating the sack of the city in the reign of **Tudhaliya III**, great-grandfather of Hattusili III.

When **Charles Texier**, discoverer of Hattusa, came upon Temple 1 in 1834, the ruins were still considerably exposed to view. It is therefore easy to understand why it is not better preserved. Had it not been built of such massive blocks of limestone, some being up to five meters long and weighing 20 tons or more, it would not have survived in its present condition. As it is, the entire superstructure of **timber** frame with mud brick filling has disappeared: indeed this is true of all Anatolian sites not preserved to a degree by fire.

Dowel holes occur in large numbers, drilled into the tops of the blocks and intended for securing the superstructure to the stone footings. The **building methods** involved are recorded in some detail in texts. Timber was clearly available on a scale and in sizes not seen for centuries. Many of the blocks forming the wall footings are carved in a curve at their base, where floor meets wall, a distinctive Hittite technique.

Stairways give evidence of several floors in all the storehouses, those on the north and west sides certainly having three. The one narrow stairway in the sanctuary led to the flat roof, which, from relevant texts, was a significant scenario for some rituals.

Built on an artificial terrace, seen from the north Temple 1 towered above its surroundings, the complex of buildings extending over some 41 hectares (103 acres). The largest structure within this complex stood on the east side: this was the **temple** proper, surrounded by numerous storerooms of narrow rectangular plan, to facilitate flooring above in the usual Near Eastern fashion. These 82 ground floor storerooms were found stripped of their contents, save only for huge jars, presumably holding the corn, **oil**, dried beans, **wine** and other provisions required for the large staff. The cult rooms within the temple itself were likewise found empty. Looting at the time of the fall of the kingdom must indeed have been thorough.

The division of the main structure of Temple 1, separated from the surrounding storerooms and covering 65 by 42 meters, into gate chamber, processional way, entranceway, inner court, stoa and cult chambers makes its plan obviously comparable with those of the numerous temples in the **Upper City** of Hattusa. The way of the royal processions can be traced by these architectural elements, with a large monolithic basin in the outer court or processional way, presumed to have been used either for ritual ablution or for libations or conceivably for both.

At the far (northeast) end of the temple stood two rooms clearly the focus of the **cult**. Reached through a portico, or stoa, of five stone piers, the more easterly of the two cult chambers contained against its rear wall a stone base: at one time considered to be a throne base, it is now agreed to have supported a divine **statue**. In the light of the arrangement of the reliefs at **Yazılıkaya** and earlier at **Alaca Höyük**, the left-hand shrine was perhaps for the god, presumed to be the **Storm-God**, and the right, with the surviving statue base, probably for the **Sun-Goddess** of **Arinna**. In the absence of inscriptions or reliefs, a considerable element of speculation is inevitable.

Along the southwest side of the main temple complex stretched a street, beneath which ran a sewer. On the other side stood a self-contained complex, its one entrance directly facing the side entrance to the temple: this "Southern District" covered 5,300 square meters, and probably included offices for **scribes**, of whose activities there are clear traces nearby, thus serving as an administrative center. That there were workshops here is hinted at by one **cuneiform tablet** mentioning a "House of Operations," also very probably housing priests and the musicians and singers required for the rituals. Storerooms and cult chambers also may have been sited here. But the almost complete dearth of finds in this "Southern District" makes complete certainty about its functions impossible. Again, the looting at the fall of the kingdom was complete.

Temple personnel are indicated for Temple I by a tablet from the corridor between the gateway and the first court listing 208 persons. Writing instruments came mostly from the rooms of the "Southern District" next to its central court. The administration of

Temple I may well have involved control of extensive estates, their produce and inhabitants, this shrine being essentially a self-supporting entity within the overriding economic control by the palace, the seat of royal **government**.

Some parallels in workmanship and architectural details can be detected with **Kültepe-Kanes** and **Acemhöyük**. Vertical pilasters at regular intervals relieved the monotony of the facades, possibly decorated also with colored panels, reminiscent of the **Bitik** vase with its depiction of a temple façade.

A *halentuwa* house is commonly mentioned in connection with major Hittite temples, a term accepted as meaning "palace." The "Southern District" hardly fits this description, though a large building standing on its own 80 meters from the gateway of Temple 1, and resembling some of the structures on **Boğazköy: Büyükkale**, may have been such.

It seems rather rash to draw parallels between Temple 1 at Boğazköy and New Kingdom temples in Egypt, perhaps especially with the Ramesseum, the mortuary temple at Thebes of **Ramesses II**, where the sanctuary in the center is indeed surrounded by streets and storehouses, arranged in groups and continuous rows. That, however, is where the resemblance ends, for the sanctuary and temple as a whole of the Ramesseum shows scant similarity to the Hittite Temple 1. If one does admit an architectural inspiration from Egypt, if certainly no slavish imitation, then Temple 1 will have to be dated to the early 13th century BC, after the confrontation between **Muwatalli II** and Ramesses, rather than to **Suppiluliuma I** or **Mursili II**.

TEMPLE PERSONNEL. A significant text is entitled *Instructions for Temple Officials*, who were obliged to be in or around the **temple** day and night. One passage reads thus: "You who are temple officials be very careful with respect to the precinct. At nightfall go promptly down to town, eat and drink. . . . But *everyone* promptly come up to spend the night in the temple. . . ."

The **statues** and votive offerings in the sanctuary had to be carefully guarded. The order to spend the night in the temple applied to all ranks. Workshops were required to maintain the cultic equipment, as were kitchens and bakeries for the ceremonial meals for deities which were so important in **festivals**. Other staff manned the offices and scribal quarters.

A **tablet** found inside the gateway of Temple 1 lists 208 persons, of whom the occupation of 144 is recorded, largely priests, singers and female musicians for the acts of worship.

Temple workshops employed artisans such as potters and carpenters. Also on the labor force of each major temple were the workers on the land, the principal wealth of each institution.

TEMPLES. The Hittite temple was literally described as the house of the **god**, and as such was treated with the utmost circumspection. Outside the times of **festivals** it was open only to authorized personnel, principally the priests. Any foreign trespasser would be executed: the essence of the offense was to look upon the image of the god or goddess in the sanctuary, the divine **statue** which was the very embodiment of the deity. For using an unclean vessel to serve the god, the penalties were drinking urine or eating excrement. It was a capital offense to fail to follow the procedures for ritual cleansing. Another capital offense was misappropriation of offerings of **food** and drink to the god or goddess. In order to guard against this, gifts legally given to an individual from the palace might be sold only after official certification of ownership.

The quality of offerings to the temples was strictly regulated. Many such would have come from the extensive estates owned and administered by the principal state temples, which played a major role in the **economy** of the Hittite state, mainly agricultural but also industrial, with their workshops. The assiduous attention of successive kings to the major temples of their realm inevitably involved them in secular as well as cultic administration. **Temple personnel** were housed in residential quarters close to the temples.

Boğazköy: Upper City included by far the largest group of Hittite temples. These were principally the work of **Tudhaliya IV**, some being new buildings but many reconstructions of temples destroyed or damaged in the fighting at the time of the usurpation of the throne by his cousin **Kurunta** (1228–1227 BC). Not all the temples were rebuilt, notably Temple 30 near the Lion Gate, one of the two largest in the Upper City: over its remains were put houses and workshops. This gives a hint that the greatest period of these temples may have been in the reign of **Hattusili III**, generally credited with the construction of the sanctuary of the **Storm-God (Temple 1)** in **Boğazköy: Lower City**. The architectural achievements of his son were nevertheless remarkable. If Hattusili III did initiate the design of the Upper City, it was laid out to a more or less symmetrical plan continued by Tudhaliya IV and even under the last Hittite king, **Suppiluliuma II**.

Some 25 temples were grouped together in the Upper City of

Hattusa, the majority in a central district, while four larger temples were sited not far within the defensive perimeter: to the west stood Temple 30 and further east Temples 3, 2 and 5, between the Sphinx Gate and the King's Gate. The symmetrical layout is demonstrated by the equal distance of 130 meters of Temple 30 from the Lion Gate and Temple 5 from the King's Gate. All these temples shared a common plan, square or rectangular, with a portal giving access to an inner court with pillared portico: this in turn gave admittance through an anteroom to the *adyton* or inner sanctuary, housing the statue of the god. To prevent direct view from the entry portal, the *adyton* was always off center. A cellar or basement room was often constructed beneath the floor of the sanctuary.

Temple 30—similar in design to Temples 2, 3 and especially 4—extended 45 meters east-west and over 30 meters north-south. The *adyton* was placed in the southeast corner, as in Temple 4 combined with an anteroom and colonnade, opening on to a large court. The inventory of Temple 30 was typical, including small **pottery** cups and jars as foundation deposits, in the Mesopotamian tradition, and three miniature **oracle** tablets. This was the last temple to be excavated by the German expedition under **Peter Neve**, with one other to the north, just south of **Büyükkale**. Temple 5, by far the largest in the Upper City, may well have been built as a private shrine for the royal family and for the ancestors of Tudhaliya IV, with three small chapels and an annex resembling a palace, the whole precinct covering almost 3,000 square meters. West of Temple 5 stood two isolated and virtually identical shrines, Temples 2 and 3, both burnt twice and rebuilt immediately after the first fire.

Both Temple 2 and Temple 3 had been decorated with many reliefs in fragments, scattered or clustered near the main entrance. Most are of greenish gabbro resembling granite, and belong to lions, probably guarding the gateway. Sphinxes also occur, with rosette-decorated pieces paralleled by the necks of the sphinxes at **Alaca Höyük**. These **sculptures** all derive from orthostats or bases of pillars. Other forms of decoration almost certainly adorned these temples, but have not survived.

Archives were deposited on the cellar floors of all these temples in the Upper City of Hattusa, almost certainly moved from shelves whose contents had been disordered in the disruption caused by Kurunta. In addition to **tablets** dealing with rituals, donations and inquiries of an oracle, there were stamp **seals**, seal impressions and clay **bullae**, many of these in two collections, most being of Suppiluliuma II. Some bullae bear obverse and reverse impressions of a seal in the form of an Iron Cross, with the names of Great Kings and Great Queens going back as far as **Tudhaliya I** and his wife, Nikkalmati, hinting at an original storage in **Büyükkale**. The largest collections of tablets were found in Temples 15 and 16, including some from a mythological text in **Hurrian-Hittite** bilingual form, in part concerned with a festival of the Storm-God of the city of Ebla in Syria. Some Akkadian fragments of the Epic of Gilgamesh may indicate a center for the training of **scribes**, in line with the evidence for Hittite bureaucracy.

In the final years of Hattusa only the larger and more important temples continued to function, houses being built on the sites of many others.

TESUB.   His status attained its apogee in the late Empire, under the influence of **Puduhepa** and through the reigns of her husband and her son **Tudhaliya IV**, when the king—on becoming a **god** at death—came to be identified with Tesub.

This god can be equated with Ba'al (Cannanite/Phoenician), Adad (Assyrian), Marduk (Babylonian) and Zeus (Greek). Tesub was a genuine Sky- and Weather-God, syncretized with the **Storm-God** who had held sway from earlier times in the Hittite realm. His role in this respect is depicted by his clasping a bunch of thunderbolts, best known with the head of the male procession in Chamber A of **Yazılıkaya**.

The ancestry of Tesub was **Hurrian**, demonstrated by his leading role in the epic cycles entitled *Kingship in Heaven* and *The Song of Ullikummi*. He became in due course the second-ranking member of the pantheon of **Urartu**, after Haldi. The reception of Tesub into the official **Hittite pantheon** in the 13th century BC is the clearest indication of the Hurrian background of the royal family in **Hattusa** during the Empire. This had been first signaled by the **marriage** of **Tudhaliya I/II** to Nikkalmati, of Hurrian family, at the dawn of the Hittite New Kingdom (Empire).

TETESHAPI.   A **Hattian** deity whose rituals are recorded from the **Middle Kingdom** onward, thus dating back to a time when Hattian influences on Hittite **religion** were still very strong. The leader in these rituals being a priestess, with the title "Sister of the City," it is likely that Teteshapi was a goddess. Forty **tablets** from **Hattusa** refer to her rituals, reflected in the **Alaca Höyük** reliefs. She was a Mistress of Animals (Greek: *Potnia Theron*). Animals not seen in the reliefs but mentioned in the texts are panther, wolf, mountain goat, lamb and piglet.

Dance, **music**, games and acrobatics were central to the **festival** in honor of Teteshapi. At Alaca Höyük the acrobats may well have performed in the courtyard in front of the reliefs. The Hittite texts illuminate the physical setting of these rituals, with references to buildings with courtyard, window and gate; an inn; a storage pit; and, significantly, a ladder, ladder men and daggers or **swords**.

Tawaniya is recorded as the **cult center** of Teteshapi, though its location at Alaca Höyük is highly debatable. This cult here seems closely connected with that of the **Storm-God** with his Hattic name Tarhu or Taru, depicted as a bull standing on an altar. Among the many deities involved in the festival of Teteshapi were the **Sun-Goddess** of **Arinna**, Mezulla, the Storm-God of **Zippalanda**, **Telepinu** and the Hattic War-God Wurunkatte.

TEXIER, CHARLES. *See* **BOĞAZKÖY: EARLY TRAVELERS; BOĞAZKÖY: EXCAVATIONS.**

TEXTILES.   Outside Egypt finds of organic material are relatively rare in excavated sites of the ancient Near East, since constant conditions, wholly dry or wet without seasonal changes, are required for preservation. Two other categories of evidence remain, pictorial and written. The former is limited in range in the reliefs of **Yazılıkaya** and elsewhere of the Hittite Empire and later examples, notably **Ivriz**. For fuller evidence one must turn to written records, of which by far the most informative are those of the Old Assyrian **trade** from **Kültepe-Kanes**.

There had clearly been a textile industry and trade on some scale in Anatolia before the arrival of Assyrian merchants. But textiles were being produced in an altogether more organized manner in Assyria, and when Assyrian traders arrived at Kanes they left their principal wives at home in charge of the family firm. The **tablets** reveal insights into the working of such firms, with instances of intermarital badinage on the completion of orders sent from Kanes, with queries about sizes and qualities of textile pieces. While **tin** and textiles constituted the staples of the Old Assyrian trade with Anatolia, analyses indicate a balance of three-to-one in favor of textiles compared with tin. They were far more important for the **economy** of Assyria, seeing that this was the major industry, with wool, the raw material, coming from there or from other parts of Mesopotamia. **Women** and children, perhaps especially girls, played a vital role as the production force. When orders could not be met in full or on time, textiles might be imported from neighboring Babylonia, where the textile industry was of even greater antiquity. Sheep-rearing must have employed a significant proportion of the population of Assyria.

Some tablets reveal a strong preference for mixed loads of textiles and tin. Some letters even stipulate that precious metals, **silver** or **gold**, arriving in Assur from Anatolia should be spent half on tin and half on textiles.

While the textiles came mainly from Assyria itself or from Babylonia, some were bought en route in north Syria, while local Anatolian textiles were traded within Anatolia, a trade in which Assyrians also played a prominent role. There is some evidence, however, that the Assyrian authorities pursued a protectionist policy, trying to hamper or prevent the circulation of Anatolian products among Assyrians, presumably because they might undercut Assyrian textiles.

Type, size, amount of wool and finishing were all points of importance in the correspondence between Kanes and Assur: regrettably, no records from Assur have been excavated. Puzur-Assur, a merchant based in Kanes, wrote to a woman named Waqartum, with detailed instructions on combing, shearing and so on: more of the fine quality textiles are requested; but the Abarnian textile which she had sent was less popular. Plainly, there was a discriminating clientele being served by the Assyrian merchants, with an element of competition playing into the hands of the customers. The large number of textiles must indicate a home industry, employing at least a number of female relations, especially daughters, as well as slave girls. While most textile production was channeled through the family firms, it appears that there may have been some transactions on the side, as it were, for the particular benefit of the merchant heading the firm. Wool was occasionally sent to Lamassi, the wife of the merchant Pusu-ken, in Assur from Anatolia, because of high **prices** in the City (Assur).

The Anatolian textiles were of inferior quality, by far the commonest brand being *pirikannu*. These, along with *saptinnu* textiles, were not welcome in Assur, and Pusu-ken was specifically forbidden to buy them, being reminded that the orders of the City were binding. Heavy fines were imposed on those breaking this regulation.

After the disappearance of the Assyrian merchants from Kanes and the other ***karum*** sites, no comparable records of the textile industry and trade survive from the Hittite Old or New Kingdom. The palace **archives** of **Hattusa**, however, record imports of textiles, perhaps parts of royal exchanges of gifts, from Babylon and Egypt, as well as linen textiles from Syria (**Amurru**) and Cyprus (**Alasiya**). Contributions from the provinces of different qualities of wool and clothing are registered, along with gowns, linen fabrics and dresses in various styles.

The thriving city and port of **Ugarit**, for nearly two centuries a Hittite protectorate, was no mere entrepot but a major center of industry, albeit directed mainly to exports. The purple dye obtained from innumerable murex shells, the source of the renowned Tyrian purple of the Phoenicians in the first millennium BC, was already being produced in the workshops of Ugarit: linen and wool were dyed, for making into garments of different designs or for export in bales. The export markets are recorded in the economic texts of Ugarit, and must have included the court at Hattusa. The textile industry, spinning and weaving, was among some hundred crafts listed in the tablets from this prosperous and cosmopolitan city.

THEOGONY. This term, signifying the birth and genealogy of **gods**, is particularly relevant in relation to **Hurrian** and Greek divinities alike, though less so to Hittite. The very concept of generations of gods can be traced back to Babylonia: ties with the West Semitic world and **Ugarit** are less clear. Among the chief protagonists, **Alalu**, **Anu** and Ea all have Babylonian names.

The Hurrian theogony begins with Alalu, who was deposed after a reign of nine years by Anu, the Sky-God; then he himself was deposed after nine years by his son **Kumarbi**, finally overthrown by **Tesub**. The change of regime was not usually effected in a non-violent manner: Kumarbi bit off the genitals of his father Anu, after pulling him down from heaven, whither he was fleeing. Yet Anu was to have his revenge, bringing about the downfall of Kumarbi in his turn.

Each ethnic group in the ancient Near East had its own peculiar cultic traditions, often associated with local divinities of the natural environment, as was true of central Anatolia, where the concepts of theogony and the traditions of Mesopotamian theology had yet to take root.

Parallels can be readily detected between the Hurrian theogony, Hesiod's *Theogony* and Phoenician mythology as related by Philo Byblius. Hesiod has the sequence of Ouranos ("Sky"), Kronos and Zeus. Castration is featured not only in the Hittite text

(Anu and Kumarbi) but also in Hesiod, in the fight between Ouranos and Kronos. Hesiod omits the generation of Alalu, but this is included by Philo Byblius; in the outline of Phoenician mythology he ascribes to a certain Sankhuniaton, giving the following sequence: the Phoenician Elioun (Greek, Hypsistos), "The Highest," is identifiable with Alalu; the Greek Ouranos, "Sky," Phoenician name not given, is identifiable with Anu; and the Phoenician El (Greek, Kronos) is the equivalent of Kumarbi. Elsewhere Ba'al-Hadad, as the chief of the gods, is the equivalent both of Tesub and of Zeus. Ea, the wise god of the Mesopotamian pantheon, is the one who in the last resort appoints and deposes celestial rulers. Phoenician mythology was the direct descendant of Canaanite traditions of the second millennium BC, which themselves had tenuous links with Hittite **religion**, essentially through Ugarit. *See also* **PANTHEON (HITTITE); PANTHEON (YAZILIKAYA).**

THEOLOGY. The Hittite kings advanced beyond the primitive concept of the **god** as god of the community, punishing the whole community for the sin of the individual. This is especially apparent in the prayers of **Mursili II**, at the time when **plague** was sweeping the land. This he readily attributes to the sins of his father, **Suppiluliuma I**, while acknowledging that these wrongdoings had been handed down to himself and thus to the next generation, though innocent in the straightforward sense of the word. Nevertheless, an awareness of individual responsibility as against collective guilt is apparent in the **Hittite Laws**. The god was lord of justice, just as the king administered justice, sparing the innocent and remitting the weight of punishment on those pleading guilty.

These theological advances developed in the context of the centralized state **cult** of the royal court at **Hattusa**, as against the older local cults, which remained relatively unsophisticated.

TIKUNANI. A minor kingdom of upper Mesopotamia, located east of the Euphrates River and perhaps northwest of the Khabur triangle. Its ruler Tunip-Tesub was a vassal of **Hattusili I**, who wrote a letter to him abbreviating his name as Tuniya, the full name presumably over taxing the **scribe** in **Hattusa**.

TILIURA. A town on the border of the **Kaska** lands, abandoned to the Kaska tribesmen in the reign of **Hantili II**, when they also overran **Nerik**. It was partially resettled by **Mursili II**, but completely so only under **Muwatalli II**. When he moved the seat of government to **Tarhuntassa**, the Kaska and other northerners rose in revolt. He then appointed his brother, the future **Hattusili III**, as effective **viceroy** of the whole northern marches. He in his turn drew up a **treaty** with the town of Tiliura, resettling the remnants of its original population there and—he recorded some years later—criticizing his father's half-measures. Kaska folk were banned from settling in or even entering Tiliura, whose importance is implied by this treaty.

Tiliura was the principal town of the Kummesmaha district, beside the river of that name, probably identifiable with the modern Devres, a tributary flowing east-northeast into the **Marrassantiya** (Kızıl Irmak). A location at Salman Höyük, near Ilgaz, is plausible: here a surface survey found **pottery** of the Middle and Late Bronze Age.

TILMEN HÖYÜK. Settlement mound located in the province of Gaziantep and district of Islahiye, near the Turco-Syrian frontier: found by Bahadir Alkim, who excavated this site from 1959. This was a fortified city with palaces of the Middle and Late Bronze Age, the earlier belonging to the more important building period.

TIMBER AND TIMBER CONSTRUCTION. Charred beams at many Anatolian sites—including **Kültepe-Kanes**, **Acemhöyük** and **Beycesultan**—give indubitable proof of the abundance of large timber for architectural construction. Deforestation was not to have serious effects in the pre-Christian era, though by Hellenistic times the demand for timber for shipbuilding was increasing. The areas surrounding major smelting sites also became steadily denuded of wood.

A foundation ritual text from **Hattusa**, albeit incomplete, seems to describe the erection of pillars and the haulage of long timbers used as beams, joists and roof battens. The term translated as "beam" is related to more elaborate sacrifices than the terms for "joist" and "roof batten." Moreover, the lumberjacks or carpenters bringing beams to the building site, for use as roof supports, received more generous payments in kind than those bringing the lighter timbers. Probably this reflected the differences in distance from source to building site, as well perhaps as difficulties of terrain. It hardly seems plausible, however, to suggest that timber was brought to Hattusa all the way from the forests bordering the Black Sea, one of the academic ideas marked by an absence of common sense. Those transporting the heavy beams received payment of one bull, three sheep, loaves of bread, three pitchers of **wine** and other drinks, a ration indeed indicating transportation over some distance, requiring a considerable time. The lighter timbers probably were available more locally, for the craftsmen bringing the joists and battens had to be content with some loaves.

The dowel holes in the masonry of **Temple 1 (Boğazköy)** and the charred timbers from other sites provide evidence of the methods of timber-frame construction, the junction with the footings and the use of mud brick above. The burnt palace of **Beycesultan** V yielded traces of the upper story, its construction and decoration, though this cannot be described as Hittite.

To this day, around Bolu and in the Black Sea region, houses can be found which can be termed log cabins. Naturally such have not survived from the second millennium BC, making archaeological surveys in that zone of Anatolia liable to be frustrating, since it will be apparent that prehistoric settlements are going undetected. The texts show that such houses were prevalent in the enemy lands north of Hatti, the homeland of the **Kaska** people. In the archives of Hattusa and in Sumerian occurs a very rare term, E.GIS.UR.RA, evidently signifying a "log cabin."   *See also* **BUILDING METHODS.**

TIN. This metal is found, for practical purposes, mostly in cassiterite ore, its name probably to be associated with a people originating in the highlands of western Iran, the Kassites, even though they must have acted, in the period of their rule in Mesopotamia from the 16th till the 11th century BC, simply as intermediaries in the long-distance tin **trade**. It is possible that they played a significant role through the centuries of Hittite dominance in central Anatolia and beyond, in bringing the much valued metal from the major sources to the east. The lack of evidence for Anatolian tin mining after the third millennium BC (Early Bronze Age) is a stumbling block, though the general picture of the production and trading of tin in Anatolia has radically changed over the past decade.

Sources of tin occur elsewhere in the Near East, though none so significant as those in Afghanistan and Kazakhstan to the east and in Bohemia and Cornwall far to the west. Tin occurs in many places in Anatolia, along with other metals; but none of these sources is rich enough to be economically viable in modern conditions. Until the 1980s no serious consideration was given to the possibility of Anatolian tin and its exploitation in the Bronze Age, for it was taken for granted that tin was imported by the Assyrian merchants who came to **Kanes** (**Nesa**) from ca.2050 BC. The **tablets** found there indicated beyond doubt that tin was imported from lands to the east, being one of the staples of this Old Assyrian trading network. The puzzling fact seems to be the extinction of an indigenous Anatolian mining industry, albeit on a limited scale, at the end of the third millennium BC, apparently succumbing to the arrival of foreign tin which could undercut the local product. Easier extraction of the ore and more sophisticated marketing seem the likeliest explanations. The evidence differs for the two trading systems, for the Anatolian tin mining is known from archaeological discoveries and analyses alone, whereas most evidence for the Assyrian trade derives from the tablets from their principal colony, Kanes. Unfortunately there is less evidence for the extraction and uses of tin after the end of the Assyrian trade around 1750 BC, though tin ingots have been recovered from Late Bronze Age shipwrecks in the Mediterranean, at Gelidonya and Ulu Burun.

Fifty kilometers east-southeast of Niğde and four kilometers from the small town of Camardi there has been found an Early Bronze Age tin mine at **Kestel**, two kilometers south of which was located a miners' village of the same period at Göltepe. Only subeconomic amounts of material remain unmined today, but some 200 tons of metallic tin were produced over one millennium during the Early Bronze Age at Kestel; and one ton of metallurgical debris, including fragments of crucibles with tin accretions, was recovered from excavations at Göltepe and at the entrance to the Kestel mine. Mining activity reached its zenith here around the mid–third millennium BC, with one batch of radiocarbon determinations giving calibrated dates of 2870–2200 BC, while another batch has given results of 3240–3100 BC.

Another source of Anatolian tin, not far from Kestel, was the Bolkardağ mining district, situated 15 kilometers southwest of Çiftehan and 100 kilometers north of Mersin. This district has proved to be perhaps the richest in a wide range of metallic ores of anywhere in Anatolia. Over 800 mines have been located, most of which yield significant percentages of tin, alongside other metals. The tin ore is commonly stannite rather than the cassiterite at Kestel, and would normally be less likely to be relevant to prehistoric mining activity, occurring as it does in veins in granite. Thus it is hard to extract. Nodules of stannite have, however, been recovered from streambeds. The dearth of dating evidence makes it impossible to evaluate with any accuracy the scale of Bronze Age workings, where mining has continued to modern times. Yet the proximity of the Bolkardağ district to the major natural trade route up from the Cilician plain (**Kizzuwadna**) through the Cilician Gates must have reinforced demand for its tin as well as its other metals.

In the Old Assyrian caravans tin was the item in more transactions than any other commodity: the value of one donkey-load of tin was equal to some four to six donkey-loads of **textiles**, dependent on their quality. Tin was often the medium for small payments made to the caravan leaders for expenses en route, the Akkadian word for "tin" being *annaku,* formerly erroneously believed to mean "lead." Profits on the tin trade would have averaged from 75 to 100 percent gross. It seems very likely that part of the tin imported from the city of Ashur was used by the Anatolian importers for alloying with **copper** from **Ergani Maden**, in spite of its distance from Kanes. It would have been used for production of tin-bronze. A major clue to an eastern source for the tin imported by the Old Assyrian merchants into Anatolia is provided by a letter ordering large amounts from the city of Shemshara in the time of Samsi-Adad I of Assyria, contemporary with **Kültepe-*Karum*** IB (later 19th century BC). The precise source remains uncertain.

A century after the end of the Old Assyrian trade **Hattusili I** came to power, seeking to expand Hittite rule to the southeast. Production of bronze seems to have ceased in central Anatolia with the end of the Assyrian caravans; but for any **army** it was an essential commodity for **weapons**, and the resurgent Hittite power would have required a considerable supply of tin to meet this need. It is very possible that one of the motives for the campaigns of Hattusili I was to secure the import of tin from the southeast, as formerly managed by Assyrian merchants, from depredations en route. If a western source of tin was available to Hattusili I, it would probably have been in Bohemia, a possible motive behind his campaign against his major western neighbor, **Arzawa**. The implication is that the Early Bronze Age tin mines of the Niğde region in Anatolia had become virtually worked out, although lead isotope analyses of Black Sea Anatolian ore samples, essentially of copper, suggest that most metal artifacts were made from ores not far from the site of discovery. It is, however, admitted that this is not a completely certain conclusion.

Circulation of tin, along with copper, in central Anatolia is attested in inventories from palace **archives** of the 13th century BC. The dispatch of tin from centers of secondary rank makes it improbable that this trade was state-regulated. *See also* **OLD ASSYRIAN CARAVAN ROUTES.**

TOPADA. One of the many **hieroglyphic** inscriptions in the kingdom of **Tabal**, it was written for the "Great King" Wasusarma himself, and records in the first person a border war against a hostile neighboring ruler.

TRADE. The Hittites, living in a largely landlocked realm, were not by nature active in external trade, which they left principally to foreign intermediaries. These were based in ports along the east Mediterranean coast, perhaps most notably **Ugarit** and **Ura**. Nor were the Hittites noted for their seamanship, relying rather on the fleets of Ugarit and other maritime cities. Overland trade was also conducted with Syria-Palestine, **Mitanni**, Assyria and Babylon, as well as with Egypt, when not seaborne. The small number of material finds demonstrating such commercial relations, however, suggests that they were intermittent. No records survive to indicate trade organized on the systematic basis of the Old Assyrian trade.

    Gold, **silver**, **copper** and lead were important natural Anatolian economic resources, from mining operations within and beyond the Hittite frontiers, of greatest utility as media of exchange or currency, especially silver. Among examples of their use was in fixing the financial penalties imposed on governmental authorities for death, injury or loss suffered by merchants passing through their jurisdiction in pursuit of their business. The lands of Ugarit and **Amurru** were particularly dangerous for traders, being infested with bandits, among them **Habiru**. Ini-Tesub, **viceroy** of **Carchemish**, was obliged at times to compensate Ugarit for mercantile losses, while himself receiving compensation from the same source, on a mutual basis dependent on responsibility for the crimes. Ini-Tesub thus had an interest in improving legal regulations designed to protect merchants and their trade.

    Merchants themselves were not always blameless, as when some from the port of Ura harassed merchants of Ugarit who failed to pay their debts, even demanding they hand over their own houses. These merchants from Ura had meanwhile been investing in real estate in Ugarit, provoking local resentment. Niqmaddu III was moved to write to his overlord, **Hattusili III**, requesting his action to remedy matters: a compromise solution retained the trading rights of these merchants from Ura, on whom Hatti depended for essential grain imports. But they were forbidden to invest in property or to sequester debtors' houses in Ugarit.

    The fine for killing and robbing a merchant was exceptionally heavy, up to 100 minas (4,000 shekels) of silver, but much lower if it was solely for killing the merchant! The real crime was removal of his goods. **Weights and measures** in the Hittite lands were modeled on those in force in Mesopotamia, though with significant difference in relative weights. A merchant's death in a quarrel or by accident incurred fines of 240 and 80 shekels respectively.

Ingots, commonly in ox hide form, were the international currency of maritime trade plying between the Levant and the Aegean lands; and one such has been found at **Hattusa**. The Hittite state **treasury income** probably benefited only marginally from the seaborne Mediterranean commerce, except through the caravans transporting crude metals to the centers of **metallurgy** in Anatolia. The Hittite court and high society, however, had a strong liking for semiprecious stones such as lapis lazuli from Afghanistan and amethyst, jasper and turquoise from the deserts near the Nile, as well as for fine woolen and linen **textiles**. All these imports arrived via the major emporia of the Near East.

Horses were from time to time imported from Babylonia, Mitanni and Egypt, but a nearer source of supply lay in the **Arzawa** lands of western Anatolia, on Homeric evidence a major horse-breeding region in the time of the Trojan War. Human imports ranged from Nubian **slaves** to doctors and **scribes**, though medical men might come for a royal consultation, then returning home.

It is hard to avoid the impression that, in spite of all the indications of commercial contacts, Hittite state and society remained remarkably little influenced by outside elements, save only in **religion**. *See also* **OLD ASSYRIAN CARAVAN ROUTES.**

TREASURY INCOME. As with all great powers in the ancient Near East, the income accruing to the royal treasury at **Hattusa** was not entirely regular and dependable. Such was war booty, largely of livestock and **metals** but also in the shape of prisoners of war: their arrival after a victorious campaign was an indirect but very real boost to the resources of the state, as much-needed manpower for a variety of purposes. Native farmers were sometimes obliged to give their labor for their overlord or for the king.

More regular sources of revenue included **taxes** in kind from agricultural land, on a range of produce, especially grain, stored in a wide scatter of government **granaries**. At times when the Hittite state was militarily strong, the tribute from vassals, from **food** to precious metals, was significant. Industrial activities, notably in **textiles,** mining and the production from centers of **metallurgy**, yielded further income.

Much of this income diminished drastically in times of military setbacks, unrest among vassals or **famine** and drought.

TREATIES. These could be international or else drawn up with a neighboring ruler or, most frequently, with a vassal. The most celebrated international treaty was that between **Hattusili III** and **Ramesses II**, drawn up in the 21st year of the latter's long reign, the common interest between the two great powers of the day being avoidance of a drain of manpower through tension along their common frontier in Syria. Egypt was anxious to secure its hold on its remaining territories in southern Syria, while Hatti looked to the threat in the east from Assyria.

Gift exchange was another means designed to promote and reinforce foreign policy, a relatively painless method of enhancing diplomatic prestige.

The outstanding example of a treaty with a neighboring land, at least nominally a vassal, was that drawn up by **Tudhaliya IV** with his cousin **Kurunta (Ulmi-Tesub)**, the ruler of **Tarhuntassa**. This was inscribed on a bronze **tablet** unique among known artifacts from the Hittite Empire, excavated beneath a pavement just inside the Sphinx Gate in **Boğazköy: Upper City** during the 1986 excavations. Its perfect preservation, with 350 lines of Hittite **cuneiform**, makes this all the more remarkable a discovery.

Treaties with vassals must have occupied much of the time of royal officials at Hattusa, the **scribes**, for they had to be redrawn with every new ruler, following death or deposition. The scribes clearly exerted direct influence on the precise wording of treaties, of which drafts as well as final versions survive. The text of international and vassal agreements with lands to the east and southeast was drawn up in Akkadian, the international language of **diplomacy**, but for the lands to the west, including **Ahhiyawa**, in Hittite, the scribes there evidently being unfamiliar with Akkadian. Many treaties were stored in the **archives** of **Temple 1 (Boğazköy)**, appropriate for the sanctity attached to agreements made in the presence of the gods. Set formulae occur for land boundaries and the mutual obligations of vassal and overlord. Many **gods and goddesses**, both of Hatti and of the vassal kingdom, are recorded as witnesses, the treaty ending with standard blessings and curses, for observance or breaking of the treaty.

A sidelight on clay tablets is provided by the indications that emendations to the text were made, of necessity when the clay was still soft. These changes came at the dictate of the king himself, who might add to the text, modify it or delete certain lines, as he saw fit. If wrapped in a damp cloth, the tablet could remain soft for a rather longer time. The presence of the king in Hattusa would, however, normally be required. Legally qualified officials may be named as signatories to many treaty clauses.

Finally, the treaty had to be inscribed in permanent form, seeing that it was a quasi-religious document. **Gold, silver** or **bronze** was used for several copies, the number often noted in the explanatory note, or colophon, attached to the treaty. Major treaties tend to include a lengthy preamble, sometimes providing the only surviving historical record for certain events of a reign or filling gaps in fragmentary texts.

TROY. This site is of course most famous for its Homeric associations as recounted in the *Iliad*, not written down until the eighth century BC. Its Turkish name is Hissarlik ("little castle/citadel"). It is now agreed that this is indeed the site of Troy, and that it can be identified with **Wilusa** of the Hittite records. It was thus involved in the Hittite world and in the complex rivalries in and around **Arzawa**. Both archaeologically and historically it can be considered primarily an Anatolian rather than an Aegean settlement at least until the 13th century BC. Nevertheless it lies on a fault-line, as it were, between Europe and Asia, the focus of academic attention not always wholly dispassionate, centered on questions related to Homer, on the one hand, and to Anatolian **historical geography**, on the other.

Originally located by Franz Kauffer (1793), Troy has seen excavations for over a century, first by **Heinrich Schliemann** (1870–1890), with further work after his death by his assistant Wilhelm Dorpfeld (1893–1894); then by Carl Blegen for the University of Cincinnati (1932–1938); and most recently in ongoing seasons under Manfred Korfmann since 1988, for the University of Tübingen and for Cincinnati. Much of this expedition's work has been concentrated outside the Citadel, in the Lower City—work that has attracted interest and controversy in almost equal measures. Regrettable acrimony has been stirred up, ostensibly by the bold reconstructions of the site publicized by Korfmann, but in all probability as much by academic jealousy, led by a university colleague in Tübingen, not an archaeologist! Opinion among archaeologists, however, has come down strongly on Korfmann's side, especially after a symposium held to thrash out these disagreements (February 2002).

The major disappointment in Troy VI (Late Bronze Age) is that the whole central area of the Citadel was destroyed in the Classical period, when the site was leveled for construction of a **temple** of Athena. Only those buildings on the perimeter, immediately inside the **fortifications**, have survived. Consequently any remains of a palace and associated structures have vanished: neither **tablets** nor **seal** impressions nor murals nor **sculptures** have been recovered. This has added fuel to the argument that Troy was an insignificant settlement, a case falsely advanced by comparing the comparative areas of a number of major Middle-Late Bronze Age citadels, when the plans cited are not on the same scale! In precise comparative terms, the Citadel of Troy VI is not much smaller in area than **Boğazköy: Büyükkale**, though none would claim that it was the center of a major state. The contemporary **Beycesultan** II, with its buildings of *megaron* plan, is of very modest extent.

Korfmann suggests—on plausible but not yet fully documented evidence—that the Lower City of Troy, stretching south from the Citadel for some 400 meters and with buildings covering an area of ca.270,000 square meters, would have had a population of 5,000–10,000, the Late Bronze Age occupation level lying beneath Hellenistic and Roman levels. Only limited areas of the Lower City, however, have yet been excavated. In late Troy VI the Lower City was defended by a palisade and ditch, with the addition of a second ditch further south in Troy VIIA. A city wall seems likely to have formed part of the defenses, together with a gateway.

The raison d'etre of Troy—whose story spans the whole third and second millennia BC and beyond—was **trade**. The presence of amber from northern Europe and lapis lazuli from Afghanistan attests long-distance trade in the Early Bronze Age, with other evidence. Maritime trade became much more significant in the Middle-Late Bronze Age, with the advent of the sailing ship. So strong were the winds and currents through the Bosphorus and Hellespont that many ships sought a haven where they could shelter, to await favorable conditions for entering the Black Sea. Troy was the answer to their need. As for the Hittites, they were involved in the long-established trade, preceding the Old Assyrian colonies in Anatolia, which ran from the Mediterranean (**Kizzuwadna**) northward through central Anatolia and on to the Black Sea outlets, whence ships could reach Troy and beyond. The evidence is lacking to do more than speculate that this trade may have been a factor in establishing the Hittite power base. **Textiles** were certainly significant items of trade from the third millennium BC. The **economy** of Troy was sustained, for purposes of basic subsistence, by a plentiful supply of fish. Modern surveys have established the prehistoric coastline, now well out from its Bronze Age line, with consequent silting of the harbor on which Troy had so heavily depended.

TUDHALIYA I/II (ca.1400–1380 BC). The reign began with a decisive victory over the supporters of the previous king, **Muwatalli I**, after his assassination. The name "Tudhaliya I/II" is a compromise to allow for the possibility of another Tudhaliya before **Tudhaliya III**, the father of **Suppiluliuma I**, and to preserve the conventional numbering of Tudhaliya III and IV.

This was not the only Hittite king to be confronted with dangers to his realm from three sectors, the west, north and southeast, embodied in **Arzawa**, **Kaska** and **Mitanni** respectively. Though fighting on three fronts in immediate succession might seem potentially fatal, the Hittite **army** had one advantage, that it was fighting on internal lines. In spite of the long years of internal discord and decline before his accession, Tudhaliya I/II must have had at his command a disciplined and effective military force, enabling him to inflict a crushing defeat by a daring night attack on an alliance of 22 rulers in the west, under the leadership of **Assuwa**, whatever its precise role in this coalition. The most permanent outcome of this campaign in western Anatolia was the inauguration of the deliberate policy of **deportation** of prisoners of war, teams of **horses** with their **chariots** and livestock to **Hattusa**—on this occasion 10,000 foot soldiers and 600 teams of horses for chariots, a significant addition to the Hittite army.

Meanwhile, in response to an invasion by Kaska tribesmen from the north, Tudhaliya I/II marched successfully against them, following up with a campaign deeper into their territory. These troubles, however, continued into the next two reigns, and are extensively recorded in the **archive** from **Maşat Höyük**.

Across the Euphrates River, in the area now forming the Turkish province of Elazığ, lay the kingdom of **Isuwa**, until its permanent annexation by **Suppiluliuma I** a thorn in the flesh of the Hittite state. At this time it looked to the **Hurrian** lands, the realm otherwise known as Mitanni, for support against the claims of Hatti. Twice during the reign of Tudhaliya I/II it rebelled and twice it was brought to heel, though on the second occasion only after it had been plundered by the Hurrian troops and after an interval of time in which the Hittite king was engaged elsewhere. He was unable to effect a permanent Hittite presence in Isuwa.

The first step needed to restore Hittite power in the southeast was to secure Hittite control of **Kizzuwadna**. That done, Tudhaliya fixed his eyes on **Aleppo**, as indicated by a **treaty** over a century later by **Muwatalli II**, a reissue of one by his father **Mursili II**, with Talmi-Sarruma, vassal ruler of that city. Treaties are particularly invaluable sources through their inclusion of a historical preamble, biased as it usually was, and this is no exception: it refers back to **Hattusili I** and **Mursili I** and then to Tudhaliya I/II, "with whom the king of Aleppo made peace." Though briefly allied with Hatti, Aleppo then accepted Mitannian suzerainty, an error which provoked a violent response from Tudhaliya. His claim to have razed the city could well be accurate; but his claim also to have destroyed **Hanigalbat** (Mitanni) must be a gross exaggeration, given the continuing activity of Mitanni east of the Euphrates. **Alalakh** Level IV with the palace of Niqmepa was, however, destroyed.

The Hittite state was once more involved as a leading player on the central stage of Near Eastern power politics, in north Syria where so many interests confronted one another. The Hittite New Kingdom and a new era had begun, however temporary the conquests by Tudhaliya I/II proved to be.

TUDHALIYA III (1360–1344 BC). Son of **Arnuwanda I** and Asmunikal and father of **Suppiluliuma I**, this king deserves better recognition for his achievements than the surviving records make possible. Faced with unparalleled attacks on his kingdom from every side, with the sack of his capital city, **Hattusa**, he nevertheless fought back, and succeeded in laying the foundations for the work of his more famous son and successor. His military triumphs place him on a level with his illustrious Old Kingdom predecessors, **Hattusili I** and **Mursili I**.

The ancient enemy in the north, the **Kaska**, came in force through the Hittite homeland to the south bend of the **Marrassantiya River**, doubtless sacking Hattusa en route. Perhaps as a result of a concentration on the northern front of opposing Hittite forces, other enemies—**Arzawa** from the southwest, **Isuwa** from the southeast, **Azzi-Hayasa** from the northeast—were able to join in the attack without immediate opposition. If Tudhaliya III rallied his followers, scattered from Hattusa, at a temporary headquarters elsewhere, it might have been at **Samuha** on the upper Marrassantiya, after expulsion of the invading men of Azzi-Hayasa.

It is from *The Deeds of Suppiluliuma*, compiled by his son **Mursili II**, that evidence can be garnered of the recovery of the Hittite realm from the invaders. The forces of Kaska and Azzi-Hayasa were the first to be confronted by Tudhaliya III, in offensives mounted from his base at Samuha.

Old age and sickness finally obliged him to hand over conduct of military operations to the capable hands of his second son, the future Suppiluliuma I.

TUDHALIYA IV (1237–1209 BC). His father **Hattusili III** seems to have chosen him as *tuhkanti* (crown prince), displacing his older brother Nerikkaili, perhaps a long planned decision. It was probably no coincidence that Tudhaliya's early career followed very closely that of his father in the borderlands of **Kaska** in the north. The young Tudhaliya seems to have been an energetic soldier, securing a victory in the north over Hatenzuwa, which his father himself had been unable to achieve. But how much credit was really owed to Tudhaliya, perhaps only 12 years old at the time, is uncertain. He may well, however, have been appointed co-regent in his father's final years. His mother, **Puduhepa**, seems to have arranged his **marriage** with a "daughter of Babylon," of acceptable status for the heir of the Great King. **Ramesses II** questioned this status of Babylon.

After his accession Tudhaliya IV found himself between two very powerful **women**, his mother with the power of the *Tawananna* (queen mother) and his Babylonian **queen**, with the women of court dividing into factions of their respective supporters. Puduhepa seems eventually to have triumphed, remaining a power in the land until her death, possibly after her sons, though this is uncertain.

Troubles faced Tudhaliya IV on all sides: in the west, where the influence of **Ahhiyawa** was rising; in the east, where Assyria posed an ongoing threat; and nearer home in the **Lower Land** where the people of **Lalanda**, described as "notorious troublemakers," rose in rebellion. His **treaty** with his vassal, Sausgamuwa of **Amurru**, reveals a perception of Egypt as still a potential threat to Hittite hegemony in Syria—an unnecessary fear, as it proved. But Tudhaliya made it plain that the treaty bound him to allegiance to himself as Hittite king and to his descendants, and to none other.

Tudhaliya reinstated his brother Nerikkaili as *tuhkanti*, doubtless to ensure his loyalty. He even before his accession considered compensation in the form of land for the sons of **Urhi-Tesub**. Additional lands and reductions of **taxes** were conferred on his cousin **Kurunta**.

The **Yalburt** inscription is one source for the activities of Tudhaliya IV in the west, where his father had been far from successful. Now there was repeated trouble with the **Seha River Land**, fomented by the king of Ahhiyawa through his port of **Millawanda/Milawata**. In due course the ruler of Millawanda, joined by marriage to the Hittite royal house, became a kind of regional governor-general or suzerain in the west, to whom the king of **Wilusa** became answerable, as well as to Tudhaliya IV. Ahhiyawa became significantly restricted in its activities on the Anatolian mainland.

Tudhaliya IV relied upon Ini-Tesub, third **viceroy** of **Carchemish** and his cousin, to secure his interests in Syria. With the death of **Shalmaneser I** (ca.1233 BC) there was reason to hope for an improvement in Assyro-Hittite relations. This did occur for a while, until the ambitions of **Tukulti-Ninurta I (1233–1197 BC)** made conflict almost inevitable. Here Tudhaliya IV blundered, relying uncritically on the support of a vassal, the ruler of **Isuwa**, who failed to send troops to reinforce the Hittite **army**, then far from its home bases, in the hills where the disastrous battle of **Nihriya** was to be fought. The outcome put an end to Hittite ambitions east of the Euphrates, though Isuwa was left in Hittite hands. After the brief usurpation of the throne in **Hattusa** by his cousin Kurunta, **Tarhuntassa** may have been lost to the Hittite Empire. Tudhaliya was obliged to acknowledge its promotion to equal rank with Carchemish.

Other problems faced this king, not least recurrent **famine**. Merneptah (1213–1204 BC), son of **Ramesses II**, referred in his Karnak inscription to a shipment of grain he had sent to "keep alive the land of Hatti." Undernourishment would not have improved the effectiveness of men recruited to the Hittite army.

Resources were undoubtedly expended to excess on building programs especially in Hattusa, and on religious endowments and **festivals**—wealth which could be ill spared.

TUDHALIYA IV: RELIGIOUS REFORMS. While to modern eyes it may seem that Tudhaliya IV, faced with dangers on more than one front, diverted essential resources from the battlefront, there were major political factors underlying his far-reaching program of religious reforms. One such was the evident requirement for concessions to **Hurrian** cultic traditions, urged on by his mother,

Puduhepa, and doubtless conceived as a favor to the population of the eastern territories under Hittite rule. Hurrians were not, however, the only intrusive element in the priesthoods, for **Luwians** were becoming increasingly influential, in large part through the dominance of their **language**. The Hittite upper class had to appease the non-Hittite majority in the Empire.

Most of the **tablets** from the royal library at **Hattusa** describing **festivals** are collations, bringing up to date much older texts, some originating in the Hittite Old Kingdom, though surviving only in fragments. The titles and colophons of these festival texts have the author of each collation always given as "My Sun Tudhaliya." Royal intervention was commonly designed to ordain new sacrifices or to augment the reserves in the **temple** storerooms. The **cult inventories** are listed in geographical order, as the royal inspectors had to proceed.

The reforms of Tudhaliya IV were intended to preserve as much as possible of earlier cultic practices, while imposing a uniformity in order to reinforce royal control and to discourage excessive local divergences from the norm. Because the real presence of a **god or goddess** existed only in or by his or her **statue**, damaged, vanished or destroyed statues had to be restored or replaced. Anthropomorphic statues were now essential for all divinities, and could not be fashioned from wood, as being too impermanent. **Iron** was the fashionable metal for the **statues**, with **gold** and **silver** brocade and appliqué ornaments. But other materials were employed, from gold and ivory in the richest shrines to wood with metal ornaments in the poorest. Such ornaments could be various jewels or lunates, solar disks or animals. **Stelae** on a hill or near a spring had henceforth to be set up in temples for their better protection. A governmental staff was dedicated to maintenance of religious statues, a new concept, with the necessary disbursement coming from the palace.

Side by side with preservation of local deities and **cults** of mountains and springs, the king sought to achieve uniformity of beliefs, to reflect the imperial unity of the state. The multiplicity of divinities had to be reduced to a limited number of categories: gods of the storm, of war and of vegetable life, goddesses of fertility. Several idols might be brought in under the same roof. Assimilation was a necessary product of these reforms: Hurrian gods and goddesses to their Anatolian equivalents and the **Hattian** Storm-God to certain attributes of the Syrian **Tesub**.

In all likelihood the religious reforms were motivated initially

by the need to restore the temples of **Hattusa** after their destruction
at the time of the usurpation of the throne by **Kurunta**. There is a
textual record of rebuilding of temples, with the king consulting an
oracle. Other texts highlight aspects of these reforms: one records
a statue of iron with eyes of gold standing on an iron lion, for
which measures of grain and **wine** were to be provided; another,
destroyed or vanished statues to be restored or replaced; another,
the rebuilding of a town with its temple, to be provided with a silver statue of its tutelary goddess; another, the opening of the storage jars installed by My Sun at harvest time or in a thunderstorm;
another, the king's ordaining a stele of silver surmounted by a solar
disk. For one temple 36 bushels of barley were provided by the
king.

It is obvious that all these donations to the numerous temples
and cult shrines must have drained much of the royal **treasury**.

TUKULTI-NINURTA I (1233–1197 BC).   Assyrian victor over the
army of **Tudhaliya IV** at the battle of **Nihriya (Nairi)** early in his
reign, ca.1232 BC. Although claiming in one text to have captured
28,800 Hittite soldiers from across the Euphrates, after this battle,
this is virtually certain to be an exaggeration. In fact he did not
pursue the defeated Hittite forces across the Euphrates, nor did he
enter the vulnerable territory of **Isuwa**. But wide territories east of
the river were permanently lost to Hittite control, including the
copper mines of **Ergani Maden**. The reason for this restraint on
the Hittite front was Assyrian concern to subdue Babylon. Like
Sennacherib over five centuries later, embroilment in Babylonia
was to lead to the Assyrian king's assassination.

TUWANUWA. This town, the Classical Tyana, is firmly located at
Ambartepe, a settlement site with seven meters' depth of occupation levels now covered by the village of Kemerhisar, south of Bor,
in the province of Niğde. Inscriptions found here include two bilingual texts in **Luwian hieroglyphs** and Old Phrygian. Another
"black stone" is inscribed in Phrygian, but is very difficult to deci-
pher. Evidently three different **scribes** were working in a Luwian
context. These inscriptions can be dated to the time of the historical
Mita (Midas), in the late eighth century BC.

In the Hittite records Tuwanuwa is first mentioned by **Telipinu**, in his account of the conquests of **Labarna**. It is later named,
in the time of **Tudhaliya III**, as the limit of invasion by forces
from **Arzawa**, via the **Lower Land**, making Tuwanuwa their fron-

tier. The *Deeds* of **Suppiluliuma I** include reference to his recapture of the town and his gathering an **army** to attack Arzawa.

Tuwanuwa was later one of the cities of **Tabal**—in the area of Tyanitis in Classical times—along with the cities of Tunna (**Porsuk Höyük**) and **Hupisna**.

- U -

UDA. A land near **Tuwanuwa** in the eastern section of the **Lower Land**. The invading troops of **Arzawa**, in the reign of **Tudhaliya III**, reached this far. Telipinu, **viceroy** of **Aleppo**, was summoned by **Suppiluliuma I** from his expedition against **Carchemish** to Uda, where the king was involved in religious **festivals**.

UGARIT. This, the major Late Bronze Age city on the Mediterranean coast of Syria, was soon identified by **cuneiform tablets** found in the French excavations carried out since 1929 at the site of Ras Shamra, three kilometers inland, and at the associated port of Minet-el-Beidha (ancient Mahadu). The excavations, following the accidental exposure of a stone-built tomb, were directed by **Claude F. A. Schaeffer** (1929–1939 and after World War II until 1970) and were resumed from 1978. The excavations are currently directed by Marguerite Yon and Yves Cabilt (University of Lyon) concurrently with reassessment of aspects of the earlier seasons' results.

Ugarit can lay claim to the first rank among all Bronze Age cities in the ancient Near East, though the Early and Middle Bronze Age levels are relatively little known. The heyday of Ugarit was in the Late Bronze Age, with the thousands of tablets dating entirely from the 15th to the 13th and very early 12th century BC. The great majority of these tablets indeed date from the last two generations of the city, up to its sudden and violent destruction by the **Sea Peoples**. Ugarit had a mixed population, its written records being even more diverse, including Sumerian, Akkadian, **Hurrian** and **Hittite** texts, as well as syllabic and alphabetic Ugaritic.

Lying just north of Canaan, yet greatly influenced by its cultural traditions, literary and religious, Ugarit thrived as an entrepot for east-west **trade**, possessing a powerful fleet deployed in the Mediterranean in trade with the Mycenaean cities. It also lay on a north-south route for overland trade between Anatolia and Syria. With the expansion of Egyptian power in the New Kingdom, from ca.1550 BC, Ugarit came under Egyptian suzerainty by the mid–15th century BC, at a time of Hittite weakness.

Thus it remained into the reign of the heretic pharaoh Akhenaten and the early years of **Suppiluliuma I** (1344–1322 BC). With the accession of a new king, Niqmaddu II, to the throne of Ugarit, however, Suppiluliuma scored a major and lasting diplomatic and political triumph, persuading the king of Ugarit to agree to his proposal that he switch his allegiance from Egypt to Hatti. This was agreed, against the backcloth of the rebellion of two vassals of Hatti, **Mukis** and **Nuhasse**, the former lying north of Ugarit and the latter inland, between the kingdom of Ugarit and the Euphrates. In this agreement was the promise, which Suppiluliuma kept, that Ugarit would be permitted to retain territory gained from neighboring enemies. Thus it came about that the extent of the kingdom of Ugarit increased three- or four fold under Hittite suzerainty.

This relationship was mutually beneficial, Ugarit securing protection from unreliable neighbors and the Hittite Empire gaining access to military manpower, enlisted on the Hittite side at **Kadesh**, and to the fleet, which served as transportation for much-needed grain in times of **famine** or scarcity to the port of **Ura** in **Kizzuwadna**. In times of danger, notably in the final years, the fleet of Ugarit gave a maritime arm to the Hittite land forces in Anatolia, deploying at least 150 ships, while mustering 1,000 **chariots**. Unlike **Aleppo** and **Carchemish**, however, Ugarit was not the seat of a **viceroyalty**. It retained a degree of independence under its own kings, coming increasingly to exercise this as the power of Hatti began to wane toward the final debacle, in which Ugarit too was to be overwhelmed (ca.1180/1176 BC).

Ugarit was more than a support for the defense of the Hittite dominions. The richest vassal of Hatti, its tribute was of major economic importance. This derived from the varied and flourishing industrial activities in and around the city, which was never wholly dependent on foreign trade. These activities are documented in the tablets and by the artifacts found in the excavations. **Gold**smiths and bronzesmiths prospered, as did the producers of linen and woolen **textiles**, exports playing a significant role in each case: one example is a bronze **sword** inscribed with the name of the pharaoh Merneptah (1213–1204 BC), son and successor of **Ramesses II**, obviously intended for dispatch to Egypt, a transaction possibly canceled by the pharaoh's death. The wealth of Ugarit depended also on the produce of the hinterland, from corn and flax, **oil** and **wine**, to **timber** from the mountainsides, this last essential not only for public works in the city but also for the large fleet.

Archaeological links with the Hittite homeland are discernible in the **postern tunnel** in the short surviving stretch of the city **fortifications**, near the royal palace, and even more clearly in the seal impressions. The postern at Ugarit is of more finely dressed masonry than that in the perimeter defenses of the **Upper City** of **Hattusa**, dating most probably to the reign of Suppiluliuma I (1344–1322 BC). The stonemason's craft had a long history in Syria, being passed on in due course to the Phoenicians. The finest Hittite masonry, in and beyond Hattusa, can be dated after the expansion of Hittite military and political power into Syria. Seal impressions exemplify Hittite royal **glyptic art**, in the form of convex-headed stamp seals with the royal monogram in cuneiform or **hieroglyphs** surrounded normally by two lines of script, cuneiform and hieroglyphic, thus providing bilingual data of some use in the decipherment of the hieroglyphs.

The clearest evidence of the external relations of Ugarit, however, is to be seen in the magnificently built stone tombs of Minetel-Beidha and Ugarit itself, excavated in the early seasons and found to contain numerous **pottery** vessels, including many Mycenaean, highlighting the importance of the maritime Aegean trade and also of the merchant community from the Mycenaean cities settled, along with other foreigners, in Ugarit. It is not impossible that such contacts were ultimately to speed the onslaught on Ugarit by the Sea Peoples, an event vividly attested by tablets found abandoned in the oven wherein they had been baked. Such contemporary record of violent attack and impending destruction is extremely rare. This great city was indeed cut off in its prime, never to rise again.

ULLIKUMMI. A stone giant or monster, appearing in part of the **Kumarbi** cycle of myths. Very probably this is to be identified on the **gold** bowl of **Hasanlu**. Ullikummi originated as **god** of the mountain Ulligamma, in the center of the zone of **Hurrian** settlement north and east of Mesopotamia. His name came to be reinterpreted as "destroyer of Kumme," the holy city of the god **Tesub**.

ULMI-TESUB. *See* **KURUNTA.**

UNDERWORLD. The chthonic element was significant in every religious tradition in the ancient world, from the first literate communities in Mesopotamia to classical Greece and pagan Rome. Hittite ritual texts reveal that it was the **gods** of the Underworld who, unlike the other deities in the Hittite lands, had a strong desire for blood from the sacrifices offered to them: thus it would be ensured that the blood would not so much be exposed to the sky as allowed to soak into the ground.

In the standardized **pantheon** which emerged in the early 14th century BC, a group of deities associated with the Underworld ranked low down the line, after the local deities. It was almost as though there was a superstitious fear about recognizing such sinister beings. In the older **Hattian** pantheon, Sulinkatte was the equivalent of **Nergal**, while **Lelwani**—a god, though later a goddess—was likewise associated with the Underworld; and Siwat, "The Lucky Day"—a euphemism for "Day of Death"—occurs especially often in the mortuary rituals.

The clearest, most familiar manifestation of the Underworld in Hittite **religion**, or more accurately in the **Hurrian cult**, occurs in Chamber B of the **Yazılıkaya** sanctuary outside the city of **Hattusa**, with the remarkable and indeed unique Sword-God, a god in human form emerging from the hilt of a dagger, its blade too shortened to be termed a **sword**. This has long been recognized as identifiable with Nergal, the god of the Underworld, one of the Mesopotamian deities imported by the Hurrians into Anatolia. From a magical ritual going far to explain the Sword-God of Chamber B at Yazılıkaya come the words: "He makes them as swords and fixes them in the ground." In another text "the bronze swords of Nergal" and "the twelve gods of the crossroads" are mentioned together: hence the twelve running gods, not soldiers as once supposed, facing the Sword-God and likewise appearing in the larger Chamber A at Yazılıkaya at the rear of the procession. Skeletons of birds were found in crevices in the rock just outside Chamber B and in the small Room C: these typically occur in rituals associated with the Underworld.

Magic features in the context of Underworld rituals and the chthonic powers, as in the employment of the substitute for preservation of the king's life or for due completion of the **royal funerary customs**. Effigies or "infernal substitutes" are prominent in these rituals. *See also* **BURIAL CUSTOMS.**

UPPER LAND. Centered in the upper **Marrassantiya** valley, in the northern sector of the modern province of Sivas, this was strategically vital to the defense of the Hittite homeland against enemies from the northwest and northeast, **Kaska** and **Azzi-Hayasa** respectively. It was probably the one bastion remaining to **Tudhaliya III** when all the rest of his kingdom had been overrun, with **Samuha** as his headquarters. This city lay east of the line of advance of the Kaska tribesmen against **Hattusa**. Even during the reign of so strong a king as **Mursili II** a Kaskan tribal leader overran and briefly annexed the Upper Land, defiantly rejecting the call to surrender: he met his defeat soon afterward.

The importance of the Upper Land is implied by the prestige attached to the governorship. When the official in that post, Arma-Tarhunda, was displaced by **Muwatalli II** to make way for his brother, the future **Hattusili III**, he protested vehemently. His son was eventually appointed to this post.

URA. A port on the coast of **Kizzuwadna**, located at Silifke or alternatively at Gilindere. This was especially important for the Hittite state in the closing years of the Empire, when it was used for the import of grain to alleviate serious **famine** in the Hittite lands. The grain was shipped through **Ugarit**, originating from **Mukis**, Canaan and Egypt. It was then transported overland by donkey caravans.

URARTU. This kingdom, centered on the land known to its own rulers as Van, flourished from the mid–ninth century BC, coming to an abrupt end not many years after the fall of Nineveh and the Assyrian Empire (612 BC). Its language is agreed to be related to **Hurrian**, though with a common ancestor rather than in direct descent. While it has been suggested that the **cyclopean masonry** characteristic of its numerous fortresses may have been derived from the comparable masonry found in the Hittite lands, notably in the gateways of **Boğazköy: Upper City**, this seems highly improbable. There are no hints of cultural connections in other respects with Late Bronze Age central Anatolia; no Urartian fortresses can be dated before the ninth century BC; and in any case **building methods** are the least likely aspect of any cultural tradition to be transferred over long distances, if only because of the necessity of obtaining stone and timber from nearby. It has to be admitted, however, that craftsmen could move long distances, as happened when workmen were imported from all over the Persian Empire for the construction of Persepolis.

Urartu became directly involved in Anatolia west of the upper Euphrates River with campaigns in the land of **Malatya** and later organization of a doomed anti-Assyrian alliance, defeated in battle by Tiglath-Pileser III (743 BC). Under Rusa II (ca.685–645 BC) Urartu enjoyed a revival. Unfortunately inscriptions from this reign are relatively meager, at least in historical content, though there are references to **Musku** and to Hatti, meaning north Syria around **Carchemish**, indicating some campaigning in the west.

The Euphrates, in the reaches between Malatya on the west side and Elazığ on the east, formed a boundary in terms of material culture, most easily recognizable from the **pottery**, which to the west includes some **Alışar IV ware**, virtually absent on the east side. On the other hand, provincial wares related to standard Urartian pottery from the central regions of the kingdom are found east of the Euphrates.

The second **god** in the ranks of the state pantheon of Urartu was none other than **Tesub/Teseba**, the Hurrian **Storm/Weather-God**, represented in **sculpture** and in **glyptic art** standing on his animal, a bull.

URHI-TESUB (1272–1267 BC). Whether or not there was any significance to the fact that this king is known by his **Hurrian** birth name rather than his adopted Hittite throne name of **Mursili III** is uncertain. But this son of the second rank, born to a concubine, never commanded universal support upon his accession.

By the rules for succession laid down by **Telipinu**, Urhi-Tesub had a perfectly legitimate claim. Initially his uncle **Hattusili III**, seasoned in government and campaigning, probably worked closely with Urhi-Tesub. He may indeed have been a decisive influence in the return of the court from **Tarhuntassa** to **Hattusa**.

However much of the accuracy of subsequent accounts of the acts of Urhi-Tesub may be questioned, he does appear to have gone against his father's wishes in a number of matters, including reinstatement of rebellious vassals to their thrones in the **Seha River Land** and **Amurru**. These changes of policy could be explicable by influences on Urhi-Tesub while a young prince susceptible to palace gossip and intrigues within the royal harem: such indeed may explain other inconsistencies in royal policy over the generations. The reinstatement of the **queen** Tanuhepa after her dismissal from office by Muwatalli II would also have been controversial.

In the east there was an ominous development, with the reduction to vassalage and later annexation of **Hanigalbat**, after successive rebellions against Assyrian overlordship in the reign of **Adad-nirari I (1295–1264 BC)**. Urhi-Tesub was obliged to accept the de facto loss of the Hittite territory.

Indignantly Urhi-Tesub rejected the claim to "brotherhood" with him of Adad-nirari I:

> With respect to brotherhood. . . . about which you speak— what does brotherhood mean? . . . . And for what reason should I write to you about brotherhood?. . . . [A]s my father and my grandfather did not write to the king of Assur about brotherhood, even so must you not write about brotherhood and Great Kingship to me.

Urhi-Tesub's lack of political sophistication in dealing with Assyria may have contributed to his downfall. Urhi-Tesub progressively reduced the areas under his uncle's administration in the north, leaving him only with his center in **Hakpissa** and the great shrine of **Nerik**, which he had regained early in Urhi-Tesub's reign. When Urhi-Tesub took these from Hattusili, the gloves were off. Urhi-Tesub marched into the **Upper Lands**, but failed to gather enough support, while many of the nobility gathered to Hattusili. Urhi-Tesub was then exiled to the **Nuhasse** lands but eventually surfaced under **Ramesses II**'s protection in Egypt, an ongoing irritant to Hattusili III and a threat to his claim to legitimacy especially in the eyes of foreign rulers.

URIAH. Perhaps the best known Hittite until the excavations began in 1906 at **Boğazköy (Hattusa)**, revealing the royal **archives** of the imperial period. One of King David's royal guard, the king, who had seduced Uriah's wife, Bath-Sheba, deliberately sent him into the forefront of the fighting, correctly expecting him to die in battle. Thus was David enabled to take Bath-Sheba as his wife, who bore him a son, Solomon. By so doing he incurred the wrath of Yahveh, conveyed by the words of Nathan the prophet, later, with Zadok the priest, to anoint Solomon king. Living in the 10th century BC, Uriah can be termed a Neo-Hittite, one of many then in Syria and the former land of Canaan.

URKESH (TELL MOZAN). Though situated near Tell Brak, in the upper Khabur basin of northeast Syria, its long history as a center of **Hurrian** culture makes Tell Mozan of direct relevance to the development of Hittite civilization from the **Middle Kingdom** onward. Its identification with ancient Urkesh is made certain by a stratified series of inscribed **seal** impressions. This is the only Hurrian city for which a dynasty of kings can be reconstructed for the late third millennium BC, even if other Hurrian cities were ruled by independent kings. Urkesh seems to have enjoyed a preeminent status.

The early rank of Urkesh is stressed by its being the seat of the god **Kumarbi**, whom his son the young god **Silver** is enjoined in an early Hurrian myth to respect:

> Kumarbi. . . . resides in Urkesh, where he rightfully resolves the lawsuits of all the lands. Your brother is **Tesup**: he is king in heaven and in the land. Your sister is **Sauska**, and she is queen in Nineveh You must not fear any of them. Only one deity you must fear, Kumarbi, who stirs up the enemy land and the wild animals.

Archaeologically, it is regrettable that the city was apparently never destroyed in antiquity, for it is in destruction levels that the richest haul of finds commonly occurs. Yet there are important building remains, including an inner city wall, a **temple** and a palace, dated to ca.2700, 2450 and 2200 BC respectively. Tupkish, the king attested by the seal inscriptions, has a Hurrian name, though his wife had an Akkadian name. He bore the title "king of Urkesh and Nawan," the latter signifying not the nearby city of Tell Brak but the highland hinterland to the north. Anatolian raw materials, especially **metals**, **timber** and stone, were brought south by major **trade** routes all converging on Urkesh, accounting for its great prosperity.

URSU (WARSUWA). A city lying west of the Euphrates River and north of **Carchemish**, it stood on a **trade** route whose control was doubtless deemed essential by **Hattusili I**, who determined to make an example of it in retaliation for the resistance of its overlord **Aleppo** to Hittite ambitions in Syria.

The so-called *Siege of Ursu Text* is less of a historical than a literary work, and as such not to be taken at face value. Unfortunately, it is only half preserved, written in Akkadian, though with clues indicating a Hittite **scribe**. It is nevertheless evident that this **siege** was conducted inefficiently. Among the many set speeches making up this composition are indications of the king's extreme frustration and anger with his commanders, while he was away in **Kizzuwadna**.

- V -

VICEROYALTIES. As a means of ensuring firm Hittite control of north Syria, **Suppiluliuma I** established two "kingdoms," in fact vicregal administrations, with his second son, Telipinu, at **Aleppo** and his third son, Piyassili, at **Carchemish**, once that city had fallen after a **siege** of eight days and a fierce battle at the end. It is interesting to note that Piyassili adopted a **Hurrian** throne name, Sarri-Kusuh, the reverse of the practice of the kings of the Empire period themselves, who, though of Hurrian descent, adopted a Hittite name on accession to the throne at Hattusa. Was this perhaps a conciliatory gesture to the population of the former territories of **Mitanni**?

Aleppo and Carchemish continued as viceregal capitals until the fall of Hatti, the latter acting as a bastion of Hittite cultural traditions in the new Neo-Hittite world. **Seal** impressions of Ini-Tesub, a later viceroy of Carchemish, have been found at **Ugarit**. Carchemish was the administrative and military center holding the north Syrian front along the Euphrates against the ever-present threat of incursions from Assyria.

Arrangements of a more temporary character might be classed as viceroyalties. Such was the cession of the territory of **Tarhuntassa** north of the Taurus range to **Kurunta** and likewise the granting by **Muwatalli II** to his brother, the future **Hattusili III**, of semi-independent powers over the lands of the north, in the face of the recurrent threat from the **Kaska** lands.

VINEYARDS. *See* **WINE.**

- W -

WAHSUSANA. A minor kingdom in the Old Assyrian period, probably centered south of the **Marrassantiya River** and southeast of **Burushattum**, perhaps in the area of Niğde. An alternative location might be further west, in the Konya Plain. At least by the period of **Kültepe-*karum*** IB a *karum* had been established in Wahsusana, though strictly subordinate to the authority of the *karum* of **Kanes**.

WARFARE. *See* **ARCHERY; ARMOR; ARMY; CHARIOTS; HELMETS; HORSES; KADESH (BATTLE OF); KIKKULI;**

SHIELDS; SIEGE WARFARE; SPEARS; SWORDS; WEAPONS AND MILITARY EQUIPMENT.

WASSUKKANNI. The royal seat and administrative capital of the kings of **Mitanni**, yet to be identified on the ground with certainty, one choice of location being **Tell Fakhariyah**. In the reign of Tusratta, Wassukkanni was captured and plundered by the Hittites under **Suppiluliuma I**.

Tell Fakhariyah, near the sources of the Khabur, is located in an area accessible for **trade** and ease of communication with the territories under Mitannian rule, though perhaps not naturally defensible. An alternative location would lie in the hill country around Mardin or probably rather to the west; but such a highland location would be less accessible. Modern science suggests a location other than Tell Fakhariyah, for neutron activation analysis of the clays used for the **tablets** inscribed with the letters of Tusratta, surely originating in Wassukkanni, shows marked differences from the clay of the Middle Assyrian tablets excavated at the site.

WATER SUPPLY. While **cisterns** provided water for a small garrison in time of **siege**, they were never large enough to meet the needs of hundreds, let alone thousands. For provision on that scale one must turn to **Hattusa** and more specifically to **Boğazköy: Upper City**, where ponds were first detected from aerial photographs. A southern group of two larger and three smaller pools was sited west-southwest of the central **temple** district and about 100 meters inside the Upper City perimeter defenses; an eastern pair of ponds lay just southeast of the Southern Citadel **(Boğazköy: Südburg)**. The lower of these two ponds measured about 60 by 90 meters, with a dam 16 meters wide at its base separating the two: waterproofing was attained with remarkable efficiency by a clay flooring and by a narrow, clay-filled trench along the embankments.

The engineering of water supply to the city below was achieved by siting the southern ponds at the highest point of the Upper City and by drawing water from a number of springs within and even beyond the perimeter. Baked clay water pipes were laid from the springs, including some in the high ground south of the Upper City. One pipeline was taken through the city defenses below the King's Gate. The maintenance of these pipelines was assisted by provision of a hole, plugged each with a stone, for each segment. This is surely yet another indication that the Upper City took a long time to construct.

WEAPONS AND MILITARY EQUIPMENT. These were adapted and developed over the generations in line with improvements in design and manufacture, while being deployed with the objectives of maximum mobility and fire power. Hittite requirements tended toward weight and fire power, while Egyptian forces demanded above all maneuverability and speed from their **chariotry**. It was this arm which proved decisive in many engagements.

Metalwork was produced by craftsmen independent of political boundaries and thus only to a limited degree controlled by the Hittite kings. **Spears** and daggers, **axes** and **swords** demonstrate particular technical improvements, with the eventual introduction of **iron**, evident in specimens recovered by excavations. Much of the evidence, however, comes in the form of depictions in reliefs, both Hittite and Egyptian, especially relevant to the study of protective equipment, comprising body **armor**, **helmets** and **shields**.

Improvements in **siege** techniques, with the use of the "**Hurrian** ram," as recorded at the siege of **Ursu** in the reign of **Hattusili I**, and with the composite bow, demonstrated a readiness to learn in the Hittite **army**. Thereafter, however, there were few developments in weaponry until the closing years of the Empire.

WEATHER-GOD. *See* **STORM-GOD.**

WEIGHTS AND MEASURES. The determination of **prices** was normally in terms of weights in **silver**, like all measures most precisely recorded in Mesopotamia. A mina of about 500 grams was used in Mesopotamia, comprising 60 shekels, whereas among the Hittites it comprised only 40 shekels, with the Hebrew ratio at 50 shekels. The probability is that the shekel was the basic, universal unit of weight, the Hittite mina therefore being much lighter than the Mesopotamian. The value of **copper** was infinitely lower than that of silver, standing at one shekel of silver for four minas of copper. With copper imported from **Alasiya (Cyprus)**, its value relative to silver was even lower (1:240).

Linear measurements were based on the cubit or forearm, about 50 centimeters. Areas were measured by multiples of cubits, called "garden plots." The Hittite builders no doubt used cubit rods of wood, stone or metal, such as those found in Mesopotamia, where they occur from ca.2200 BC. Cubits might be divided into palms of four or five fingers and sometimes into fingers and smaller units. Shekels and barleycorns were used for fractions of area, weight and capacity. The Mesopotamian measure of capacity

(Akkadian *qu*) was approximately one liter.

WHEELED VEHICLES. Heavy wagons and carts, four- and two-wheeled respectively and to be distinguished from **chariots**, were economically essential in Anatolia in Hittite times. It is recorded that village communities were obliged to supply manufactured items to the administrative center, or palace: among these were parts of wagons. It is a fair presumption that these were required in part at least for supply purposes on campaign. Agriculture, however, was also relevant. Such wagons and carts were inefficient in terms of their weight-to-load ratio, and consequently slow-moving; but they could negotiate fairly rough ground, like the comparable solid-wheeled carts widely in use in Anatolia until a very few years ago. Wooden axles had continued in use for millennia, though many of the modern carts, drawn by oxen or water buffalo, had steel axles. Likewise long-lasting, from pre-Hittite to modern times, has been the standard design of the solid wheel, the tripartite disk, with the nave or hub carved from the solid wood and projecting only slightly. Two painted **pottery** models of oxen—of the 15th or 16th century BC, from **Boğazköy: Büyükkale** IV—illustrate the method of controlling the bovids, drawing carts and wagons with nose ropes.

Egyptian **temple** reliefs of the New Kingdom provide the best-known pictures of solid-wheeled vehicles, in scenes of the attack on **Kadesh** in Syria by Seti I, father of **Ramesses II**, and of the famous battle there in which the latter was vaingloriously depicted in the thick of the fray: the Hittite **army** was shown with solid-wheeled vehicles, evidently used as troop carriers, bringing the infantry to the battlefield. A third Egyptian king, Ramesses III, depicted the **Sea Peoples** on the façade of his mortuary temple of Medinet Habu, early in the 12th century BC: women and children are being conveyed overland in solid-wheeled ox-drawn carts.

Wheeled vehicles were in the first instance introduced from outside into Anatolia, where the evidence for their presence before the second millennium BC is very limited. **Seal** impressions from **Kültepe-*Karum*** II include designs of vehicles of the primitive cross-bar type as well as spoked-wheel vehicles, implying that the skills of the wheelwright were being developed from the end of the Early Bronze Age in central Anatolia at least, leading to fully developed Hittite chariotry from ca.1650 BC, under **Hattusili I** and his successors. Copper/bronze models said to come from southeastern Anatolia date to the third millennium BC. The earliest trace of the wheel in Anatolia appears to be a clay wheel model from **Malatya (Arslantepe)**, while three seal impressions among thousands dumped in one room at the same site depict a sledge drawn by a bovid.

The evidence for the origins of wheeled carts and wagons is fourfold, comprising actual remains, wheel ruts, models and representations. All these are significant, though model wheels may in some cases be better classed as spindle whorls, and are thus the least conclusive. The strong case for a Near Eastern, more specifically Mesopotamian, origin rests on the representation of a wagon as one of the earliest Sumerian pictograms, dating around 3400 BC. This argument, however, rests in part on an **absolute chronology** which has remained much as before for Mesopotamia but with higher dating for relevant evidence from the steppes and from Europe, moving these data back from the third to the mid-fourth millennium BC. Two sites merit special mention: at Flintbek, near Kiel in north Germany, have been found wheel ruts; and at Bronocice, in the upper Vistula basin of Poland, occurs pottery with representations of wagons, albeit in rather stylized form. Of fairly similar date are various steppe sites with remains of wheeled vehicles, roughly contemporary with the Eanna IVA **tablets** from Uruk-Warka. Although a claim of a mid–fifth millennium BC context for clay wheel models, up to 12 centimeters in diameter, found in Romania seems to have been ignored, it may deserve mention.

An origin for wheeled vehicles, carts and wagons, in the early fourth millennium BC in the zone stretching across the steppes into eastern and northern Europe seems more likely than one in Mesopotamia, a land cut about by waterways, where the easiest mode of transport was indeed by water. Only a discovery of remains of a wheeled vehicle in earlier, secure context in Mesopotamia or elsewhere in the Near East would undermine the above conclusion.

An additional line of inquiry is based on **Proto-Indo-European** roots, which include no fewer than six related to wheeled vehicles, this linguistic evidence indicating their origin no later than the early fourth millennium BC. If this claim is given due weight, a Mesopotamian origin for wheeled vehicles would appear to be ruled out. Three terms (*hurgi, keklos* and *rot-eh*) refer to "wheel," while *h-ih-s* represents "thill" (the draft pole to which the yoke is attached); the term for "axle" is none other than *aks-*, while that for "convey in a vehicle" is *wegheti*. This basic vocabulary extends from India to Scotland, thus antedating the dispersal from the Proto-Indo-European homeland. The root Anatolian term for "wheel" is *hurgi*.

WILUSA. This land lay in the extreme northwest of Anatolia, including the Troad, and features quite prominently in the affairs of the region during the 13th century BC, though never a state of the first rank. Linguistic evidence indicates that Wilusa lay outside the **Luwian**-speaking zone: it therefore seems reasonable to see this as a hint that it was not strictly part of the **Arzawa** lands. This could be one factor behind the loyalty to Hatti of Wilusa as a vassal state, whose geographical location made it especially valuable to the Hittites. After his campaign, led by the general Gassu, **Muwatalli II** restored Hittite control over Wilusa, establishing Alaksandu as ruler and drawing up a **treaty** with him, in which the past loyalty of Wilusa to **Hattusa** is stressed. Troubles in Wilusa later came to a head in the time of **Tudhaliya IV**, when Walmu was the vassal ruler: he was deposed, fleeing to **Millawanda**, where a new, pro-Hittite ruler had come to power, possibly allied by **marriage** to the Hittite royal house. Significantly, Walmu was apparently answerable both to Tudhaliya in Hattusa and to Milawat, an arrangement which would not have been tolerated by earlier Hittite kings, who demanded exclusive fealty to themselves and who did not differentiate between their vassals in terms of status.

The location of Wilusa, commanding the sea route through to the Black Sea, provided it with a source of wealth but also the danger of attack by envious, rapacious neighbors. In the 13th century BC these were above all the Mycenaeans, almost certainly identifiable with **Ahhiyawa**. As long as this power flourished, Wilusa was in constant danger of attack. Its links across the Dardanelles with Europe were archaeologically clearest in the 12th century BC, after the heyday of Mycenaean power in the maritime region of western Anatolia and the downfall of the Hittite Empire.

If Hissarlik—the site of **Heinrich Schliemann**'s and later excavations—is indeed to be identified with Homeric **Troy**, then it must surely be with Troy VIH, imposing in its architectural remains in contrast with those of the following levels, and destroyed most probably around 1250 BC. The last two names in the list of states comprising the alliance defeated by **Tudhaliya I/II** (ca.1400 BC)—Wilusiya and Taruisa—have been identified with the Greek names (W)ilios or Ilion and Troia (Troy). The implication is that the name of Wilusa, clearly in the first instance that of a land or minor state, came to be given to the city we know as Troy. Mycenaean-Greek elements in western Anatolia seem implied by the very name of Alaksandu, vassal ruler of Wilusa. On the identification of Wilusa as Ilios and thus Troy a divergent theory distinguishes Truisa from Wilusa, with the former lying not far east of the latter.

One of the sources of the wealth of Troy was the plentiful supply of fish, an attraction to covetous neighbors. The sea came further inland than today, and ships would have plied to and fro between the port and Mycenaean harbors, as well as in the more hazardous maritime trade with the Black Sea.

Wilusa lay at the junction of two continents and the meeting place at various times of different populations, among them the ancestors of both Lydians and Etruscans. In the 13th century BC its situation gave it a pivotal role for Hittite policy in the west, not least for curbing the designs of **Ahhiyawa**.

WINCKLER, HUGO (1863–1913). He was the leading figure in the earliest seasons' excavations at **Boğazköy (Hattusa)** by the German expedition: it was to him that the Turkish authorities granted the excavation permit, after the personal intervention of Kaiser Wilhelm II. **Ludwig Curtius** became his assistant. As he phrased it, Winckler was "full of resentment against anyone who was more successful than himself and intolerant of scientific opponents. Every aspect of civilization arose from Babylon (he urged). . . ." His chronic health problem certainly made him irascible.

In 1906, after provisioning in Ankara, Winckler and his associates set off very late in the season, on 14 October. The ride took five days. On 19 October excavations began. Winckler was a brilliant philologist, who had already cracked the code of the inscriptions of **Mitanni**, but as a field excavator he was more akin to Belzoni a century earlier in Egypt than to **Heinrich Schliemann**. Like many after him, all that concerned him was the written records, here on clay **tablets**. He worked all day at translating the tablets brought to him in his tent as they were unearthed. The texts in Akkadian presented no problems, though **Hittite** was yet to be deciphered.

A more thoroughly prepared expedition was to be planned for 1907. By then Winckler had become convinced that he was investigating the Hittite capital, but he needed funds. Curtius wrote that "Winckler himself did not take the slightest part in the actual excavating. . . . **Makridi** saw no reason to give us any information about the place or the manner in which these tablets had been discovered." Curtius observed "looting" of tablet fragments from

Temple 1 by Hassan the foreman. Curtius realized that these tablets had fallen in rows from the shelves of an **archive**, and were not mere rubble fill.

Winckler dug once more at Boğazköy (1911–1912), already fatally ill. In his will he mentioned years of work on deciphering **cuneiform** Hittite, but no notes could be found. He might be described as a brilliant but flawed genius.

WINE AND VINEYARDS. Grape pips have been excavated in Georgia and in the land which later became **Isuwa**, indicating that viticulture was being practiced as early as the fourth millennium BC, at least in the highlands of Trans-Caucasia and the lands east of the upper Euphrates. It is tempting to envisage many of the huge storage jars (*pithoi*) found in palaces and **temples** in the Hittite lands as containing wine. It seems likely that by the time of the Empire wine was in abundant supply, for wine and emmer wheat were priced the same for a given volume, twice the price of barley but the same as one cheese.

The vine is native to Anatolia, hardy enough to survive the bitter winter cold, in contrast with the more tender Mediterranean olive: it cannot, however, endure damp summers, explaining its absence from the Black Sea littoral. Wine and fruits were a major source of farmers' wealth, and there were harsh penalties for burning a vineyard or orchard.

Quantity was not the sole consideration: fine vintages were highly esteemed. This is dramatically illustrated by the death penalty inflicted by **Hattusili I** on his cupbearer, a senior palace official, for passing off inferior wine, no doubt to his own benefit, as the finest vintage which the king had ordered for the **queen** mother.

Royal funerals and **festivals** required a supply of fine wine. A bull-headed tankard of **gold** or **silver** was downed by the king when he "drank the god" at the climax of major festivals. Beer and wine were poured out to quench the flames of the royal funeral pyre; and those collecting the charred bones were given food and drink, presumably including wine. Homer mentions quenching the pyre with wine at the funeral of the Greek hero Patroclus, with a similar ritual at that of the Trojan warrior Hector (*Iliad* XXIII.233 and XXIV.782-end).

WOMEN IN STATE AND SOCIETY. The status and activities of women varied considerably in space and time through the lands of the ancient Near East. In many ways their position was regulated by law or social custom, although individual circumstances and personality played their roles, not least in the Hittite state. Inevitably much more is known about women of wealth or in positions of influence or even power than about the vast majority, for the most part living on the land. This is hardly remarkable: exactly the same applies to men.

Mesopotamian influence gives the first clear light, in the form of the senior wives of the Old Assyrian merchants, who remained at home in Assur, while their husbands went to **Kanes** or beyond, to operate the Old Assyrian **trade** in Anatolia. These merchants picked up local wives to give them company during absences of some years from their homeland. It does not require much imagination to suppose that such liaisons did not go unnoticed in Assur; but it seems they were not allowed to interfere with the functioning of the family firm. The **tablets** from Kanes indicate the business abilities and down-to-earth efficiency of those women left in Assyria, effectively in charge of production and shipments at that end of the line. It is with the production of **textiles** that the clearest evidence of the role of Assyrian women and their workforce, including young girls and **slaves**, is available. These responsible women would have learned the textile business, manufacturing and trading, from childhood. Although in the records they appear compliant with their husbands' requirements in terms of fabrics, sizes and quantities per order, some tablets hint at lively arguments, even if they were difficult to conduct effectively over such a long distance as the route from Assur to Kanes. In comparison, consignments of **tin** or **copper** were relatively straightforward.

There was no Anatolian equivalent of that privileged order of Mesopotamian women from rich families of the Old Babylonian period, contemporary with the Assyrian trade to Kanes, who led sheltered, comfortable but celibate lives, the *naditu*, of whom much is known from the **archives** of the city of Sippar.

The whole question of matrilinear versus patrilinear succession is bound up with the problems surrounding Indo-European origins and immigration into Anatolia, of course including the Hittites. In spite of the undoubted **Hattian** elements in early Hittite society, there is no proof of matrilinear succession in the Hittite Old Kingdom nor indeed in the New Kingdom, or Empire. This latter is more surprising in the light of the certain **Hurrian** impact on the state **religion**, on the royal blood line and on literature and probably also on **music**, inadequate as the evidence may be. In some parts of Anatolia traces of matriarchy survived, according to Herodotus as late as the fifth century BC in Lycia, formerly the **Lukka** lands; and the **goddess** of fertility, the crops and the earth, Demeter, survived as Diana of the Ephesians in the New Testament (Acts 19), where the economic threat to those employed in serving the cult aroused strong opposition to Saint Paul. **Kubaba** (Kybele) is another non-Indo-European Anatolian goddess. Such survivals in cultic context had little practical relevance to the status and well-being or otherwise of women in ancient Anatolia, in and beyond the Hittite lands.

If the Hittite royal family had been a model for the status of all their female subjects, their lot would have been quite a happy one, for the **queens** enjoyed high status, in particular after the death of the queen mother, who retained the title of Tawananna after the death of her husband, the reigning king, when he "became a god." At first this title was apparently not restricted to the king's wife, as is evident in the reign of **Hattusili I**. Only later did it become standardized, after **Telipinu**, in his *Proclamation*, had laid down the rules governing the royal succession, which was to descend through the male line, even through the son of a second-rank wife rather than the first, senior wife who held the queenship, failing a male heir by her. Succession through the female line to a son-in-law was to be permitted only if no male heir at all was available.

Women within the Hittite royal family could be at the center of bitter antagonisms, as happened with the sister of Hattusili I, when he removed the status of royal heir from his nephew; and with the stepmother of **Mursili II**, when, jealous of the political status of the king's consort and queen, she brought about her death. By contrast, **Puduhepa** proved a consistently loyal, forceful and pious support to her husband, **Hattusili III**, in sickness and in health.

The family and the institution of **marriage** were inevitably at the heart of Hittite society, the latter naturally with an emphasis on economic considerations. While the husband, following Indo-European traditions, was head of the family, he did not have unfettered powers. The most glaring exception was in a case of adultery by the wife after consummation of the marriage, when the penalty was death. The fate of a wife committing adultery before consummation of the marriage was at the discretion of the husband. Betrothal might take place, at a very early age, when the boy's father would hand over a gift to the girl's family. If, however, the girl later decided she did not wish to proceed to marry her betrothed, she could so decide without her father's consent, the one stipulation being the return of the betrothal gift. At marriage the bride's father had to provide her with a dowry and the bridegroom with a symbolic gift. One Hittite marriage custom, paralleled in Assyria, was that the bride, while normally going to live under the same roof with her husband, might alternatively remain in her father's house. In that event, if she were to die, her dowry would, it seems, pass to her children; but if living with her husband, it would go to him. This implies two degrees of marriage.

The objective of marriage was to perpetuate the family line. Failure by either party to consummate the marriage was regarded as breach of contract, with severe financial penalties. In line with the levirate marriage custom of the **Bible**, it was the duty of the brother-in-law to marry his brother's widow, especially in the absence of an heir. Widows had few rights when it came to remarriage, the only invariable prohibitions being on intercourse with fathers or sons.

Inevitably much less is known of the status and indeed the lives of the majority of the population, those engaged in agriculture and stockbreeding, including women. Their labor was vital to the **economy**, yet the rate of hire for a woman worker at the harvest was precisely half that for a plow ox.

While certainty is impossible, the evidence tends to imply a slightly happier lot for Hittite women compared with those living in Mesopotamia. This is consistent with a more humane legal ethos. *See also* **HITTITE LAWS.**

WOOLLEY, (Sir) CHARLES LEONARD (1880–1960). The well-known field archaeologist, who did much to bring the ancient Near East outside Egypt to the wider public. Although best known for his 12 seasons' excavations at Ur in southern Iraq (1923–1934), he had earlier directed the British Museum excavations at the site of **Carchemish** (1911–1914, 1920), identified in 1876 by George Smith on his last journey. Taking over the directorship from **D. G. Hogarth** and then R. Campbell Thompson, he was assisted by **T. E. Lawrence** ("Lawrence of Arabia" as he was to become). The excavations had hurriedly to be abandoned before the outbreak of World War I and again after a brief resumption of work on the site, in each instance resulting in the loss of most of the site records, inevitably affecting the publications.

His final excavations (1937–1939, 1946–1949) were carried out in the Plain of Antioch (Amuq) at **Alalakh** (Tell Atchana), a site chosen by himself with his foreman from Ur, Hamoudi, with that unerring eye for ground for which he had become known. This was taken in good part by the Oriental Institute of Chicago expedition to the Amuq, which had been seeking just such a site. Woolley also excavated in Egypt at **Tell el-Amarna** (1921–1922), near Ur at Ubaid (1922) and on the Mediterranean coast of Syria at Al-Mina (1936–1937). At Ur he had developed conservation of delicate artifacts, including harps and lyres, by the use of paraffin wax.

WRIGHT, WILLIAM. He published a short article on the Hittites (1878) and then a book entitled *The Empire of the Hittites, with Decipherment of the Hittite Inscriptions by Professor A. H. Sayce* (1884). The Hittites were erroneously centered by him in north Syria, with the belief that they then somehow spread northward into Anatolia, the precise opposite of the truth.

WURUSEMU. A **Hattian** goddess, equated with the **Sun-Goddess** of **Arinna** and associated with the **Underworld**. She was married to the father of the **gods** of **Nerik** and **Zippalanda**. She was also styled "Sun-Goddess of the Earth," the **Hattic** root *wur-* signifying "earth."

- Y -

YALBURT. Northeast of Ilgin and about 60 kilometers northwest of Konya lies this Hittite spring-basin of **Tudhaliya IV**. His **hieroglyphic** inscription, carved on the sides of the rectangular stone basin and extending across 18 blocks, narrates a campaign he waged against the **Lukka** lands. In addition to the name Luk(k)a, three towns—Awarna, Wiyanawanda and Talawa—are mentioned. Awarna is the Lycian Arnna and Classical Xanthos, and the other two are identifiable with the Lycian Oenoanda and Tlos. These lie west of the limit of Hittite territory at the accession of Tudhaliya IV. This is one of two major historical inscriptions brought to public attention in 1988, greatly expanding knowledge of the hieroglyphic script of the Empire.

YARAŞLI. This site stands in a naturally defensible position on an eastern spur of the Karaca Dağ (1,724 meters), north of the Salt Lake and about 100 kilometers south of Ankara. The site was first discovered by W. M. Calder and rediscovered by Michael Ballance and Alan Hall during an epigraphic survey (1957).

The circuit of the solid rubble perimeter wall is about 1,400 meters and the area enclosed about 500 by 200 meters or more. A gate stands in the middle of the south side; and a high glacis is impressively preserved on the east side. At the south corner is a probable **postern**. A citadel adjoins the northwest sector of the lower town.

James Mellaart, reporting on his visit to Yaraşlı, strongly advocated (in 1983) its identification with **Sallapa**, where the **army** of **Mursili II** was joined by that of Sarri-Kusuh from **Carchemish**, en route for campaigning in **Arzawa**. Yaraşlı would have been a significant protection for the western frontier of Hatti. Yet Mellaart admitted that the **historical geography**, as so widely in Anatolia, was obscure, and that alternative identifications were possible.

YAZILIKAYA. Situated two kilometers northeast of the city of **Hattusa**, and approached by a likely processional road of Hittite date, this can justly be described as the most famous of all known Hittite monuments. When **Charles Texier** visited the site in 1834—the first traveler to do so in modern times—he believed that the reliefs depicted a fight involving the Amazons, the heroic women of Classical mythology, with which he was familiar, in common with all educated men and women of his time. Subsequent visitors recorded the reliefs of this open-air shrine with varying success. *See* **BOĞAZKÖY: EARLY TRAVELERS.**

There is some written evidence related to the Yazılıkaya shrine. In one **cuneiform tablet Hattusili III** for the second time requested a sculptor from the Kassite king of Babylon, for a maker of images for his new "family house," while in another clay tablet **Suppiluliuma II** mentions that he had fashioned a portrait of his father, **Tudhaliya IV**, on or in a rock structure. More probably, however, this refers to **Boğazköy: Südburg**. Babylonian influence on Hittite **sculpture** may seem surprising, given the lack of stone in the plains of Mesopotamia; but skilled artists and craftsmen had been active there over many centuries, by contrast with the relatively parvenu Hittite civilization. A theory that Egyptian influence was conveyed through the **Tell el-Amarna (Akhetaten)** boundary stones and reliefs, and that it is reflected not only at Yazılıkaya but also in other Hittite rock reliefs, including **Sirkeli**, **Hemite**, **Hanyeri-Gezbel** and **Karabel**, seems rather far-fetched, though perhaps not completely to be ruled out. The tradition of boundary markers was after all equally typical and at a rather earlier date of

Kassite Babylon, with its elaborately decorated *kudurru*.

Chamber A is the larger of the two areas of this rock shrine, originally approached through an entrance structure of which only the lower stone courses survive. Exposed for centuries, the reliefs here are badly worn and damaged, though the subject matter can be distinguished. The smaller area, Chamber B, is a cleft in the rock not more than 2.7 meters wide: here the reliefs are better preserved, because not exposed until excavated in the mid–19th century.

The obvious feature of the composition of the figures depicted in Chamber A, an unusual arrangement for the ancient Near East, is that there are two processions meeting in the center, rather than just one long row of figures approaching a deity seated on a throne. The Male Procession is headed by **Tesub**, the **Hurrian Storm/Weather-God**; the Female Procession by **Hebat/Hepat**, the Hurrian Mother Goddess metamorphosed, probably through the agency of **Puduhepa**, **queen** of **Hattusili III**, into the **Sun-Goddess** of **Arinna**. A detailed description of the **pantheon** is given elsewhere. Suffice it here to mention some of the participants in these two processions of divinities. From front to rear of the Male Procession stand the Grain-God **Kumarbi**, the goddess of War and Love **Sausga**, the bulls **Seri and Hurri** and the **Under-world**-God **Nergal**. In the Female Procession, immediately behind Hebat, stands **Sarruma**, son of Tesub and Hebat, followed in due course by goddesses of writing and destiny. One might compare these last with the god of tablets, who brings up the rear of the Male Procession. Other deities are for the most part related to one another as a divine family network.

In Chamber B the main elements comprise: the remarkable Sword-God, its figure emerging from the hilt of a very short **sword** or dagger; a row of running figures resembling soldiers but undoubtedly divine; and the pair of the king, Tudhaliya IV, held in protective embrace by his guardian god, Sarruma. This theme of divine protection of the sovereign is probably of Egyptian inspiration, occurring as it does in Hittite art for the first time in the reign of **Muwatalli II**, possibly immediately following the battle of **Kadesh**. Significantly, all the main figures in Chamber B face north, toward the end wall of this chamber, where stands an empty **statue** base with a cartouche (royal monogram) of Tudhaliya IV. Moreover, there is a clear association with the Underworld and thus with **royal funerary** customs. Thus Chamber B, whatever the precise interpretation of Chamber A which may emerge from ongoing discussion, is virtually certain to be the funerary shrine for

Tudhaliya IV designed by his son Suppiluliuma II, perhaps with advice from the then aged Puduhepa. This is infinitely more plausible than any suggestion that Chamber B was designed by Tudhaliya IV for his father Hattusili III, even if Chamber A dates back to that reign. The reason is simple: no Hittite king "became a god" or was portrayed in public during his lifetime.

Certainly the skills of the Hittite stonemasons were directly relevant to the art of the sculptors of Yazılıkaya and other monuments. Stylistic analysis of Yazılıkaya indicates the work of two leading sculptors and their assistants, which have been given the sobriquets of **Fraktin** Master and Yazılıkaya Master. The former, working during the minority of Tudhaliya IV and almost certainly under the instructions of the queen mother Puduhepa, demonstrates a rather more conservative style, while adapting to changes in style at Yazılıkaya. The most striking feature of the work of the Yazılıkaya Master appears to be the influence of the **seal** cutters, demonstrating the essential homogeneity of Hittite art, irrespective of material or scale. This homogeneity recurs in the **Gold** Tomb at **Carchemish**, of Neo-Hittite date.

The **hieroglyphs** of Yazılıkaya are significant for more than one reason. The differing yet recognizable character of the different signs makes it virtually certain that those carving them were illiterate, which is hardly surprising, seeing that literacy was largely restricted to the priesthoods. The pictorial character of the hieroglyphs meant that they formed part of the artistic design, over and beyond their meaning, affecting their size and arrangement. If the deities portrayed had all been completely familiar to those who would be entering the shrine, there would have been less reason for these hieroglyphic inscriptions. But, through the determination of Puduhepa supported by her husband Hattusili III, foreign elements had been introduced to the official **cult** of the Hittite court, whether or not they were instantly welcomed. These were the Hurrian importations from **Kizzuwadna**. Their very unfamiliarity to the people of **Hattusa** made written labels essential. The most striking example is the juxtaposition of the calf of Sarruma alongside his father, the Storm-God Tesub; to ensure understanding, this innovation was inscribed in detail. It clearly had a political significance.

Debate on the meaning and purpose of the Yazılıkaya shrine has continued since the 19th century, beginning with Charles Texier's theory of a meeting between the Amazons and Paphlagonians. Later in the 19th century other theories were aired, that the reliefs represented the feast of the Saka (Scyths), from the northern steppes; or alternatively the conclusion of the **treaty** between Medes and Lydians in the time of Astyages (sixth century BC); or that Sandon and Mylitta, alias Ba'al and Astarte, were the two leading divinities, with their entourage.

The modern era of research into and understanding of the Hittites may be said to begin with the new and highly penetrating insight of **Archibald H. Sayce**, when he asserted that the reliefs of north Syria, especially **Hama(th)** and **Carchemish**, could be linked with those of Yazılıkaya, indicating an extensive North Syrian–Asia Minor (Anatolian) cultural zone. Sayce announced his claim in a lecture to the Society of Biblical Archaeology in London (1876), repeated years later in his *Reminiscences* (London, 1923), pp. 161ff. Later on, R. P. de Cara proposed the theory (Rome, 1891) that the Yazılıkaya reliefs were contemporary with the 19th Dynasty of Egypt; and that one relief in Chamber B depicts the seal in the treaty between **Ramesses II** and Khetasar (i.e., Hattusili III).

Discoveries since the German expedition began work at Boğazköy-Hattusa have naturally led to a spate of interpretations of the Yazılıkaya shrine, both of the reliefs and of the **temple** structure at the entrance. These may perhaps be summed up as the alternative suggestions that the shrine was associated with the New Year or spring **festival** or else with funerary rites for Tudhaliya IV and possibly also for his predecessors. The former theory has now been abandoned, the suggestion that Yazılıkaya was the *akitu* house, dedicated to the festivities and rituals associated with the New Year. The evidence refuting this interpretation of Yazılıkaya lies in the ritual texts, which reveal that the Hittite equivalent of the Mesopotamian *akitu* festivities lay in the twice-yearly procession to the inscribed **stela**, or *huwasi* stone. The building housing such a sacred stela was termed a *huwasi*.

By far the likeliest interpretation of Yazılıkaya explains it as the one and only *hesti*-house, evidently of a funerary character. It is surely significant that **Mursili II** records his celebration of the greatest **festival** of the Hittite religious calendar—the *purulli* festival held each spring—in the *hesti*-house in honor of **Lelwani**, goddess of the Underworld and death. The *hesti* rituals probably antedate the Hurrian innovations introduced by Puduhepa in the early 13th century BC. The *hesti*-house is described in the ritual text as having a gate house and inner room and as being reached by the king in a light **chariot** along a "great road." This shrine was originally dedicated to **Hattian** deities of the Underworld, including Lelwani: other Hattian deities were later also involved, including the Sun-Goddess and **Telipinu**. In the unruly years before **Suppiluliuma I**—so Hattusili III records—the *hesti*-house was far enough away from the center of Hattusa to escape damage. This accords with the location of Yazılıkaya. The funerary function of this great shrine is beyond doubt as far as Chamber B is concerned, clearly a chapel in honor of the deified Tudhaliya IV, and identifiable as the "permanent peak" recorded in a text of Suppiluliuma II explicitly as a shrine in honor of his royal father. The suggestion that the plinth and its **statue** at the north end of Chamber B were added by Suppiluliuma II to a preexisting relief-decorated chapel designed and executed for Tudhaliya IV seems less plausible.

Four phases have been distinguished in the lifetime of the Yazılıkaya shrine, with possibly a greater unity of function for the whole before the death of Tudhaliya IV. Conceivably Yazılıkaya was a double temple dedicated to Tesub and Hebat. It is perhaps harder to accept the suggestion that purification rites would have been performed here, if avoidance of contamination would have dictated a more remote site.

YEŞEMEK. This large quarry and stone-carving workshop lies 22 kilometers southeast of Islahiye, in Gaziantep province. Literally hundreds of **statues**, gate lions, sphinxes and relief blocks, in varying stages of completion and awaiting transportation, date mostly to the Neo-Hittite period but in part to the Empire period.

- Z -

ZALPA (ZALPUWA). Situated probably at or near the estuary of the **Marrassantiya River**, the modern Kızıl Irmak, on the Black Sea coast. The evidence for its location rests partly on the legend associated with it, which may perhaps refer to events in the prehistoric past of the city of **Kanes**.

According to this legend, the **queen** of Kanes gave birth to 30 sons, whom she put into a box which she floated on the river, whereby it was carried downstream to the sea at Zalpa. There the **gods** found the box, and raised the boys to manhood. Meanwhile, the queen of Kanes had given birth to 30 daughters, deciding to bring them up herself. The sons, now men, set out to find their mother. Once they arrived at Kanes, she failed to recognize them, and she gave them her 30 daughters. Only the youngest son warned against incest: though the text is broken here, he seems not to have been heeded.

Kanes does seem at one time indeed to have been ruled by a queen (*rubatum*), though captured by **Anitta** from a king. Other old Hittite texts indicate a location for Zalpa by the sea. Whether the legend of the queen and her offspring conceals memories of early migrations into central Anatolia from the north seems less plausible than might once have been the case, seeing that the early Indo-Europeans evidently arrived in Anatolia much earlier than the later third millennium BC, as formerly suggested.

The kingdom or principality of Zalpa was evidently prominent in the early years of Hittite power, though fading out thereafter. It was clearly significant in the period of the Old Assyrian merchant colonies. The so-called Anitta Inscription records that the kingdom of **Nesa** (i.e. Kanes) was ravaged and subdued by Uhna, king of Zalpa, perhaps in alliance with the king of Hatti. This conquest may be reflected in the destruction of **Kültepe-Kanes-*Karum* II,** dramatically mirrored in the archaeological record. One tentative theory is that Nesa may have cut off the **trade** routes to the more northerly Anatolian kingdoms. By the end of his reign Anitta had subjugated all lands from Zalpa in the north to Ullanma in the south. Then, however, he was faced by an alliance of Hatti and Zalpa. The latter was defeated, its ruler being brought back to Nesa as a prisoner of war; Hattusa was put under **siege**.

Later on, **Hattusili I** records marching against Zalpa, destroying it and seizing its gods. This was not, however, to be the end of the story, for Zalpa was able to profit from the inevitable rivalries within the Hittite royal family: Hakkarpili, one of the sons of Hattusili I, in spite of having been appointed a local governor in accordance with common Hittite practice, was involved in a rebellion against his father. Though the outcome is not documented, this was presumably suppressed.

ZIDANTA I (ca.1560 BC–?). First having to dispose of the legitimate heir of **Hantili I** and his sons in order to seize the throne for himself, this king had a brief reign, from which it seems no records survive. He paid the price for his crimes, being murdered by his own son, **Ammuna**. Thus a pattern of bloodshed became established around the **kingship**.

ZINCIRLI (SAM'AL). A German expedition before World War I excavated this outstanding Neo-Hittite citadel near the Amanus range, the best preserved of all excavated Neo-Hittite cities. Its public buildings were mostly the work of two of its kings, Kilamu and Barrakib, contemporaries of Shalmaneser III and Tiglath-Pileser III of Assyria respectively, thus dating to the ninth–eighth centuries BC.

The citadel was defended by an approximately oval wall with semi-circular towers, with an inner wall along the south sector and two fortified gateways, the outer one decorated with carved stone orthostats. On the highest part of the citadel a large *bit hilani* was later replaced by a building constructed by a ruler of Zincirli and the kingdom of Sam'al, of which it was the center. Subsequently this was probably used by the Assyrian governor, whose troops were quartered in the adjacent barracks in the upper story, with their **horses** below and **chariots** parked perhaps just outside.

The palace of Kilamu, at the northwest corner of the citadel, was enlarged a century later by Barrakib, to comprise two *bit hilani* side by side, facing a large court entered originally by a portal with guardian lions. Barrakib built a more grandiose access to the south, with a vast court enclosed by colonnades and with his principal palace, on the *bit hilani* plan, at the northwest corner. Inscriptions clarify the dating of these buildings.

The Neo-Hittite cities, with the expansion of Assyrian power in the ninth and again in the eighth century BC, tended to experience conflicts between pro- and anti-Assyrian parties, the former ultimately prevailing. This occurred at Zincirli, where Barrakib set up a **stela** in Aramaic, commemorating his forebear Panammu I and Bar-Sur, perhaps his son, who was slain, along with most of his family, in a revolt of the anti-Assyrian party led by one named Azriyau (ca.739 BC). He in turn was defeated and slain in the following year by Tiglath-Pileser III. Barrakib had recognized the futility of trying to resist the advancing power of Assyria under an exceptionally capable ruler.

After the greatest days of Zincirli were over, Esarhaddon of Assyria set up a victory stela to commemorate his conquest of Egypt (670 BC).

ZIPPALANDA. This is one of the many towns well known from the written records of Hittite times, not pinpointed on the ground until recently, when it has been identified with a settlement mound near Kerkenes Dağ in the province of Yozgat. It was an administrative center in the Hittite Old Kingdom, evidently of Hattic origin, and the seat of a royal prince together with "the son of **Ankuwa**." This strengthened the case for locating Zippalanda not far north of

Ankuwa (**Alışar Höyük**) and for identifying Mount Daha—with which it is closely associated—with nearby Kerkenes Dağ. **Alaca Höyük** is too far from Kerkenes Dağ to be a plausible location.

Zippalanda was principally a religious center, though military personnel are recorded, as well as craftsmen and men engaged in hunting and stock breeding. It seems that it was one of the old Hattic holy cities enjoying special privileges in the Old Kingdom, along with **Arinna** and **Nerik**, joined by **Hattusa** and **Tarhuntassa** in the closing generations of the Hittite Empire.

The major buildings recorded in the **tablets** from Hattusa concerning Zippalanda are the **temple** of the **Storm-God** and the *halentu* (residence or palace), apparently in the upper and lower towns respectively, though this location, the opposite from that at Hattusa, must be treated with caution. The whole territory of Zippalanda includes a number of cult stations or shrines, inside and outside the city and mostly toward Mount Daha. Around the whole territory, it seems, there ran a perimeter wall less defensive than religious in function, in this respect resembling the walls of Alaca Höyük, and perhaps reinforcing the identification of that site with the most famous of the holy cities, Arinna.

The Hittite king was involved in performing the ceremonies connected with the **festivals** of the official **cult** at Zippalanda—the *purulli*-festival, the great spring and autumn imperial festivals, the month festival and perhaps also the *Ki-Lam* (hunting) festival. Local festivals and daily cults are only indirectly mentioned.

Appendix: Hittite Collections

In contrast with the abundance of material from Mesopotamia (Iraq and northeast Syria) and Egypt, as well as from the southern Levant, Hittite material is much less widely dispersed. Many of the finds from Mesopotamia and Egypt in European and American museums and other collections derive from early excavations, plunder or purchases in the antiquities market, in Cairo, Baghdad or elsewhere.

The relative rarity of Hittite material in museums outside the Near East is explicable by its originating almost entirely from one country, Turkey, and predominantly from one site, Boğazköy (Hattusa). The major exception is the material, tablets and seals with their impressions, from Ras Shamra (Ugarit) in Syria. In view of the date (1906) of the first season of the German expedition at Boğazköy, the paucity of finds discovered in the 19th century, the epic age of discovery in Egypt and Mesopotamia, is understandable.

Hittite tablets are less numerous than the 30,000 or so fragments from Boğazköy might suggest: five or six pieces on average make up a whole tablet; and Hittitologists are still investigating possible joins.

The great majority of Hittite tablets are now housed in the Museum of Anatolian Civilizations in Ankara and in the Istanbul Museum, in the former capital of the Ottoman Empire. In the latter are to be found finds from the early, pre–World War I German excavations at Boğazköy. The numerous tablets allowed by the Turkish authorities to be taken to Berlin for study have since been returned to Turkey.

Owing to chance discoveries and plundering in central Anatolia (Cappadocia), tablets and painted pottery of the period of the Old Assyrian merchant colonies found their way abroad, largely ending up in Paris in the collections of the Louvre, the British Museum acquiring a modest number.

Hittite tablets and other items are thus relatively rare outside Turkey, where they can be studied on receipt of an official research permit. Elsewhere, the Oriental Institute of the University of Chicago possesses some tablets, and has long been the principal center of Hittitology in North America. Cuneiform tablets are to be found also at such places as Yale University and the New York Public Library; but for the most part they are classed as "Babylonian," from Mesopotamia, where the scribal schools were more numerous than in the Hittite Empire.

Those readers seeking information on Hittite tablets and other material would be well advised to consult the Oriental Institute of the University of Chicago, the University Museum of Philadelphia, the British Museum in London, the Louvre in Paris or the Berlin Museum.

Bibliography

Contents

Abbreviations

AA	*Anadolu Arastirmalari (Jahrbuch für Orientforschung)*
AJA	*American Journal of Archaeology*
AS	*Anatolian Studies*
BASOR	*Bulletin of the American Schools of Oriental Research*
BIAA	British Institute of Archaeology at Ankara
JAOS	*Journal of the American Oriental Society*
JCS	*Journal of Cuneiform Studies*
JESHO	*Journal of Economic and Social History of the Orient*
JIES	*Journal of Indo-European Studies*
JNES	*Journal of Near Eastern Studies*
Kbo	*Keilschrifttexte aus Boghazkoi*
KUB	*Keilschrifturkunden aus Boghazkoi*
MDOG	*Mitteilungen der deutschen Orient-Gesellschaft*
RA	*Revue d'Assyriologie et d'Archeologie Orientale*
RHA	*Revue Hittite et Asianique*
SMEA	*Studi Micenei ed Egeo-Anatolici*
StBoT	*Studien zu den Bogazkoy-Texten*
VBoT	*Verstreute Boghazkoi-Texte*
WVDOG	*Wissenschaftliche Veröffentlichungen der deutschen Orient-Gesellschaft*
ZA	*Zeitschrift für Assyriologie und Vorderasiatische Archäologie*

General Works

Akurgal, Ekrem. *Ancient Civilizations and Ruins of Turkey.* Istanbul: Mobil Oil Turk, 1969.

Bienkowski, Piotr, and Alan Millard (eds.). *Dictionary of the Ancient Near East.* London: British Museum Press, 2000.

Burney, Charles. *From Village to Empire—An Introduction to Near Eastern Archaeology.* Oxford: Phaidon, 1977.

Burney, Charles, and David Marshall Lang. *The Peoples of the Hills: Ancient Ararat and Caucasus.* London: Weidenfeld and Nicolson, 1971.

Cambridge Ancient History, Vols. 1, 2, 3/1, 3/2, 4, 6 (rev. ed). Cambridge: Cambridge University Press, 1972-1994.

Hallo, William, and William Simpson. *The Ancient Near East.* New York: Harcourt, Brace, Jovanavich, 1971.

Kuhrt, Amelie. *The Ancient Near East. Vol.1: ca.3000-ca.1200 BC; Vol.2: ca.1200-330 BC.* London: Routledge, 1995.

Lloyd, Seton. *Ancient Turkey—A Traveller's History of Anatolia.* London: British Museum Publications, 1989.

Matthews, Roger (ed.). *Ancient Anatolia—Fifty Years' Work by the British Institute of Archaeology at Ankara.* London: BIAA, 1998.

McDonagh, Bernard. *Blue Guide—Turkey.* London: A. and C. Black, 3rd ed., 2001.

Mellaart, James. *The Archaeology of Ancient Turkey.* Oxford: Bodley Head, 1978.

Meyers, E. M. (ed.). *The Oxford Encyclopedia of Archaeology in the Near East.* New York: Oxford University Press, 1997.

Özdoğan, Mehmet, and Nezih Başgelen (eds.). *Neolithic in Turkey— The Cradle of Civilization: New Discoveries.* Ancient Anatolian Civilizations Series 3. Istanbul: Arkeoloji ve Sanat Yayinları, 1999. [Background to the Bronze Age.]

Sasson, J. M. (ed.). *Civilizations of the Ancient Near East* (4 volumes). New York: Scribners, 1995.

Turkish Republic Ministry of Culture: General Directorate of Monuments and Museums. *Woman in Anatolia—9,000 Years of the Anatolian Woman.* Istanbul Topkapı Sarayı Museum: Catalogue for exhibition, 29 November 1993 to 28 February 1994. Istanbul, 1993.

Yakar, Jak. *Ethnoarchaeology in Anatolia: Rural Socio-Economy in the Bronze and Iron Ages.* Tel Aviv: Sonia and Marcia Nadler Institute of Tel Aviv, 2000.

General Works on Hittite Civilization

Alp, Sedat, and A. Suel (eds.). *Acts of the Third International Congress of Hittitology, Çorum, September 16-22, 1996.* Ankara, 1998.

Bryce, Trevor R. *The Kingdom of the Hittites.* Oxford: Oxford University Press, 1998.

———. *Life and Society in the Hittite World.* Oxford: Oxford University Press, 2002.

Cornelius, F. *Geschichte der Hethiter: Mit besonderer Berücksichtigung der geographischen Verhältnisse und der Rechtsgeschichte.* Darmstadt: Wissenschaftliche Buchgesellschaft, 1979.

Giorgadze, G. G. "The Hittite kingdom." In Diakonoff, I. M., and Philip L. Kohl (eds.). *Early Antiquity.* Chicago: University of Chicago Press, 1991: 266-285.

Gorny, Ronald L. "Environment, archaeology and history in Hittite Anatolia." *Biblical Archaeologist* 52 (1989): 78-96.

Gurney, Oliver R. *The Hittites.* Harmondsworth, England: Penguin Books, rev. ed., 1990.

Hawkins, David. "Les hittites et leur empire." *Dossiers d'Archéologie* 1996-1997, Part I: 30-35.

Hoffner, H. A. "The Hittites and Hurrians." In D. J. Wiseman (ed.), *Peoples of Old Testament Times.* Society of Old Testament Study. Oxford: Clarendon Press, 1973: 197-228.

————. "Hittites." In A. J. Hoesth, G. L. Mattingly and E. M. Yamauchi (eds.), *Peoples of the Old Testament World.* Grand Rapids, Mich., 1994: 127-155.

Klengel, Horst. *Geschichte des Hethitischen Reiches.* Handbuch der Orientalistik 1, 034. Leiden: E. J. Brill, 1999.

Klock-Fontanille, I. *Les Hittites.* Paris: Presses Universitaires de France, 1998.

McMahon, Gregory. "The History of the Hittites." *Biblical Archaeologist* 52 (1989): 62-77.

Macqueen, James G. *The Hittites and Their Contemporaries in Asia Minor.* London: Thames and Hudson, rev. ed., 1986.

Wilhelm, Gernot (ed.). *Akten des IV. Internationalen Kongresses für Hethitologie, Wurzburg, October 4-8, 1999. StBoT* 45. Wiesbaden: Harrassowitz, 2001. Review by Alice Mouton [in French], *Bibliotheca Orientalis* 59 (2000): 581-586.

Yener, K. A., and H. A. Hoffner (eds.). *Recent Developments in Hittite Archaeology and History: Papers in Memory of Hans Gustav Güterbock.* Indiana: Eisenbrauns, 2002.

Collections of Texts in Translation

Bryce, Trevor R. *The Major Historical Texts of Early Hittite History.* Brisbane, 1982. Brisbane: University of Queensland, 1983.

Hawkins, J. David , and Halet Çambel. *Corpus of Hieroglyphic Luwian Inscriptions—Volume I: Inscriptions of the Iron Age.* Untersuchungen zu indogermanischen Sprach und Kultur-wissenschaft [Studies in Indo-European Language and Culture: New Series, 8]. Berlin: W. de Gruyter, 1999-2000.

Houwink ten Cate, P. H. J. *The Records of the Early Hittite Empire.* Leiden: E. J. Brill, 1970.

Jakob-Rost, Liane. *Keilschrifttexte aus Boghazkoy im Vorderasiatischen Museum.* Vorderasiatische Schriftdenkmäler der Staatlichen Museen zu Berlin, neue Folge, Heft 12. Mainz: Philipp von Zabern, 1997. Review by H. A. Hoffner, *JNES* 59 (2000): 124-126.

Laroche, Emmanuel. *Catalogue des Textes Hittites* [*CTH*]. Paris, 1971.

―――. Supplement to *Catalogue*. *RHA* 30 (1972): 94-133.

Copies of Texts/Tablets

Keilsschrifttexte aus Boghazkoi [*KBo*]. Leipzig and Berlin. ("Cuneiform texts from Boğazköy.")

Keilschrifturkunden aus Boghazkoi [*KUB*]. Berlin. ("Cuneiform documents from Boğazköy.")

Verstreute Boghazkoi-Texte [*VBoT*]. ("Scattered Boğazköy texts.")

Tablet Archives

For a brief assessment, *see* Bryce, Trevor R. *The Kingdom of the Hittites.* Oxford: Oxford University Press, 1998: 416-427.

Indo-European Background and Horse Domestication

A. The wider background

Diakonov, I. M. "On the original home of the speakers of Indo-European." *JIES* 13 (1975): 92-174.

Drews, Robert, (ed.) *Greater Anatolia and the Indo–Hittite Language Family.* Papers presented to a colloquium hosted by the University of Richmond, Virginia, March 18-19, 2000. *JIES* Monograph Series no. 38. Washington, D.C.: Institute for the Study of Man, 2001.

Gamkrelidze, Thomas V., and Vjaceslav V. Ivanov. *Indo-European and the Indo-Europeans.* Translated J. Nicols. Trends in Linguistics, Studies and Monographs 80. Berlin: Mouton de Gruyter, 1995.˙

Mallory, J. P. *In Search of the Indo-Europeans—Language, Archaeology and Myth.* London: Thames and Hudson, 1989.

Puhvel, Jaan. "Anatolian: autochthon or interloper?" *JIES* 22 (1994): 251-263.

Renfrew, Colin. *The Archaeology of Language: The Puzzle of Indo-European Origins.* London: Jonathan Cape, 1987.

Sturtevant, E. H. "The Indo-Hittite hypothesis." *Language* 38 (1962): 205-210.

B. Anatolia

Gamkrelidze, Thomas V. "Proto-Indo-Europeans in Anatolia." *JIES* 18 (1990): 341-350.
Mellaart, James. "Anatolia and the Indo-Europeans." *JIES* 9 (1981): 135-149.
Singer, Itamar. "Hittites and Hattians in Anatolia at the beginning of the second millennium BC." *JIES* 9 (1981): 119-134.
Steiner, G. "The role of the Hittites in ancient Anatolia." *JIES* 9 (1981): 150-173.
———. "The immigration of the first Indo-Europeans into Anatolia reconsidered." *JIES* 18 (1990): 185-214.
Yakar, Jak. "Anatolia and the 'Great Movement' of Indo-Europeans, ca.2300 BCE." *Tel Aviv* 3 (1976): 151-160.
———. "The Indo-Europeans and their impact on Anatolian cultural development." *JIES* 9 (1981): 94-112.

C. Horses

Anthony, David W., and Dorcas R. Brown. "Eneolithic horse exploitation in the Eurasian steppes—diet, ritual and riding." *Antiquity* 74, no. 238 (2000): 75-86.
Hansel, Bernhard ,and Stephan Zimmer (eds.). *Die Indogermanen und das Pferd.* Budapest: Archaeolingua Hauptreite vol.4 (Festschrift Bernfried Schlerath), 1994.
Vila, C., J. A.Leonard et al. "Mitochondrial DNA analyses of domesticated horses." *Science* 291, no. 5503 (2001): 474-477.

Old Assyrian Trade and Colonies

Balkan, Kemal. *Letter of King Anum-Hirbi of Mama to King Warshama of Kanesh.* Ankara: Turkish Historical Foundation, 1957.
Dercksen, J. G. *The Old Assyrian Copper Trade in Anatolia.* Leiden: E. J. Brill, 1996.
Garelli, Paul. *Les Assyriens en Cappadoce.* Bulletin de l'Institut Français d'Archéologie d'Istanbul, 19. Paris: Maisonneuve, 1963.
Larsen, M. T. *Old Assyrian Caravan Procedures.* Istanbul: Netherlands Institute, 1967.
———. "The Old Assyrian colonies in Anatolia." Review article on Orlin 1970. *JAOS* 94 (1974): 468 -475.
———. *The Old Assyrian City-State and its Colonies.* Copenhagen, 1976.

Michel, C. *Correspondance des Marchands de Kanis au Début du IIe Millènaire avant J.-C.* Paris: Les Editions du Cerf, 2001.

Orlin, Louis L. *Assyrian Colonies in Cappadocia.* The Hague: Mouton, 1970.

Özgüç, Tahsin. "The art and architecture of ancient Kanish." *Anatolia/ Anadolu* 8 (1966): 27-48.

Soldt, W. H. van (ed.). *Veenhof Anniversary Volume: Studies Presented to Klaas R. Veenhof on the Occasion of His Sixty-Fifth Birthday.* Leiden: Netherlands Near Eastern Institute, 2001.

Veenhof, K. R. *Aspects of Old Assyrian Trade and its Terminology.* Leiden: E. J .Brill, 1972.

———. "Prices and trade: the Old Assyrian evidence." *Altorientalische Forschungen* 15 (1988): 243-263.

Government, Law and Kingship

A. Administration

Beckman, G. "The Hittite assembly." *JAOS* 102 (1982): 435-442.

———. "Hittite administration in Syria in the light of the texts from Hattusa, Ugarit and Emar." In M. W. Chavalas, and J. L. Hayes (eds.), *New Horizons in the Study of Ancient Syria.* Bibliotheca Mesopotamica 25 (1992): 41-49.

———. "Hittite provincial administration in Anatolia and Syria: the view from Maşat and Emar." In *Atti del II Congresso Internazionale di Hittitologia.* Studia Mediterranea 9. Pavia (1995): 19-35.

Easton, Donald F. "Hittite land donations and Tabarna seals." *JCS* 33 (1981): 3-43.

Gurney, O. R. "The Hittite Empire." In M. T. Larsen (ed.), *Power and Propaganda—A Symposium on Ancient Empires.* Mesopotamia: Copenhagen Studies in Assyriology, vol. 7. Copenhagen: Academic Press, 1979: 151-165.

Imparati, Fiorella. "Aspects de l'organisation de l'état Hittite dans les documents juridiques et administratifs." *JESHO* 25 (1982): 225-267.

Singer, Itamar. "The *agrig* in the Hittite texts." *AS* 34 (1984): 97-127.

B. Laws

Güterbock, Hans G. "Authority and law in the Hittite kingdom." *JAOS* Supplement 17 (1954).

336 • BIBLIOGRAPHY

Hoffner, Harry. *The Hittite Laws—A Critical Edition.* Studies in Near Eastern Archaeology and Civilization, 23. Leiden: E. J. Brill, 1997.
Justins, Carol. Review of Hoffner 1997. *JIES* 30 (2002): 179-188.
Neufeld, E. *The Hittite Laws.* London: Luzac, 1951.

C. Kingship

Beckman, G. "Royal ideology and state administration in Hittite Anatolia." In J. M.Sasson (ed.), *Civilizations of the Ancient Near East* (1995): 529-543.
Gonnet, H. "La titulaire royale Hittite au IIe millénnaire avant J-C." *Hethitica* 3 (1979): 3-108.
Gurney, O. R. "Hittite kingship." In S. H. Hooke (ed.), *Myth, Ritual and Kingship.* Oxford: Oxford University Press, 1958: 105-121.
Puhvel, Jaan. "Hittite regal titles: Hattic or Indo-European?" *JIES* 17 (1989): 351-361.
Starke, F. "Halmasuit im Anitta-Texte und die hethitische Ideologie vom Königtum." *ZA* 69 (1979): 45-120.

D. Royal family

Bin-Nun, S. R. "The Anatolian background of the Tawananna's position in the Hittite kingdom." *RHA* 30 (1972): 54-80.
———. *The Tawananna in the Hittite Kingdom.* Heidelberg, 1975.
Singer, Itamar. "The title 'Great Princess' in the Hittite Empire." *Ugarit-Forschungen* 23 (1991): 327-338.

Political History, Chronology etc.

A. General

Beal, Richard H. "Studies in Hittite history." *JCS* 35 (1983): 115-126.
Bryce, Trevor R. "The boundaries of Hatti and Hittite border policy." *Tel Aviv* 13-14 (1986-1987): 85-102.
McMahon, G. "Hittite history." *Biblical Archaeologist* 52 (1989): 62-77.

B. Old Kingdom

Bryce, Trevor R. "Hattusili I and the problems of the royal succession." *AS* 31 (1981): 9-17.
Collins, Billie Jean. "Hattusili I, the lion king." *JCS* 50 (1998): 15-20.

Imparati, F, and C. Saporetti. "L'autobiografia di Hattusili I." *Studi Classici e Orientali* 14 (1965): 44-85.

C. New Kingdom (Empire)

Archi, A. "The propaganda of Hattusili III." *SMEA* 14 (1971): 185-215.
Darga, M. "Puduhepa, an Anatolian queen of the 13th century BC." In *Mélanges Mansel.* Ankara: Turkish Historical Foundation Press, 1974: 939-961.
Güterbock, H. G. "The Deeds of Suppiluliuma as told by his son, Mursili II." *JCS* 10 (1956): 41-68, 75-98, 107-130.
Houwink ten Cate, P. H. J. "The early and late phases of Urhi-Tesub's career." In *Festschrift Güterbock 1* (1974): 123-150.
Imparati, F., "Apology of Hattusili III or designation of his successor?" In *Festschrift Houwink ten Cate* (1995): 143-155.

D. Western Anatolia

Bryce, Trevor R. "Some geographical and political aspects of Mursili's Arzawan campaign." *AS* 24 (1974): 103-116.
——— ."A reinterpretation of the Milawata letter in the light of the new join piece." *AS* 35 (1985): 13-23.
Singer, Itamar. "Western Anatolia in the thirteenth century BC according to the Hittite sources." *AS* 33 (1983): 205-217.
Yakar, Jak. "Hittite involvement in western Anatolia." *AS* 26 (1976): 117-128.

E. Kizzuwadna and Syria

Beal, Richard H. "The history of Kizzuwatna and the date of the Sunassura treaty." *Orientalia* 55 (1986): 424-455.
Singer, Itamar. "A concise history of Amurru." Appendix III to Izre'el, S. *Amurru Akkadian: A Linguistic Study, vol.*2: 135-195. Atlanta, Ga., 1991.
——— . "The 'Land of Amurru' and the 'Lands of Amurru' in the Sausgamuwa treaty." *Iraq* 53 (1991): 69-74.

F. Chronology

Astour, Michael C. *Hittite History and Absolute Chronology of the Bronze Age.* Studies in Mediterranean Archaeology and Literature. Partille, Sweden: Astroms, 1989.

Astrom, P. (ed.). *High, Middle or Low? Acts of an International Colloquium on Absolute Chronology Held at the University of Gothenburg, 20-22 August 1987.* Gothenburg, 1987.

Bietak, M. (ed.). *High, Middle or Low? Acts of the Second International Colloquium on Absolute Chronology: The Bronze Age in the Eastern Mediterranean.* Vienna, 1992.

Bryce, Trevor R. "Some observations on the chronology of Suppiluliuma's reign." *AS* 39 (1989): 19-30.

Otten, Heinrich. *Die hethitischen historischen Quellen und die altorientalische Chronologie.* Mainz, 1968.

External Relations, Diplomacy and Gift Exchange

A. General

Imparati, F. "La politique extérieure des Hittites: tendances et problèmes." *Hethitica* 8 (1987): 187ff.

Liverani, M. *Prestige and Interest: International Relations in the Near East ca. 1600-1100 BC.* Pavia, 1990.

Zaccagnini, C. "Aspects of ceremonial exchange in the Near East during the second millennium BC." In M. Rowlands, M. T. Larsen and K. Kristiansen (eds.). *Centre and Periphery in the Ancient World.* Cambridge: Cambridge University Press (1987): 57-65.

B. Diplomacy

Beckman, G. *Hittite Diplomatic Texts.* Atlanta, Ga.: Society of Biblical Literature, 1996.

Briend, J., R. Lebrun and E. Puech. *Traités et Serments dans le Proche-Orient Ancien.* Paris, 1992.

Kestermont, G. *Diplomatique et Droit Interne en Asie Occidentale (1600-1200 BC).* Louvain, 1974.

C. Relations with Syria, Assyria and Mesopotamia

Beckman, Gary. "Mesopotamians and Mesopotamian learning at Hattusa." *JCS* 35 (1983): 97-114.

Harrak, Amir. *Assyria and Hanigalbat.* Hildesheim: Olms Publishers, 1987.

Nadav, Na'aman. "The historical introduction of the Aleppo treaty reconsidered." *JCS* 32 (1980): 34-42.

D. Relations with Egypt

Izre'el, S. *The Amarna Scholarly Tablets.* Cuneiform Monographs, 9. Groningen: Styx Publications, 1997.
Kitchen, K. A. *Suppiluliuma and the Amarna Pharaohs: A Study in Relative Chronology.* Liverpool Monographs in Archaeology and Oriental Studies, 5. Liverpool: Liverpool University Press, 1982.
Rowton, M. B. "The background of the treaty between Ramesses II and Hattusili III." *JCS* 13 (1959): 1-11.
Spalinger, A. "Egyptian-Hittite relations at the close of the Amarna period and some notes on Hittite military strategy in north Syria." *Bulletin of the Egyptological Seminar* 1 (1979): 55-89.
————."Considerations of the Hittite treaty between Egypt and Hatti." *Studien zur altägyptischen Kultur* 9 (1981): 299-358.

E. Tarhuntassa

Van den Hout, T. "A chronology of the Tarhuntassa treaties." *JCS* 41 (1989): 100-114.
Houwink ten Cate, P. H. J. "The Bronze Tablet of Tudhaliyas IV and its geographical and historical relations." *ZA* 82 (1992): 233-270.
Otten, Heinrich. *Die Bronzetafel aus Boğazköy: ein Staatsvertrag Tudhaliyas IV.* Wiesbaden: *StBoT, Beiheft 1,* 1988.
Singer, I., "Great Kings of Tarhuntassa." *SMEA* 38 (1999): 63-71.

F. The northern frontier region

Alp, Sedat. "Die hethitische Tontafelentdeckungen auf dem Maşat-Hüyük." *Belleten* 44 (1980): 25-59.
————. *Hethitische Briefe aus Maşat-Höyük.* Ankara, 1991.
Schuler, E. von. *Die Kaskaer.* Berlin, 1965.

G. Relations with the west

Cline, E. "Hittite objects in the Bronze Age Aegean." *AS* 41 (1991): 133-143.
Güterbock, H. G., M. J. Mellink and E. T. Vermeule. "The Hittites and the Aegean world." *AJA* 87 (1983): 133-143.
Heinhold-Krahmer, S. *Arzawa: Untersuchungen zu seiner Geschichte nach den hethitischen Quellen.* Heidelberg, 1977.

Jewell, E. R. *The Archaeology and History of Western Anatolia During the Second Millennium BC.* Ann Arbor, Mich.: Ph.D. dissertation, University of Michigan, 1974.

Kosak, S. "The Hittites and the Greeks." *Linguistica* 20 (1980): 35-47.

———. "Western neighbours of the Hittites." *Eretz Israel* 15 (1981): 12-16.

Historiography

Beckman, G. "The Siege of Ursu text and Old Hittite historiography." *JCS* 47 (1995): 23-34.

Cancik, Hubert. *Mythische und Historische Wahrheit: Interpretationen zu texten der hethitischen, biblischen und griechischen Historiographie.* Stuttgart: Katholisches Bibelwerk, 1970.

Cancik, C. *Grundzüge der hethitischen und alttestamentlichen Geschichtsschreibung.* Wiesbaden, 1976.

Dentan, R. C. (ed.). *The Idea of History in the Ancient Near East.* New Haven, Conn.: 1955. Reprinted 1983.

Hoffner, H. A. "Propaganda and political justification in Hittite historiography." In H. Goedicke and J. J. M. Roberts (eds.). *Essays in the History, Literature and Religion of the Ancient Near East.* Baltimore and London, 1975: 49-62.

———. "Histories and historians of the ancient Near East: the Hittites." *Orientalia* 49 (1980): 283-332.

Wyatt, Nicolas. "Some observations on the idea of history among the West Semitic peoples." *Ugarit-Forschungen* 11 (1979): 825-832.

Economy: Trade and Food Production

A. Trade

Archi, Alfonso. "Anatolia in the second millennium BC." In *Circulation of Goods in Non-Palatial Context in the Ancient Near East.* Ed. by the same. Rome: Edizione dell' Ateneo, 1984: 195-206.

Heltzer, M. "Metal trade of Ugarit and the problem of transportation of commercial goods." *Iraq* 39 (1977): 203-211.

Leemans, W. F. *Foreign Trade in the Old Babylonian Period.* Leiden: E. J. Brill, 1960.

Polanyi, Karl, C .M. Arensberg and H. W. Pearson (eds.). *Trade and Market in the Early Empires – Economies in History and Theory.* Glencoe, Ill.: Free Press, 1957.

Polanyi, Karl. *The Livelihood of Man.* Edited by H. W. Pearson. New York: Academic Press, 1977.

Postgate, J. N. "Learning the lessons of the future: trade in prehistory viewed from history." *Bibliotheca Orientalis* 60 (2003): 5-25.

Sabloff, J. A. and C. C. Lamberg-Karlovsky (eds.). *Ancient Civilization and Trade.* Albuquerque: University of New Mexico Press, 1975.

B. Food production

Beckman, G. "Herding and herdsmen in Hittite culture." In E. Neu and C .Ruster (eds.). *Festschrift Heinrich Otten II.* Wiesbaden, 1988: 33-44.

Hoffner, H. A. *Alimenta Hethaeorum: Food Production in Hittite Asia Minor.* New Haven, Conn: 1974.

————."Oil in Hittite texts". *Biblical Archaeologist* 58 (1995): 108.

Hongo, H. "Patterns of animal husbandry at Kaman-Kalehöyük, Turkey: continuity and change during the second and first millennia BC." In H. I. H. Prince Takahito Mikasa (ed.). *Essays on Ancient Anatolia in the Second Millennium BC.* Wiesbaden: Harrassowitz. *Bulletin of the Middle Eastern Culture Center in Japan,* vol.10: 239-278.

Natural Environment

Brice, W. C. *South-West Asia.* Systematic Regional Geography series. Edited by J. F. Unstead, vol. 8. London: University of London Press, 1966.

————. (ed.). *The Environmental History of the Near and Middle East Since the Last Ice Age.* London: Academic Press, 1978.

Butzer, Karl. "Environmental change, climate history and human modification." In J. M. Sasson (ed.). *Civilizations of the Ancient Near East.* New York: Scribners, 1995.

Dalfes, H. Nuzhet, George Kukla and Harvey Weiss. *Third Millennium BC Climate Change and Old World Collapse.* NATO ASI Series. Series 1: Global Environmental Change, vol. 49. Berlin: Springer, 1997.

Matthews, Roger. "Zebu: harbingers of doom in Bronze Age western Asia?" *Antiquity* 76 (2002): 438-446.

Neumann, J., and S. Parpola. "Climatic change and the eleventh-tenth century eclipse of Assyria and Babylonia." *JNES* 46 (1987): 161-182.

Warfare

A. General

Goetze, A. "Warfare in Asia Minor." *Iraq* 25 (1963): 124-130.
Miller, R., E. McEwan and C. Bergman "Experimental approaches to ancient Near Eastern archery." *World Archaeology* 18 (1986): 178-195.
Yadin, Yigael. *The Art of Warfare in Biblical Lands in the Light of Archaeological Discoveries.* London: Weidenfeld and Nicolson, 1963.

B. Hittite warfare

Beal, R. H. *The Organization of the Hittite Military.* Heidelberg: *TdH* 20, 1992.
Houwink ten Cate, P. H. J. "The history of warfare according to Hittite sources: the annals of Hattusilis I," Parts I and II. *Anatolica* 10 (1983): 91-109; *Anatolica* 11 (1984): 47-83.
Korosec, V. "The warfare of the Hittites from the legal point of view." *Iraq* 25 (1963): 159-166.

C. Chariotry

Anthony, D. W. "Horse, wagon and chariot: Indo-European languages and archaeology." *Antiquity* 69 (1995): 554-565.
——— et al. "Birth of the chariot." *Archaeology* 48 (1995): 36-41.
Bakker, Jan Alber, et al. "The earliest evidence of wheeled vehicles in Europe and the Near East." *Antiquity* 73 (1999): 778-790.
Littauer, M. A. and J. H. Crouwel. *Wheeled Vehicles and Ridden Animals in the Ancient Near East.* Leiden: E. J. Brill, 1979.
———. "The origin of the true chariot." *Antiquity* 70 (1996): 934-939.
Moorey, P. R. S. "The emergence of the light, horse-drawn chariot in the Near East, ca. 2000-1500 BC." *World Archaeology* 18 (1986): 196-210.

D. Battle of Kadesh

Fecht, G. "Ramses II und die Schlacht bei Qadesh." *Göttinger Miszellen* 80 (1984): 23-53.
Goedicke, Hans (ed.). *Perspectives on the Battle of Kadesh.* Baltimore,

Md.: Halgo, 1985.

Murnane, W. J. *The Road to Kadesh.* Chicago, 1985; rev. 2nd ed., 1990.

Religion, Magic and Divination

A. General

Beckman, G. "The religion of the Hittites." *Biblical Archaeologist* 52 (1989): 98-108.

Gurney, O. R. *Some Aspects of Hittite Religion.* Oxford: Schweich Lectures, 1977.

Haas, V. *Geschichte der hethitischen Religion.* Leiden: E. J. Brill, 1994.

Popko, M. *Religions of Asia Minor.* Translated from Polish by Iwona Zych. Warsaw: Academic Publications Dialog, 1995.

B. Various aspects

Haas, V. "Death and afterlife in Hittite thought." In J. M. Sasson (ed.). *Civilizations of the Ancient Near East.* New York: Scribners, 1995: 2021-2030.

Laroche, E. "La réforme religieuse de Tudhaliya IV et sa signification politique." In F. Dunand and P. Levêque (eds.). *Les Syncrétismes dans les Religions de l'Antiquité—Colloque de Besançon 22-23 Octobre 1973.* Leiden: E. J. Brill, 1975: 87-94.

Macqueen, J. G. "Hattian mythology and Hittite monarchy." *AS* 9 (1959): 171-188.

Singer, Itamar. *Hittite Prayers.* Writings from the Ancient World Society of Biblical Literature, 11 (2002).

Tsevat, Mattiahu. "Two Old Testament Stories and their Hittite Analogies." *JAOS* 103 (1983): 321-326.

C. Gods and goddesses

Danmanville, Jenny. "Iconographie d'Istar-Sausga en Anatolie ancienne." *RA* 56 (1962): 9-30, 113-131, 175-190.

Deighton, Hilary J. *The "Weather-God" in Hittite Anatolia.* Oxford: British Archaeological Reports International Series 143 (1982).

Houwink ten Cate, P. H. J. "The Hittite Storm-God: his role and his rule according to Hittite cuneiform sources." In D.Meijer (ed.)., *Natural Phenomena—Their Meaning and Depiction in the Ancient*

Near East. Amsterdam, 1992: 83-148.

Laroche, E. "Le panthéon de Yazılıkaya." *JCS* 6 (1952): 115-123.

———. "Le dieu anatolien Sarruma." *Syria* 40 (1963): 277-302.

———. "Les dieux de Yazılıkaya." *RHA* 28 (1969): 61-109.

McMahon, G. *The Hittite State Cult of the Tutelary Deities*. Chicago: Oriental Institute of Chicago Assyriological Studies 25 (1991).

D.   Cults of hearth and ancestors

Archi, A. "Il colto di focolare presso gli Ititi." *SMEA* 16 (1975): 77-87.

Gonnet, Hatice. "Le culte des ancêtres en Anatolie Hittite au IIe mill. avant notre ère." *Anatolica* 21 (1995): 189-195.

Takaoğlu, Turan. "Hearth structures in the religious pattern of Early Bronze Age northeast Anatolia." *AS* 50 (2000): 11-16.

Van der Toorn, Karel. "Gods and ancestors in Emar and Nuzi." *ZA* 84 (1994): 38-59.

Volpe, A della. "From the hearth to the creation of boundaries." *JIES* 18 (1990): 157-184.

E.   Magic and medicine

Beckman, G. "From cradle to grave: women's role in Hittite medicine and magic." *Journal of Ancient Civilizations* 8 (1993): 25-39. Published by Institute for History of Ancient Civilizations, N. E. Normal University, Changchun, Jilin Province, People's Republic of China.

Frantz-Szabo, G. "Hittite witchcraft, magic and divination." In. J. M. Sasson (ed.). *Civilizations of the Ancient Near East*. New York: Scribners; 1995: 2007-2019.

Unal, A. "The role of magic in the ancient Anatolian religions according to the cuneiform texts from Boğazköy-Khattusha." In H. I. H. Prince Takahito Mikasa (ed.), *Essays on Anatolian Studies in the Second Millennium BC*. Wiesbaden, 1988: 52-75.

F.   Divination

Archi, A. "Il sistema KIN. . ." *Oriens Antiquus* 13 (1974): 113-144.

Oppenheim, A. Leo. *The Interpretation of Dreams in the Ancient Near East*. American Philosophical Society Transactions NS, vol.46, part 3 (1956).

Soysal, Oğuz. "Analysis of a Hittite oracular document." *ZA* 90 (2000): 85-122.

G. Festivals

Archi, A. "Fêtes de printemps et d'automne et réintegration rituelle d'images de culte dans l'Anatolie Hittite." *Ugarit-Forschungen* 5 (1973): 7-27.
Carter, C. "Athletic contests in Hittite religious festivals." *JNES* 47 (1988): 85-87.
Güterbock, H. G. "An outline of the Hittite AN.TAH.SUM festival." *JNES* 19 (1960): 80-89.
Singer, Itamar. *The Hittite KI.LAM. Festival.* Wiesbaden, 1983-1984.

Funerary Customs

Bittel, Kurt. Report on Osmankayasi: *see BOĞAZKÖY: EXCAVATION REPORTS (WVDOG 71 [1958]).*
Christmann-Franck, L. "Le rituel des funerailles royales Hittites." *RHA* 29 (1971): 61-111.
Emre, Kutlu. *Yanarlar—A Hittite Cemetery near Afyon.* Ankara: Turkish Historical Foundation, 1978.
Mellink, Machteld, J. *A Hittite Cemetery at Gordion.* Philadelphia, 1956.
Orthmann, Winfried. *Das Graberfeld bei Ilica.* Wiesbaden, 1967.
Otten, Heinrich. *Hethitische Totenrituale.* Berlin, 1958.

Art and Architecture

A. General

Akurgal, Ekrem. *The Art of the Hittites.* London, 1962. Translation of *Die Kunst der Hethiter.* Munich: Hirmer, 1961.
Alexander, Robert L. "Sausga and the Hittite ivory from Megiddo." *JNES* 50 (1991): 161-182.
Bittel, Kurt. "Hittite art." In *Encyclopedia of World Art,* vol. 7, columns 559-575. New York: McGraw-Hill, 1963.
———. *Die Hethiter. Die Kunst Anatoliens vom Ende des 3 bis zum Anfang des 1 Jahrtausends vor Christus.* Munich: C. H . Beck, 1976.
Canby, J. V. "Hittite art." *Biblical Archaeologist* 52 (1989): 109-129.
Güterbock, H. G. "Narration in Anatolian, Syrian and Assyrian art." *AJA* 61 (1957): 62-71.
Vieyra, Maurice. *Hittite Art, 2300-750 BC.* London: Alec Tiranti, 1965.

B. Sculpture

Alexander, Robert L. *The Sculptures and Sculptors of Yazılıkaya.*
Cranbury, N.J.: Associated University Presses, 1986.
————. "A Great Queen on the sphinx piers at Alaca Höyük." *AS* 39
(1989): 151-158.
Canby, J. V. "The sculptors of the Hittite capital." *Oriens Antiquus* 15
(1976): 33-42.
Güterbock, H. G. "Yazılıkaya: a propos a new interpretation." *JNES*
34 (1975): 273-277.
Mellink, M. J. "Hittite friezes and gate sculptures," in *Festschrift
Güterbock 1* (1974): 201-214.
Sipahi, T. "Eine althethitische Reliefvase vom Huseyindede Tepesi."
Istanbuler Mitteilungen 50 (2000): 63-85.
Unal, A. "The textual illustration of the 'jester scene' on the sculptures
of Alaca Höyük." *AS* 44 (1994): 207-218.

C. Eflatun Pınar

Alexander, Robert L. "The Mountain-God at Eflatun Pınar." *Anatolica 2*
(1968): 77-86.
Bittel, Kurt. "Beitrag zu Eflatun-Pınar." *Bibliotheca Orientalis* 10
(1953): 2-5.
Borker-Klahn, J., and Chr. Borker. "Eflatun Pınar, zu Rekonstruktion,
Deutung und Datierung." *Jahrbuch der Deutschen Archäolog-
ischen Instituts* 90 (1976): 1-41.
Laroche, E. "Eflatun Pınar." *Anadolu (Anatolia)* 3 (1958): 43-47.
Mellaart, James. "The Late Bronze Age monuments of Eflatun Pınar
and Fasillar near Beyşehir." *AS* 12 (1962): 111-117.

D. Rock reliefs

Archi, A. "Felsrelief von Hemite." *SMEA* 14 (1971): 71-74.
Borker-Klahn, J. "Imamkulu gelesen und datiert?" *ZA* 67 (1977): 64-
72.
Bossert, H. T. "Das hethitische Felsrelief bei Hanyeri (Gezbel)."
Orientalia 23 (1954): 129-147.
Kohlmeyer, Kay. "Felsbilder der hethitischen Grossreichzeit." *Acta
Praehistorica et Archaeologica* 15 (1983): 7-154.
Wafler, M. "Zum Felsrelief von Imamkulu." *MDOG zu Berlin* 107
(1975): 17-26.

E. Architecture

Frankfort, Henri. *The Art and Architecture of the Ancient Orient.* Harmondsworth , England: Penguin Books, 4th ed., 1970.

Naumann, Rudolf. *Architektur Kleinasiens von ihren Anfangen bis zum Ende der hethitischen Zeit.* Tübingen: Ernst Wasmuth, 2nd edition, 1971.

Unal, A. " 'You should build for eternity': new light on the Hittite architects and their work." *JCS* 40 (1988): 97-106.

F. Glyptic (seals)

Özgüç, Nimet. *The Anatolian Group of Cylinder Seal Impressions from Kültepe.* Ankara: Turkish Historical Foundation Reports, Series 5, no. 22 (1965).

———. *Seals and Seal Impressions of Level IB from Karum Kanis.* Ankara: Turkish Historical Foundation Reports, Series 5, no. 25 (1968).

Teissier, Beatrice. *Sealing and Seals from Kültepe Karum Level II.* Leiden: Netherlands Historical-Archaeological Institute in Istanbul, 1994.

Metals and Metalwork

Cernyh, E. N., et al. "The Circumpontic metallurgical province as a system." *East and West* 41 (1991): 11-45.

Emre, Kutlu, and Aykut Cinaroğlu. "A group of metal Hittite vessels from Kinik-Kastmonu." In Mellink, M. J., E. Porada and T. Özgüç (eds.). *Aspects of Art and Iconography (Festschrift Nimet Özgüç)*: 675-713.

Emre, Kutlu. "New lead figurines and moulds from Kültepe and Kizilhamza." In *Aspects of Art and Iconography*: 169-177.

de Jesus, Prentiss S. *The Development of Prehistoric Mining and Metallurgy in Anatolia.* Oxford: British Archaeological Reports International Series 74 (i and ii), 1980.

Kaptan, Ergun. "Tin and ancient tin mining in Turkey." *Anatolica 21* (1995): 197-203.

Lordkipanidze, Otar. "The Golden Fleece: myth, euhemeristic explanation and archaeology." *Oxford Journal of Archaeology* 20 (2001): 1-38.

Maxwell-Hyslop, K. R. "The metals AMUTU and ASIU in the Kültepe texts." *AS* 22 (1972): 159-162.

Muhly, J. D. *Copper and Tin.* New Haven, Transactions of the Connecticut Academy of Arts and Sciences, 43 (1973): 155-535.

———."Iron in Anatolia and the nature of the Hittite iron industry." *AS* 35 (1985): 67-84.

———."Metalle B. Archäologisch." [in English], in Erich Ebeling, Bruno Meissner et al. (eds.), *Reallexicon der Assyriologie,* Band 8. Berlin: Walter de Gruyter, 1993—1997: 119-136.

Ramage, Andrew, and Paul Craddock. *King Croesus' Gold— Excavations at Sardis and the History of Gold Refining.* Cambridge, Mass.: Harvard University Press, 2000.

Sayre, E. V., et al. "Stable lead isotope studies of Black Sea Anatolian ore sources. . ." *Archaeometry* 43 (2001): 77-115.

Wertime, T. A.,and J. D. Muhly (eds.). *The Coming of the Age of Iron.* New Haven, Conn.: Yale University Press, 1980.

Yalçin, Ünsal. "Early iron metallurgy in Anatolia." *AS* 49 (1999): 177-187. Proceedings of 4th Anatolian Iron Ages Colloquium 1997.

Yener, K.Aslihan. "The production, exchange and utilization of silver and lead metals in ancient Anatolia: a source identification project." *Anatolica* 10 (1983): 1-16.

———. *The Domestication of Metals—The Rise of Complex Metal Industries in Anatolia (4500-2000 BC).* Culture and History of the Ancient Near East, series. Edited B. Halpern et al. Leiden: E. J. Brill, 2000.

Yener, K. Aslihan and Hadi Özbal. "Tin in the Turkish Taurus mountains: the Bolkardağ mining district." *Antiquity* 61 (1987): 220-226.

Pottery

A. *Various sites and regions*

Emre, Kutlu. "The pottery of the Assyrian colony period according to the building levels of the Kanis Karum." *Anadolu (Anatolia)* 7 (1963): 87-99.

Knappett, Carl. "Characterizing ceramic change at Kilise Tepe." BIAA *Anatolian Archaeology* 3 (1997): 10.

Makkay, Jan. "Pottery links between late Neolithic cultures of the North-West Pontic and Anatolia, and the origins of the Hittites." *Anatolica* 19 (1993): 117-128.

Mellaart, James. "Iron Age pottery from southern Anatolia." *Belleten* 19 (1955): 115-136.

———. "Bronze Age pottery from the Konya Plain and

neighbourhood." *Belleten* 22 (1958): 311-345.

Russell, H. F. *Pre-Classical Pottery of Eastern Anatolia.* Oxford: British Archaeological Reports International Series, 85, 1980.

B. Boğazköy

Boehmer, R.M. *Die Reliefkeramik von Boğazköy–Grabungskampagnen 1906-12, 1931-39, 1952-78.* Berlin: Mann, 1983.

Fischer, F. *Die Hethitische Keramik von Boğazköy. WVDOG 75.* Berlin: Mann, 1963.

Müller-Karpe, A. *Hethitische Töpferei: ein Beitrag zur Kenntnis spatgrossreichzeitlicher Keramik und Topfereibetriebe unter Zugrundelugung der Grabungsergebnisse 1979-82 in Bogazkoy.* Marburg: Hitzeroth, 1982.

Orthmann, Winfried. *Frühe Keramik von Boğazköy. WVDOG 74.* Berlin: Mann, 1963.

Parzinger, H., and R. Sanz. *Die Oberstadt von Hattusa. Hethitische Keramik aus dem zentralen Tempelviertel. Funde aus den Grabungen 1982-1987.* Bogazkoy-Hattusa 15. Berlin: Gebruder Mann, 1992.

C. Gordion

Henrickson, R. C. "Continuity and discontinuity in the ceramic tradition at Gordion during the Iron Age." In D.H.French and A. Çilingiroğlu, (eds.). *Anatolian Iron Ages 3* (1994): 95-129.

———. "Hittite potters and pottery: the view from Late Bronze Age Gordion." *Biblical Archaeologist* 58 (1995): 82-90.

Henrickson, R. C., and M. J. Blackman. "Large scale production of pottery at Gordion: a comparison of Late Bronze and Early Phrygian industries." *Paléorient* 22 (1996): 67-87.

Excavation Reports

Alaca Höyük

Arik, R. O. *Les Fouilles d'Alaca Hüyük Rapport Préliminaire sur les Travaux en 1935.* Ankara: Turkish Historical Foundation, 1937.

Kosay, H.Z. *Ausgrabungen von Alaca Hüyük.* Ankara: Turkish Historical Foundation, 1944.

———.*Les Fouilles d'Alaca Hüyük. Rapport Préliminaire sur les Travaux en 1937-39.* Ankara: Turkish Historical Foundation, 1951.

Koşay, H.Z., and M. Akok. *Ausgrabungen von Alaca Hüyük 1940-1948.* Ankara: Historical Foundation, 1966.
———. *Alacahöyük Excavations 1963-1967.* Ankara: Turkish Historical Foundation, 1973.

Alişar Höyük

Schmidt, E. F. *Anatolia Through the Ages: Discoveries at the Alishar Mound, 1927-29.* Chicago: Oriental Institute, 1931.
———. *Alishar Hüyük: Seasons 1928-29 (Parts I-II).* Chicago: Oriental Institute, 1932-1933.
Von der Osten, H. H. *Discoveries in Anatolia, 1930-31.* Chicago: Oriental Institute Communications 14, 1933.
———. *The Alishar Hüyük: Seasons 1930-32 (Parts I-III).* Chicago: Oriental Institute, 1937.

Beycesultan

Lloyd, Seton, and James Mellaart. *Beycesultan, Vol. I.* London: BIAA Occasional Publications 6, 1962.
———. *Beycesultan, Vol .II.* London: BIAA Occasional Publications 8, 1965.
Lloyd, Seton. *Beycesultan,Vol. III.(Part I).* London: BIAA Occasional Publications 11, 1972.
Mellaart, J. and A.Murray. *Beycesultan, Vol.III (Part II).* London: BIAA Occasional Publications 12, 1995.

Carchemish

Hogarth, D. G. *Carchemish I: Introductory.* London: British Museum, 1914.
Woolley, C. L. *Carchemish Part II: The Town Defences.* London: British Museum, 1921.
———. *Carchemish Part III: The Excavations of the Inner Town.* London: British Museum, 1952.

Eskiyapar

Özgüç, Tahsin, and Raci Temizer. "The Eskiyapar treasure." In *Aspects of Art and Iconography in Anatolia and Its Neighbours (Festschrift Nimet Özgüç).* Ankara: Turkish Historical Foundation, 1993: 613-628.

Hama

Fugmann, E. *Hama 2:1. L'Architecture des Périodes Pré-Hellenistiques.* Copenhagen: Carlsberg Foundation, 1958.

Riis, P. J. *Hama 2:3. Les Cimetières à Crémation.* Copenhagen: Carlsberg Foundation, 1948.

Horoztepe

Özgüç, Tahsin, and Mahmut Akok. *Horoztepe—An Early Bronze Age Settlement and Cemetery.* Ankara: Turkish Historical Foundation, 1958.

Ikiztepe

Alkim, U. B., O. Bilgi and H. Alkim. *Ikiztepe I: The First and Second Season (1974-1975).* Ankara, 1988.

Inandiktepe

Özgüç, Tahsin. *Inandiktepe—An Important Cult Center in the Old Hittite Period.* Ankara: Turkish Historical Foundation, 1988.

KaraHüyük (Elbistan)

Özgüç, Tahsin, and Nimet Özgüç. *KaraHüyük Hafriyati Raporu, 1947.* Ankara: Turkish Historical Foundation, 1949.

Kilise Tepe

Postgate, J. N. "Between the plateau and the sea: Kilise Tepe 1994-1997." In Roger Matthews (ed.), *Ancient Anatolia.* London: BIAA (1998): 127-141.

Korucutepe

Van Loon, Maurits N. (ed.). *Korucutepe I-III.* Amsterdam: North Holland Publishing, 1975-1980.

Kültepe

Özgüç, T., and N. Özgüç. *Ausgrabungen in Kültepe 1948/1949.* Ankara: Turkish Historical Foundation, 1950-1953.

Özgüç, Tahsin. *Kültepe-Kanis: New Researches at the Center of the Assyrian Trade Colonies.* Ankara: Turkish Historical Foundation, 1959.

————. *Kültepe-Kanis II: New Researches at the Trading Center of the Ancient Near East.* Ankara: Turkish Historical Foundation, 1986.

Malatya (Arslantepe)

Delaporte, L. *Malatya, Arslantepe.* Paris, 1940.

Frangipane, Marcella, and J. D.Hawkins. "Melid." In Erich Ebeling and Bruno Meisner (eds.), *Reallexicon der Assyriologie* 8. Berlin, 1993-1997: 35-52.

Maşat Höyük

Özgüç, Tahsin. *Excavations at Maşat Höyük and Investigations in Its Vicinity.* Ankara: Turkish Historical Foundation, 1978.

————. *Maşat Höyük II—A Hittite Center Northeast of Boğazköy.* Ankara: Turkish Historical Foundation, 1982.

Mersin

Garstang, John. *Prehistoric Mersin.* Oxford: Oxford University Press, 1953.

Norşuntepe

Hauptmann, Harald. Reports [in German] on the excavations: *Istanbuler Mitteilungen* 19-20 (1969): 21-78; and in *Keban* 3 (1972), *Keban* 5 (1976) and *Keban* 6 (1979).

————. "Die Grabungen auf dem Norşuntepe 1974." *Keban* 7 (1982): 41-94.

Porsuk Höyük

Crespin, A.-S. "The Porsuk area at the beginning of the Iron Age." *AS* 49 (1999): 61-71.

Pelon, Olivier. "Occupation Hittite et début de l'age du fer à Porsuk."

In Le Guen-Pollet, B., and O. Pelon (eds.), *La Cappadoce Meridionale Jusqu'à la Fin de l'Époque Romaine. État des Recherches*: 15-18. Paris, 1991.

Sakçegözü

Du Plat Taylor, Joan, M. V.Seton-Williams and J. Waechter. "The excavations at Sakçegözü." *Iraq* XII (1950): 53-138.
Garstang, John. Interim reports: *Liverpool Annals of Archaeology and Anthropology* 1 (108), 5 (1912) and 24 (1937).

Tarsus

French, E. "A reassessment of the Mycenaean pottery at Tarsus." *AS* 25 (1975): 53-75.
Goldman, Hetty. *Excavations at Gozlu Kule—Tarsus 2.* Princeton, N.J.: Princeton University Press, 1956.

Tell Halaf

Oppenheim, Max Freiherr. *Tell Halaf: A New Culture in Oldest Mesopotamia.* London: Putnam, 1933.
Dornemann, R. H. "Halaf, Tell." In Meyers, E. M. (ed.), *The Oxford Encyclopedia of Archaeology in the Near East* 2 : 460-462.

Ugarit (Ras Shamra)

Curtis, Adrian. *Ugarit—Ras Shamra.* Cities of the Biblical World. Cambridge: Lutterworth Press, 1985.
Schaeffer, C. F. A., et al. *Ugaritica III.* Mission de Ras Shamra. Paris: Imprimerie Nationale, 1956. [For Hittite royal seals and seal impressions.].

Zincirli

Von Luschan, F., C. Humann, R. Koldewey and N. Andrae. Five reports in *Könligichen Museen zu Berlin: Mitteilungen aus den Orientalischen Sammlungen,* Heft 11-15. [Excavation results, inscriptions, architecture and small finds.]

Aspects of Various Sites

A. Troy

Beekes, Robert. "The prehistory of the Lydians, the origins of the Etruscans, Troy and Aeneas." *Bibliotheca Orientalis* 59 (2002): 205-241.

Bryce, T. R. "Review of Mellink 1986." *Bibliotheca Orientalis* 45 (1988): 668-680.

Easton, Donald F., J. D. Hawkins, A. G. Sherratt and E. S. Sherratt. "Troy in recent perspective." *AS* 52 (2002): 75-110.

Easton, D. F. "Has the Trojan War been found?" Review of Michael Wood . *Antiquity* 59 (1985): 188-196.

Mellink, Machteld J. (ed.). *Troy and the Trojan War*. Bryn Mawr Pa.: Bryn Mawr College, 1986.

Wood, Michael. *In Search of the Trojan War*. London: British Broadcasting Corporation, 1985.

B. Beycesultan

Mellaart, James. "The second millennium chronology of Beycesultan." *AS* 20 (1970): 55-67.

———."Western Anatolia, Beycesultan and the Hittites." In Festschrift *Mélanges Mansel*. Ankara, 1974: 493-526

C. Emar

Adamthwaite, M. R. *Late Hittite Emar*. Ancient Near Eastern Studies Supplement 8. Louvain: Peeters, 2001.

Margueron, J.-C. "Maquettes architecturales de Meskene-Emar." *Syria* 53 (1976): 193-232.

———. "Emar, capital of Astata in the fourteenth century BCE." *Biblical Archaeologist* 58 (1995): 126-138.

D. Ugarit

Heltzer, Michael. *The Rural Community in Ancient Ugarit*. Wiesbaden: Dr. Ludwig Reichert, 1976.

———. *The Internal Organization of the Kingdom of Ugarit*. Wiesbaden: Dr. Ludwig Reichert, 1982.

Pardee, Dennis. "Ugaritic studies at the end of the twentieth century." *BASOR* 320 (2000): 49-86.

Saade, G. *Ougarit—Metropole Cananeénne*. Beirut, 1979.
Watson, Wilfred G. E., and Nicholas Wyatt. *Handbook of Ugaritic Studies*. Handbuch der Orientalistik, Abteilung 1, Band 39. Leiden: E. J. Brill, 1999.

E. *Other sites*

Emre, Kutlu. "The Hittite dam of Karakuyu." *Bulletin of the Middle East Culture Center in Japan* 7 (1993): 1-42.
Özgüç, Tahsin. "The Bitik vase." *Anadolu (Anatolia)* 2 (1957): 57-78.

Boğazköy Excavation Reports in Order of Publication

The earlier reports appeared in *Wissenschaftliche Veröffentlichungen der deutschen Orient-Gesellschaft* [*WVDOG*], the later in the series *Ergebnisse der Ausgrabungen*, edited by Kurt Bittel.

Puchstein, Otto. *Boghaskoi, Die Bauwerke*. Leipzig, 1912.
Bittel, Kurt, and H. G. Güterbock. *Boğazköy: Neue Untersuchungen in der Hethitischen Haupstadt*. Berlin, 1935.
Bittel, Kurt. *Boğazköy I—Die Kleinfunde der Grabungen 1906-12. I. Funde Hethitischer Zeit*. Leipzig: J. C. Hinrichs, 1937.
Bittel, Kurt and Rudolf Naumann. *Boğazköy II—Neue Untersuchungen hethitischer Architektur*. Berlin, 1938.
————.*Boğazköy-Hattusa I: Architektur, Topographie, Landeskunde und Siedlungsgeschichte*. *WVDOG* 63. Stuttgart: W. Kohlhammer, 1952.
————. *Boğazköy III—Funde aus den Grabungen 1952-55*. Berlin, 1957.
Bittel, Kurt, et al. *Die Hethitischen Grabfunden von Osmankayasi WVDOG* 71. Berlin: Mann, 1958.
Bittel, Kurt, Rudolf Naumann and Heinz Otto. *Yazılıkaya*. *WVDOG* 61. Osnabruck, 1967.
Beran, Thomas. *Die Hethitische Glyptik von Boğazköy*. *WVDOG* 76. Berlin: Mann, 1967.
Schirmer, Wulf. *Die Bebauung am Unteren Büyükkale Nordwesthang in Boğazköy*. *WVDOG* 81. Berlin: Mann, 1969.
Boehmer, Rainer Michael. *Die Kleinfunde von Boğazköy*. *WVDOG* 87. Berlin: Mann, 1972.
Seidl, Ursula. *Gefassmarken von Boğazköy*. *WVDOG* 88. Berlin: Mann, 1972.
Bittel, Kurt, et al. *Das Hethitische Felsheiligtum Yazılıkaya*. Berlin:

Mann, 1975.

Boehmer, R .M. *Die Kleinfunde aus der Unterstadt von Boğazköy.* Berlin: Mann, 1979.

Von den Driesch, Angela, and Joachim Boessneck. *Reste von Haus— und Jagdtieren aus der Unterstadt von Boğazköy—Hattusa Grabungen 1958-1977.* Berlin: Mann, 1981

Neve, Peter. *Büyükkale—Die Bauwerke. Grabungen 1954-1966.* Berlin: Mann, 1982.

Boehmer, R. M. and H. G. Güterbock. *Glyptik aus dem Stadtgebiet von Boğazköy.* Berlin: Mann, 1987.

Hawkins, J. D. *The Hieroglyphic Inscription of the Sacred Pool Complex at Hattusa (SUDBURG).* StBoT Beiheft 3. Wiesbaden: Harrassowitz, 1995.

Neve, P. J. *Die Oberstadt von Hattusa. Die Bauwerke I. Das zentrale Tempelviertel.* Boğazköy-Hattusa 16. Berlin: Gebruder Mann, 1999.

Boğazköy: Shorter Reports and General Works

Bittel, Kurt. *Hattusha, the Capital of the Hittites.* New York: Oxford University Press, 1970.

———. "The Great Temple of Hattusha-Boğazköy." *AJA* 80 (1976): 66-73.

———. *Hattuscha, Haupstadt der Hethiter: Geschichte und Kultur einer altorientalischen Grossmacht.* Cologne: Dumont, 1983.

Hawkins, John David. "The new inscription from the Südburg of Boğazköy-Hattusa." *Archäologischer Anzeiger* (1990): 305-314.

Neve, Peter. "Boğazköy-Hattusha: new results of the excavations in the Upper City." *Anatolica* 16 (1989-1990): 7-19.

———. *Hattusa Stadt der Götter und Tempel.* Mainz am Rhein, 1993.

———. Lecture on excavations in the Upper City, in *Proceedings of the British Academy* 80 (1993): 105-132.

Seeher, Jürgen. *Hattusha Guide—A Day in the Hittite Capital.* Istanbul: Ege Yayınları, 1999; rev. ed., 2002.

Early Research

A. General

Campbell, J. *The Hittites, Their Inscriptions and Their History, I-II.* London, 1891.

Ceram, C. W. [Kurt W. Marek]. *Narrow Pass, Black Mountain.*

Translated from the German by R. and C. Winston. London: Victor Gollancz with Sidgwick and Jackson, 1956.

Garstang, John. *The Hittite Empire. A survey of the History, Geography and Monuments of Hittite Asia Minor and Syria.* London: Constable, 1929.

Lloyd, Seton. *Foundations in the Dust.* Revised and enlarged edition. London: Thames and Hudson, 1980.

B. Travelers

Chantre, Ernest. *Recherches Archéologiques dans l'Asie Occidentale. Mission en Cappadoce, 1893-1894.* Paris, 1898.

Hamilton, W. T. *Researches in Asia Minor, Pontus and Armenia, with some Account of their Antiquities and Geology.* London, 1842.

Humann, K., and O. Puchstein. *Reise in Kleinasien und Nord-Syrien.* Berlin, 1890.

Von der Osten, Hans Henning. *Explorations in Central Anatolia, Season of 1926.* Chicago: Oriental Institute Publications 5, 1929.

———. *Explorations in Hittite Asia Minor, 1927-29.* Chicago: Oriental Institute Communications 6 and 8, 1929-1930.

———. *Discoveries in Anatolia, 1930-31.* Chicago: Oriental Institute Communication 14, 1933.

Perrot, Georges, Edmond Guillaume and Jules Delbet. *Exploration Archéologique de la Galatie et de la Bithynie, d'une partie de la Mysie, de la Phrygie, de Cappadoce et de Pont, exécutée en 1861.* Paris, 1872.

Texier, Charles. *Description de l'Asie Mineure, faite par ordre du Gouvernement français de 1833-37, et publieé par le Ministère de l'Instruction Publique. Beaux-Arts, Monuments Historiques, Plans et Topographie des Cités Antiques.* Gravures de Lemaitre. 3 volumes. Paris, 1839-1849.

Thompson, R. C. "A journey by some unmapped routes in the western Hittite country between Angora and Ereğli." *Proceedings of the Society for Biblical Archaeology* 32 (1910)-33 (1911).

C. Languages

Hrozny, Bedrich. "Die Lösung des hethitischen Problems." *MDOG* 56 (1915): 17-50.

———. *Die Sprache der Hethiter.* Leipzig, 1917.

Knudtzon, Jorgen Alexander. *Die Zwei Arzawa Briefe: Die Altesten*

Urkunden in Indogermmanische Sprache. Leipzig, 1902.

Sayce, Archibald H. "On the Hamathite inscriptions." *Transactions of the Society for Biblical Archaeology* 5 (1877).

Wright, William. "The decipherment of the Hittite inscriptions." *British Weekly* (March 1887).

Festschrifts

Festschrift Alp. Otten, H., E. Akurgal, H. Ertem and A. Suel (eds.). *Hittite and Other Anatolian and Near Eastern Studies in Honor of Sedat Alp.* Ankara: Turkish Historical Foundation, 1992.

Festschrift Bittel. Boehmer, R. M., and H. Hauptmann (eds.). *Beiträge zur Altertumskunde Kleinasiens–Festschrift für Kurt Bittel [Contributions on the Study of the Antiquity of Asia Minor].* Mainz: Philipp von Zabern, 1983.

Festschrift Boehmer. Finkbeiner, U., R. Dittmann and H. Hauptmann (eds.). *Beitrage zur Kulturgeschichte Vorderasiens. Festschrift für Rainer Michael Boehmer [Contributions on the Cultural History of the Near East].* Mainz am Rhein, 1995.

Festschrift Güterbock 1. Bittel, Kurt, P. H. J. Houwink ten Cate and E. Reiner (eds.). *Anatolian Studies Presented to Hans Gustav Güterbock on the Occasion of His Sixty-Fifth Birthday.* Istanbul: Netherlands Historical-Archaeological Institute in the Near East, 1974.

Festschrift Güterbock 2. Hoffner, H. A. and G. M. Beckman (eds.). *Kannissuwar: A Tribute to Hans G .Güterbock on His Seventy-Fifth Birthday.* Chicago, 1986.

Festschrift Houwink ten Cate. Van den Hout, T., and J. de Roos (eds.). *Studio Historiae Ardens—Ancient Near Eastern Studies Presented to Philo H. J .Houwink ten Cate on the Occasion of His 65th Birthday.* Istanbul: Netherlands Historical-Archaeological Institute in the Near East, 1995.

Festschrift Laroche. *Florilegium Anatolicum (Mélanges Offerts á Emmanuel Laroche).* Paris: Boccard, 1979.

Festschrift Mansel. *Mélanges Mansel I-II.* [Studies presented to Arif Mufit Mansel.] Ankara: Turkish Historical Foundation, 1974.

Festschrift Meriggi. Carruba, O. (ed.). *Studia Mediterranea Piero Meriggi Dicata.* 2 volumes. Pavia, 1979.

Festschrift Neve. *Istanbuler Mitteilungen* 43 (1993).

Festschrift Otten 1. Neu, E., and C. Ruster (eds.). *Festschrift Heinrich Otten.* Wiesbaden: Harrassowitz, 1973.

Festschrift Otten 2. Neu, E., and C. Ruster (eds.). *Documentum Asiae*

Minoris Antiquae. Wiesbaden: Harrassowitz, 1988.
Festschrift Nimet Özgüç. Mellink, M. J., E. Porada and T. Özgüç (eds.). *Aspects of Art and Iconography—Anatolia and Its Neighbours. Studies in Honor of Nimet Özgüç.* Ankara: Turkish Historical Foundation, 1993.
Festschrift Tahsin Özgüç. Emre, Kutlu, Machteld Mellink, Barthel Hrouda and Nimet Özgüç (eds.). *Anatolia and the Ancient Near East—Studies in Honor of Tahsin Özgüç.* Ankara: Turkish Historical Foundation, 1989.
Festschrift Popko. Taracha, P. (ed.). *Silva Anatolica—Anatolian Studies presented to Maciej Popko on the Occasion of His 65th Birthday.* Warsaw, 2002.

Daily Life, etc.

Canby, J. V. "Falconry (hawking) in Hittite lands." *JNES* 61 (2002): 161-201.
Hoffner, Harry. "The *Arzana* house." In *Festschrift Güterbock 1* (1974): 113-121.
Imparati, F. "Private life among the Hittites." In J. M. Sasson (ed.). *Civilizations of the Ancient Near East.* New York: Scribners, 1995: 571-586.
Klengel, H. "The economy of the Hittite household (E)." *Oikumene* 5 (1986): 23-31.

Literature and Mythology

Archi, A. "Hittite and Hurrian literatures: an overview." In J. M. Sasson (ed.). *Civilizations of the Ancient Near East.* New York: Scribners, 1995: 2367-2377.
Beckman, G. "Mythologie A.II. Bei den Hethitern." [In English] in Erich Ebeling and Bruno Meissner (eds.), *Reallexicon der Assyriologie* 8. Berlin, 1993-1997: 564-572.
Güterbock, H. G. "Hittite version of the Hurrian Kumarbi myths: oriental forerunners of Hesiod." *AJA* 52 (1948): 123-134.
———. "The Song of Ullikummi: revised text of the Hittite version of a Hurrian myth." *JCS* 5 (1951): 135-61; *JCS* 6 (1952): 8-42.
———. "Hittite mythology." In S.N. Kramer (ed.). *Mythologies of the Ancient World.* Garden City, N.Y.: Doubleday, 1961: 141-179.
Hoffner, H. A. *Hittite Myths.* Atlanta: Scholars Press, 1998, 2nd ed.
Unal, A. "The power of narrative in Hittite literature." *Biblical Archaeologist* 52 (1989): 130-143.

Languages and Writing

Adrados, F. R. "The archaic structure of Hittite: the crux of the problem." *JIES* 10 (1982): 1-35.

Beckman, G. "The Hittite language and its decipherment." *Bulletin of the Canadian Society for Mesopotamian Studies* 31 (1996): 23-30.

Goetze, Albrecht. "The linguistic continuity of Anatolia as shown by its proper names." *JCS* 8 (1954): 74-81.

Hawkins, J. D. "Writing in Anatolia: imported and indigenous systems." *World Archaeology* 17 (1985): 363-376.

Justins, Carol F. "The impact of non-Indo-European languages on Anatolia." In Edgar C. Polomé and Werner Winter (eds.). *Reconstructing Languages and Cultures* (1992): 443-467.

Kammenhuber, A. "The linguistic situation of the second millennium BC in ancient Anatolia." *Journal of the Royal Asiatic Society* (1975): 116-120.

Kimball, S. E. *Hittite Historical Phonology*. Innsbruck: Institut für Sprachwissenschaft, 1999.

Polomé, Edgar C., and Werner Winter (eds.). *Reconstructing Languages and Cultures*. Trends in Linguistics–Studies and Monographs 58. Berlin: Mouton de Gruyter, 1992.

Thieme, P. "The 'Aryan' gods of the Mitanni treaties." *JAOS* 80 (1960): 301-317.

Personal Names (Onomastica)

Donbaz, Veysel. "Old Assyrian influence on the Hittite onomasticon and toponyms." *AA* 14 (1996): 229-241.

Hoffner, H. A. "Name, Namengebung. C. Bei den Hethitern." [In English] In Erich Ebeling and Bruno Meisner (eds.), *Reallexicon der Assyriologie* 9. Berlin, 2001: 116-121.

Khossian, Aram V. "The outline of Anatolian onomastics." *SMEA* 24 (1984): 225-227. [Memorial volume for Piero Meriggi (1899-1982)].

Laroche, E. *Les Noms des Hittites*. Paris, 1966.

Popko, M. Reviews of van Gessel. *Onomasticon of the Hittite Pantheon*. *Bibliotheca Orientalis* 55 (1998): 855-858; and 59 (2002): 117-118.

Salvini, Mirjo. *The Habiru Prism of King Tunip-Tessup of Tikunani*. Rome: Istituto per gli Studi Micenei ed Egeo-Anatolici, 1996.

Van Gessel, Ben H. L. *Onomasticon of the Hittite Pantheon*. Parts 1-2

(1998); part 3 (2001). Leiden: E. J. Brill.
Wilhelm, Gernot. "Name, Namengebung. D. Bei den Hurritern." In Erich Ebeling and Bruno Meissner (eds.), *Reallexicon der Assyriologie* 9. Berlin, 2001: 121-127

Hurrians

Buccellati, G., and M. Kelly Buccellati. "Urkesh, the first Hurrian capital." *Biblical Archaeologist* 60 (1997): 77-96.
———. "The royal storehouse of Urkesh: the glyptic evidence from the southwestern wing." *Archiv für Orientforschung* 42-43 (1995-1996): 1-32.
Burney, Charles. "Hurrians and Indo-Europeans in their historical and archaeological context." In *Special Volume in Commemoration of the 70th Birthday of Professor Hideo Fujii*. Kokushikan, Japan: Institute for Cultural Studies of Ancient Iraq (1997): 175-193.
Güterbock, H. G. "The Hurrian element in the Hittite Empire." *Journal of World History* 2 (1954): 383-394.
Mascheroni, Lorenza M. "Scribi hurriti a Boğazköy: una verifica prosopografica." *SMEA* 24 (1984): 151-173.
Wilhelm, Gernot, and Diana Stein. *The Hurrians.* Translated from German by Jennifer Barnes. Warminster, England: Aris and Phillips, 1989.

Early Trans-Caucasian Culture

Burney, Charles. "Hurrians and Proto-Indo-Europeans: the ethnic context of the Early Trans-Caucasian culture." In *Festschrift Tahsin Özgüç* (1989): 45-51.
———. "The highland sheep are sweeter . . ." In *Cultural Interaction in the Ancient Near East.* Papers read at a symposium held at the University of Melbourne, Department of Classics and Archaeology, 29-30 September 1994. *Abr-Nahrain* Supplement Series Volume 5: 1-15.
Diamant, S., and J. Rutter. "Horned objects in Anatolia and the Near East and possible connections with the Minoan horns of consecration." *AS* 19 (1969): 147-177.
Edens, C. "Transcaucasia at the end of the Early Bronze Age." *BASOR* 299/300 (1995): 53-64.

The Fall of Hatti and the Sea Peoples

A. Decline and fall of Hatti

Drews, Richard. *The End of the Bronze Age*: *Changes in Warfare and the Catastrophe ca. 1200 BC*. Princeton, N.J.: Princeton University Press, 1993.

Hawkins, J. David. "The inscriptions of the Kızıldağ and the Karadağ in the light of the Yalburt inscription." In *Festschrift Alp* (1992): 259-275.

――――. "Anatolia: the end of the Hittite Empire and after." In Eva Braun-Holzinger and Hartmut Matthaus (eds.), *Kulturelle und Sprachliche Kontakte*. Colloquium im Johannes Gutenberg-Universitat 11-12 Dezember 1998. Mainz: Bibliopolis, 2002.

Singer, Itamar. "The battle of Nihriya and the end of the Hittite Empire." *ZA* 75 (1985): 100-123.

――――. "New evidence on the end of the Hittite Empire." In E. D. Oren (ed.). *The Sea Peoples and Their World*. Philadelphia, 2000: 21-33.

Ward, A.W., and M. S. Joukowsky. *The Crisis Years—The 12th Century BC*. Dubuque, Iowa. 1989.

Woodhuizen, Fred C. "The late Hittite Empire in the light of recently discovered hieroglyphic texts." *JIES* 22 (1994): 53-81.

B. Sea Peoples

Astour, M. C. "New evidence on the last days of Ugarit." *AJA* 69 (1965): 253-258.

Cifola, B. "Ramesses III and the Sea Peoples: a structural analysis of the Medinet Habu inscriptions." *Orientalia* 57 (1988): 275-306.

Drews, Richard. "Oxcarts, ships and migration theories." *JNES* 59 (2000): 161-190.

Mellink, Machteld J. (ed.). *Dark Ages and Nomads*. Istanbul: Netherlands Institute, 1964.

Oren, Eliezer D. (ed.). *The Sea Peoples and Their World: A Reassessment*. Philadelphia: University Museum, University of Pennsylvania, 2000.

Sandars, Nancy K. *The Sea Peoples: Warriors of the Ancient Mediterranean, 1250-1150 BC*. Rev. ed. London: Thames and Hudson, 1985.

Neo-Hittite Civilization

A. General

Akurgal, Ekrem. *The Birth of Greek Art.* London, 1968.
Bunnens, Guy (ed.). *Essays on Syria in the Iron Age. Ancient Near Eastern Studies* [formerly *Abr-Nahrain*] Supplement Louvain: Peeters Press, 2000
Çilingiroğlu, Altan, David French and Roger Matthews (eds.). *Anatolian Iron Ages 1-4.* London: BIAA. Proceedings of colloquia held under the chairmanship of Professor Çilingiroğlu at Izmir (1984, 1987), Van (1990) and Mersin (1997), with many contributions on Urartu, Phrygia and related topics. The 1997 colloquium is published as *AS* 49 (1999). Forthcoming: papers from Van 2001 colloquium.
Hawkins, J. D. "The Neo-Hittite states in Syria and Anatolia." In *Cambridge Ancient History* III, 1: 372-441.
Yakar, Jak. "Anatolian civilization following the disintegration of the Hittite Empire: an archaeological appraisal." *Tel Aviv* 20 (1993): 3-28.

B. Carchemish

Hawkins, J. D. "Building inscriptons of Carchemish: the Long Wall of Sculpture and Great Staircase." *AS* 22 (1972): 87-114.
————. "Karkamis." In Erich Ebeling and Bruno Meissner (eds.), *Reallexicon der Assyriologie* 5. Berlin, 1980: 426-446.
————. "Kuzi-Tesub and the 'Great Kings' of Carchemish." *AS* 38 (1988): 99-108.
————. "Karkamish and Karatepe: Neo-Hittite city-states in north Syria." In J. M. Sasson (ed.). *Ancient Civilizations of the Near East.* New York: Scribners, 1995: 1295-1307.
————. "'Great Kings' and 'Country-Lords' at Malatya and Karkamish." In *Festschrift Houwink ten Cate* (1995): 73-85.

C. Tabal

Hawkins, J. D. "Problems of hieroglyphic Luwian inscriptions." *AS* 29 (1979): 153-167.
————. "The Kululu lead strips: economic documents in hieroglyphic Luwian." *AS* 37 (1987): 135-162.
Özgüç, Tahsin. *Kültepe and Its Vicinity in the Iron Age.* Ankara:

Turkish Historical Foundation, 1971.

D. Karatepe

Barnett, Richard D. "Karatepe, the key to the Hittite hieroglyphs." *AS* 3 (1953): 53-95.
Çambel, H. and A. Özyar. *Karatepe-Aslantaş Azatiwataya.. Die Bildwerke*. Mainz am Rhein: Philipp von Zabern, 2003.
Hawkins, J. D. "On the problems of Karatepe: the hieroglyphic text." *AS* 28 (1978): 103-119.
Winter, Irene J. "On the problems of Karatepe: the reliefs and their context." *AS* 29 (1979): 115-151.

About the Author

Charles Burney, after graduating in history and archaeology from King's College, Cambridge, gained wide firsthand experience of Near Eastern archaeology on excavations in Egypt, Cyprus, Jordan, Turkey, Iraq and Iran. After carrying out extensive archaeological surveys in northern and eastern Turkey, he was appointed to a junior post in the University of Manchester, thereafter as senior lecturer in Near Eastern Archaeology. He has directed excavations in northwestern Iran as well as at a site in the territory of the Iron Age kingdom of Urartu (Ararat) in eastern Turkey, where one of his former students is currently directing excavation of a major Urartian fortress beside Lake Van.

From 1954 he carried out his archaeological reconnaissances by bicycle over nontarmac roads for three years and later by Land-Rover. The acquisition of a reasonable command of spoken Turkish was essential, not least in the villages.

In Manchester, his philosophy as a teacher was to provide his B.A. students with a broad view in both time and space, from Turkey, the Caucasus and Iran to Egypt, the Levant and Iraq and from the Neolithic period until ca.500 BC. This approach is no longer very fashionable in a time of increasing specialization.

Married in 1960, with twins now in their thirties, he lives in the United Kingdom, in Buxton (Derbyshire) and in a cottage beside the sea in the Isle of Skye, with his wife, Brigit, and Labrador dog, Fergus.